Narrative Commentaries

General Editor
Ivor H. Jones

The Acts of the Apostles

The Acts of
the Apostles

JAMES D. G. DUNN

TRINITY PRESS INTERNATIONAL
VALLEY FORGE, PENNSYLVANIA

Copyright © James D. G. Dunn 1996

Extracts from the Revised English Bible are © 1989
by the Delegates of the Oxford University Press and the
Syndics of the Cambridge University Press and are used
by permission

Library of Congress Cataloging-in-Publication
data available
1-56338-192-3

First Published 1996
by Epworth Press
20 Ivatt Way
Peterborough PE3 7PG

First U.S. Edition published 1996 by
Trinity Press International
P.O. Box 851
Valley Forge, PA 19482

Trinity Press International is a division of the
Morehouse Publishing Group

Typeset by Regent Typesetting, London
and printed in Great Britain by
Biddles Ltd, Guildford and King's Lynn

CONTENTS

BKP/JB

2/26/99

Contents

GENERAL INTRODUCTION

The *Epworth Preachers' Commentaries* that Greville P. Lewis edited so successfully in the 1950s and 1960s having now served their turn, the Epworth Press has commissioned a team of distinguished academics who are also preachers and teachers to create a new series of commentaries that will serve the 1990s and beyond. We have seized the opportunity offered by the publication in 1989 of the Revised English Bible to use this very readable and scholarly version as the basis of our commentaries, and we are grateful to the Oxford and Cambridge University Presses for the requisite licence. Our authors will nevertheless be free to cite and discuss other translations wherever they think that these will illuminate the original text.

Just as the books that make up the Bible differ in their provenance and purpose, so our authors will necessarily differ in the structure and bearing of their commentaries. But they will all strive to get as close as possible to the intention of the original writers, expounding their texts in the light of the place, time, circumstances, and culture that gave them birth, and showing why each work was received by Jews and Christians into their respective Canons of Holy Scripture. They will seek to make full use of the dramatic advance in biblical scholarship world-wide but at the same time to explain technical terms in the language of the common reader, and to suggest ways in which scripture can help towards the living of a Christian life today. They will endeavour to produce commentaries that can be used with confidence in ecumenical, multiracial, and multifaith situations, and not by scholars only but by preachers, teachers, students, church members, and anyone who wants to improve his or her understanding of the Bible.

Ivor H. Jones

INTRODUCTION

The Acts of the Apostles is the most exciting book in the New Testament, probably in the whole Christian Bible. It tells of the beginnings of Christianity with a vigour and vividness which often leaves the new reader breathless. It is a story of men (almost entirely men) who are filled with divine power, inspired to speak with an effectiveness far beyond native ability, guided and sustained at crucial moments by heavenly visions, their mission punctuated by miraculous healings and rescues, their initial success staggering and their progress to the centre of the civilized world (Rome) remorseless. Its particular hero and the one whose character is most clearly drawn is Saul who becomes Paul, persecutor become advocate, Pharisee become apologist, ardent Jew become missionary to Gentiles. His conversion, his travels and many crises, his preaching and encounters, disappointment and success, even his long drawn out defence in the final chapters, is the stuff of adventure yarns.

Acts is a book which even today still stirs the passions when read in Christian congregations and groups, evoking the same mixed responses that Paul's own message received: some being persuaded by what is said, others disbelieving (28.24). Some sighing, 'Oh that the church today could know again the same empowering of the Spirit.' Others doubting, 'Could it really have been as Acts narrates?' The rest probably somewhere in between, wondering how comfortable or disconcerted they would be should either alternative prove to be the case. But few, surely, can remain unimpressed or unmoved by the Acts account, whether as a superb adventure tale or as a historical narrative, in its portrayal of a Christianity which excites and provokes. Is this Christianity as it really was in the beginning, as we should continue to envisage it, or even as it should be?

What is this book then? What do we need to know about it before we can read it to best effect?

§1 *The author, recipient, date and text of Acts*

The book does not tell us who its author was; in this it is more like the Gospels than the Epistles in the New Testament. From earliest times, at least from the end of the second century AD, the tradition has been that the author was Luke, the one described as 'the beloved physician' in Col. 4.14 (cf. II Tim. 4.11; Philemon 24). The evidence available to us from Acts does not enable a firm judgment on the point. But there are two features within the document itself which are particularly relevant.

One is the presence of 'we/us' sections in the second (the Pauline) half of the narrative, where the impression certainly seems to be given that the narrator was personally present at and involved in the events described (16.10–17; 20.5–15; 21.8–18; 27.1–28.16). Most critical studies ascribe this feature to artistic invention or literary convention, but the abruptness of the transitions from third person to first person and back again are better explained in terms of personal presence and absence, and overall it is hard to avoid the conclusion that the narrator intended his readers to infer his personal involvement in the episodes described.

The other is the fact that Acts is the second of a two-volume work – Luke-Acts. This is clearly signalled in the opening sentence of the latter volume (1.1–2), as also by the stylistic characteristics which permeate both volumes, and is confirmed by the several obviously deliberate points of parallel between the two volumes which effectively lock them together (see below §3). We can therefore take the prologue to the Gospel (Luke 1.1–4) and conclude that the claim indicated there, of careful research after sources and eyewitness information, applies also to the Acts.

In other words, it makes not a lot of difference whether we can or cannot give a particular name to the author of Acts or describe his character and precise relation to the story he tells. It is enough to know that he was personally close to the events, often/usually(?) able to draw on eyewitness recollections, and that he went about his task with considerable care and with due sense of responsibility. Since we cannot be sure who he was, we will stick with the traditional identification of the author as 'Luke'.

Like the Gospel, Acts is addressed to one Theophilus. Who he was we now have no means of knowing, other than that the manner of Luke's address in Luke 1.3 ('most excellent') suggests that he was a man of some rank and influence (cf. the address in Acts 23.26, 24.3

and 26.25). There is no suggestion that the two volumes were for Theophilus' personal use alone. The hope would rather be that Theophilus would act as a sponsor, formal or otherwise, for the work. He must have been either a Christian or a strong sympathizer. His sponsorship would not have made much difference in the various Christian churches who would soon learn of and seek out their own copies, but it could have made a difference in drawing attention to the volume among the literate and governing classes in some parts of the Empire. The address, however, does not help us much in resolving the question of why Luke wrote his two books (below §2).

Not much hangs on the date of the composition, but a date in the middle of the second generation of Christianity (the 80s) fits best with the evidence: (1) a volume written some time after the Gospel of Luke, itself usually thought to be dependent on Mark's Gospel (usually dated to the late 60s or early 70s), (2) by someone who had probably been a companion of Paul, and (3) whose portrayal of earliest Christianity seems to reflect the concerns of the post-Pauline generation after that stormy petrel had disappeared from the scene.

All New Testament writings come down to us in different textual forms, from manuscripts and translations dating chiefly from the fourth century onwards. Usually the differences between them though multitudinous are insignificant. But in the case of Acts, a text form of Acts (usually called the 'Western' text) can be discerned which consistently seeks to clarify and smooth the earlier text by numerous elaborations. These do not belong to the original text, and so are rarely referred to in the following commentary, but are often interesting and tell us how Acts was received and used within early Western Christianity. Those interested can find regular reference to the 'Western' elaborations in Johnson's commentary and technical evaluation of the textual tradition in Metzger's commentary.

§2 *Why did Luke write this book?*

Luke indicates his own answer to this question – again in the very opening sentence: (1) his concern evidently was to trace out the continuation of and the continuities with the work which Jesus began (1.1–2). As we shall see when we turn to the beginning of his narrative, this does indeed seem to be his fundamental concern: *to identify the movement whose early history he describes as clearly as possible by its*

reference to Jesus. This also means by reference to his message, the
kingdom of God (see on 1.3), to his death and resurrection, the
central emphasis of the gospel as preached consistently through
Acts, to his name, the banner under which they marched forward,
and to his Spirit, the major force behind the evangelism and its
success. Since Jesus is also Messiah of his people, that means also,
not least, to identify the Jewish sect of Jesus the Nazarene by
reference to Israel's God (as the fulfilment of his purposes), to
Israel's heritage (the law and the prophets), to Israel's mission (to be
a light to the Gentiles) and to Israel's hope (resurrection) (see further
§5 below).

Other objectives fall within this overarching objective. (2) Prominent among them is the intention *to describe the spread of the new movement and the success of its evangelism in the power of the Spirit*, following
the programme set out in 1.8. (3) This includes *the developing schism*
with the leaders of Judaism in Jerusalem (chs 3–7) and in most cases
with the chief representatives of 'the Jews' in other centres (chs 13–
25). But Luke nowhere shows this to be a final schism (see 28.17–31).
Rather it is more a case of sibling rivalry or 'sectarian' tension –
integral, in fact, to Christianity's emerging identity. So Luke had no
qualms in portraying Paul asserting his own identity as a Jew (21.39;
22.3) and protesting his loyalty to the ancestral traditions of his
people to the end (22.3; 23.6; 24.11–17; 25.8; 26.4–7; 28.17).

(4) It also includes *the beginning, justification and development of the
mission to the Gentiles*, with its various crucial moments of decision
for a Jewish sect (particularly chs 10–11, 15), and with the sequence
of confrontations with false understandings of God, particularly in
Samaria, Lystra and Athens (chs 8, 14 and 17), and with the false
practices of magic in Samaria, Cyprus and Ephesus (chs 8, 13, 19).
The whole plot unfolds at the instigation of God (see on 2.23 and
4.12) and mission to the Gentiles is the central feature of Paul's commission (9.15–16; 22.21; 26.16–18, 23). That it is the God of Israel is
always taken for granted, and the proclamation of this God as
creator and judge to pagans and idolaters is a major feature (the
speeches of chs 10, 14 and 17).

(5) Included also is a deliberate attempt to underline *the unity of the
expanding movement*, despite the tensions caused by a Jewish mission
to Gentiles. Its object is achieved by emphasizing the centrality and
oversight of the Jerusalem church (as in 8.14 and 11.22) and of 'the
apostles' (1.26; 2.42; 8.1; 9.27; 11.1; 15.2, 6, 22–23; 16.4), and by drawing a discrete veil over the tensions provoked by 'the Hellenists' (6.1)

and Stephen (8.2), not to mention those involving Paul (see below §4(2)).

(6) So too the overarching objective includes *an apologetic strand in relation to the power of Rome*. In contrast to the repeated antagonism of Jews, Roman officials are regularly portrayed in a positive light, particularly in the unresolved trial of Paul in chs 21–28. Pilate's verdict on Jesus' innocence is repeated from the Gospel (3.13). The centurion of Caesarea and the proconsul of Cyprus are equally attracted to the new movement (ch. 10; 13.4–12). The magistrates in Philippi are depicted as having to eat humble pie because they had infringed Paul's citizen rights (16.35–39), and the Christians are exempted from any blame for the riot in Ephesus (19.21–41). Above all, the ruling of Gallio in 18.12–17, that the disputes between Paul and his fellow Jews were an internal affair, not liable to prosecution under Roman law, is sustained by procurator Festus and king Agrippa (25.19, 25; 26.30–32). Luke's story fades out on the picture of Paul preaching and teaching freely in Rome, with the legal term 'unhindered' literally the last word (28.31). Paul, and so also the movement he represented, was evidently no threat to Roman law or state, and could be left free to get on with its own business. Equally, Luke's Christian readers could take confidence from what he wrote that Roman law and government were no real threat to their movement and mission (Walaskay).

Some have focussed attention on these last features and suggested that Luke wrote Acts primarily as a brief for Paul's defence in his final trial before Nero (which would push the date of Acts back to the early 60s). However, that would hardly explain why Paul is not introduced till the narrative is well advanced, why there is so much repetition of what would be irrelevant themes, and why the subject of Paul's trial fades almost entirely from view in the last two chapters of the book. It is not just the political status of Christianity which Luke was concerned to defend; his concern much more was to define its theological identity.

(7) In some contrast, definition of believers' social identity as such does not seem to have been a major interest for Luke. He does note examples of wealthy recruits, like Barnabas and Lydia (4.36–37; 16.14–15), to the new sect, and concern for those in need is a recurring feature (2.45; 6.3–4; 11.28–30; 24.17; cf. particularly Luke 4.18; 6.20). But the social tensions in such episodes as 6.1 (different language groups), 8.4–8, 12 (Jews and Samaritans), 14.8–18 (encounter with unsophisticated highland townsfolk) and 16.16–19

(slave girl manipulated by owners) are left unstated. Nevertheless, it is true that, for example, his portrayal of the primitive community of goods and the emphasis he put upon Peter's acceptance of the hospitality of the uncircumcised Cornelius would have provided precedents for the social behaviour of his Christian readers (cf. Esler).

§3 *Literary structure*

In commenting on the character and structure of Luke's narrative we will have frequent occasion to call attention to Luke's skill as a story-teller (e.g. 3.1–10; 5.21–26; 14.8–18; 16.11–40; 19.23–41; 21.27–40). The influence over the centuries of the picture he portrayed and its continuing impact today bear their own witness. It may be useful here, however, to draw attention to some of the more striking features of Luke's overall construction.

Particularly notable is the care Luke has evidently taken to draw out whole sequences of parallels: within Acts between Peter and Paul –

Peter	Paul
2.22–39	13.26–41
3.1–10	14.8–11
4.8	13.9
5.15	19.12
8.17	19.6
8.18–24	13.6–11
9.36–41	20.9–12
12.6–11	16.25–34

– and in relation to the Gospel with Jesus also –

Luke	Acts
3.21–22	2.1–4
4.14–21	2.14–39/13.16–41
4.40	28.9
5.17–26	3.1–10/14.8–11
8.40–56	9.36–41/20.9–12
22.66–71	6.8–15
22.69	7.56
23.34, 46	7.59–60

See further the Introductions to ch. 1 and chs 21–28; also on 1.1–5 as a whole.

Less frequently noted are the number of features in the Gospel which Luke chose to omit or to refer to only briefly, because, evidently, he wanted to reserve their impact until Acts. Thus, although, as is generally agreed, he used much of Mark's Gospel as one of the sources for his own Gospel, he nevertheless omitted the accusation at Jesus' trial that Jesus had threatened to destroy the Temple (Mark 14.58), presumably because he wanted to reserve the confrontation and split over the Temple until the Stephen episode (chs 6–7; see on 6.14). Likewise, he omitted Mark 7, the episode which in Mark spells the end of the ritual distinction between clean and unclean, presumably because he wanted to reserve the full impact of Peter's 'conversion' on this point until the Cornelius episode (see Introduction to ch. 10). So too Luke may have omitted the account of John the Baptist's death in Mark 6.17–29 because he wanted to save its impact for Acts 24.24–26. Finally we may note that he restricted the allusion to Isa. 6.9–10 in Luke 8.10 (contrast Mark 4.12 and Matt. 13.14–15), presumably because he wished to reserve the impact of the full quotation of Isa. 6.9–10 until Acts 28.25–27. As a feature of Luke's technique we may compare his holding back of the information in 22.17–20 for the more dramatic second telling of Paul's conversion-commission.

One interesting corollary which follows from these observations is that Luke and Acts were evidently intended to make a matching pair, and a pair complete in itself. It would be difficult to envisage how Luke could have extended such motifs into a third volume or to identify any other loose ends which he may have intended to tie up in a projected third volume. So too this second volume seems to fade out into an open-ended future (28.30–31), the effect of which a third volume would destroy. We may conclude from such structural observations that Acts was intended by Luke to be the climax and completion of his career as historian and epitomizer of earliest Christianity.

§4 *What kind of history?*

Luke's narrative can certainly be described as a history, but that title ('history') raises issues which Luke himself probably never envisaged. This is because the concept of historiography and of what is proper to a history has changed significantly over the centuries. It is not that ancient historians were any less interested in what had happened in significant periods and events of the past than are modern historians. Nor is it the case that modern historians are any less biased and tendentious in their reconstructions and portrayals of characters and events than ancient historians; we may think, for example, of the current diverse historical recountings and evaluations of such figures as Winston Churchill or Margaret Thatcher. In other words, the issues confronting us over the kind of history which Acts is cannot be simply reduced to a black and white choice between unadorned fact and unadulterated fiction. That has never been the case with responsible historical writing, and it is not the case with Acts. Good history has never been simply a matter of pedantic communication of information.

The issue is rather what counted as responsible history writing in the ancient world. What would Luke's readers have expected from him? How would they have read Acts? We can derive the answer in part from the New Testament itself.

(1) However conventional Luke's claims for the carefulness of his research and the reliability of his findings (Luke 1.1–4), we have good reason to conclude that Luke did try to live up to these claims. At the very least we can be confident of the broad outlines of his narrative. This is borne out by the comparisons we can make between the Gospel of Luke and the other two Synoptic Gospels (Matthew and Mark): they indicate a homogeneity and overlap of material which points to the conclusion that Luke had access to early reminiscences of Jesus' ministry and used them in such a way that the outline of particular incidents and substance of particular teachings remains clear. Although Acts is a different format (a form of history, not a Gospel), the explicit detail of persons and titles, of times and places, particularly from ch. 13 onwards, attests the similar effectiveness of Luke's sources of information (probably including his own personal involvement in various episodes), so that the reader can justifiably be confident of the historical basis of most of his narratives. In the following pages, the introduction to each chapter usually draws attention to the pertinent features.

(2) At the same time, comparison between the Gospels indicates that Luke, like the other Evangelists, did not see his task limited to the collection and passing on of tradition. Rather we see a readiness to edit the available traditions – to locate in different places, to omit or add, to expand or contract, to elaborate and interpret. The method

and technique is well illustrated within Acts itself by the triple telling of the story of Paul's conversion (chs 9, 22, 26), where both the common outline and detailed core of the story are clear enough, but also the freedom in the manipulation of detail to bring out different emphases. That the same author can include such retellings within the same volume tells us much of what he regarded as good historical as well as good storytelling technique (see also on 11.4–14).

In Acts, Luke's freedom in regard to tradition is shown by his practice of telescoping events (see Introduction to 8.1–3), by his playing down the probable seriousness of the crisis for the Jerusalem church occasioned by the activities of the Hellenists and Stephen in particular (chs 6–8), by his smoothing out initial relations between Paul and the Jerusalem church (9.23–30), by his ignoring the confrontations between Paul and other Christian Jews at Antioch and Galatia (of which we learn from Paul's letter to the Galatians), by his failure to mention Paul's letter-writing activity and the tensions they indicate particularly in Paul's relations with the church in Corinth (see e.g. on 20.1–2), and by his side-lining of the principal reason why Paul made his final journey to Jerusalem (to deliver the collection; see Introduction to ch. 20). Luke evidently had a different agenda from that of Paul, Luke presumably wanting to highlight the unity of the Nazarene sect in its expansion, whereas Paul's letters were occasioned more by the conflicts and tensions which his church planting occasioned. So too we should not be surprised at the different details and divergent tendencies as between Luke's portrayal of his great hero and the self-portrayal of Paul himself in his letters; that even the closest collaborators in a great enterprise have different impressions and divergent evaluations of their common endeavours is a recurrent feature of history both ancient and modern.

(3) The most sensitive area of unease over Luke's portrayal of Christian origins is the speeches or sermons which constitute a major feature of his narrative (they take up about 30% of the space) and which carry the most heavy weight of the book's theology. It is at this point that conventions of ancient historiography differ most markedly from those of the modern period. In ancient historiography speeches served not only to indicate what the person was known to have said, but also what the writer thought he was likely to have said. They also played a role within the drama of the unfolding narrative, being included for rhetorical effect, to entertain as well

as to inform the reader; the ancient historians show varying degrees of responsibility and irresponsibility in this practice. For example, the Jewish historian Josephus, a contemporary of Luke, places two quite different speeches in the mouth of Herod in his parallel accounts of the same episode (*Jewish War* 1.373–9; *Antiquities* 15.127–46). At this point the line between the ancient historian and the dramatist becomes quite fine and the ancient history becomes more like the historical novel than the modern history, where much stricter controls apply over what can and cannot, should and should not be attributed. Much quoted in discussions on this question are the words of the Greek historian Thucydides, often regarded as the greatest of ancient historians. In his *History of the Peloponnesian War* 1.22.1 he writes:

> As to the speeches which were made either before or during the war, it was hard for me, and for others who reported them to me, to recollect the exact words. I have therefore put into the mouth of each speaker the sentiments proper to the occasion, expressed as I thought he would be likely to express them, while at the same time I endeavoured, as nearly as I could, to give the general import of what was actually said (Bruce [1990] 34 using B. Jowett's translation).

In Acts we can see fairly clearly how Luke worked within these ancient conventions. In all cases the style of the speeches is Lukan through and through; they are, properly speaking, Lukan compositions. At the same time, in most cases the individuality and distinctiveness of the material points to the conclusion that Luke has been able to draw on and incorporate tradition – not necessarily any specific record or recollection as such, but tradition related to and representative of the individual's views and well suited to the occasion. In almost all cases we cannot but be impressed by the combination of brevity (speeches which take only three or four minutes to deliver) and roundedness; they are neither outlines nor abbreviations, but cameos. Given the conventions of the time, the readers would not expect any more. Twentieth- and twenty-first-century readers, accustomed to modern conventions, should neither expect more nor judge Luke unfavourably on this score.

This also means that the speeches of Acts can be used only with care as sources for earliest Christian proclamation and teaching. They represent Luke's impression of that theology, but it is theology seen through Luke's eyes and reflecting also his own concerns. In the following commentary the Introduction to the chapter or section containing a significant speech summarizes both the (Lukan) theological emphases and the indications of earlier tradition.

§5 *The teaching of Acts*

What then is the theology of Acts? What is the overall message that Luke wanted Theophilus and his other readers to take away from his book? We may sum it up under several headings.

(1) The creator is God of all, sovereign in the ordering of times and seasons (4.24; 14.15; 17.24–27). He is the God of Israel, and Jesus is the climax of his purpose for Israel and the focus of his purpose for the nations at large; note the divine 'must' (see on 4.12) and the divine purpose (see on 4.27–28; also Squires). The gospel to the Gentiles calls on them to recognize the true character of God and to repent in face of the judgment to come (8.10, 18–24; 10.25–26, 34–43; 14.15–17; 17.22–31; 19.26).

(2) Jesus is at the centre of the narrative. Not that much attention is paid to his earlier ministry (already dealt with fully in the Gospel), nor that much is made of his continuing function as ascended. But his death and rejection by the leaders of his own people (see on 2.23) and subsequent vindication by God (see on 2.24) was fore-ordained by God (again the divine 'must'; see on 4.12). And the subject of the book, 'Christianity' (to use the later title for convenience), is the continuation of what began with Jesus (1.1–2), its chief identity marker is its relation to Jesus (it is named with his name; see Introduction to ch. 3), and its principal testimony is to his resurrection (2.24–32; 4.1–2, 33; 10.40–41; 13.30–37; 17.18, 30–31; 23.6; 26.6–8, 23), to which the major theme of 'witness' is most closely linked (see on 1.8).

(3) The Christianity of Acts is characterized by mission from start to finish (1.8; 28.30–31), by the effectiveness and expansion of 'the word' (see on 4.4). That mission begins with the empowering of the Holy Spirit (1.5, 8; 2.1–42). Its direction and success is dependent on and enabled by the Holy Spirit (4.8, 31; 5.32; 6.5; 7.55; 8.29, 39; 10.19–20, 47; 13.2, 4, 9; 15.28; 16.6–7; 20.22). The crucial factor in conversion is the gift of the Spirit, the manifest evidence of the Spirit's presence knitting converts into the established communities (2.38; 8.14–17; 9.17; 10.44–48; 11.15–18; 18.24–19.6), and the grace and insight enabled by the Spirit maintaining the unity of the burgeoning movement (2.43–47; 9.31; 11.23–24; 13.52; 20.28). Spirit-inspired

prophecy and prophets are vital features of the ongoing life of the churches (2.17–18; 3.25; 11.27; 13.1; 15.32; 19.6; 21.9–10).

(4) Integral to the self-understanding of this Christianity is its recognition that it is an extension of Israel (cf. Maddox). It is the heir of key promises and fulfilment of important prophecies in their common scriptures (2.16–21, 25–28; 3.21–25; 4.25–26; 8.32–35; 13.33–41, 47; 15.15–18; 28.25–27). It claims that 'the hope of Israel' (28.20) has already begun to be fulfilled in Jesus (1.16; 3.18; 7.52; 13.27). It is not antagonistic to the law, even though so accused by Israel's current leaders (6.13–14; 18.13; 21.21, 28; 24.6); but each charge is countered (7.38, 53; 18.15, 18; 21.24–26; 22.3, 12; 23.29; 24.14; 25.8; 28.17, 23). Its mission is Israel's mission to the nations, an essential aspect of Israel's own restoration (1.6–8; 2.39; 3.17–26; 11.18; 15.14–18; 23.6; 24.14–15; 26.18, 23; 28.23). Its message for Greeks as well as Jews (see on 20.21) offends the majority of the Jews in many centres (12.3, 11; 13.50; 14.2, 4, 19; 17.5; 18.6, 12; 19.9; 20.3, 19; 22.30; 23.12). But the Jews continue to have first claim upon its message (2.39; 3.22, 25–26; 5.31; and see on 13.5), and many are convinced (2.41, 47; 4.4; 5.14; 6.7; 9.31; 13.43; 14.1; 16.1; 17.4, 11–12; 18.4, 8; 19.9; 20.21; 21.20; 23.9; 26.20; 28.24). And the dialogue with the Jews has to be an ongoing dialogue in search of mutual self-understanding in relation to God's Messiah and in response to his Spirit (17.2–4, 11; 18.4, 19, 28; 19.8; 23.6; 24.14–15; 26.6–8, 19–29; 28.17–31). This true understanding of 'the way of the Lord' is set over against not only the deficient insights of the less well instructed (18.24–19.6), but also the false claims of corrupt or syncretistic forms of Judaism (8.9–24; 13.6–12; 19.11–20).

It is important to recognize that for Luke these are the three most fundamental features – (the name of) Jesus, (the power of) the Spirit, and continuity with Israel – which mark out the movement whose beginnings he records and which define its identity most clearly.

(5) Among other distinctive features of Luke's portrayal of Christian beginnings the following are particularly worthy of note:

(*a*) the limitation of Jesus' resurrection appearances to Jerusalem, the clear differentiation in character and time of Jesus' ascension from his resurrection, and the tradition of Pentecost (see Introduction to ch. 1);

(*b*) the limitation of full apostolic status to those who had been with Jesus from the beginning (1.21–22), with the consequential implicit denial that Paul was an apostle like the twelve (despite 14.4,

14), and the attribution to Peter of the decisive breakthrough to the Gentiles (10.1–11.18; 15.7–11);

(*c*) the restriction of Luke's attention to particular individuals, giving no doubt a selective view of Christianity's development – the Acts of Peter, of Stephen and Philip, and of Paul; '

(*d*) the primitive christologies incorporated in the early speeches (2.22, 33, 36; 3.13–15, 19–21; 7.55–56; 10.38, 42; 13.33), including that of the prophet like Moses (3.22–23; 7.37), and the absence of any salvific function attributed to the cross in the evangelistic and apologetic speeches of Acts, beyond that of Jesus' suffering prior to his vindication (2.23–24; 3.14–15; 4.10; 5.30; 8.32–33; 10.39–40; 13.28–30);

(*e*) the primacy of 'salvation' as the dominant metaphor for what the gospel achieves (particularly 2.21, 47; 4.12; 11.14; 13.26, 47; 15.1, 11; 16.17, 30–31) and the centrality of the gift of the Spirit in conversion (see (3) above), without diminishing the importance of repentance (2.38; 3.19; 5.31; 8.22; 11.18; 17.30; 20.21; 26.20), faith (4.4; 9.42; 10.43; 11.17, 21; 13.12, 48; 14.1, 9, 23, 27; 15.7, 9; 16.31, 34; 18.8, 27; 19.2, 4; 20.21; 26.18) or baptism (2.38, 41; 8.12–13, 36, 38; 9.18; 10.47–48; 16.15, 33; 18.8; 19.5; 22.16);

(*f*) not simply the emphasis on prophecy (see above §5(3)), but also Luke's conceptualization of the tangibility of spiritual phenomena (1.3, 9; 2.33; 8.18; 10.45–46; 12.9; cf. Luke 3.22; 24.39);

(*g*) likewise the somewhat enthusiastic and uncritical blurring of prophecy and glossolalia (2.4, 16–18; 10.46; 19.6), acceptance of visions in crucial decision-making (9.10–12; 10.3–6, 10–14; 11.5–14; 16.9–10; 18.9–10; 22.17–21), and delight in the miraculous, particularly the signs and wonders of the early phase (see on 2.22; also 5.15 and 19.11–12), in contrast to the critical treatment of magic (8.18–24; 13.4–12; 16.16–18; 19.13–20; see also on 5.15);

(*h*) also in some contrast, the emphasis on Jerusalem as the mother church of Christianity and on 'the apostles'/'the twelve' as the focus of continuity (6.2; see Introduction to ch. 1 and on 1.2), and on the unity and orderliness of the churches from the first, as indicated by the handling of the problems posed in chapters 5 and 6, the monitoring and approval of developments in Samaria and Antioch (8.14–17; 11.22–24), the solution to the problem of mixed Jew-Gentile churches (15.19–16.5), the integration of Paul (9.26–29; 11.29–30; 16.4) and of his churches (by the appointment of elders; 14.23; 20.17) and of otherwise detached groups (as illustrated in 18.24–19.7) – features regarded by some as evidence of an 'early catholic' perspective (but note also points (*f*) and (*g*) above);

(*i*) the lack of much concern to indicate how Christian ethics developed, marked by the use of the Old Testament for its predictive rather than prescriptive value, and by the complete absence of any talk of 'love', *agape* (Acts is the only New Testament writing in which neither verb nor noun occur);

(*j*) the fading of any sense of eschatological intensity and urgency beyond the references in 2.17–21 and 3.19–21, with even talk of judgment presented more as a doctrine of 'the last things' than a matter of urgent crisis (10.42; 17.31; 24.25), and the appropriate balance of emphasis indicated at beginning and end (1.6–8; 28.30–31).

In the commentary itself care will be taken in the Introductions to each chapter to highlight the chief features of Luke's narrative, including the main theological points and evaluation of its historical and dramatic force.

§6 *Bibliography*

Sources

The Greek text used has been the Nestle-Aland 26th and 27th editions. English translations referred to are Jerusalem Bible (JB), New Jerusalem Bible (NJB), New English Bible (NEB), Revised English Bible (REB), New International Version (NIV), Revised Standard Version (RSV), New Revised Standard Version (NRSV). Most of these include the Apocrypha.

Invaluable for Jewish background and thought are the texts collected in the two-volume *Old Testament Pseudepigrapha*, edited by J. H. Charlesworth (London: Darton, Longman & Todd 1983, 1985) or the briefer collection edited by H. F. D. Sparks, *The Apocryphal Old Testament* (Oxford: Clarendon 1984). The most convenient text for the Qumran Scrolls is G. Vermes, *The Dead Sea Scrolls in English* (Penguin, [4]1995), and for the early rabbinic writings is still H. Danby, *The Mishnah* (Oxford: Clarendon 1933). The writings of the Alexandrian Jewish philosopher, Paul's older contemporary, Philo, are cited from the twelve-volume Loeb edition, and of the Jewish historian, Luke's contemporary, Josephus, from the corresponding nine-volume Loeb edition. *The Apostolic Fathers* likewise can be consulted in the two-volume Loeb edition, and other classical Greek texts, cited sparingly, also use the equivalent Loeb editions.

Commentaries

There are several valuable commentaries available in English. The most technical is the long awaited International Critical Commentary in two volumes by the doyen of British New Testament scholars, C. K. Barrett, *Acts* (Edinburgh: T. & T. Clark 1994, 1997). On the textual variations see particularly B. M. Metzger, *A Textual Commentary on the Greek New Testament* (London: United Bible Societies ²1975).

Also technical are the two commentaries which well represent the traditions of German critical evaluation of Acts – H. Conzelmann, *The Acts of the Apostles* (Hermeneia; Philadelphia: Fortress 1987), and E. Haenchen, *The Acts of the Apostles* (Oxford: Blackwell 1971). Less technical, but in the same category is G. Lüdemann's *Early Christianity according to the Traditions in Acts* (London: SCM Press/ Philadephia: Fortress 1989), which concentrates on sifting tradition from redaction.

A counterbalance to these is the more conservative commentary on the Greek text by F. F. Bruce, *The Acts of the Apostles* (Grand Rapids: Eerdmans/Leicester: Apollos ³1990), with its popular complement and fuller exposition, *The Book of the Acts* (Grand Rapids: Eerdmans ²1988). The older two-volume commentary edited by K. Lake and H. J. Cadbury remains of value, particularly the latter volume of additional notes, which appeared as volumes 4 and 5 of *The Beginnings of Christianity, Part I, The Acts of the Apostles*, edited by F. J. Foakes Jackson and K. Lake (London: Macmillan 1933).

Highly recommended as spanning the division between technical and popular, and for its overall balance, is the Sacra Pagina (Roman Catholic) commentary by L. T. Johnson, *The Acts of the Apostles* (Collegeville, Minnesota: Liturgical 1992).

Of popular treatments in English mention may also be made particularly of the New Clarendon Bible by R. P. C. Hanson, *The Acts* (Oxford: Clarendon 1967), and the Tyndale Commentary by I. H. Marshall, *Acts* (Leicester: Inter-Varsity 1980). The two volumes by R. C. Tannehill, *The Narrative Unity of Luke-Acts: A Literary Interpretation* (Philadelphia: Fortress 1986, 1990) provides a well regarded analysis of the narrative of Acts.

Those who can cope with German are recommended to the two-volume Ökumenischer Taschenbuchkommentar by A. Weiser, *Die Apostelgeschichte* (Gütersloh: Gütersloher 1981, 1985), the two-volume Evangelisch-Katholischer Kommentar by R. Pesch,

Die Apostelgeschichte (Zürich: Benziger/Neukirchen-Vluyn: Neukirchener 1986), and the more popular Neue Testament Deutsch volume by J. Roloff, *Die Apostelgeschichte* (Göttingen: Vandenhoeck & Ruprecht 1981).

Selected studies

Thorough introductions are provided, e.g., by W. G. Kümmel, *Introduction to the New Testament* (Nashville: Abingdon/London: SCM Press 1975) and L. T. Johnson, 'Luke-Acts, Book of', *Anchor Bible Dictionary* (New York: Doubleday 1992) IV.403–20, the latter in particular reminding us of the importance of reading Acts as part of a two-volume project. For analysis of various features of Acts as illumined by its historical background the five-volume series, *The Book of Acts in its First-Century Setting*, edited by B. W. Winter (Grand Rapids: Eerdmans/Carlisle: Paternoster 1993–96) can be recommended. A. N. Sherwin-White, *Roman Society and Roman Law in the New Testament* (Oxford: Clarendon 1963) is still valuable on the legal background to Acts. The classic study of Luke's style remains H. J. Cadbury, *The Making of Luke-Acts* (New York: Macmillan 1927).

On questions of Acts historical reliability, particularly the speeches, the principal critical impetus came from M. Dibelius, *Studies in the Acts of the Apostles* (London: SCM Press 1956). In contrast, the Tübingen scholar M. Hengel, *Acts and the History of Earliest Christianity* (London: SCM Press/Philadephia: Fortress 1979) has been consistently more confident in using Acts as a historical source. The equivalent debate in English scholarship is between treating Acts primarily as literature, as, for example, R. I. Pervo, *Profit with Delight: The Literary Genre of the Acts of the Apostles* (Philadelphia: Fortress 1987) – Acts as a historical novel or romance – and treating it primarily as history, as particularly by C. J. Hemer, *The Book of Acts in the Setting of Hellenistic History* (Tübingen: J. C. B. Mohr 1989). The recent thorough study by G. E. Sterling, *Historiography and Self-Definition: Josephos, Luke-Acts and Apologetic Historiography* (Leiden: Brill 1992), concludes that Luke-Acts is best classified as 'apologetic history'.

For general histories of earliest Christianity reference may be made to F. F. Bruce, *New Testament History* (London: Nelson/Pickering & Inglis 1969), S. Brown, *The Origins of Christianity* (Oxford University Press 1984, ²1993), H. Conzelmann, *History of Primitive Christianity* (London: Darton, Longman & Todd 1973), L. Goppelt,

Apostolic and Post-Apostolic Times (London: A. & C. Black 1970), and C. Rowland, *Christian Origins* (London: SPCK, 1985).

On the particular issues surrounding Stephen and the Hellenists, the spread of debate is well represented by M. Simon, *St Stephen and the Hellenists in the Primitive Church* (London: Longmans 1958), M. Hengel, *Between Jesus and Paul* (London: SCM Press/Philadelphia: Fortress 1983), E. Richard, *Acts 6:1–8:4. The Author's Method of Composition* (Missoula, Montana: Scholars 1978), and C. C. Hill, *Hellenists and Hebrews: Reappraising Division within the Earliest Church* (Minneapolis: Fortress 1992).

For the life of Paul the following will give a good example of scholarly opinion: G. Bornkamm, *Paul* (New York: Harper/London: Hodder 1971), F. F. Bruce, *Paul: Apostle of the Free Spirit* (Exeter: Paternoster 1977), M. Hengel, *The Pre-Christian Paul* (London: SCM Press/Philadelphia: Trinity Press International 1991), M. Dibelius, *Paul* (London: Longmans Green 1953), and J. Knox, *Chapters in a Life of Paul* (London: SCM Press 1950, revised 1989).

Overviews of Luke's theology and purpose include the collection of important, some classic essays in *Studies in Luke Acts*, edited by L. E. Keck and J. L. Martyn (Nashville: Abingdon 1966), R. Maddox, *The Purpose of Luke-Acts* (Edinburgh: T. & T. Clark 1982), I. H. Marshall, *Luke: Historian and Theologian* (Exeter: Paternoster 1970), R. F. O'Toole, *The Unity of Luke's Theology* (Wilmington, Delaware: Michael Glazier 1984), and H. C. Kee, *Good News to the Ends of the Earth: The Theology of Acts* (London: SCM Press/Philadelphia: Trinity Press International 1990). For the interplay of Lukan emphases within New Testament theology see the author's *Unity and Diversity in the New Testament* (London: SCM Press/Philadephia: Trinity Press International ²1990).

On the theme which runs most persistently through Acts and the following pages, the relation between Judaism and Christianity as portrayed by Luke, the spectrum runs through an amazingly diverse range, from the view that Luke was bitterly and unyieldingly hostile to the Jews, to a much more positive evaluation of their interdependence – from J. T. Sanders, *The Jews in Luke-Acts* (London: SCM Press/Philadephia: Fortress 1987), through J. B. Tyson, *Images of Judaism in Luke-Acts* (Columbia, S.Carolina: University of South Carolina 1992), the two volumes by S. G. Wilson, *The Gentiles and the Gentile Mission in Luke-Acts* (Cambridge University Press 1973) and *Luke and the Law* (Cambridge University Press 1983), and R. L. Brawley, *Luke-Acts and the Jews: Conflict, Apology, and Conciliation*

(Atlanta: Scholars 1987), to the three controversial volumes by J. Jervell, *Luke and the People of God* (Minneapolis: Augsburg 1972), *The Unknown Paul: Essays on Luke-Acts and Early Christian History* (Minneapolis: Augsburg 1984), and *The Theology of Acts* (Cambridge University Press 1996). Mention should also be made of the more specific study by J. A. Weatherly, *Jewish Responsibility for the Death of Jesus in Luke-Acts* (Sheffield Academic 1994). For these issues within a wider New Testament framework see the author's *The Partings of the Ways between Christianity and Judaism* (London: SCM Press/ Philadelphia: Trinity Press International 1991).

On the particular issues raised by Luke's portrayal of the Spirit, readers might wish to consult the author's earlier studies – *Baptism in the Holy Spirit* (London: SCM Press/Philadelphia: Westminster 1970), and *Jesus and the Spirit: A Study of the Religious and Charismatic Experience of Jesus and the First Christians as Reflected in the New Testament* (London: SCM Press/Philadelphia: Westminster 1975). Individual monographs of value on other specific aspects, whose titles are self explanatory, include S. Brown, *Apostasy and Perseverance in the Theology of Luke* (Rome: Pontifical Biblical Institute 1969); R. J. Cassidy, *Society and Politics in the Acts of the Apostles* (New York: Orbis 1987); P. F. Esler, *Community and Gospel in Luke-Acts: The Social and Political Motivations of Lucan Theology* (Cambridge University Press 1987); S. R. Garrett, *The Demise of the Devil: Magic and the Demonic in Luke's Writings* (Minneapolis: Fortress 1989); M. L. Soards, *The Speeches in Acts: Their Content, Context, and Concerns* (Louisville: Westminster 1994); F. S. Spencer, *The Portrait of Philip in Acts* (Sheffield Academic 1992); J. T. Squires, *The Plan of God in Luke-Acts* (Cambridge University Press 1993); P. W. Walaskay, *'And So We Came to Rome': The Political Perspective of St Luke* (Cambridge University Press 1983); and R. F. Zehnle, *Peter's Pentecost Discourse: Tradition and Lukan Reinterpretation in Peter's Speeches of Acts 2 and 3* (Nashville: Abingdon 1971).

PART I
Beginning in Jerusalem
1–5

It began in Jerusalem. That is the first clear message which Luke wants his readers to understand. That is why he locates the first obvious section of his narrative (chs 1–5) entirely in Jerusalem. Equally deliberate will be his ending of his narrative in Rome (ch. 28). For his whole account hangs between these two poles, and the character of his narrative is shaped by this tension.

The very identity of his subject matter is determined by the same tension between beginning and goal. What is the 'it' which began in Jerusalem? (1) We today want most naturally to answer, '*Christianity*', and to label Luke's account as 'the first history of Christianity'. And indeed, so it is. But it is not a history as we understand history, as we have already observed (Introduction §4) and as we will have plenty of occasion to confirm. More to the point, such a title is anachronistic. That is to say, to use the term 'Christianity' at this stage is historically inaccurate. Properly speaking, 'Christianity' did not yet exist. The term 'Christians' was first coined some way into Luke's story (11.26; 26.28; cf. I Peter 4.16), and the term 'Christianity' itself first appears in our sources in the 110s (by Ignatius, *Magnesians* 10.1–3; *Romans* 3.3; *Philadelphians* 6.1) – that is, some eighty years after the events narrated by Luke in chs 1–5 here. The term is important as indicating the extent to which the identity of the new movement was bound up with 'Christ', but that simply confirms emphases made by Luke by other means from the first (see on 1.1 and Introduction §5(2)).

If we are to let our description be determined by Luke's preferred terms we could speak of the history of (2) '*the church*', so long as we appreciate that by 'the church' Luke always means the assembly (cf. 19.32, 39, 41) or community of believers in a particular place – in Jerusalem (e.g. 5.11; 12.1; 15.4, 22; 18.22), or in Antioch (13.1; 15.3), or

1

in Ephesus (20.17), or, once, in a region, 'the whole of Judaea' (9.31). Notable here is the fact that Luke also includes reference to 'the church/assembly (of Israel) in the wilderness' (7.38). (3) Another term which sums up identity in a single action and attitude is *'the believers'* (see on 2.44). Luke also occasionally speaks of 'the faith' (13.8; 14.22; 16.5), but in each case a better translation is 'their (or his) faith'. (4) *'The disciples'* first appears in ch. 6 (see on 6.1).

(5) Alternatively, if we limit ourselves to terms actually used at the time, within the narrative itself, rather than by Luke as narrator, we would have to speak of the beginning of *'the way'* (8.36; 9.2; 19.9, 23; 22.4; 24.14, 22), that is, the way of Jesus of Nazareth (cf. 18.25–26; see also on 9.2), or (6) of 'the *sect of the Nazarenes'* (24.5, 14; 28.22). This is a reminder that, in Jewish eyes at least, the new movement centring on the name of the Nazarene (see on 4.10) was simply another sect, like the 'sects' of the Sadducees or the Pharisees (cf. 5.17; 15.5; 26.5). Which is also to say that at this beginning stage we are not yet talking of a new religion, far less a religion sprung full grown into existence at the first Christian Easter or Pentecost. We are talking rather of a movement within the first-century Judaism of the land of Israel, a messianic movement (Jews who were followers of the way of Jesus of Nazareth), indeed, from Christian perspective at least, a renewal movement, whose potential for renewal within the religion of Israel has never been fully realized. (7) Similar conclusions can be drawn from Luke's use of the title *'the saints'* (see on 9.13). (8) A related term is *'brothers'*; but see on 1.15.

'Beginning in Jerusalem', therefore, describes not simply a geo-graphical location. It is also a theological description. It indicates that the identity of the movement whose beginnings Luke now sets out to relate was and remains largely determined by those beginnings. Even when the movement has made its ironically triumphant entry into the capital of the civilized world (Rome), it is still 'the hope of Israel' (28.20) which is at stake. The historical narrative which follows this opening tells of a geographical expansion of that move-ment. The underlying theological narrative, however, is of how that 'hope of Israel' was re-expressed, how the identity of the Jewish way of Jesus was opened and enlarged to embrace the wider world of the Gentiles. The tension thus set up between Jerusalem and Rome, between beginning and goal, becomes the theological drama which underlies the more surface drama of expansion and rejection, of bold proclamation, persecution and shipwreck.

The Prologue: Awaiting the Spirit
1.1–26

The beginning begins with an introduction, a prelude to the majestic (and sometimes sombre) themes which will be given their first full expression in ch. 2. The first chapter of Acts thus fulfils the same role in Luke's second volume that the first two chapters of Luke's Gospel fulfil in his first volume. As the birth narratives are prologue to the account of Jesus' ministry (Luke 1–2), begun by his being anointed with the Holy Spirit and with power at the river Jordan (Acts 10.38), so the account of the fifty days between Easter and Pentecost are prologue to the account of Jesus' first followers being anointed with the Holy Spirit and with power for their ministry.

Chapter 1 also shares with the birth narratives of the Gospel a problem for the historian. The problem is that the theological shaping of the account is so extensive that we cannot be sure just how much is rooted in sound historical memory of any participants. On the whole, in Acts we can be confident that at least most of the basic narrative data is derived from good eyewitness recollection. But here it would appear that the theological emphases have been given top priority – precisely in order to drive home several points relating to the theological character of the new movement's beginnings. In which case, since Luke has been the less concerned with brute facts, the less able are we to say what they were.

The historical problems can be briefly summarized.

(1) The restriction of the disciples to Jerusalem (1.4). The implication is that the disciples remained in Jerusalem between Easter and Pentecost – an inference confirmed by Luke 24.49. But all the other Gospels contain accounts of appearances of the risen Jesus elsewhere, in Galilee in particular. Luke must have known of at least some of these accounts, but he seems to have modified the tradition (cf. Luke 24.6 with Mark 16.7) in order to focus everything in Jerusalem. There must be no uncertainty that it began in Jerusalem.

(2) The separation of ascension from resurrection by forty days (1.3) is a feature confined to Acts. Elsewhere either Jesus' ascension is

portrayed as the other side of the same coin (e.g. John 20.17; Acts 2.32–33; Phil. 2.9), or else it follows his resurrection very quickly (Matt. 28; Luke 24!). In contrast, the earliest account of resurrection appearances (I Cor. 15.3–8) implies that they spanned a much longer period. 'More than 500' (I Cor. 15.6) sounds like a gathering which already reflected the initial growth of the new movement (according to Acts 1.15, there were only about 120 awaiting the coming of the Spirit). The appearance to 'all the apostles' (I Cor. 15.7) also probably relates to the first missionary expansion out of Jerusalem, linked with the Hellenists (Acts 8.4; 11.19–21). And for the appearance to Paul to have been accepted by others as a genuine appearance suggests that it must have followed sufficiently closely to the previous appearance for Paul's claim to have been the last so honoured (I Cor. 15.8) to be credible.

(3) The third major historical problem relates to the death of Judas and his replacement. The difficulty of correlating the other account of Judas' death (Matt. 27.6–10) with the one given here (Acts 1.18) are obvious. Given the state of our traditions it is no longer possible to gain a clear account of Judas' actual end. More important for the Acts narrative is the oddity of the disciples' action in replacing Judas. Why was it done without any command from the risen Christ? Why was it done prior to the coming of the Spirit? Why was it done precisely in the period when neither risen Lord nor outpoured Spirit were there to direct them? There is evidently something important below the surface of the narrative to which these anomalies are probably intended to alert the reader. And finally we should just note the often commented feature that for all their concern to fill Judas' place, we never hear one word more about this new apostle as such. Here again the reader has to ask, What should this fact say about the importance or necessity of this act carried out in the interregnum between Christ and Spirit?

All that being said, however, we can be confident of the basic historical data utilized by Luke. (1) That it *did* begin in Jerusalem is sufficiently clear from other evidence (see Introduction to ch. 2). Luke's editing has the effect of bringing out the theological significance of this historical fact. (2) There was a period during which the risen Christ was seen by/appeared to individuals or groups, including not least 'the twelve', and this period did come to an end. This is also the clear implication of the early tradition cited by Paul in I Cor. 15.3–7 and by Paul's own 'last of all' claim in I Cor. 15.8. (3) Judas did die! Yet, despite his defection, it was a matter of theological principle for the first Christians to be able to speak of an unbroken group of 'the twelve' as a fundamental factor in Christian beginnings (I Cor. 15.5; Rev. 21.14). The very oddity of what is narrated in Acts 1.23–26 may even indicate that these were actions of bewildered men uncertain what to do, waiting for something to happen, and taking the only action they could in the meantime.

More important for an appreciation of Acts 1, however, is a sensitivity to the theological claims which Luke embodies in his narrative. These can be highlighted most simply by following the course of Luke's narrative. And since Luke's emphases in these opening paragraphs help shape the reader's appreciation of the subsequent narrative it is worth pausing longer over them than space really allows.

The transition from the previous volume
1.1–5

Luke's first objective is to ensure that his readers recognize the continuity with his earlier account of Jesus' ministry (the Gospel of Luke). This is not merely a concern for narrative continuity. It is first and foremost a theological concern. The reader must understand that the history of 'the way' about to be narrated cannot be detached from what has gone before. Quite the contrary: what began in Jerusalem really began with Jesus. Failure to appreciate this theological (as well as historical) fact will mean failure to understand the character and purpose of both the narrative and its subject matter.

1.1   The point is made at once by referring back to 'the first part of my work', literally 'the first (or former) word', which Luke had previously written, and to the same person (see Introduction §1). The implication is that Acts is the second volume in the sequence, picking up where the first left off, but continuing the same story and with the same end in view (cf. Luke 1.1–4). The inference is strengthened by the second half of the verse: the account is 'of all that Jesus did and taught from the beginning', or, better, 'all that Jesus began to do and teach' (translations and commentators are divided on the proper translation). Either way the implication is of an unbroken continuity from the beginning of Jesus' ministry through into the history of those who gave the lead in following the way of the Nazarene.

1.2   The continuity is re-enforced by emphasizing four further features. (1) The overlap period with the former account runs right up to the end of the forty days. The double narration of Jesus' ascension (at the end of the Gospel and beginning of Acts) thus functions as a kind of clamp, binding the two accounts together. (2) The overlap period was filled with instruction from Jesus himself (1.3). It is Jesus himself who forms the overlap and ensures that what is to follow is in direct continuity with what went before. (3) The instruction was given 'through the Holy Spirit'. This is a unique theological note within the New Testament: the claim that Jesus' post-resurrection ministry was also inspired or even required the inspiration of the Spirit (but cf. Rom. 1.4; I Tim. 3.16; I Peter 3.18–19). But its function is not so much to say anything about the risen Christ as to ensure that the link from the opening of Jesus' ministry (Luke 3.22; 4.18–21) to the beginning of the church in Jerusalem (Acts 2) is as complete as possible.

(4) Not least of importance was the claim that the instruction was given to 'the apostles'. More than any other Evangelist, Luke had emphasized the role of the disciples of Jesus as 'the apostles' (Luke 6.13; 9.10; 17.5; 22.4; 24.10). And in Acts 'the apostles' become the ones who hold everything together and ensure continuity in the initial expansion (e.g. Acts 2.42–43; 6.6; 8.1, 14; 9.27; 15.22–23). Hence the importance of 1.15–26 (see Introduction to 1.15–26). In later decades and centuries, Gnostic Christians wanted to claim that Jesus had given much more (secret) teaching during a longer eighteen-month period, of which they (the Gnostics) were now the custodians. So it was important to be able to refer to this passage in maintaining that the only custodians recognized by the early church traditions were the apostles.

1.3   A second concern of Luke here is to reassert the tangible character of Jesus' resurrection: 'he presented himself alive to them by many convincing proofs' (NRSV). This again serves the purpose of clamping Luke's two documents together, since the sort of 'convincing proof' that he evidently had in mind was already given in Luke 24.39–43. But the primary concern here was evidently to root the church's beginnings in the certainty of Christ's resurrection. That the resurrection appearances were experienced in such a physical way is the testimony of Luke alone; in contrast we might note Matt. 28.17 ('some were doubtful') and Paul's reminder that the resurrection body is different in character from the body of this life (I Cor. 15.44–50).

Why Luke should make this distinctive emphasis is less clear. Possibly it was in response to some fresh or increasing scepticism about the bodily character of Christ's resurrection. Or possibly it is a reflection of Luke's own perspective on spiritual experience, since elsewhere he seems to emphasize the tangible character of such experience (e.g. Luke 3.22 – 'in bodily form'; Acts 2.1–4; 12.9). It would be somewhat disturbing if belief in the resurrection of Jesus had been dependent in every case on such tangible manifestations. But Luke is a lone voice within the New Testament at this point. Which is not to say that Luke is mistaken in putting such an emphasis on the tangibility of spiritual manifestations. Simply to say that other attestations of the resurrection did not feel the same need.

On the 'forty days' of Jesus' appearances see above (Introduction to ch. 1) and below (1.9–11).

The subject of the risen Jesus' teaching during the forty days is given as 'the kingdom of God', or, as many would prefer, 'God's rule as king'. This is a further striking point of continuity between the Gospel and Acts. If any phrase characterizes Jesus' teaching during his ministry after Jordan it is 'the kingdom of God' (Luke 4.43; 6.20; 7.28; 8.1, 10; 9.2, 11, etc.). And the same phrase recurs sufficiently regularly in Acts as the theme of the expanding mission, not least of the hero of the second half of Acts (Paul), to be more than accidental (8.12; 14.22; 19.8; 20.25; 28.23). Particularly noticeable is its appearance in the very last verse of Acts (28.31): the continuity of gospel theme runs not just through Acts but beyond into the phase following the closure of Acts. This is all the more striking since the phrase occurs so infrequently elsewhere in the New Testament, and still more rarely as characterizing the evangelistic preaching. Here again, then, we can detect a particularly Lukan emphasis as he attempts to reinforce the closeness of the bond between Jesus' preaching and that of the apostles' mission. As will become clear in 1.6, the phrase also plays a part in defining the tension which characterized the new movement's identity.

1.4   It is unclear what Luke means by the first phrase – 'while he was in their company'. Most recent commentators prefer the rendering, 'while he was eating with them' (cf. Acts 10.41). This would reinforce the link back to the table-fellowship which characterized Jesus' earlier ministry (e.g. Luke 7.31–50; 14; 15.2), not least Luke's earlier account of Jesus' appearance to the twelve (Luke 24.30, 35, 41–43), and the importance of 'breaking bread' in the earliest church from the first (Acts 2.42, 46). The continuity of table-fellowship between Jesus and his church, both in its symbolical significance and in its practical implementation, has been one of the primary marks of Christianity from the first.

Otherwise what the phrase entails remains unclear. The tense of the verb, as indeed the flow of the narrative, could imply a continuous presence. But all other accounts of post-Easter appearances indicate much briefer encounters. At this point it doesn't make much difference. Luke's main point is to stress the continuity between Jesus' earlier ministry and the mission of the church, and the language used makes that point clearly enough.

On the significance of the apostles staying in Jerusalem, see above (Introduction to ch. 1 [p.3]).

'The promise of the Father' (REB – 'the gift promised by the Father') is another phrase which binds the end of Luke (Luke 24.49) closely into the beginning of Acts (Acts 3.33, 39). But still more it binds this new phase of the work begun by Jesus into the purpose and plan of God from long before. The sort of passages Luke would no doubt have had in mind would be Ezek. 36.27 and, of course, Joel 2.28–29 (Acts 2.16–21). As will become steadily clearer as we progress through Acts, it is of utmost importance for Luke that the Christian mission be recognized not as a departure from God's earlier purpose through Israel, but as its completion. The Acts of the Apostles not only continue the work of Jesus, but in the power of the same Spirit, and in accordance with the purpose of the one God of Israel.

1.5   The final point of continuity emphasized by this opening paragraph is that between the Pentecost narrative to follow in this Luke's second volume (Acts 2) and the opening of Jesus' ministry in his earlier volume (Luke 3.16). As the repeated references back to John's baptism indicate (Acts 1.22; 10.37; 13.24; 18.25; 19.3–4), it is a point of major concern for Luke to remind his readers that 'the way' of the Nazarene began with John the Baptist. This new phase is not discontinuous or an unexpected departure from the earlier one (see further on Acts 18.24–19.7).

It is equally Luke's concern that his readers should appreciate that the expansion he goes on to narrate has been made possible only in the power of the Spirit (1.8) which as much marks out the new phase of God's purpose as John's baptism marked out the previous phase. Hence the repetition in 11.16 of the comparison (John's baptism in water and the anticipated baptism in Holy Spirit) at the most crucial breakthrough to wider mission (chs 10–11). In both cases the metaphor of baptism associated with the Spirit emphasizes not just the idea of immersion in Spirit (rather than water) but the inauguration of a decisive new stage in the purpose and mission of God (the use of the metaphor in Acts does not validate a more general use of the metaphor, but cf. I Cor. 12.13). That Luke's version here (and in 11.16) has changed the speaker from the Baptist (Luke 3.16) to Jesus is of significance only to the extent of emphasizing that while John the Baptist marks the beginning of the gospel, it is Jesus himself who constitutes the continuity into this new phase and validates its new departures. Quite what the significance of the omission of the phrase 'and fire' (Luke 3.16) amounts to is unclear: it could imply the transformation of the firey baptism into something less fearful (cf. Luke 3.16–17; 12.49–50; but note also Acts 14.22) or more symbolic (cf. Acts 2.3).

The new direction clarified
1.6–8

This section is evidently the climax of the instructions given by Jesus during the forty days in company with the apostles. That 1.8 provides a contents page for the rest of Acts has long been recognized. But more attention needs to be given to 1.6–7. For 1.8 functions as a correction of the false perspective or misleading emphasis articulated in 1.6. The full significance of 1.8 therefore depends on the prior understanding of what it is in 1.6 which is being corrected. The climax of Jesus' resurrection teaching for Luke can be properly appreciated only if both parts of 1.6–8 are given full weight.

1.6 It is not by chance that the question put by those gathered with Jesus (for the last time in this fashion) again focusses on 'the kingdom' (cf. 1.3). Of course, it confirms the importance of 'the kingdom' as a leitmotif linking Gospel and Acts (see on 1.3). But, more important here, it also introduces the readers of Acts to the first point of tension involved in the understanding of the way of the Nazarene. The kingdom of God as preached by Jesus could very readily have been understood in terms of Israel, as God's kingly rule focussed in and expressed through Israel. Or, as that would usually be understood within Israel, as the restoration of Israel to its old glories (Sir. 48.10 – 'to restore the tribes of Jacob'), the kingdom ruled by the son of David outstripping in glory the kingdom ruled by the first David. Such could have been the inference to be drawn from such sayings of Jesus as Luke 12.32, 19.11–27 and 22.29–30. And it is certainly the implication of the question here – that the experience of Jesus raised from the dead and his teaching on the kingdom had given them to believe (or confirmed them in their belief) that the kingdom (REB 'sovereignty') was about to be restored to Israel. Such an expectation indicates a hope fully in continuity with the hope of Israel's prophets (the restoration of Israel), but still constricted by the terms of that earlier hope.

1.7   It is important to note that the hope of the kingdom in these terms is corrected or qualified by Jesus, but not denied or rejected. The implication is that the question (1.6) arose, not improperly, out of or in response to Jesus' teaching on the kingly rule of God (1.3). And here Jesus simply dismisses speculation about timing, not the thought itself. In other words, the idea that the kingdom of God is related to the restoration of Israel is in effect reaffirmed. In this way is set up the tension regarding the identity of the church: in what sense is it a continuation of Israel, its presence and expansion a fulfilment of Israel's hope? And in what sense does the kingdom of God transcend hope for the restoration of Israel?

Not least of importance is the firm assertion that such matters lie wholly within the authority of God. Luke's monotheism brooks no qualification. The outworking of Luke's narrative simply reflects the unbrokenness of God's purpose, but also its clarification. Since the effective implementation of God's kingly authority almost inevitably carries overtones of final judgment (cf. Luke 22.29–30), there is probably also a warning against speculating about the end or the radical transformation of human history. Trust in God's sovereignty is not to be made dependent on human expectation of a particular timetable or outcome (cf. Mark 13.32; Luke 19.11). For the present it is enough that God's rule is expressed in and through his Spirit.

1.8   does indeed provide the outline which Luke's account will follow – the beginnings in Jerusalem (chs 1–5), the first stirrings resulting in expansion more widely into Judaea and then, wonder of wonders, into apostate Samaria (chs 6–12), and finally to 'the farthest corners of the earth' (13–28). The last phrase (literally 'to the end of the earth') certainly envisages a world-wide mission, with perhaps a specific echo of Isa. 49.6 intended (cf. Luke 2.32; Acts 13.47; 26.23). The implication, then, is that Paul's success in bringing the gospel to Rome was the most significant step on the way to that goal, but not the goal itself (though the phrase was used a century earlier in reference to Rome in *Psalms of Solomon* 8.15). The wider vocation of the servant of Yahweh to be 'a light to the nations' (Isa. 42.6–7 = Acts 26.18; Isa. 49.6) looked still further beyond Rome. Here again we may recall the deliberate way Luke ends his account by speaking of the open and unhindered preaching of the kingdom of God in the heart of Rome itself (28.31). In other words, the answer provided by 1.8 (and the whole of the following narrative) to the question of 1.6 is that the question itself is not closed. The gospel goes on, the proclamation of the kingdom continues. The hope and mission of Israel has not yet been completely fulfilled (cf. 28.20). Part of the tension in Luke's redefinition is that the apostles maintain the continuity by staying in Jerusalem (cf. particularly 8.1) and do not themselves take the message to the end of the earth.

In the meantime, however, the priority is clear: not speculation about 'dates or times' (1.7) but 'witness'. The term assumes critical importance, particularly in the early chapters of Acts, and reinforces the importance of the opening transition passage (1.1–5). For the role of witness is consistently related to the resurrection appearances of Jesus (1.22; 2.32; 3.15; 5.32; 10.41; 13.31; 22.15; 26.16). Here again there is an element of correction in the direction which might have been plotted from 1.1–5 alone. For the commission given to the apostles and their companions is not to re-proclaim the *teaching* of Jesus given during that time, but to proclaim *Jesus himself* in his resurrection.

Not least of importance is the reiteration of the promise of the Spirit (twice within four verses, not to mention Luke 24.49). What it means to thus experience the Spirit is now clarified. The Spirit is the power of God within creation and human life. The impact of the Spirit is therefore characteristically one of transformation, of enabling what would be impossible in human strength alone. In this case it is an enabling to live and speak in such a way as bears witness to the risen Christ. It is only in the strength of this power which comes from on high that the mission of witness can be carried

11

through. The prominence of the Spirit in Luke's narrative from Pentecost onwards makes clear beyond doubt that for Luke the mission of the church could not hope to be effective without this empowering from God (the Spirit of God) which transcends human ability and transforms human inability.

Jesus' departure
1.9–11

By making the narrative run on without a break, Luke indicates that 1.7–8 was Jesus' final word. The account of the ascension thus functions to bring to a clear and unequivocal end this phase of the two-volume story. It is here, strictly speaking, that the account of Jesus' earthly ministry ends. The interlocking nature of the two volumes is reinforced.

Luke's account of the ascension poses two principal problems. (1) We have earlier observed that the forty day period is peculiar to Luke and that the resurrection appearances seem to have continued for a longer period. What then is the explanation for Luke's account here? We can hardly be sure, but one possible answer is that Luke wished to emphasize the distinctiveness of the different epochs of God's purpose. The next fixed date in the calendar of earliest Christian remembrance was Pentecost (see Introduction to ch. 2). That began the phase of a Spirit-empowered church. To mark it out clearly from the preceding epoch, the ministry of Jesus, it was desirable, therefore, to draw a clear line under that ministry, indicating beyond doubt that it had ceased, at least in the form of the personal presence of Jesus on earth. The intervening few days (1.15–26) would then make clear the absence of both Jesus and the Spirit.

If there is anything in this we should not conclude that Luke is dealing casually with his material or falsifying history. Quite what the history actually was is hard to tell, when all that we otherwise hear of is episodic seeings of and encounters with Jesus. And Luke may well have been confronted with the same difficulty; he later describes the appearance to Saul/Paul as a 'heavenly vision' (26.19). More important, then, to make quite clear that that period of revelatory encounter with the risen Christ had ceased. Apart from anything else, there might be endless confusion between experiences of the Spirit and experiences of the risen Christ (a few have seen Pentecost as a variant tradition of the appearance to more than 500 – I Cor. 15.6); and the scope for new and divergent teachings to be rooted in a claimed succession of further resurrection appearances would be endless (as the later Gnostic documents show). At this point the theological imperative takes precedence over a disparate tradition whose historical connectedness is unclear.

(2) The other problem is how the ascension should be conceptualized. It was no problem for Luke, of course, since he presumably shared the common perception of the cosmos, where heaven was literally above the earth, so that 'going to heaven' meant quite literally 'ascension' ('taken up into heaven' – 1.11). The problem arises for the modern interpreter, however, since heaven is no longer conceived as 'up there', except in a metaphorical or pictorial sense. The problem is compounded since, according to 1.11, the return of Jesus (the second coming) will be patterned on his departure to heaven. What then are we today to make of an 'ascension' in a day of space rockets and satellites?

The simplest answer is that we should not confuse metaphor and fact. All talk of the divine and of heaven has to be metaphorical; human speech can never encompass a dimension of reality which so completely transcends our own. This was as true of the ancients as it is today. In trying to speak of heaven they, like us, spoke of what was beyond every day experience. With their more limited perspective on the cosmos, it was sufficient to express that 'beyond' in terms of beyond what eye can see. The metaphor of transcendence could be expressed quite fully enough for them by envisaging it as literal 'up-above'-ness. The result was that they framed their visions of heaven in these terms; they could not conceive of going to heaven as otherwise than ascending to heaven. Consequently the interpretation of Luke's account here involves no denial of what he says, but simply a reconceptualizing of what he recounts. Nor does it mean that we have to abandon the language of 'ascension'. It simply means that we give more weight to its metaphorical and symbolical character. What all this means for a conceptualization of the coming again of Christ needs to be thought through more than it has been.

1.9   The account here is normally described as an ascension. It could equally be described as a 'rapture' or 'translation'. Transportation by cloud (a cloud 'received or supported or took him up') was a regular feature of visions of heaven (e.g. Dan. 7.13; I Thess. 4.17). Various heroes of the past were thought to have been translated to heaven in similar fashion – notably Enoch (cf. the interpretation of Gen. 5.24 in *II Enoch* 3.1) and Elijah (II Kings 2.11, a whirlwind). And there was speculation current in the first century as to whether Moses had been taken to heaven in a similar way (Josephus, *Antiquities* 4.326). That Jesus had certainly already died, but had also been raised from the dead prior to his ascension, makes this variation on the pattern unique.

It is also notable that no account is given of Jesus' being transformed into a more glorious form – a regular feature of such heavenly transportations (cf. *II Enoch* 22.8; *Ascension of Isaiah* 9.9; not to mention Luke 9.29). What is not clear, and Luke makes no effort to clarify the issue, is whether Jesus' resurrection body was somehow different during the forty days (cf. again Luke 24.39–43), or whether it was in this tangibly physical form that he was transported to heaven. The issue is caught up with that of Luke's own conceptuality of spiritual encounters (see Introduction §5(5f)) and the preceding discussion of the metaphorical significance of the term 'ascension'.

1.10   The two men in white robes are presumably intended to be understood as angels – frequent participants in the opening to Luke's previous volume (e.g. Luke 1.11, 26; 2.9) and prominent participants in the later narratives of Acts (5.19; 8.26; 10.3; 12.7; 27.23). Here again we are caught up in the ancient Jewish world's way of conceptualizing encounters with the divine and one of the ways of conceptualizing the experience of inspiration from beyond (cf. Revelation). Johnson, however, thinks that Luke intended an allusion rather to Moses and Elijah, a plausible suggestion in view of the above parallels and of Luke 9.30–31. The allusion would be strengthened by the fact that both Moses and Elijah commissioned their successors, Joshua and Elijah, who in turn received their spirit (Deut. 34.9; I Kings 19.16; II Kings 1.9–12). As with Elijah (and Jesus in John's Gospel), Jesus must depart before the Spirit of Jesus can be more widely dispersed.

1.11   It is important to note again that Luke's perspective extends far beyond the success of the gospel in reaching Rome. Beyond his own end point (Rome), he looked not only for witness to be borne to the end of the earth (1.8), but also for a climax beyond. The opening of Acts (Christ's departure) is to be matched in the real story extending beyond Acts narrative history with a final closure (Christ's return). The ascension of Jesus thus fulfils a double role in Luke's narrative: it both brings the epoch of Jesus' own ministry on earth to a close, and it points forward to the equivalent closure of the interim period of the church's witness in the return of Jesus. Luke does not say, but presumably the coming of Christ will correlate with the coming of the kingdom and provide the final answer to the disciples' question of 1.6, leaving it open in the meantime.

Waiting in Jerusalem
1.12–14

Luke's task in describing the period between ascension and Pentecost is to give the impression of its character as an interval between Jesus and the Spirit, empty of either. He does this first by indicating a period of prayerful waiting.

1.12 The fact that the ascension took place outside Jerusalem had not been made clear in the previous narrative. So the mention of the return to Jerusalem here allows a reaffirmation of the earlier emphasis (1.4) that the apostles never stirred from Jerusalem (see Introduction to ch. 1), and thus underlines once again the importance of the continuity with Israel's past and the previous phases of God's purpose which Jerusalem symbolized.

The identification of the site of the ascension as the Mount of Olives may belong to early Christian memory (cf. Luke 19.29; 21.37), but it may also reflect the eschatological significance attributed to the Mount of Olives in Zech. 14.4–5. The note that Olivet was only a sabbath day's journey from Jerusalem (between 1.1 kilometers and three-quarters of a mile) further reinforces the impression (no doubt intended by Luke) that the movement of Jesus' disciples thus far was still wholly contained within the bounds of observant Judaism.

1.13 'The upper room' presumably refers to a room already mentioned, that is, 'the large upper room' (though the Greek word is different) of Luke 22.12. Despite Barrett, there is no reason why we should avoid the implication that the room was large enough for the apostles (about to be named) to live there during the next few days. After all, they were all Galileans (1.11), and historical continuity between their time with Jesus and the establishment of the Jerusalem church following Pentecost implies that they probably stuck together during what, on any reconstruction of events, must have been a difficult interim period.

The list of disciples is the same as in Luke 6.14–16. The only differences are: (1) the two brothers, James and John, are now grouped with Peter, leaving Andrew, Peter's brother, separated from Peter; (2) the next four are the same as in Luke 6, but now grouped in two pairs – Philip and Thomas, Bartholomew and Matthew (cf. Matt. 10.3); (3) the final three are in the same order, with Judas, of course omitted. That Simon is described as 'the zealot' indicates a further point of continuity with traditional Judaism, since the term denotes someone 'zealous' for the distinctive traditions of Israel (cf. Acts 21.20; 22.3; Gal. 1.14); at the time it did not yet refer to membership of the Zealots, a faction which only emerged in the period leading into the Jewish revolt of AD 66. The implication is that Peter, James and John formed a central or leadership group – an inference borne out by their association elsewhere (Luke 8.45; 9.28) and by their role in the subsequent chapters. Whether the grouping in pairs of the second foursome signifies anything is now impossible to say.

1.14   The emphasis on their being all 'of one accord' is typical of Luke (the word is almost exclusive to Acts, where it appears ten times); as is also the importance which he places on prayer throughout his two books (Luke 1.10; 3.21; 5.16; 6.12; 9.18, 28–29; 11.1; 22.41; Acts 1.24–25; 2.42; 4.24–30; 6.6; 8.15; 9.11; 10.2, 9; 12.5, 12; 13.3; 16.25; 20.36; 21.5). That women (their wives?) were present is also in accord with Luke's description of their prominence in Jesus' earlier mission (Luke 8.2–3; 23.49, 55–56; 24.1–10, 22).

The mention of Jesus' mother and brothers being present is somewhat surprising. The implication of such few references as there are to them during Jesus' ministry (particularly Mark 3.20–21, 31–35) is that they were hostile to Jesus' ministry. Presumably we are intended to deduce that they had become reconciled to Jesus either before his death or afterwards. The explicit mention of Mary indicates that she had a prominent place within the Jerusalem church, along with the apostles, from the first.

James, Jesus' eldest brother, will be included, of course, though it is noticeable that Luke does not pick him out here, despite his later prominence as the leader of the Jerusalem church (see on 12.17). When he in particular became a disciple or believer in Jesus is not clear. The traditional view is that he was converted by the appearance of the risen Jesus to him (I Cor. 15.7), but that is by no means certain. Apart from the appearance to Paul, all the other appearances were to those who already had been followers. At the very least, however, the mention of Jesus' family being present in the upper room provides further reinforcement of the continuity with what had gone before. The new phase of the work begun by Jesus did not mean a breach with Jesus' family. On the contrary they were thoroughly involved in it from the first.

The twelfth man
1.15–26

In the interval between Jesus and the Spirit the only action taken (or narrated), apart from prayer, is the replacement of Judas as the twelfth apostle. The very manner of its narration, particularly the awkwardness of the insertion of the report of Judas' death, indicates the character of the period in Luke's account.

On the one hand, as noted earlier (Introduction to ch. 1), there is the oddity of such an important action being taken precisely in the intervening period, after Christ's departure and prior to the Spirit's coming. It is not that Jesus' departure as such meant that access to Jesus' presence and power was no longer possible (contrast e.g. Acts 3.16; 18.9–10). So Luke's failure to refer to such direction from the ascended Christ will not have been accidental. On the contrary, the resort to the ancient method of lots (1.26) underscores their plight; for all the difference of epoch that Jesus had brought about, they were no better off than the ancient Israelites (see on 1.26).

On the other hand, the fact that the one clear action taken in the ten day interval is to complete the band of twelve apostles is surely intended to imply an attitude wholly in accord with that of the question in 1.6. The implication is that a restored band of twelve is assumed to be necessary if the apostles are to form the core of a reconstituted Israel, representatives of the new twelve tribes (note again Luke 22.29). The negative corollary is that in this pre-Pentecost period the remaining apostles were still no further on than they were in 1.6, still needing the redirection which Jesus himself had indicated in 1.7–8. The positive corollary is that by reconstituting the twelve, Luke reaffirms yet once more the continuity between the church about to emerge and the Israel of old. There is a similar ambivalence in the impression given by Luke 1–2.

In short, the overall impression given by the account is of an uncertainty, awkwardness and powerlessness – just what needed to be remedied by the coming of the Spirit at Pentecost.

1.15   Putting the spotlight on Peter at this point may be deliberate as confirming that Peter's leadership went back to Jesus' initial choice of the twelve (Luke 6.14); it did not result solely from the events at Pentecost. The term 'brothers' is now used for the whole group (so also 6.3; 9.30; 10.23; 11.1, 12, 29; 12.17; 14.2; 15.1, 3, 7, 13, 22, 23, 32, 33, 36, 40; 16.2, 40; 17.6, 10, 14; 18.18, 27; 21.7, 17, 20; 18.14, 15), but Luke continues to use it for their relationship with fellow Jews (2.29, 37; 3.17; 7.2; 13.15, 26, 38; 22.1, 5; 23.1, 5, 6; 28.17, 21). It therefore nicely reflects the tension between continuity and redefinition underlying Luke's account (nicely caught, e.g., by its use in 9.17 and 22.13, and by the interplay sustained to the end in 28.14–21).

It is unclear how the larger group (about 120) relate to the previous (1.3–6) and future events (2.1–4). But however much Luke may have wanted to make the apostles the custodians of the tradition of Jesus' teaching (see on 1.2), he certainly made no effort to limit the outpouring of the Spirit to the twelve.

1.16   Continuity of divine purpose is most clearly affirmed by identifying events, not least unexpected events, with scriptural prophecies. The point is reinforced in several ways: (1) the divinely determined necessity of fulfilment (similarly Luke 22.37; 24.26, 44; Acts 1.21; 3.18; 17.3); (2) the Holy Spirit as inspiring author of the prophecy (the only reference to the Spirit in the interval between ascension and Pentecost); and (3) the reminder that the human speaker of the prophecy was David himself (cf. 4.25). See further on 1.20.

1.17   There is obviously some play between the 'lot', the portion of ministry which Judas was assigned and the lots to be cast in 1.26. The implication is that Matthias took over Judas' ministry (1.20, 25). But at this point there may just be a deliberate ambiguity, that Judas fulfilled all too well the ministry he had actually been given (cf. 2.23; and note 1.25 – 'he went to his own place'). What then that says about Matthias as Judas' replacement is less clear.

1.18–19 The tradition diverges so much from that contained in Matt. 27.3–10 that it is impossible to work back to a common account: who bought the field and when? how did Judas die, and was it by suicide or by accident? The two accounts set alongside each other show just how far accounts of what must have been one event can diverge in the tradition process (common to both: the fact of Judas' death, somehow connected to a field known as the 'field of blood'). But they also show how little concerned were the Evangelists to reproduce 'bare data' or unreflected-upon tradition. Here it is the divergent purposes of the Evangelists which have determined how such information as was available to them was used. Matthew's purpose was to demonstrate another example of prophecy fulfilled (Zech. 11.12–13; cf. Jer. 32.6–15; 18.2–3).

In contrast, Luke, unlike Matthew (27.3), makes no attempt to depict Judas as repenting for his act of betrayal. On the contrary, Judas had been possessed by Satan (Luke 22.3), is shown as unrepentant (he bought a plot of land or small farm with 'the reward of his wickedness'), his death is depicted in classic terms as the death of an evil man (cf. II Sam. 20.10; Wisd. Sol. 4.19; II Macc. 9.9), and he 'went to his own place' (1.25 – presumably hell). In Acts Judas stands with Herod (12.23), less so Ananias and Sapphira (5.1–10), as a fearful warning.

1.20 The Psalms cited are 69.26 and 109.8 (Luke uses the Greek version, partly no doubt for his readers' benefit). The former is one of the more commonly cited Psalms in the New Testament: 69.9 (John 2.17; Rom. 15.3); 69.22–23 (Rom. 11.9–10). The section quoted here and in Romans (69.22–28) is a malediction against David's enemies. Its use probably reflects the prior conclusion that the earlier part of the Psalm foreshadowed the suffering and rejection of Jesus (cf. 69.21 with Luke 23.36). Which probably means that the Psalm emerged as a messianic psalm in the course of earliest Christian reflection on the sufferings of the Christ (cf. Luke 24.26–27) which Luke has been able to turn to good account here.

This is the only clear use of Ps. 109 in the New Testament. It is a similar psalm of cursing against enemies, and as a psalm attributed to David, it invited a similar use to that of Ps. 69.

The logic is the same in both cases: not necessarily that these psalms were prophecies as such to which one could look for further fulfilments; but rather that as Davidic psalms, which shed such light on key events that had already taken place, they could be recognized as prophecies. The function of prophecy here assumed may thus be seen as more confirmative than predictive, to be recognized as prophecy after the event rather than clearly indicating what will happen beforehand.

1.21–22   Most important here is the qualification which is laid down for apostleship. (1) An apostle must have been one of those who followed Jesus continually (2) from the baptism of John until the ascension, and thus (3) also be a witness of Jesus' resurrection. The emphasis on continuity could hardly be clearer. Once again John's baptism is treated as the starting point for what is distinctive about Jesus' ministry and the ministry he instituted (see on 1.5). And once again the centrality of the resurrection as the focal point of witness is re-emphasized (see on 1.8). Clearly implied is the central and crucial role of the apostles in safeguarding that continuity and providing the authoritative continuity with 'all that Jesus began to do and teach' or 'did and taught from the beginning' (1.1; see also on 1.2). Notable also is the fact that Luke does not hesitate to speak of Judas as having had an 'apostleship' (1.25), with the corollary that even one of the apostles can defect and end as evil men end. It is this breach in the apostolic circle which makes the replacement of Judas necessary.

It should be appreciated that this definition of apostleship is something of a development which goes beyond what we find in Paul's writings. Both are agreed on the centrality of the resurrection and of commissioning from the risen Christ (cf. I Cor. 9.1; 15.8–9). But Luke's first two qualifications do not feature in Paul's definition of apostleship. Much more important for him was the role of the apostle as missionary and church founder (again I Cor. 9.1–2; 15.8–11), reflecting what was probably the term's original force ('apostle' = one sent, that is, missionary). Luke does not diminish the missionary thrust (1.8), but the redefinition involved, here of apostle as safeguarder of authoritative tradition, almost certainly reflects later concerns and leaves Luke with some embarrassment over the status of Paul, who also fails the first two qualifications (see further on 14.4). It also helps explain how it is that 'the apostles' can disappear so completely from view in the latter half of Acts: as guarantors of the continuity and the teaching of Jesus, and not themselves missionaries, their task is largely done in the first half of Acts.

1.23–26   We know and hear nothing more of either candidate. Since Luke also says nothing more of the majority of those listed in 1.13, perhaps not too much should be made of this. On the other hand, having made so much of the event and its importance, his subsequent silence is surprising – unless the intended implication is that the action reflected the in-between state of the ten days in contrast to the subsequent confidence (chs 2–5). Bearing in mind the observations of the preceding paragraph, it is worth noting that James, the brother of Jesus, is not put forward. Of the three most prominent and influential people in the subsequent narrative (Peter, James brother of Jesus, and Paul), only one met the qualifications to become one of 'the apostles'!

The prayer (1.24–25) is addressed to God ('knower of hearts'; cf. 15.8) and seems to be the expression of proper piety (cf. e.g. Deut. 8.2; Ps. 139.23). That fact and the traditional role of lots (1.26) as a means of discerning God's will (e.g. Lev. 16.7–10; Num. 26.55; I Sam. 10.20–21) means that the action of Peter and the others cannot be disparaged as an act of unbelief. And it remains possible that Luke intended the narrative to be understood in wholly positive terms. Yet it is striking that when Luke uses very similar terms in 15.7–8 (God who knows the heart and chooses) that which attests his choice and will is the giving of the Holy Spirit. On balance, therefore, it appears as though this action in filling the twelfth man's place was intended by Luke to stand in contrast with the immediately following account of the disciples and apostles being filled with the Holy Spirit and marked out and empowered for ministry.

When the Spirit Came
2.1–47

It began with the Spirit. The reiterated promises of the prologue (1.5, 8), followed by the downbeat of the in-between time (1.12–26), have prepared the way for the climax of Pentecost. This is clearly Luke's second great theme, and more important than the first. It began with the Spirit. For without the Spirit there would be no story to tell. Without the Spirit there would be no church, no way to follow. Without the Spirit there would be no witness bearing, in Jerusalem or anywhere else. Again history and theology combine to reinforce the significance of each other.

The theological notes are clear. (1) The timing of the Spirit's coming on the Day of Pentecost. (2) The symbolism of a crowd gathered 'from every nation under heaven' hearing of God's mighty works in their own tongues (2.5–6). 'To the end of the earth' (1.8) is already foreshadowed. (3) Peter's sermon tying together outpouring of the Spirit with exalted Christ (particularly 2.33), reaffirming the direct continuity between David and his greater descendant on the one hand and the explosion of new life and power on the other. (4) The immediate success of Peter's sermon (2.41), and the quality of the new church's common life, built round the apostles' teaching, the breaking of bread together and common prayer and worship (2.42).

Here, however, we can be more confident that Luke was able to draw on good historical tradition for the heart of the narrative. (1) That the new movement was a renewal movement of the Spirit, enthusiastic and charismatic, is clearly attested and assumed elsewhere in the New Testament (e.g. Rom. 8.4–27; Gal. 3.2–5; Heb. 2.4; I Peter 1.12; I John 3.24). Our knowledge of such movements at other times, in Christianity and other religions, would have suggested to us anyway that such a movement probably began with a significant group experience of enthusiasm or ecstasy. (2) That such an experience happened in Jerusalem, and helped establish

Jerusalem as the centre of the new movement, is confirmed by the fact that no other or alternative founding centre for Christianity is even so much as hinted at in Christian source documents. Even Paul, whose relations with Jerusalem were often frosty (to say the least), always regarded Jerusalem as the spiritual centre of the gospel he proclaimed (Rom. 11.26; 15.19, 25–27; Gal. 2.1–2). (3) That it took place on the first Pentecost after Jesus' crucifixion is also likely. With any longer interval the cohesion of the disciples would have been greatly strained. Pentecost was the next great pilgrim feast when followers of Jesus were likely anyway to gather in Jerusalem in hopes of some further confirmation of their new faith in Jesus as risen. Why else would the first Christians take over the Jewish feast of Pentecost, rather than the feast of Booths, if it did not have special associations for them (cf. Acts 20.16)? And the use of the imagery of firstfruits for the Spirit by Paul (Rom. 8.23) suggests an already traditional association between the Spirit and Pentecost (the feast of firstfruits) at the time of Paul. We could also note the echo of the language used in the Pentecost narrative – the Spirit outpoured (Acts 2.17–18, 33; cf. 10.45) in Rom. 5.5 and Titus 3.6, baptized in Spirit (Acts 1.5) in I Cor. 12.13 – suggesting deliberate echoes of a more established tradition.

For the traditions used in the sermon and in the final summary passage see the introductions to these sections.

The day of Pentecost
2.1–4

Pentecost was a festival full of potential significance for the first Christians. It is striking, then, how little of that significance Luke points up in his account. (1) As the feast of firstfruits (the dedication of the first sheaf of the wheat harvest) it could have encouraged thought of the Spirit as the beginning of God's work of redemption (as in Rom. 8.23). (2) With the symbolism of wind (2.2) and breath could have come the thought of the Spirit as the breath of new life (as in 'the Johannine Pentecost' in John 20.22, deliberately echoing Gen. 2.7). (3) The powerful symbolism of fire for cleansing/purifying present in the earlier form of the Baptist's prediction (Luke 3.16), where it appears to echo such prophetic oracles as Isa. 4.4, 30.27–28 and 66.15–18, has been largely evacuated in the portrayal of 'tongues of fire' (Acts 2.3).

(4) At some point within Judaism Pentecost came to be celebrated as the giving of the law and renewal of the covenant, in which case there would have been scope to insert the idea of the Spirit as replacing the law and inaugurating the new covenant (cf. II Cor. 3.3–6). Indeed, a later Jewish tradition elaborates the account of the giving of the law in ways not dissimilar to Luke's account of many languages being spoken, and there have been suggestions that Luke's account is influenced by such traditions. The traditions, however, cannot be dated to the first century, and there is no clear evidence of Luke using or alluding to them (for details see e.g. Lake and Cadbury 5.116 and Barrett 111–12).

(5) A more plausible allusion would be to the division of speech at Babel (Gen. 11.1–9) – the Pentecost miracle as its reversal. The problem here is that Luke evidently did not think of the tongues as a single language (Acts 2.6, 11; contrast *Testament of Judah* 25.3).

(6) The imagery Luke was concerned with is that bound up in talk of the Spirit as 'the promise of the Father', the fulfilment of the Baptist's talk of Spirit-baptism as hallmark of the Coming One's ministry, just as water baptism had been John's own hallmark (1.4–5), and the promised empowering for witness (see on 1.8). (7) As his later emphasis on the Spirit makes clear (2.38–39; 8.14–17; 9.17; 10.44–47; 19.1–6), Luke was also concerned to indicate that without the coming of the Spirit into a life there can be no discipleship.

2.1   Pentecost was one of the three pilgrim feasts of the Jewish religious year, when devout Jews, where possible, would seek to celebrate the festival in Jerusalem (particularly Lev. 23.15–21; Deut. 16.9–12). It took place fifty days after Passover (*pentekoste* = 50th). 'All' are present, with nothing in the preceding context to indicate that the 'all' should be understood as any other than the 120 or so, indicated in 1.15. Without further detail we should presumably understand the 'one place' where they were gathered to be the upper room of 1.13.

2.2   The same word in both Hebrew (*ruah*) and Greek (*pneuma*) means both wind and breath and spirit. Hence the play on words particularly in Ezek. 37.9–10 and John 3.8 and 20.22. The sound is not the wind itself but a sound 'like' that of a wind. The play of allusion is enhanced by talk of it 'filling the whole house' (cf. 2.4).

2.3   Again to be noted is the description, 'tongues like fire', not fire as such. What is being described is, strictly speaking, a vision. The subject of 'sat' is singular, which probably indicates a single entity (a single flame?) divided among each of those present. There is presumably another play between 'tongues' of fire and speaking in 'other tongues' (2.4).

2.4   Note again the emphasis on 'all'. Despite Luke's emphasis on the importance of 'the apostles' elsewhere (see on 1.2) he seems to take some pains to ensure that his readers do not think the Spirit of Pentecost was given only to the apostles.

The imagery of being 'filled with the Spirit' is one of Luke's favourite ways of speaking of the experience of the Spirit (Luke 1.41, 67; 4.8, 31; 9.17; 13.9) and presumably comes in part at least from the experience itself, as one of emptiness being transformed into one of overflowing. We may assume the same reason behind the characteristic water or liquid imagery associated with the Spirit (e.g. Isa. 44.3; Ezek. 39.29; John 7.37–39; I Cor 12.13). It is just that experience of refreshing and revitalizing which has traditionally been attributed to and recognized as a mark of God's Spirit.

That the experience also involves glossolalia is again a common feature of such experiences, glossolalia understood as automatic speech, or articulation without conscious manipulation or monitoring of speech patterns. Elsewhere in the New Testament it is understood to be unknown, probably angelic language (I Cor. 13.1; 14.2, 9), and 'tongue' in the sense of 'language' is an established usage. But only Luke (Acts 2.6, 11) presents glossolalia as speaking in known foreign languages. The rise of Pentecostalism in the early twentieth century saw many similar reports. None of them have been well authenticated, but the fact that such reports can be circulated today indicates that even here Luke could be drawing on very early impressions or reports.

The reaction of the crowd
2.5–13

The crowd here function very much in the role of the chorus in a contemporary play. (1) They are there in a representative capacity – to represent every nation under heaven (2.5), able to hear 'the great things of God' in their own language. The awkward insertion of the list of nations at 2.9–11 (including Judaea!) reinforces the choral effect but also enhances the theological point, since the fifteen nations named stretch in a rough circle round Jerusalem, from Parthians, Medes and Elamites in the east round in an anticlockwise circle with Egypt, Cyrene, Rome, Crete and Arabia circumscribing the second half of the circle (west to south). There is possibly an echo of some record of Jewish dispersion (cf. Philo, *Embassy to Gaius* 281–2). (2) At the same time the fact that all there gathered are explicitly described as 'Jews' (2.5), 'Jews and proselytes' (2.10–11) effectively renews the tension bound up in Luke's presentation of the new movement (see Introduction to chs 1–5). He wished to assert, or at least to foreshadow its universal sweep (cf. 1.8). But he wished also to indicate that the initial phase of its expansion was confined to Jews, restricted within the Judaism of the time, dispersed as the latter was throughout the world (there were more Jews living outside the land of Israel than in it). (3) Also chorus-, or at least drama-like, is the final verse (2.13), the sub-group within the crowd (chorus) who provide comic relief (as well as the link to the next section). The underlying theological point, however, is that the manifestations of the Spirit are not self-evident in themselves, but ambiguous and capable of different interpretations. Eph. 5.18 plays on just the same ambiguity as here.

2.5   It is possible that Luke thought the crowd was composed of pilgrims (present in Jerusalem for the feast), but his language is more naturally understood of diaspora Jews now resident in Jerusalem (cf. 6.1). Only those from Rome are described as 'visitors' (2.10). Either way, however, it is their origin in the diaspora which gives them their symbolic significance for Luke's account.

2.6   The 'sound' is unspecified. It could be that of the wind-like sound in 2.2. Or, more likely, it could be the noise generated by the glossolalia – reinforcing the impression that what was in view was an ecstatic experience. This impression is put beyond doubt by 2.13; those who had been filled with the Spirit gave the impression of being drunk.

2.7 The reference to 'Galileans' alludes not only to a particular dialect (Galilean 'Scots' to Judaean 'English'; cf. Luke 22.59). More important is the sharpening of the antithesis between the small regional beginnings of the Nazarene movement and the world-wide outreach about to be foreshadowed.

The repeated references to 'Jews', 'Judaea', 'Jews' (2.5, 9, 11) reinforce the tension between a still Jerusalem- and Israel-focussed message and its universal potential.

2.12–13 In dramatic terms, both reactions open the door to the next scene.

Peter's first sermon
2.14–36

The structure of the sermon is straightforward. Each section focusses on a quotation from the scriptures.

(*a*) Introduction (2.14–21), answering the charge of drunkenness – Joel 2.28–32;

(*b*) Central section (2.22–32), on Jesus' resurrection – Ps. 16.8–11;

(*c*) Climax (2.33–36), linking the christology to the outpoured Spirit – Ps. 110.1.

(*d*) We should also note that in an important sense the sermon is not completed until 2.39, where there is obviously a deliberate echo of Joel 2.32 answering to the initial quotation and rounding off the whole in a pleasing rhetorical fashion.

Bearing in mind the general remarks on the speeches in Acts (Introduction §4.3), we are looking here not at a transcript of what Peter said on the occasion but at a cameo representation (it would take only about three minutes to declaim these verses) of the sort of thing Peter would have said, and may indeed have said in his earliest preaching. Although the sermon is in Luke's own words there are several indications that he was able to draw on earlier tradition. (1) The speech is a good example of a Jewish sermon – a midrash on Joel 2.28–32, with Acts 2.39 rounding it off. (2) The full quotation from Joel is only alluded to elsewhere (particularly Rom. 10.13 and Titus 3.6), which suggests that the fuller thought given by the whole passage early on became an established part of Christian tradition. And while Ps. 16.8–11 could be part of Luke's own theological armoury (used only here and in Acts 13.35), Ps. 110.1 certainly belongs to early Christian reflection on what had happened to Jesus (see on 2.33–35). (3) The eschatology is surprising in Acts (see on 2.16–20). (4) The christology itself seems primitive at a number of points: the personal name, 'Jesus the Nazarene' (2.22), 'Jesus' (2.32), 'this Jesus' (2.36); 'a man attested by God . . . signs that God did through him' (2.22); 'the Messiah' – still a title (2.31); Jesus as the bestower of the Spirit, consequent upon his exaltation (2.33); the resurrection/ascension as evidence that 'God has made him both Lord and Messiah' (2.36). Given the more developed christology at the period of Luke's writing, it is unlikely that he was wishing to promote these emphases. It is more likely that he drew them from traditions or memories which his inquiry (or common knowlege) had brought to light.

So far as Luke's own theological emphases are concerned we should note that he takes the opportunity of the sermon to reinforce the tensions within the Jerusalem church and its earliest evangelism. On the one hand, the quotation from Joel speaks of an outpouring of the Spirit on all flesh in the context of cosmic convulsions (2.17, 19–20). On the other, the addressees are repeatedly identified as 'Judaeans', 'inhabitants of Jerusalem', 'Israelites', 'the whole house of Israel' (2.14, 22, [29], 36). See further on 2.39.

2.14–15   The comic interlude character of 2.13 is reinforced by the light-heartedness of the answer ('It is only nine in the morning!' – 2.15). The sermon, however, is interested primarily in the event of Pentecost, not the miraculous speech.

2.16–18   The quotation from Joel has two interesting modifications. (1) In 2.17, the 'afterward' of Joel 2.28's Hebrew is replaced by 'in the last days' (cf. Isa. 2.2; Micah 4.1). Since Luke elsewhere in Acts seems to play down the idea that 'the last days' were already in train, we may conclude that the modification belongs to Luke's source and expresses an authentic reminiscence of the eschatological fervour which the experience of the Spirit evoked in the first Christians. (2) Luke adds 'and they shall prophesy' at the end of 2.18. This could well be Luke's own addition, since he elsewhere emphasizes the importance of prophecy ('prophet' occurs fifty-nine times in Luke Acts), including the Spirit's role as inspirer of prophecy (Luke 1.67; Acts 19.6). But the Spirit of prophecy is a traditional understanding of the Spirit (cf. particularly Num. 11.29) which was widely shared in earliest Christianity (I Cor. 12.10; 14.1–5; I Thess. 5.19–20; I Peter 1.10–11; Rev. 19.10).

2.19–20   It is noticeable that Luke does not omit this section of the Joel passage despite the absence of cosmic convulsions in the account of Pentecost. Does it imply that such descriptions were understood as dramatic 'sound-effects' to heighten the eschatological significance of the event referred to, and not to be taken literally? If so it would be an important precedent for interpretation of similar imagery in other prophecies of the end time. The impression given by the passage, that 'the great and terrible day of the Lord' (the day of judgment) was imminent, again indicates very early tradition, since Luke elsewhere envisages a long period of evangelism before any final manifestation of God's rule (cf. 1.6–8).

2.21   'The Lord' in the Joel passage is God. But in the context of the sermon, particularly given its climax (2.34–36), 'the Lord' should presumably be understood as the exalted Jesus (cf. I Cor. 1.8; Phil. 1.6, 10). In which case (as in Rom. 10.9–13) this could be the first occasion in which an Old Testament passage referring to God is referred to Jesus, the exalted Christ understood as a plenipotentiary representative of God (cf. 7.59–60). This would also mean that the christology of the sermon embraces a rich spectrum of emphasis (cf. particularly 2.22 and 36).

As in the first extensive scriptural quotation in the Gospel (Luke 3.4–6), so here, Luke extends the quotation to include the reference to salvation – a central motif for him. The story of Jesus and about the Spirit is the story of salvation or it amounts to nothing.

2.22   together with 10.36–39 are the only passages in the Acts speeches which say anything about Jesus' pre-crucifixion ministry. It is noticeable here that the feature picked out is his miracles, signs and wonders (more balanced in 10.36–39), in echo of the Joel prophecy (2.19). The emphasis makes sense in a context of enthusiasm engendered by the experience of Pentecost, but it also accords with

Luke's own emphasis on the dramatic and faith-producing effect of 'signs and wonders' (2.43; 4.30; 5.12; 6.8; 14.3; 15.12; with allusion perhaps to the LXX of Ex. 7.3, 9; 11.9–10).

2.23   The precise focus of responsibility here is unclear: who handed over Jesus to whom? Who are the 'lawless men'? In any event, it is clear that responsibility is pinned on the Jews addressed ('you killed'). It is this charge which causes some commentators to accuse Luke of anti-Jewish sentiment, since it is repeated in other speeches (2.36; 3.14–15, 17; 4.10; 5.30; 10.39; 13.28), and since, more to the point, crucifixion was a form of capital punishment solely in the hands of the Roman authorities (the 'lawless men'?). At the same time, the sermon takes care to attribute ultimate responsibility to God – not just his 'foreknowledge', but his 'definite plan' (see on 4.27–28). This may be another expression of the tension Luke sees throughout his account between Christianity as both an intra-Jewish affair and a work of God transcending its specific Jewish beginnings.

2.24   The characteristic response in the early Acts sermons to the downbeat of the charge of judicial murder is the upbeat of God's riposte in raising Jesus from the dead (3.15; 4.10; 5.30; 10.40; 13.30). There is a clear echo of Ps. 18.4–5 here ('the pains of death' LXX), indicating that the explicit quotation from Ps. 16 (2.25–28) evoked further reflection on David as a type of the Messiah.

2.25–28   The quotation is from Ps. 16.8–11, where David expresses his confidence in God's care and protection. 'The Lord' here is David's God, David himself being understood as speaking for the Messiah. The confusion of reference of 'Lord' (cf. 2.20–21) and of David (both representing the Messiah and speaking of him as 'my Lord' – 2.34–35) simply illustrates the fluidity of concept and characterization at this stage.

2.29–32   Given that the principal messianic hope of the period was focussed in a Davidic (or royal) Messiah, it was natural that any belief in Jesus as Messiah should look to David's words to make sense of what had happened to Jesus. The argument of 2.29–31 justifying the application of Ps. 16.10–11 to Jesus is quite lucid: since David's words evidently did not apply to himself (he remains dead!), and since he had been promised an unbroken succession

(II Sam. 7.12–13; Ps. 132.11; see also on 7.46–47), he must have spoken the words prophetically in the person of his greater descendant. The conclusion (2.32) repeats the central claim (2.24), now linked into the theme of the apostles as witnesses (see on 1.8).

2.33–35 Despite the clear distinction between resurrection and ascension in ch. 1, the sermon here assumes that resurrection carries with it exaltation. This is expressed here in the characteristic terms drawn from Ps. 110.1, a key verse in earliest Christian self-understanding and apologetic (particularly Mark 12.36; I Cor. 15.25; Heb. 1.13), with a repeat of the justification used in 2.29.

A unique feature at this point, however, is the thought of the exalted Jesus both receiving the promised Spirit from God and pouring it forth on the disciples (but cf. Eph. 4.8). Elsewhere the earliest Christians were uncertain how to depict the relation between the exalted Christ and the Spirit (cf. Rom. 1.4; 8.11; I Cor. 15.45); and elsewhere God is characteristically the one who gives the Spirit (including Acts 5.32 and 15.8; elsewhere e.g. II Cor. 1.22 and I Thess. 4.8). The usage here may reflect a very early stage of influence still continuing from the Baptist's prediction (1.5). At all events, Luke certainly gives his own understanding of how the original Baptist's prediction was fulfilled – that is, a bestowal of the Spirit, as a bestowal by Jesus, but not during his earthly ministry, even his ministry between Easter and ascension, only after his ascension. In this way Luke again ensures that the two acts of Jesus' ministry (Luke and Acts) are not divorced from each other, and that the experience of the Spirit cannot be understood other than as a demonstration of Jesus as God's plenipotentiary. Also characteristic of Luke's portrayal of the Spirit is his identification of what the exalted Christ poured forth not with the Spirit as such, but with the visible/audible manifestations of the Spirit.

2.36 The proclamation is of Jesus. Its climactic point, therefore, is the significance of the Pentecost event for their understanding of the status and significance of Jesus. The idea that the resurrection/ascension constituted Jesus' installation as Lord is present wherever the Ps. 110.1 passage is echoed (e.g. Rom. 10.9–10; Phil. 2.9–11; Heb. 10.12–13). More unusual is the thought that it constituted Jesus also as Messiah (contrast even Rom. 1.3–4, another early formulation). The emphasis may indeed reflect a very early attempt to express the theological significance of the overpowering experience of resurrected Christ and Pentecostal Spirit. At any rate it would be unwise to take the text out of context and to use it as a building block in some overarching dogmatic christology (see also on 13.33).

The effect of the first sermon
2.37–42

What precisely was the effect of the earliest preaching we are hardly in a position to say now. There can be no doubt that the sect of the Nazarenes grew very quickly initially, and such growth must have been the effect of charismatic lives and preaching on the part of the first believers. Luke, however, is probably describing a prototypical response. That is, he uses the corollary of the first sermon to depict what good preaching should look and pray for: repentance among hearers, a normative sequence of baptism and Holy Spirit, converts, and a model fellowship resulting.

2.37   The action is limited to 'the apostles', with the answering emphasis on 'the apostles' teaching' (2.42) rounding off the passage. 'Brothers' again expresses the ambivalence of a brotherhood of fellow-Jews and fellow-believers (see on 1.15).

2.38   The four part 'order of salvation' is clear: (1) the preaching climaxes in (2) a call for repentance, (3) to be expressed in baptism, and (4) to which the Spirit is given.

(2) The call for repentance here presupposes the Pentecost audience's sense of remorse over the death of Jesus. But for Luke it again ties together a characteristic emphasis of Jesus' own preaching with the ongoing preaching of the church (Luke 5.32; 11.32; 13.3, 5; 15.7, 10; Acts 3.19; 5.31; 8.22; 11.18; 17.30; 20.21; 26.20). We may contrast Paul and John who make little or no mention of repentance in their representation or recollection of early gospel preaching.

(3) Baptism is now Christian baptism ('in the name of Jesus Christ' – similarly 8.16; 10.48; 19.5). That is, the name of Jesus was probably named over the baptisands indicating the one under whose authority they now were being placed (cf. I Cor. 1.12–13). Though the apostles and the other beneficiaries of the Spirit's coming described earlier did not themselves receive baptism in the name of Jesus (John's baptism followed by Spirit baptism being deemed

sufficient), the clear implication of the episode described in chs 3–4 is that this name of Jesus at once became the defining mark of the new movement (see Introduction to ch. 3), and that the 120 or so as well as those baptized on the day of Pentecost saw themselves equally as under the name of Jesus.

There is no reason whatsoever to doubt that John's baptism was thus transformed into Christian baptism at the very beginning of the new movement (the New Testament knows of no unbaptized believer). Despite the antithetical form of the original Baptist's prediction (Luke 3.16; Acts 1.5), there never seems to have been any question of the Pentecostal baptism in Spirit rendering baptism in the name of Jesus unnecessary. The first Christians attributed the inspiration for this adoption and transformation of the Baptist's rite to the risen Christ (Matt. 28.19), though the formula used in Acts ('in the name of Jesus Christ') suggests that the three-fold formula of 'the great commission' (Matt. 28.19) also reflects later developments.

The precise relation between the repentance, baptism and forgiveness of sins is unclear. The implication of Luke 24.47 and Acts 3.19 and 5.31 is that the primary link is between repentance and forgiveness, with baptism as the medium by which the repentance is expressed (cf. Luke 3.3, 8).

(4) Once again it is the gift of the Spirit to which the 'order of salvation' builds up. It is that which completes or seals the initiation into the fellowship inaugurated by Pentecost. Whatever the precise relation between baptism and the gift of the Spirit intended here, it is evident from the other stories recounted by Luke in which both baptism and the gift of the Spirit feature (8.14–17; 10.44–48; 19.1–6), that the chief point in each case is the gift of the Spirit.

2.39   Reference to 'the promise' ties 'the gift of the Spirit' received at conversion-initiation into the Pentecostal Spirit. It is the same Spirit alluded to in 1.4 and 2.33 which is given to the one who repents and is baptized.

The mention of who the promise had in view ('you, and your children, and all who are far away') is a further expression of the tension in the identity of the new movement. The reverse echo of the ancient covenant threat formula (Ex. 20.5; 34.7) implies thought of a promise to successive generations of Israel. But the ambiguity of the third phrase (cf. Isa. 57.19; Joel 2.32) may deliberately embrace thought both of the return of exiled Israel and of foreigners responding to Israel's message (cf. Deut. 30.1–6; Isa. 56.3–8). In which case the thought still hangs between a consummation conceived in terms of the restoration of Israel (cf. 1.6, 21–26) and the outreach of the gospel to Gentiles which takes place later in Acts (22.21; cf. Eph. 2.17). The promise then would embrace the original promise to the patriarchs, that Abraham would be a blessing to the nations, and foreshadows the argument of Gal. 3.6–14 (see further on Acts 3.25). At this stage, however, as with 2.5, it is the universal outreach of the gospel which is in view rather than an outreach specifically to Gentiles as such.

2.40   The echo of Deut. 32.5 and Ps. 78.8 is probably deliberate, since both passages chide Israel for false and faithless dealings with their God.

2.41   As elsewhere in Acts (8.12–13, 38; 10.47–48; 16.15, 33; 18.8) baptism proceeds immediately without further instruction. It functions, in other words, as the response to the proclaimed message, as an expression of repentance and commitment, rather than as ratification of a decision made at an earlier date.

Numbers in ancient historians tended to be more impressionistic (or propagandistic) rather than to provide what we today would regard as an accurate accounting. We may compare the obviously inflated numbers reported by both sides in the Iran/Iraq War of the early 1980s. But even so we can be confident that there was a large initial movement of successful recruitment by the new sect (see also 2.47).

An impression of the earliest Christian community
2.42–47

The portrayal may be somewhat idealized in this section, particularly 2.42, as many commentators think, and the vocabulary is certainly Luke's throughout. But anyone who is familiar with movements of enthusiastic spiritual renewal will recognize authentic notes: the enthusiasm of the members of the renewal group, with sense of overflowing joy (2.46), desire to come together frequently (2.44, 46), eating together and worshipping (2.46–47), and including the readiness for unreserved commitment to one another in a shared common life (2.44–45). We may even be able to recognize here well rooted memories of a kind of holy awe which struck onlookers who witnessed this common life. And typical of such movements are reports of healings and other miracles (2.43).

2.42 There may be a deliberate liturgical roundedness to this description.

'The apostles' again are the medium and guarantors of the teaching – presumably focussed on fresh interpretation of the scriptures (as in 2.14–36) and beginning to order the memories of Jesus' teaching and ministry into forms suitable for instruction, worship, and proclamation.

'Fellowship' is the first occurrence of a word classically linked to the Spirit by Paul – 'the fellowship of the Spirit' (II Cor. 13.13; Phil. 2.1), meaning shared participation in the Spirit. It was Pentecost which saw the beginning of this fundamental character of Christian community as growing out of the shared experience of the Spirit.

'Breaking of the bread' is often taken as a reference specifically to the Lord's Supper, and thus as affirming a eucharistically focussed Christian community from the first. Luke's later uses of the same phrase, however (see on 20.7a, 11–12 and 27.35–36), indicate rather that he had in mind shared meals (so also 2.46), presumably in continuance in some degree at least of the meals characteristic of Jesus' earlier ministry (see on 1.4). We may assume that on some occasions at least the meal included a shared commemoration of the Last Supper (cf. I Cor. 11.23–26). But Luke has not gone out of his way to make this plain.

It is reference to 'the prayers' which more than anything evokes the picture of a more established or regular liturgical practice. What is meant is not clear. Devout Jews probably observed three times of prayer every day (cf. Dan. 6.10). But perhaps Luke implies a more spontaneous prayer whenever believers came together.

2.43 Talk of 'fear/awe' conjures up a sense of the numinous (cf. 5.5, 11; 19.17). On 'wonders and signs' see 2.22. Note again the focus on the apostles as the agents of the miracle working.

2.44 Another name emerges for the new movement – 'the believers', or, more precisely, those who have made a commitment of faith (so also 4.32; 5.14; 15.5; 19.18; 21.20, 25; 22.19; see also

Introduction §5(5e)). This is rather striking since belief was not mentioned as a qualification for membership of the Jesus movement. It is obviously being taken for granted (*a*) that it is faith in Jesus, that is, in the Jesus proclaimed in the preaching, and (*b*) that response to this preaching involved a determined act of commitment (presumably expressed in baptism – more explicit in 18.8).

2.44–45 A community of goods would not be an unexpected feature of a group wholly committed to one another and to what the group represented. The most obvious and immediate parallel is the community of goods practised not very far away at Qumran (described most clearly in Josephus, *Jewish War* 2.122 – 'the individual's possessions join the common stock and all, like brothers, enjoy a single patrimony'). The most obvious difference is that the first Christian sharing of goods was not obligatory (as at Qumran), but wholly spontaneous, an expression of eschatological enthusiasm (note that they did not merely contribute income but sold off property). The procedure is indicated by the Greek: not that everything was sold off at once and put in a common fund, but that possessions were sold off over a period as need arose. The impression is strong of a group whose economic basis (regular jobs and income) was far from secure, but whose imminent expectation (Jesus Messiah returning soon?) allowed them to cope by short-term measures (see also on 3.6). As Johnson notes, the description of 'all things in common' has been influential throughout the history of Christianity.

2.46–47 The scene is almost idyllic, but the first wave of an enthusiastic movement often has that character, especially in retrospect. Luke makes a point of emphasizing that they did not shut themselves off from the rest of the people, wrapped up solely in their own affairs. They attended the Temple daily; their worship was directed towards God; and they aroused no antagonism among the rest of the populace. There is no hint of new or strange forms of worship. The note of continuity has no counter melody. This movement, begun at Pentecost, is thoroughly embedded in the heart of Israel's capital and religion. At the same time the house meetings indicate the beginning of a different structure or organization and worship.

Their daily focus on the Temple might indicate that they thought Jesus would return to the Temple (Mal. 3.1). The experience of joy (2.46) was a feature of the early movement (cf. Luke 1.14, 44, 47;

10.21; Acts 16.34; I Peter. 1.6, 8); but it also occurs in the Psalms as an expression of the joy of worship in the Temple (Pss. 42.4; 47.1; 63.5; 100.2; etc.).

The first believers are described as 'those being saved' (cf. I Cor. 1.21; 15.2), both echoing the last verse of the Joel quotation, and indicating that salvation was understood from the beginning as a process, of which conversion, baptism and the gift of the Spirit was only the start.

The Power of the Name (1)
3.1–26

What was this new movement which had been launched by the Pentecost event and which had seen such a huge initial success? In boundary-defining terms its most distinctive feature thus far was the requirement of baptism, baptism 'in the name of Jesus Christ' (2.38; cf. 2.21). It is not surprising, then, that in his first sustained, connected episode from the life of the new movement Luke focusses on the name of Jesus (3.6, 16; 4.7, 10, 12, 17–18, 30). It is this, the name of Jesus, which thus so early, indeed from the first, or so it would appear, identified those who banded themselves round the apostles (see also 5.28, 40–41; 8.12, 16; 9.14–16, 21, 27–28; 10.43, 48; 15.14, 17, 26; 16.18; 19.5, 17; 21.13; 22.16; 26.9). And since the name was generally understood to represent the person in the ancient world, at once the point is made that it is Jesus himself, or, more precisely, the first believers' relation to Jesus, his name named over them as their distinguishing mark, and their consequent authority to call upon him, which identified them as a distinct group (hence in 24.5, 'the Nazarenes', followers of 'the Nazarene'; see on 4.10). To bring this point out is the underlying rationale of the following narrative, the name linking chs 3–4 into a structural unity.

There is also a second linking feature. Luke has already indicated his conviction that 'wonders and signs' were a foundational feature of both Jesus' ministry and of the Pentecostal Spirit's empowering (2.19, 22, 43). So it is not surprising that the first episode of the new movement he chooses to relate is a miraculous healing. Indeed, it is the miracles of the next four chapters which provide the momentum for the story; they provide the occasion both for the preaching and for the reaction of the authorities (cf. also 4.30; 5.12; 6.8). This need not be considered a contrivance on Luke's part: enthusiastic renewal movements have often helped generate an atmosphere in which unexpected healings take place. But Luke has certainly focussed attention on this feature.

While the portrayal is exciting for readers past and present, the exclusiveness of the focus on the miraculous makes it more difficult for those of more humdrum days to sense a full rapport with the earliest church. The question cannot be easily kept down: are miracles of that character (5.1–11 as well as 3.1–10) an inevitable consequence of the outpouring of the Spirit (cf. Rom. 15.19; I Cor. 12.9–10; Gal. 3.5; Heb. 2.4)? And if so, what does that say about churches of later days where such miracles are lacking? The history of Christianity carries not a few examples of groups who have been inspired by Luke's accounts to make claims for their own miraculous ministry but whose sequel is very different from Luke's. Thus, even while being carried along by Luke's own enthusiasm, it is hard to avoid a slight sense of unease and a wish that Luke's account had given more attention to other features of the earliest Christian community, and to the elements of common life and worship which have proved more enduring.

The narrative technique – a kind of 'fast-forward' blur (2.43–47; 4.32–37; 5.12–16) interspersed with slow paced dramatic episodes (3.1–4.31; 5.1–11, 17–42) – makes it difficult to gain any clear sense of how much time was passing. The period covered by chs 1–5 may have been only a few weeks, or at most months.

The second miracle
3.1–10

There is a beautiful and moving simplicity about this report which both tugs the heart strings and gives delight. Particularly affecting are the balance between devotion and practical piety (Temple, hour of prayer, almsgiving), the exchange between the lame man and Peter in 3.3–6, and the contrast between the opening depiction of the man lame from birth being carried and placed daily at the gate of the Temple, but unable to enter for himself, and the closing description of the same man entering the Temple healed, walking and leaping and praising God. Luke demonstrates the skills of a superb storyteller in choosing to use this episode as the first sequel to Pentecost. The account itself he was probably able to draw from accounts of Peter's miracles which were familiar in Judaea (cf. 9.32–42), but Luke uses it here to draw out one of his deliberate parallels between Peter and Paul (cf. 14.8–10).

The deeper resonances of the story play on the fact that a lame man was unable to serve as a priest (Lev. 21.18), and for that reason

was also debarred from membership of the Qumran community (e.g.
1QSa 2.5–6). Hence the significance of Jesus' own healing and social
ministry (Luke 7.22; 14.13, 21). Not least of the significance of the
episode is that here too the healing makes possible the man's full
participation in the cult (3.8): the word used for the 'perfect health,
wholeness' to which the man is restored (3.16) may be a cultic word,
used to describe unblemished animals suitable for use in sacrifice (cf.
Zech. 11.16); cf. also the subplot of the story of the eunuch in 8.26–40.
In so saying, the importance of the Temple and what it stood for is
reaffirmed.

3.1   Peter and John are the principal focus of the next two chapters,
though it is Peter who carries the action, with John as a more
shadowy accompanying figure. So much so that we gain little
impression of his character. The Pentecost event evidently confirmed
Peter in the leadership role which went back to his time with Jesus
(see also 1.15). As the next chapters also indicate, these two can be
regarded as the chief representatives of the new Nazarene way.

Luke specifically states that they were going to the Temple 'at the
hour of prayer'. This was the time at which the evening sacrifice was
offered, during which prayers would be said (Ex. 29.39, 41; Num.
28.4; Dan. 9.21; Judith 9.1). There can be no other inference intended
than that Peter and John were going to the Temple to be part of the
worshipping crowd, that is, to take part in the Temple cultus.
Evidently, they had not yet come to the conclusion that Jesus' death
on the cross was itself a sacrifice which rendered all other sacrifices
unnecessary (Heb. 10.1–18). Again the theological sub-text is clear:
the new movement which sprang to powerful life at Pentecost was
still thoroughly part of the religion of Israel, still centred on the
Jerusalem Temple and its cult, even as that group within Israel
which named the name of Jesus Messiah.

3.2   The seriousness of the man's condition is emphasized: from
birth; and not just lame (walked with a limp), but helpless (he had to
be carried).

It is unclear what gate to the Temple is referred to here as 'the
Beautiful Gate'. Most assume that either the Nicanor Gate, leading
from the Court of Gentiles into the Court of Women, or the gate leading from the Court of Women into the Court of Israel is meant. The
setting of the sequel in Solomon's portico (3.11) suggests the former.

3.2–5   One of the most impressive features of Judaism past and present is the major emphasis it places on provision for the poor and disadvantaged (classically the widow, orphan and stranger – e.g. Deut. 24.10–22; Isa. 10.2; 58.6–7; Jer. 7.6; Mal. 3.5). Almsgiving was therefore a principal act of religious responsibility (e.g. Sir. 3.30; 29.12; Tobit 12.9; 14.11); hence also Acts 9.36, 10.2 and 24.17.

3.6   The representation of apostolic poverty is partly at least a story-telling device, to bring out the real treasure which the first Christians enjoyed. But it may also reflect the rather parlous state of the first believers in Jerusalem, dependent on selling off possessions in order to live (see on 2.44–45).

As already noted, the name of Jesus Christ dominates the subsequent narrative (3.16; 4.7, 10, 12, 17–18, 30). In its first appearance it is spoken as a solemn formula of identification – 'Jesus Christ the Nazarene' (elsewhere only in 4.10). Here we see something of the ancient idea of the power vested in a name. Indeed, the narrative of chs 3–4 is one of the best illustrations of the ancient belief in the power of the name (note again 4.7). The claims made for the name of Jesus are very strong: it is his name which healed the man (3.16; 4.10; cf. 4.30); only this name can achieve salvation (4.12). Evidently the name represents the person and carries his authority. There is no implication of magic here, any more than in 2.38: if anything, Luke goes out of his way to exclude the inference (Peter makes no use of physical aids; and cf. 19.13–16). We today may recognize echoes of this sense of the power of the name in talk of a person's 'good name' and in the strenuous efforts individuals will make to clear their name of misrepresentation or slander.

3.6b–9   Part of the storyteller's artifice is the repeated mention of the lame man 'walking' (four times in 3.6–8, and again in 3.12). Mention of his 'leaping' is probably with deliberate echo of Isa. 35.6 (LXX). The 'immediately' of 3.7 is a favourite Lukan word and emphasizes his understanding of the 'sign and wonder' character of the miracles he records (e.g. Luke 4.39; 5.25; 13.13; Acts 12.23; 16.26).

3.10   In describing the resulting astonishment of the people, Luke uses the unusual word *ekstasis*, which elsewhere denotes an ecstatic vision (Acts 10.10; 11.5; 22.17). It can also denote 'astonishment', but its formation (literally 'standing out of oneself') implies a numinous character. In this way Luke evokes again the 'holy' as a quality almost tangibly attaching to the new movement (cf. 5.5, 11, 15). It also provides another point of parallel with his previous account of Jesus (Luke 5.26 being the only other time Luke uses the term).

The second sermon
3.11–26

Like the first speech (2.14–36), the second is presented as a spontaneous response to an unexpected opportunity. This is characteristic of the Acts speeches, but no doubt the early success of Christianity was marked by such infectious spontaneous enthusiasm expressed in earliest witness-bearing.

The sermon attributed to Peter in Solomon's portico has a number of unusual features. For one thing, its structure is rather surprising. It falls into two clear parts: (*a*) an introduction picking up from the healing which has just taken place; and (*b*) the body of the sermon. But the introduction includes the regular reference to the death and resurrection of Jesus, within which the full exposition of the first sermon is compressed into two verses. The body of the sermon is presented rather as an elaboration of the call to repentance (3.19), which elsewhere forms the climax of the speech (2.38; 17.30), with the final paragraph (3.22–26) as a kind of coda developing an independent apologetic line. And, quite unusual among the Acts speeches, the corollary does not immediately focus on the reaction of the hearers (4.1–4).

Much more striking is the evidence that Luke has been able to draw on some very old tradition in framing this sermon, above all the christology which hardly occurs anywhere else in the New Testament and which has a distinctly primitive ring, particularly the titles used of Jesus (Zehnle). (1) He is called *pais*, 'servant' – only here in the New Testament (see further on 3.13). (2) He is also called 'the holy and just one' (3.14), epithets seldom used of Jesus elsewhere ('holy' – Luke 4.34; John 6.69; 'just' – Matt. 27.19; Acts 7.52; 22.14; I John 2.1). (3) Equally uncommon, he is called the *archegos*, 'leader or originator' (3.15; 5.31), a title which appears elsewhere only in Heb. 2.10 and 12.2.

(4) Even more striking is the language of 3.19–21, which contains several ancient motifs: the call for a repentance which will secure times of refreshing, the return of Jesus and universal restoration (cf.

Testament of Moses 1.18); and 'the Lord', clearly God is meant, who will send the Christ (not the usual way of speaking of the second coming), now in heaven awaiting his recall on to the earth's stage. (5) Also striking is the presentation of Jesus as fulfilment of Moses' promise that the Lord God would raise up a prophet like himself (3.22–23, referring to Deut. 18.15–16), a promise explicitly cited else-where only at 7.37. This is a line of christology which seems to have been left behind quite quickly in early Christian apologetic as 'prophet' was seen to be an inadequate expression of Jesus' full significance. (6) And quite unique in the New Testament is the closing argument that Jesus as God's servant fulfils the covenant promise to Abraham, of blessing for all the nations (Gen. 22.18), but to Israel first (3.24–26).

It is difficult to avoid the conclusion that Luke had some very old tradition at his disposal in framing this speech of Peter. The fact that he has evidently made an effort to uncover and use such material is a clear indication that he felt under some constraint in formulating such speeches. The very marked primitiveness of the christology indicates that Luke was probably conscious of some dangers of anachronism and that he did not intend the sermon to be a model for preaching in his own day. We can say no more than that, and need say no more than that. So far as Luke and his readers were con-cerned, it would not matter whether Peter said just these words on just that occasion. It was enough that the words gave a fair represen-tation of what Peter would or might have said at that stage.

At the same time the sermon serves very well one of Luke's chief concerns: to demonstrate that the new movement operating under the name of Jesus was in full continuity with the Israel which had given it birth. (1) The speech is delivered within the Temple precincts (3.11). (2) The audience are again addressed as 'fellow Israelites' (3.12) and 'brothers' (3.17), and latterly they are specifi-cally described as 'the sons of the prophets and of the covenant' (3.25); note also the evocation of 'the people' in 3.23. (3) It is 'the God of Abraham and of Isaac and of Jacob, the God of our fathers' who is the chief actor behind and within the events referred to (3.13, 15, 18, 19–20, 22, 25–26). (4) The emphasis on fulfilment of prophecy is sus-tained through the body of the sermon (3.18–26). (5) 'The times of refreshing' and 'times for restoration of all things' (3.20–21), given the further exposition of 3.22–26, may be a further elucidation of the issues posed in 1.6–7 (where the same two words for 'time' are used); the restoration foretold by the prophets presumably must include, if not focus on, the restoration of Israel (cf. 15.16). (6) In particular, Jesus is the fulfilment of the Moses prophecy (3.22–23), and the eschatological fulfilment of the central covenant promise (3.24–26). Those who fail to listen to him will be cut off from the people (3.23); that is, response to Jesus becomes the defining norm for Israel's continuity.

Here too the sustained character of this emphasis cannot be accidental. Luke is using old tradition which contained this emphasis, but in so using it he makes it his own and affirms its continuing centrality within Christianity's own self-definition.

3.11   Solomon's portico was an impressive colonnade along the east side of the Temple platform, overlooking the Kidron valley, ideal as a gathering place. Since the gate (3.2) most likely led from the outer court of the Temple into the inner court we probably have to envisage a lapse of time following the healing, with this new development taking place after the time of sacrifice and when Peter and John were on their way out again. 'All the people' will be a typical storyteller's hyperbole.

3.12   Note the assumption that piety could be a factor in bringing about a healing. By means of the speech Luke makes a particular point of denying any thought of piety as a kind of manipulation of divine power (see also 3.16).

3.13   That the God of Israel is identified as the God of the patriarchs (similarly 24.14) defines Israel's own identity by reference to the initial promises to Abraham (Gen. 12.3; 15; etc.) and to the covenant God of Moses and the Exodus (Ex. 3.6, 13–15; cited also by Jesus in Luke 20.37). By thus appealing to God so defined, the speech claims that Jesus and those who name his name are also part of this Israel. Highly effective is the way the speech climaxes in an explicit appeal to the same covenant promises to Abraham and the patriarchs (3.25). The bracketing double emphasis underlines the point: what has happened is what the fathers had been promised from the first.

The language is almost certainly drawn from the LXX of Isa. 52.13: 'my servant (*pais*) . . . will be glorified', since talk of God glorifying Jesus is quite exceptional in the New Testament outside John's Gospel, and the title *pais* for Jesus is limited to these two chapters in Acts (3.13, 26; 4.25, 27, 30). This allusion to the famous Servant song of Isa. 52.13–53.12 is probably very early since it expresses only a theology of suffering and vindication (3.13–15), rather like that of the righteous *pais* (Wisd. 2.13) of Wisd. 2.12–20 and 5.1–5. Whereas other allusions to Isa. 53 in connection with Jesus' suffering, while still early, use it to express a theology of atonement (cf. Mark 10.45; Rom. 4.24–25; I Peter 2.22–25). See also on 8.30–34.

3.13–15 The accusation against the audience is more carefully formulated than in 2.23, 36. Initially the talk is only of their having handed over Jesus and denied him, the details (reference to Pilate and the events of the trial) reflecting Luke's own account (Luke 23.13–25). But the climax is the same harsh charge of murder (3.15), allowing the same sharp antithesis as in 2.23–24 – 'but God . . .'. In addition, however, Luke will hardly have been unmindful of the apologetic value of accounts which played down Roman responsibility for the execution of an innocent man. Apart from anything else, they would reinforce the impression that the Jesus movement was not a threat to Roman authority (see Introduction §2(4)). On the titles used for Jesus see Introduction to this section. Note again the motif of witness-bearing (see on 1.8).

3.16 Important here is the bringing together of two of the key identity markers of the new movement – faith and the name. Significant then is the variation played on their relationship. It was the name of Jesus which was decisive; the power of the name is reiterated (see on 3.6). But it is immediately qualified by stressing the importance of faith; left unclear is whether the faith is that of Peter and John or the faith of the lame man (probably the former; cf. 3.5 with 14.9). There is, however, a further variation and qualification, since the healing is then ascribed to this faith, but the faith itself is described as 'through him'. Evidently there is some concern here to avoid any concept of magic or of self achievement (cf. 3.12). The attitude of open trust is an important medium through which the healing power flows, but the faith itself is divinely enabled, and the effective power is the power of him whose name is named.

3.17 The severity of the accusation of murder is softened by allowing that the act was one of ignorance (as in Luke 23.34; Acts 13.27; cf. I Cor. 2.8). The charge is not simply of failure to recognize what to the believer seems obvious, since the significance of Jesus' ministry only became clear to the disciples in the light of Jesus' resurrection. But it would still be irritating to the non-believer.

45

3.18   The other way to limit the seriousness of the accusation is to affirm that it had to happen (see on 2.23). Here the point is made in terms of the familiar proof from prophecy argument (as in Luke 24.23 and Acts 26.22–23). Only by uncovering such scriptures could the first disciples make sense of what had happened to Jesus on the cross (cf. I Cor. 15.3; I Peter 1.10–12). According to Acts, this was the first time the point would have been made to a Jerusalem audience. Since the claim was both novel and astounding (a suffering Messiah!), such an initial claim would have to be backed up by a good deal of documentation and argument (cf. Luke 24.27). Here the cameo character of the Acts speeches becomes evident. In putting the material of the sermon together, Luke evidently wanted to draw the thread of continuity all the way through, from Abraham (3.13, 25), through Moses (3.22), Samuel and all the prophets (3.18, 21, 24). It is the whole sweep of earlier revelation which bears witness to Jesus the Christ.

3.19   There seems to be a deliberate attempt here to bring out the full force of the Hebrew word, 'turn or return', since both Greek words used at this point can translate the same Hebrew concept. The first word, 'repent', may therefore have here the more Greek sense, to 'change one's mind', with further implication of regret for the previous opinion. While it is the second word which carries the fuller sense of the Hebrew concept – a radical change of direction, a turning round of direction of life – an important feature of the prophets' message (e.g. Isa. 55.7; Ezek. 18.32; Hos. 6.1; Joel 2.13; Zech. 1.3). As in Luke 24.47, the wiping out of sins, an expressive metaphor drawn from Jewish usage (Pss. 51.1, 9; 109.14; Isa. 43.25), is a direct consequence of the repentance.

3.20–21   As in the last verse there seem to be strong intimations of a train of thought first formulated by someone to whom semitic idiom came naturally – 'from the face of the Lord (= God)', 'send the Messiah appointed for you', 'all that God spoke by the mouth of his holy prophets'. The two 'time' phrases, 'times of refreshing' and 'times for restoration', are without parallel in the rest of the New Testament, though the latter presumably echoes Mal. 4.5–6. Since we lack the information to fill out their meaning and to distinguish them from each other, it remains uncertain how the two should be related to each other. At most we could guess that the 'times of refreshing' (times of respite? – cf. Ex. 8.15; Mark 13.20) are to precede the 'times of restoration', the latter referring to a complex of events, including 'the great and terrible day of the Lord' (Mal. 4.5; cf. Acts 2.20) and the Christ's return. Even so, the portrayal is of Jesus received by heaven, and just awaiting the signal to return as the Christ to bring about and be part of the restoration of all things. As with 2.17, this is an eschatology, and a relatively imminent eschatology, which Luke does not seem to promote elsewhere. All told, the language catches rather effectively a sense of trembling, expectant excitement at the prospect of the Christ recently departed but ready to return soon to bring history to its ordained climax.

3.22–23 The quotation is a combination of Deut. 18.15–16, 19 and Lev. 23.29. The promise of a prophet like Moses was surprisingly not much reflected on in the Jewish writings of the period, though it features in Qumran expectation (4QTest/4Q175 5–8; cf. 1QS 9.11). But the Deut. 18 texts seem to have attracted early Christian attention and that early reflection, though it never became a central feature of christology (prophet being an inadequate term to describe Christ's significance), nevertheless left traces at various points in the tradition (cf. Mark 9.7; John 6.14; 7.52; Acts 7.37). At this point the talk of 'raising up' in the original text (the word used to describe Jesus' resurrection) allows the play on the idea that the resurrection either establishes Jesus as the Moses prophet (cf. 2.36) or proves that he (already) was so. Lev. 23.29 originally had nothing to do with the hope of a prophet like Moses, which makes the combination of such a severe warning with the prophet like Moses prophecy all the more powerful: it is response to the new Moses which determines membership of the people.

3.24 is not just a repetition of 3.18 but has in view the whole eschatological programme indicated in 3.19–21. Samuel is mentioned as being the first great prophet after Moses and the first of Israel's great sequence of prophets.

3.25 The identification of the audience as 'sons' both of the prophets and of the covenant again emphasizes the completeness of the continuity: they stand in a line from Abraham, through the prophets; the original covenant promise to Abraham still stands and has been reaffirmed by the prophets. The implication is clear: Jesus and those who now name his name stand at and as the climax of that unbroken line of divine purpose.

The text evokes the repeated promise to Abraham Isaac and Jacob (Gen. 12.3; 18.18; 22.18; 26.4; 28.14), though the particular citation is drawn immediately from Gen. 22.18 and 26.4. It is particularly striking that this speech, with its phrasing and vocabulary stretching back to the earliest days of the Nazarene movement, should now incorporate a text which is particularly associated with Paul's own justification for his Gentile mission (especially Gal. 3.6–14). This certainly indicates a Lukan device to root the later Gentile mission in the beginnings of Christianity. It thus also fills out further Luke's own sense of the tension within the self-understanding of a movement which is so thoroughly rooted in its Jewish heritage and yet so committed to bring the gospel of Jesus Christ to 'all the families of the earth'. In other words, it was as fundamental to Luke as it was to Paul that the Christian mission be seen as an outworking of the original covenant promise given to Abraham (cf. Luke 1.55, 73; Acts 7.5–6, 16–17). Nevertheless, the ancient character of the speech as a whole means that we cannot rule out the possibility that this Pauline-Lukan conviction goes much further back into Christianity's beginnings. The promise that Abraham would be a blessing to the nations may have provided one of the earliest points of light within earliest Christian theologizing which grew into the great floodlight which directed Paul on his mission.

3.26   Having thus opened the windows to the universal mission to come, the speech is quickly concluded by ensuring that the continuity from Abraham to the families of the earth runs through present Israel. 'To you first' (the words in a position of emphasis) God sent his servant. This was the initial purpose of the resurrection (the play on 3.22 is reinforced by the repetition of the same word – 'raised up'). The blessing of the world comes through Israel. The blessing of the world begins with the blessing of Israel (cf. 2.39). Hence even Paul, sent to the Gentiles, always preaches first to the Jews (see on 13.5).

A condition or means is stated: 'in turning you from your wickedness'. The implication of the context is that the wickedness in view is that referred to in 3.17–19 – the wickedness of killing the Author of life (3.15). But it is stated in broad terms which no devout Jew would quarrel with – similar to the prayers of general confession used Sunday by Sunday in many Christian worship services.

The Power of the Name (2)
4.1–37

The transition
4.1–4

Luke occasionally uses the device of seeming to interrupt the speech he is recording, even though the speech in its cameo form is already complete (most noticeably 10.44 and 22.22). Here the interruption is from the Temple authorities and results in the arrest of Peter and John (4.1–3). This leads directly into the first formal defence of the new movement's testimony (4.5–22). But the paragraph ends with the report of the success of the second sermon (4.4), bringing the preceding phase of the narrative to a proper close. The paragraph thus serves, in a way analogous to 1.1–11, as a transition and overlapping bracket which bonds the two halves of a single narrative together.

Luke was well enough informed to know that the Sadducees were hostile to the idea of resurrection (4.2; cf. Luke 20.27–40; Acts 23.6–9). He evidently intended to focus the opposition to the new movement in those whose power was located in and dependent on the Temple, the high priests and their supporters (4.5–6, 23 and 5.17, 21, 27; contrast 5.33–40). This prepares the way for the decisive breach in chs 6–7, but there is no reason to doubt that Luke was able to draw on good tradition on this point, since the passion narratives in the Gospels are agreed that the opposition to Jesus was also primarily priestly in composition.

4.1 Of the three groups mentioned – priests, the captain of the Temple police (Levites) and Sadducees – the first two are obviously representatives of the Temple authorities. Of the Sadducees we know surprisingly little, but enough to know that they were the aristocratic priestly party or faction (5.17) within the land of Israel, though not all were priests; they probably named themselves after Zadok the priest (I Sam. 8.17; 15.24; I Kings 1.34). This opposition is juxtaposed over against 'the people', apparently listening without complaint (4.1–2). The distinction is presumably deliberate. The two groups identified in 3.17 (the audience/people and their rulers) as together responsible (in ignorance) for Jesus' death now begin to divide. The implication is that the promise to 'all the people' whom Peter addressed (3.11–12) can still be fulfilled for the people (3.25–26), even if their leaders refuse to listen and thus cut themselves off from the people (3.23). The theme is continued in 4.10, 17 and 21, though 4.27 strikes a jarring counter note.

4.2   The focus of the opposition's 'annoyance' is the proclamation of the resurrection. The point is carefully framed: 'they were proclaiming in Jesus the resurrection which is from the dead'. The raising up of which Moses had spoken was 'the resurrection (same word) which is from the dead', not just the sending of another prophet, but a whole new category, opening up a quite different prospect. The point of the proclamation is that this raising up had happened and happened only in the one case, that of Jesus. The formulation thus provides the double emphasis: that Jesus is the defining centre of the new movement; and that his resurrection is the key point of emphasis and differentiation in its preaching (cf. 4.33).

4.3   No charge is levelled against the apostles, and Luke gives no suggestion that a riot was threatened. But Temple officials would certainly be able to exercise such arbitrary authority within the Temple precincts. The timing ('evening') indicates that several hours had elapsed since the ninth hour (even though Peter's speech would have taken less than two minutes to deliver).

4.4   As already in 2.41 and regularly thereafter (4.29; 6.4; 8.4; 10.36, 44; 11.19; 14.25; 16.6; 17.11) the message preached by the first Christian evangelists is described simply as 'the word' (similarly 'the word of God' – 4.31; 6.2, 7; 8.14; 11.1; 13.5, 7, 44, 46, 48; 16.32; 17.13; 18.11; 'the word of the Lord' – 8.25; 12.24; 13.49; 15.35; 19.10, 20). Their response is described simply as 'belief', but with an implication of a commitment (in baptism) to the one preached and the community who named his name. On the number (5,000) see on 2.41.

The first defence
4.5–22

The account of the first public encounter between the authorities and the spokesman for the new movement is carefully structured. The reference to 'rulers' (4.5, 8) links back to the first part of the two-chapter narrative (3.17), but also, and more important, the terminology used ('the rulers were gathered' – 4.5) directly anticipates (and thus gives more force to) the subsequent citation of Ps. 2.2 (4.26). The description of Peter as 'filled with the Holy Spirit' for his defence (4.8) clearly recalls the promise of Luke 11.11–12 (cf. 21.14–15). And particularly striking is the contrast between the boldness of the unlettered apostles (4.8–13, 19–20) and the confusion and weakness of all the most powerful people in the city (4.13–18, 21).

It is the name of Jesus, however, which continues to be the central linking thread of the narrative. The question regarding the healing of the lame man is posed to Peter in terms of the name: 'By what name did you do this?' (4.7). And Peter's reply focusses almost entirely on the name, attributing to it not only the success of the healing, but also, astonishingly, exclusive power of universal salvation (4.10, 12). Likewise in the second phase of the hearing it is the name of Jesus which the authorities are shown to fear: the point is underlined by the technique of narrating the warning not to speak in the name of Jesus twice (4.17–18). In contrast, in the immediate sequel, Peter's community is shown to express unabashed confidence in the power of the name of Jesus (4.30).

In all this the sovereign perspective of the storyteller is evident: the early details show awareness of what is to follow; and he knows the inner debates of the council, even though Peter and John had been put outside (4.15–17). At the same time Luke was aware that the initial opposition to the new movement was mainly priestly in motivation. The description of Peter's and John's super confidence is stylized but could also reflect the burgeoning boldness of those still swept along on a wave of spiritual enthusiasm. And though the claims made in 4.11–12 seem to express the product of a longer period of reflection than the narrative has allowed, the 'stone testimonial' (Ps. 118.22) did become an important Christian proof text, most notably linked to the name of Peter (I Peter 2.7), and the sweeping claim of 4.12 has the ring of enthusiastic hyperbole. Here again, then, we may assume that Luke is providing what would have been regarded in his own time as a highly responsible historical account.

4.5–6   The historical facts behind this description are unclear. It is usually assumed that a formal meeting of the Sanhedrin is being described, but we simply do not know how much of the formal constitution of the Sanhedrin as described in later rabbinic sources applied prior to the destruction of the Temple in AD 70. The Greek term, *sunedrion* (used in 4.15) may be better taken to describe simply a 'council', a gathering of some senior figures called together by the high priest and his immediate advisers. Why, after all, would the highest court in the land be formally convened to deal with a minor matter (not even a disturbance) as related in ch. 3?

Luke's account may therefore be more firmly rooted than at first appears. 'The elders (leading citizens) and scribes (lawyers)' could be involved in either case. But the mention of Annas in lead position (despite having been succeeded by his son in law, Caiaphas, as High Priest in AD 18) and of the other members of 'the high priest's family' (John may also have been a son of Annas) catches well both the considerable political power which was vested in a few families and the degree to which the council may simply have been a rather *ad hoc* gathering instigated by the family of Annas.

The mention of Jerusalem is just a reminder to the reader that the focal point for everything so far has been Jerusalem, with all the overtones of continuity with Israel's history and heritage (see Introduction to ch. 1).

4.7   The question provides the cue for what follows. Note again the way 'power' and 'name' are used as almost synonymous (see on 3.6).

4.8   The description of Peter as 'filled with the Holy Spirit' clearly envisages a welling up of inspired speech, and provides one of the several parallels between Peter and Paul (13.9; see Introduction to ch. 3). The fact that the phrase is used prior to this utterance, rather than prior to Peter's two previous speeches, obviously indicates the influence of Luke 12.11–12 in Luke's narrative. Since Luke goes on to describe a further filling with the Spirit in 4.31 he obviously felt no inconsistency between these descriptions and the previous account of the Pentecostal filling (2.4). This need not mean that he saw all these fillings as merely temporary, as though the Spirit departed as quickly as it came. The imagery of the language suggests more an occasional 'topping up' of a Spirit once for all bestowed at Pentecost. Or perhaps we should simply recognize language expressive of spiritual experience, where crises of varying magnitudes can call forth an unexpectedly confident response, with an enabling sensed to be not of one's self. In movements of spiritual or charismatic renewal, experiences of inspired utterance have not been uncommon.

4.9–10   In the midst of the explanation by reference to the power of the name of Jesus the same kerygmatic core as in 2.23–24 and 3.13–15 is summarily inserted – 'whom you crucified, whom God raised from the dead' (see on 2.23 and 24). The full name, 'Jesus Christ the Nazarene' echoes 3.6, the only other time it is used (but see also 2.22; 6.14; 22.8; 26.9). Again Luke takes the opportunity to reiterate that the significance of this name is for 'all the people of Israel' (see on 3.6).

4.11   The sentence is almost a direct quotation from Ps. 118.22, but the middle clause has been made more forceful and turned into a repetition of the charge of rejection (as in 3.13–14) – not just rejected (passed over as unsuitable), but rejected with contempt (as in Luke 23.11 where the same verb is used), 'by you the builders'. This passage from Ps. 118 was one of the Old Testament verses which must have sounded with immediate and amazing relevance in the ears of the first Christians – far more so than the usually contrived interpretations read into the prophets in the Qumran commentaries. It is appended to the parable of the wicked tenants in all three of the Synoptic Gospels (Matt. 21.42; Mark 12.10–11; Luke 20.17) and cited by I Peter 2.4, 7, where it makes a natural pair with another 'stone testimony' (Isa. 8.14).

4.12   The 'healing' (*sozein*) of the lame man (4.9) by the name of Jesus now becomes the basis for the most sweeping and extravagant claim that 'salvation' (the same word) is henceforth not possible by any other name. That such a flush of exclusivist triumphalism should have been expressed thus so early is not impossible in the wave of enthusiasm which launched Christianity, but its character as an expression of enthusiastic hyperbole (whether Peter's or Luke's) should be noted. In fact, however, the saying is just an exaggerated and more pointed expression of what had already been attributed to Jesus in Luke 7.22–23: that healing of the lame was a particularly potent image of the power of the new age to come; and that this power in marked degree was focussed in and channelled through Jesus himself. It should also be noted that 4.12 is formulated as a confession ('by which we must be saved'), rather than as an evangelistic either-or (believe this or lose salvation). Moreover, it is formulated as a yielding to the same divine sovereignty ('must') which has been a feature of Luke's account so far (Acts 1.16, 21; 2.23; 3.18, 21; also 5.29; 9.6, 16; 14.22; 16.30; 17.3; 19.21; 23.11; 27.24); Jesus is now to be seen as the central vehicle for God's saving purpose on a universal scale.

4.13   'Boldness' now becomes a key term linking this phase of the narrative to its climax in 4.29–31. It also foreshadows the boldness with which Jesus will continue to be proclaimed beyond the end of Acts (28.31). The contrast with their uneducated state is strongly drawn, but does reflect the astonishing fact that Christianity began with a small group of Galileans whose level of educational attainment cannot have been very high. We should not ourselves over-exaggerate the contrast however: Peter and John were from artisan class (John's father had a small business with hired help, according to Mark 1.20); so they were hardly 'country bumpkins'.

What has made the difference, the narrator informs us, is that 'they had been with Jesus'. How much this tells us of the authorities' information regarding the new movement we can hardly say. The point is theological: that it was the influence of Jesus which had made the difference. This also illuminates their use of Jesus' name: it was not simply the utterance of a formula which anyone could use, far less use to their own ends; on the contrary, they could use Jesus' name precisely because they knew Jesus and thus what his name expressed and what it could be used for. The point will be later reinforced by the half-amusing half-frightening story in 19.13–16.

4.14–18   As part of the inquiry, the (formerly) lame man has been brought in also. The value of miracle as proof of saving/healing power is taken for granted by Luke: they could not speak against it. Luke of course knew well that a response was possible (as in Luke 11.15), but it is the overwhelming effect in these first days of the new movement's manifest spiritual power which he wants to underline in these chapters. The feebleness of the response (4.17), the response of the rulers and leading authorities in the land, is the appropriate dramatic corollary which highlights the main theme all the more strikingly.

4.19–20   The boldness of Peter and John (4.13) is dramatically illustrated. The scene would not be an unfamiliar one to Luke's wider
readership. In a classic parallel (much quoted by commentators), and
no doubt widely known, Socrates had told his judges, 'I will obey
God/the god rather than you' (Plato, *Apology* 29d). The boldness of
saints and martyrs before much more threatening power is a
favourite theme in Jewish and Christian writings (e.g. Dan. 3.16–18;
II Macc. 7). To recognize this, of course, is not to consign the whole
tradition to the level of artistic or novellistic striving for effect. The
tradition, already well documented before this, could be inspiration
as much for a Peter and John in a lesser confrontation as for Luke the
dramatic historian. At the same time Luke takes the opportunity to
underline that the preaching from the first was a witness bearing, a
testifying to personal experience and born of personal involvement:
'it is not possible for us to remain silent about what we have seen
and heard'.

4.21–22   The weakness of the authorities' position (but also their
self-restraint within the law) is re-emphasized for a final time. And
the contrast between a hostile leadership and a responsive people is
reiterated. But the final emphasis is on the effect of the miracle. This
healing was a 'sign' – all the more effective as being wrought on
someone who had been lame for forty years. And it had been recognized as such by 'the people' who all glorified God because of it. Any
scope for questioning the 'sign'-ificance of the claimed miracle is
completely overwhelmed by the undisputably beneficial effect of
what had happened.

The sequel
4.23–31

The climax to the long narrative (stretching from 3.1) is now reached.
The central feature, the prayer of 4.24–30, is an excellent example of
Luke's skill in providing a passage which dramatically ties the whole
sequence together, wonderfully fits the mood of the scene and is
highly appropriate to the time and circumstances. (1) The prayer
functions as a kind of choral finale: they all praise and pray with one
voice (4.24). It would be foolish to ask how they could have said in
unison a prayer which was obviously so fitted to the occasion (and

so not a traditional and well known liturgical form). As in 2.7–11, Luke is using the liberty of a dramatic historian, not attempting to act as a modern archivist.

(2) The passage is used to bring to a climax and round off a number of motifs which have formed the warp and woof of the narrative and which provide continuity of theme with preceding episodes: (*a*) David as a primary resource of prophetic inspiration (1.16; 2.25; 4.25); (*b*) 'the rulers gathered together' (4.26) echoes the role call at the beginning of the previous scene (4.5); (**c**) this alliance of Gentile and Jewish rulers, including Herod (Antipas) and Pilate, ties the account back to Luke's passion narrative (Luke 23.1–25; the episode with Herod is peculiar to Luke), and provides the counterpoise to the repeated assertion that the divine purpose was wholly in control throughout (4.28; cf. 2.23; 3.18; 4.12); (*d*) the theme of boldness in witnessing (4.13, 29, 31) and use of 'the word' absolutely for the message proclaimed (4.4, 29, 31); (*e*) healing, 'signs and wonders' (2.19, 22, 43; 4.16, 22, 30); (*f*) the repeated filling with the Spirit (2.4; 4.8, 31); and not least (*g*) the final clinching reference to the most important leitmotif, the name of Jesus (3.6, 16; 4.7, 10, 12, 17–18, 30).

(3) As usual, however, Luke seems to have been able to draw on earlier material. (*a*) The model provided by prayers recorded in similar circumstances (particularly Isa. 37.16–20) may have inspired several early prayers in the highly charged early days of the new movement as it understood itself by means of such precedents. That one such prayer became established in early Christian worship where Luke encountered it and from which he drew the opening and the overall model is not at all far-fetched. (*b*) Noteworthy is the fact that the prayer is directed to God (4.24), and that 'Lord', not only in the Old Testament text quoted (4.26), but also in the prayer itself (4.29), refers clearly to God and not to Jesus (in contrast to 2.21, 36 and 4.33), with Jesus clearly designated as God's holy servant through whom God works (4.29–30; cf. 2.22). (*c*) Striking again is the use of *pais*, 'servant', for Jesus (in the New Testament it appears as a title for Jesus only in 3.13, 26 and 4.27 and 30), and the clear awareness of the original force of the title 'Christ', the anointed one (4.26–27). (*d*) In view of the positive role of 'the people' earlier (4.1–2, 21), the unusual phrase ('the peoples of Israel') and their association with the Gentiles in opposition to Jesus (4.27) may belong more to the material Luke takes over than to Luke's own contrivance. (*e*) It may even be possible to discern early tradition behind the dramatic experience referred to in 4.31 (the place where they were being

physically shaken). It is the reports of such events, rather than necessarily the events themselves, which attest the sense of immediacy of divine presence and power characteristic of the early days of prophetic or revival movements.

4.23   The return to friends (not just the twelve) after a crisis is a natural action which features elsewhere in the Acts narratives (12.12; 16.40).

4.24   The opening of the prayer echoes a regular theme in Jewish confession and worship of the one God, creator of all (see Ex. 20.11; II Kings 19.15; Neh. 9.6; Ps. 146.6; Isa. 37.16). Luke resumes the motif later in 14.15 and 17.24. Luke uses the address 'sovereign Lord' (*despotes*) again in Luke 2.29.

4.25   The allusion to David as speaking under inspiration is another means of underlining the continuity between the Spirit active in the scriptures and the Spirit inspiring contemporary testimony (4.8, 31). It is the same Spirit. The point is reinforced by the fact that David is also designated as God's servant (*pais*). Implicit is a claim that Jesus is another David, another *pais* (4.27, 30).

4.25–26   This is the only time Ps. 2.1–2 (from LXX) is cited as a proof text in the New Testament, so it is not possible to say whether its place here is something Luke drew from tradition or whether he drew it in himself in constructing the narrative beginning with the echo of Ps. 2.2 (4.5).

4.27–28   Once again the attribution of fault to the Jewish and Gentile authorities is balanced by the assertion that what happened was fully in accord with God's own predetermined counsel and action. In the New Testament, thought of the divine counsel is particularly Lukan (Luke 7.30; Acts 2.23; 5.38–39; 13.36; 20.27). Here it is reinforced (as in 2.23) by a 'fore-' compound ('foreordained'), another regular feature of Lukan theology and style (cf. 1.16; 2.31; 3.18, 20; 7.52; 10.41; 13.24; 22.14; 26.16).

4.29–30   What is asked for is a cooperative outreach, but with God as the prime mover: that he will grant his servants (*douloi*) to speak his word boldly; and that he himself will exercise healing and miraculous power through the name of his servant (*pais*) Jesus. A theological balance is also maintained between word and action; it is typical of Luke – the actions in view are healings, signs and wonders (see on 2.22) – but it could well reflect the balance of emphasis sought by the first enthusiastic believers themselves (cf. 6.1).

4.31   For Peter, presumably, this was the third time he had been filled by the Spirit (2.4; 4.8)! What is in view is primarily an experience of being inspired, of speaking with a spontaneity and boldness which transcended normal speech. Despite the association of bold speech and signs and wonders in the previous two verses, the almost invariable manifestation of the Spirit in Acts is inspired speech (2.4; 4.8; 6.10; 10.45–46; 13.2, 9; 18.25; 19.6; 20.23; 21.4, 11), whereas, somewhat surprisingly, the miracles of Acts are never attributed to the Spirit as such (though note 10.38).

Another snapshot of the earliest community
4.32–37

Luke evidently thought it important to give such an extensive account of one brief episode (3.1–4.31), no doubt because for him it caught the spirit of the new community who now ranged themselves under the name of Jesus. But now he 'fast forwards' again, as he had after the previous episode of Pentecost (2.43–47), to give another overall impression of the community as a whole. The same impression (as in 2.43–47) of an idyllic scene rouses the same suspicion that Luke looks back through rose-tinted spectacles. But all generations tend to view the past as 'the good old days', and the founding epoch of such a movement, continuing steadily to grow through Luke's own time, would naturally tend to evoke impressions of a golden age. The sense of looking back through a golden haze, with the picture painted in impressionistic rather than portrait terms, will be partly deliberate, partly inevitable. To complain that the details are obscure in a 'broad brush' style is like complaining that the details of Monet's famous water lilies lack all precision.

Yet, one episode does stand out from the general hazy impression, an episode which evidently impressed itself on the corporate memory of the first believers and which Luke was able to retrieve with some precision of detail (4.36–37). A prominent landowner, a diaspora Jew, had evidently made a successful career before buying land in and around Jerusalem. Having allied himself to the new movement, through faith commitment and baptism in Jesus' name, he sold one of his fields and contributed the proceeds to the common fund. The episode was readily recalled, no doubt, since Barnabas became such an important figure in the early church (see on 4.36–37). But it may very well also be the case that he was the first man of substantial wealth and position who became a member of the Jesus people and that his contribution was the first substantial gift to the common fund. Another reason why Luke uses it here, of course, is because it provides an immediate link into the next episode (5.1–11).

4.32   Luke liked to emphasize the unanimity of mind and purpose of the first believers (see 1.14 and the similar emphasis of the earlier summary account in 2.46). Looking back, he saw the sort of spirit which Paul encouraged among his churches (I Cor. 10.24, 33; 13.5; Phil. 2.4) to have been literally lived out in the first church. Charismatic movements, particularly in the first flush of enthusiasm, are capable of building a communal life on such altruistic principles. For the description 'the believers' see 2.44.

4.33   Once again at the centre of the testimony given is 'the resurrection of the Lord Jesus' (see on 1.8 and 4.2). As in 2.47 the great Pauline term 'grace' (the outreach of God's generous power) is used in a rather un-Pauline way ('grace upon them').

4.34–35   The term 'needy' (only here in the New Testament) may be a deliberate allusion to Deut. 15.4: the new congregation of the Nazarene fulfilled Israel's hope for a people blessed by the Lord.

As with 2.45, the tenses used for the verbs (imperfect in Greek) indicate not a one-off sale of all property, but a continuing practice where financial needs of the new group were met by individuals selling off property from time to time and contributing the proceeds to the communal fund. One naturally wonders whether part at least of the rapid growth of the movement was made up of 'rice Christians', those attracted to Jesus' disciples by the prospect of free handouts. The question is not so sceptical as it might seem, since Luke himself goes out of his way in the next two chapters to report that the idyll had several darker features.

4.36–37   Enter one of the most attractive figures from the earliest days of Christianity. Joseph Barnabas features regularly later on in Acts as an absolutely crucial figure in the early expansion of

Christianity beyond Israel and out to the Gentiles. According to Acts, he gave Saul/Paul decisive backing following his conversion and drew him into the apostolic company, despite their natural reservations (9.27). He was the bridge man who as representative of the Jerusalem church was able to ensure that the new breakthrough at Syrian Antioch kept on the right lines (11.22). Thereafter he brought Saul/Paul to join the leadership at Antioch (11.25–26). He was the initial leader of the mission team who undertook what became the first significant penetration of the gospel into the Gentile world (13.1–2, etc.), and together with Paul was able to hold the line at the Jerusalem council on behalf of the Gentile believers (ch. 15). His vital role in keeping the expansion linked to the Jerusalem church is attested not only in 11.30, but also in Gal. 2.1, 9. The rupture with Paul (Acts 15.39; Gal. 2.13) does not seem to have lasted (cf. I Cor. 9.6; Col. 4.10). The warmth of the testimony on Barnabas' behalf, both here ('son of encouragement') and in 11.24 ('a good man, full of the Holy Spirit and of faith') is unusual even in Acts and surely indicates a man of rare quality, a community builder, able to promote and sustain warm and constructive personal relations.

The description of Barnabas as 'a Levite, a native of Cyprus', both sets him in contrast with the hostile priests of 4.1, and points forward to the future mission beyond the land of Israel (ch. 13).

The repetition of the phrase 'laid at the apostles' feet (4.35, 37; 5.2) may indicate an element of formality which became established in the practice of making substantial contribution to the fund.

Defining the Boundaries
5.1–42

Throughout the opening section of his account (chs 1–5) Luke has been attempting to define and characterize the new movement which sprang into life at Pentecost. One of his principal concerns throughout all four chapters so far has been to insist that the new sect is in full continuity with Israel of old, is the fulfilment of Israel's prophetic hope, and is thus in full accord with the purpose of God. The movement itself he has already marked out by two essential defining features: those round Peter and the other apostles were from the first those who had put themselves under the name of Jesus Messiah and were filled with God's Spirit. He has also made a point of distinguishing the power of Jesus' name from magic or human manipulation (3.6, 16) and of marking out the priestly authorities as the opponents of those who named this name (4.1, 5–6).

Now in this final chapter in the opening phase of the new movement Luke seeks to round off his initial description by giving these boundaries greater clarity. First, by representing the power of the new community as holy and aweful in character, brooking no human deceit or manipulation (5.1–16). And secondly, by defining the opposition more sharply as the high priest's faction, from which Gamaliel a leading Pharisee stood out. The latter seems willing to recognize what Luke's account affirms: that this undertaking is of God (5.17–39). Luke's account reaches its conclusion by juxtaposing two of the new sect's principal defining features: its representatives speak in the name of Jesus, 'teaching and preaching Jesus as the Christ' (5.40–42); and they do so in the Temple every day (5.42), implicitly affirming yet once more that the new movement is in full continuity with Israel's heritage and understands that heritage better than its priestly guardians.

Infringing the holy
5.1–11

For the Christian reader, this is one of the most unnerving episodes in the whole of the New Testament. The portrayal of two individuals caught out in what seems a not so very serious deception and immediately struck down dead, and without opportunity for repentance, is a profoundly shocking picture for those who have inherited long traditions of concern for 'due process of law'. What we must appreciate, however, is that here we are in a wholly different world from what most of us are used to. It is the world of 'the holy' (to echo the title of Rudolf Otto's famous study), a world where the spiritual realm has an almost tangible presence of raw, uncontainable energy, and where infringement of the holy can have devastating results.

Such holiness adheres particularly to the holy place or the holy object, set apart to God and therefore touched with something of the fearful power of his presence, the cosmic power of the Creator focussed in a particular place or object. Classic examples in the Old Testament are the restrictions on the people to prevent them approaching or touching Mount Sinai in Ex. 19.10–25, the cautionary tales of Nadab and Abihu in Lev. 10.1–3 and of Achan in Josh. 7, and the equally unnerving story of Uzzah's fate when he tried to steady the ark of the covenant in II Sam. 6.6–7. The Temple itself was the focus of holiness within the religion of Israel, as the Stephen affair would recall (cf. 6.13). The sense of awe which many today, including non-religious, feel when visiting an ancient shrine or mighty cathedral is of a piece with this, the subconscious awareness of the numinous producing an almost physical sensation. One of the reasons why many today want to restrict priesthood as much as possible is because they see the priest as a focus of the holy. In other, particularly animist religions we would have to compare and contrast the power of the taboo and the frightening power of the ju-ju and of voodoo.

The episode here reinforces the impression that the beginnings of Christianity were marked by the power of the holy creating a kind of numinous aura round the principal participants. In such circumstances, for anyone to infringe the boundaries of what was permissible was to invite a fearful retribution, not from the guardians of the holy but from the holy thing itself. We may see something of this also in Paul in the treatment he expects for the one guilty of grave immorality in I Cor. 5.3–5 (where Paul seems ready to play the role attributed to Peter in 5.9), as also perhaps in the effect of unworthy partaking in the Lord's Supper in I Cor. 11.29–30. How much of the effect is due to psychological processes in those suddenly confronted with the fact that they have infringed the holy is another question which does not change the basic facts of the case.

It is quite possible, therefore, that in the highly charged spiritual atmosphere generated by the beginning of the sect of the Nazarene there were cautionary tales told of the fearful results of infringing the holy. And this is what Luke has obviously picked up here. Whatever the source, however, the story fits with his own perception of the tangible character of the spiritual. And as a cautionary tale it serves to highlight the standards of integrity expected in the new movement. More important, the episode marks out the new church as evincing that aura of holiness which particularly in its beginnings marked out tabernacle and Temple with its Holy of Holies (Ex. 33.12–23; 34.29–35; II Chron. 7.1–3). The ground is being prepared for the first dramatic split between new church and old Temple which Luke will go on to recount in chs 6–7.

5.1–2 The story flows on immediately from the preceding account of Joseph Barnabas' generosity, the antecedant making the action of Ananias and Sapphira all the more blameworthy. In view of the sequel (5.7–10), Luke makes a point of noting the wife's complicity. They were in effect breaching the strict rules regarding vows (Num. 30.1–2; Deut. 23.21–23; cf. Mark 7.11–12; 1QS 6.24–25), but for Luke the episode is about a much more immediate confrontation with spiritual power.

5.3–4 Peter's reaction brings out two important aspects of the episode. First, the deception lay not in failure to contribute all the proceeds of the property sale to the common fund; they could have retained some of the proceeds without blame (5.4). The deception was rather in pretending that they were contributing all the proceeds while in reality retaining some for themselves. This makes clear that contribution to the common fund was neither compulsory, nor were contributors expected to give all their income or resources. Later on, for example, it becomes obvious that Mary, mother of John Mark, had not sold off her obviously rather substantial house (12.12–13). The whole affair of the common fund was evidently much more spontaneous and *ad hoc* in character.

Secondly, the encounter between Ananias and Peter is presented as actually a conflict between Satan and the Holy Spirit (5.3). Ananias, like Judas (Luke 22.3), is the (presumably willing) mouthpiece of Satan (already a familiar title for the chief adversary to God – Luke 10.18; 11.18; 22.31). The lie told to Peter was in fact told to the Spirit who presumably inspired Peter to recognize Ananias' deception. In this way Luke indicates his appreciation that the church is not a merely human institution and that behind its public affairs spiritual forces of incalculable power are ranged. The manner in which these forces manifest themselves in this instance brings to visible expression processes of integrity and corruption which usually work in more hidden ways. The episode thus has the character of revelation.

5.5   The recognition on Ananias' part that he had lied not merely to a fellow human being but to God had devastating consequences. It is not said that he was struck down, so we could well envisage his death as the effect of a profound shock. But Luke takes care to reinforce the sense of the holy by noting the awe and dread of those who heard of the unhappy event (as in 2.43 and 19.17).

5.6   There is an eerie ring to the conclusion of both parts of the episode in the references to 'the young men', who are otherwise nowhere mentioned (but cf. 2.17). Is there, perhaps, an allusion to the conclusion of the story of Nadab and Abihu in Lev. 10.4–5, where the sons of Aaron's uncle are called on to remove the bodies of those who had so rashly infringed the holy? If so the deliberate evocation of the raw energy of the holy is even more emphasized (cf. Lev. 10.6–7).

5.7–11   The second half of the story is modelled on the first. The accusation (5.9) is, if anything, more severe: not merely a lie to the Spirit, but an agreement to tempt the Spirit of the Lord (probably God here), an echo of the wilderness story (e.g. Ex. 17.2; Num. 20.22; Ps. 78.41, 56). Moreover, in this case Peter pronounces a sentence of death (5.9). As the spokesman for the outraged Spirit, he does not regard the death of Ananias as an unfortunate or regretable outcome from which he should try to save Sapphira. The deed had been calculating and perverse. The sanctity of the new gathering of God's people (not merely its moral standards) was at stake. The infringement of the holy had to be seen to be such in all its seriousness. But the effect is the same: the sudden death; the mysterious 'young men' again waiting in the wings; and the holy awe which came upon 'the whole church' (cf. 9.31) and all who heard the shocking story. The title 'church' is used for the first time, but refers only to the Jerusalem community.

The holy community
5.12–16

Following on the cautionary tale of Ananias and Sapphira, it is not surprising that Luke focusses this third brief characterization of the atmosphere of the earliest days on the 'signs and wonders' performed then. It is not merely that he wished to portray earliest Christianity as a successful miracle working movement. The underlying intention is still to highlight the church, or the apostles in particular, as a vehicle of the holy. Nor was it merely their success as miracle workers which he wanted to trumpet. Rather it is the fact that the Lord was so manifestly among them, in an almost tangible way, making them the focus and medium of his presence. That Luke himself saw that divine presence most manifest in the 'signs and wonders' produced is partly a reflection of the heady and potent spiritual atmosphere of these first days and partly an expression of Luke's own high evaluation of signs and wonders.

5.12   For the importance Luke places on 'signs and wonders' see on 2.22, 3.6 and Introduction to ch. 3. 'Through the hands' is almost a reflex phrase, it being simply taken for granted that most healings involved some touching or imposition of the healer's hands (cf. 3.7; 8.17; 19.6). The united character of the new movement is reiterated (as in 2.46), but the emphasis has greater significance here in view of the episode just narrated.

The mention of Solomon's portico is hardly accidental. It implies that the leaders of the new movement saw the Temple, or at least the huge Temple platform, as the natural place for them to be in these last or interim days. So it reinforces one of Luke's primary themes: that from the first the new movement saw itself as in no way at odds with the principal symbol of Israel's religion.

5.13   The initial clause is at first puzzling: who were 'the rest' who feared to join the united gathering of believers? Presumably other Jews; but Luke is not interested in clarifying the question. The point for him is to maintain the sense of that same holy atmosphere as constantly enveloping the first church, and evoking both respect, wonder and fear among the residents of Jerusalem.

5.14   is a variation of the formula used in 2.47. That the addition is 'to the Lord' (presumably Jesus here, as by implication 2.47) re-emphasizes the fact that 'the Lord' is the central identity marker of the new movement. Again the title 'believers' is used (as in 2.44 and 4.32).

5.15   Description of the most fearful of the miracles of judgment wrought within the Nazarene sect (5.1–11) is followed by reference to the most bizarre of the healing miracles – healing through Peter's shadow. But the atmosphere evoked is more or less the same – of an aura of holy power emanating from the new movement and its principal representative. There is no reason to think that Luke has contrived the account. The fervour and heightened susceptibility which attends prophetic movements or movements of spiritual renewal, particularly in their initial enthusiasm, can arouse such excitement and expectation (cf. Luke 4.14–15, 37, 40–41; 5.15; etc.). And Luke was no doubt able to draw on various memories of such enthusiastic scenes. Such beliefs lie behind the ancient tradition of venerating relics within Christian history. The account here also enabled Luke to draw out a further parallel between Peter and Paul (cf. 19.12). We today might have hoped for a somewhat more discriminating attitude on Luke's part to the signs and wonders he so evidently delighted in. But the boundary he wanted to draw is different: elsewhere between miracle and magic (3.6, 16; 8.18–24; 13.8–12; 19.11–20); here the boundary of holy awe, marking off those open to the power of the risen Lord in their lives from those abusive of it (5.1–11), frightened by it (5.13), or hostile to it (5.17).

5.16   This is the first indication, apart from 2.9, of the news (not yet message) of what was happening in Jerusalem reaching beyond Jerusalem, the first hint that the programme of 1.8 will be fulfilled. It is also the first mention in Acts of the healings so characteristic of Jesus' ministry – exorcisms. As with the one who allowed himself to become an agent of Satan (5.3), so with those possessed by 'unclean spirits', the encounter between Holy Spirit and unclean spirit results in the defeat of the latter. The holiness of the new community who name the name of Jesus remains unimpaired.

The second confrontation with the high priest
5.17–32

The principal object of this episode is to sharpen the sense of conflict between the apostles and their opponents and to focus that opposition in the high priest and his entourage. Luke does this, first, by repeated mention of the high priest himself as the apostles' implacable foe, not just waiting to be called upon to arbitrate some complaint against the apostles, but actually provoking and directing the action against them (5.17, 21, 27). 'All those with him' include particularly the Sadducees and the rest of the high priests (5.17, 24), emphasizing that the opposition to the apostles is focussed in the Temple authorities. Over against them stand the people, open to and welcoming of the apostles' message (5.13, 20, 25, 26), and even the Pharisee, Gamaliel, held in honour by all the people (5.34). The second way in which Luke sharpens the contrast between high priest and apostles is by emphasizing the intemperate nature of the opposition – 'filled with jealousy' (5.17), 'enraged' and wanting to kill the apostles (5.33). The contrast with the apostles standing daily in the Temple and speaking the words of life (5.20, 21, 25, 42) is stark and deliberately so.

5.17–18   The high priest himself is the instigator of the action, and with his supporters arrests the apostles and puts them in the public prison. In contrast with 4.5–6, no mention is made of the elders and scribes. On the Sadducees see 4.1. Here they are described as a 'sect', the term also used by Josephus to describe the three or four principal religious and political parties within Israel (*Jewish War* 2.118; *Antiquities* 13.171), but also by Luke to describe the Pharisees later (15.5), as indeed also the Nazarenes themselves (24.5). No reason is given for the arrest, though it is later indicated as a breach of conditions of parole (5.28); but such arbitrary exercise of supreme power was quite typical of authorities of the time.

5.19–20   This account of angelic deliverance has some puzzling features. It is surprisingly similar to, but much briefer than the account in 12.6–11 – an unusual doublet in Acts, where Luke seems content to fill out his comparison between Peter and Paul by means of single parallel incidents (here 16.25–34). The brevity means that the story is told in brusque, matter-of-fact terms, with nothing of the sense of the numinous which pervades both the immediately preceding context and the parallel in 12.6–11. Untypical of Luke, also, is the fact that he makes so little of it as a miracle; contrast 12.9 (it really was an angel in the prison).

It is possible that Luke heard two versions of the same episode and decided to make use of both (cf. his account of two missions of Jesus' disciples in Luke 9 and 10). But we cannot exclude the possibility that the matter of fact account is a way of hinting that 'the angel or messenger (same word) of the Lord' was actually an early sympathizer with the new movement within the prison staff. If such a one had already found spiritual renewal through the apostles' preaching it would be understandable that he should want them to continue the public proclamation of 'the words of this life' (for this summary use of 'life' cf. 3.15 and 11.18). The first believers would no doubt take great delight in retelling the story in their own circles using the politically tactful *double entendre*.

5.21–26   The contrast between the open boldness of the apostles teaching in the Temple and the perplexity of the Temple authorities bears the mark of a supremely gifted storyteller. The climax is the still more striking contrast between the hostility of the Temple authorities and the enthusiastic support of the people: the people might have stoned the Temple officials to protect the apostles!

Unusually 5.21 contain two words for the gathering convened – *sunedrion* and *gerousia*. Whatever the precise historical facts regarding the history of the Sanhedrin at this time (see on 4.5–6) Luke was evidently indicating the full weight of political, legal and religious authority ('all the council of the sons of Israel') being brought to bear against the apostles.

5.27–28   The charge, that the apostles were trying to pin blood guilt on the priestly authorities, would have made more sense had Luke narrated any intervening example of the apostles repeating that accusation. They had certainly made such a public accusation earlier (2.23; 3.13–15; and particularly 4.10), but not once in Luke's narrative since their previous caution (4.18). Luke probably intends his readers to assume that the emphasis was a regular feature of the apostles' preaching (4.29, 33; 5.12, 21). But the main effect of the high priest's question is to underscore the widespread impact of their teaching. Their teaching had filled Jerusalem – a hint that the church was ready for its next phase of expansion.

5.29 As in 2.7–11 and 4.24–30, Luke evokes a kind of choral effect, as not just Peter but all the apostles speak in unison. The description is hardly intended as literal. It is simply one of Luke's artistic touches to heighten the drama of the confrontation between the high priest and 'all the council of the sons of Israel' (5.21) ranged on one side, and Peter and the apostles ranged on the other. Here indeed is a fundamental conflict about the destiny and identity of Israel.

5.29–32 This is not just a reply, as in 4.19–20, but a brief speech which encapsulates the chief points made in the previous speeches. Indeed, it is almost as though Luke has stitched together this brief response from emphases and echoes drawn from these speeches. At the same time he has shaped these echoes to highlight his own emphases and included some striking variations, which do not appear to be arbitrarily conceived and presumably reflect Luke's awareness of various traditions from the early period. Moreover, as with all the speeches he records, this one too, for all its brevity, is a beautifully shaped cameo, its artistry marked by the way it rounds off with the same word as it began ('obey').

The speech begins (5.29) with a reiteration of the last response (4.19–20). But the evocation of other confrontations between human authority and those commissioned by God (e.g. Ex. 3.15; Dan. 3.26 LXX; see also on 4.19–20) is more starkly marked. Luke includes his favourite *dei* ('it is necessary') as indicating a divinely inspired compulsion in accord with the divine purpose (see on 4.12).

It emphasizes that all the determinative action was God's from start to finish – 'God' is named four times in the four verses. God raised Jesus, whom you killed (5.30) – the reverse order from the earlier speeches (2.23–24; 3.15; 4.10). God exalted Jesus to his right hand (5.31 – a direct echo of 2.33). God has given the Holy Spirit (5.32; in some contrast to 2.33, which see).

The christology puts first emphasis on the resurrection, as usual (5.30), and implies rather more of a distinction between resurrection and exaltation than in 2.32–33, but, of course, in line with 1.1–11. The talk of Jesus' being killed by being hung on a tree (similarly 10.39) probably alludes to Deut. 21.22–23, and may provide the first hint that this text was used to discredit the claim that a crucified man could be Messiah (implied also in Gal. 3.13). The speech also picks up the same ancient title, 'author, leader', as in 3.15. But it adds 'Saviour', a title which only reappears in 13.23, and elsewhere seems to be almost wholly confined to second and third generation sources (only in Phil. 3.20 of the undisputed Pauline letters). At the same time, however, it sums up one of Luke's favourite motifs (salvation; see on 4.12). In contrast to 2.33, where God gives Jesus the Spirit to pour out on others, here Jesus is exalted to give repentance (contrast 11.18) and forgiveness.

The order of salvation, repentance resulting in forgiveness of sins, and the gift of the Spirit echoes the sequence of 2.38 (and 3.19). But an unusual note is that the Spirit is given 'to those who obey him'. Not too much should be made of this as though Luke envisaged the Spirit as given in response to a procedure properly followed. The key here is to recognize that the word used is the same as the word with which the speech began, a rather unusual word for 'obey'. Its use in 5.32, therefore, is determined mostly by rhetorical considerations. But the theological point is that the Spirit and the sort of boldness that was shown by Peter and the apostles go together: where such boldness is displayed (forthright proclamation of Christ in the face of hostile religious authorities) one can be sure that the Spirit is behind it (cf. 4.8, 31; Luke 12.11–12); alternatively expressed, it is such readiness for full commitment to his cause (characteristically expressed in baptism in his name) which opens the individual to the Spirit's infilling and enabling.

Not least of Luke's concerns is reflected in the emphasis on continuity with Israel's history and hopes: 'the God of our fathers' (5.30; cf. 4.13); 'to give repentance to Israel and forgiveness of sins' (5.31; cf. 2.39 and 3.25–26). In formulating the second of these phrases Luke will no doubt already have had in mind the description with which he would sum up the (for him) first great breakthrough of the gospel to the Gentiles (11.18). But at this stage in particular the focus is exclusively on Israel as the primary beneficiaries of the gospel's blessing, with the implication that the church is Israel in so far as it repents and receives forgiveness and the Spirit.

Finally, the authorization and responsibility of the disciples as 'witnesses' is reiterated (5.32), picking up the thread begun at 1.8 and woven through the early chapters (1.22; 2.32; 3.15; 4.33). But care is taken also to underline one of Luke's major themes: that this witness is only possible in the power and at the inspiration of the Holy Spirit (1.8; 2.11, 32–33; 4.8, 31; cf. again Luke 12.11–12).

The Jerusalem church's position secured
5.33–42

Although this paragraph is a continuation of the same scene it is one which deserves to be picked out. For in it Luke shows how the hostility and rage of the religious authorities were stemmed by the intervention of Gamaliel the Pharisee. In terms of the unfolding drama, this has the effect of isolating the opposition to the new church and limiting it to the political faction whose power base was the Temple. For the first time in the narrative, the leadership of Israel is split, and it is this which enables the church to maintain its position within Jerusalem despite priestly opposition.

A feature of Luke's two-volume account is the number of episodes he narrates which feature Pharisees sympathetic or open to Jesus (Luke 7.36; 11.37; 13.31; 14.1), without playing down the more frequent recollections of Pharisaic hostility to Jesus. This probably constitutes Luke's own way of protesting against a too undifferentiated opposition to the Pharisees which prevailed in other early Christian traditions. If so, the protest would no doubt have been stimulated by Luke's own awareness that Pharisees did in fact associate themselves with the new movement (Acts 15.5; 26.5!) and were otherwise closer in sympathy to it than the Sadducees and those who identified their cause with that of the high priest (so also 23.6–9). That Luke is thus able to heighten the drama of his account is insufficient ground for arguing that the whole motif (of Pharisaic sympathy) is a Lukan contrivance. On the contrary, the fact that the Jerusalem believers were able to establish themselves so effectively in Jerusalem must indicate a measure of sympathy for them among the opinion formers of the capital. Whatever we make of the speech used by Gamaliel as such (5.35–39), therefore, it is very likely that the substance of the account is rooted in well-informed recollections of the time.

At all events, Luke is able to use the tradition to end his account of the opening phase of Christianity in a position of equilibrium – firmly established in the Temple, and despite alarms still daily teaching and preaching Jesus as the Christ in the Temple, the symbolical heart of Israel. He will end his whole account in the same way (28.31).

5.33   The language indicates the intemperance of the council and heightens the contrast with the apostles' boldness and Gamaliel's temperate counsel. The vivid quality of storytelling is evident, though we should recall that religious convictions when crossed can provoke extreme passions.

5.34   Gamaliel was indeed a leading and highly regarded member of the Pharisees in that period, and, according to 22.3, the teacher of Paul. Whether as a Pharisee he would have had sufficient authority to give orders in the council is unclear, but we do not know enough of the composition and rules governing the council (or Sanhedrin) at this period for us to dispute Luke's version (see on 4.5–6). That the Pharisees, particularly a highly regarded one like Gamaliel, were held in high honour by the people is also attested by Josephus (*Antiquities* 8.15, 17).

Gamaliel is described as a 'teacher of the law', which properly characterizes the Pharisees' *raison d'être*. The description attached to one who speaks on behalf of the new sect also indicates, however, that the law was no issue between the Pharisees and the earliest Jerusalem church. The contrast with Jesus' own ministry (Luke 6.1–11), as also with the later phase of the Christian mission (15.5), is somewhat surprising. But it can be taken as a further indication that the first Jerusalem believers were all devout Jews and loyal to the law (see also 10.14), that is, properly speaking still a sect within Judaism, marked out only by the distinctiveness of their beliefs regarding Jesus.

5.35–39   Gamaliel's argument is simple. Do not prejudge the new movement. Let time disclose its character. If it is not of God, it will fail. If it is of God, opposition to it cannot succeed (cf. Mishnah, *Aboth* 4.11). In other words, Gamaliel takes seriously the claim of Peter (5.29). The way in which 5.38–39 answers to 5.29 makes for a pleasing rhetorical roundedness.

More to the point, what is at stake here is perception as to what God's will actually is (the reference to this 'plan' in 5.38 is probably a deliberate echo of the same word used of God's plan in 2.23 and 4.28). On this point Luke's contrast between Sadducees and Pharisees reflects what is the more widely recognized contrast – that is, between a priestly contentment with the Torah as such, and a recognition that Torah needs interpretation. So here, the high priest is confident enough in the established forms and patterns as still expressing God's will; a word of new revelation is by definition ruled out. Gamaliel, the Pharisee, on the other hand, recognizes that changing times may require redefinition of God's will or at least openness to that possibility. Needless to say, this is a constantly recurring conflict within Jewish and Christian history (hence always the importance of prophet alongside priest). What is interesting here is that it is the Pharisee who stands on the side of openness to development and even radical change.

The two precedents cited by Gamaliel (5.36–37) are known also from Josephus' history of the period, and the details given here accord in broad outline with those of Josephus (*Antiquities* 20.97–98; 18.4–8). The problem is, however, that according to Josephus the first mentioned episode took place some years later than Gamaliel's speech (Theudas' folly was enacted in AD 44, some ten years later), while the second episode took place before Theudas (the census was taken in AD 6), not after it, as Gamaliel states here. The fact that Luke's details are historically anachronistic, however, should cause no disquiet. The character and quality of historiography of the time did not depend on the precision of detail which the modern historian presupposes to be fundamental. The point of the speech remains unaffected by questions of historical sequence. As ever in the Acts speeches, what matters is that Gamaliel (or someone of his stature) must have said and probably did say something like this to counter and prevent high priestly hostility against the new sect having more serious effect (the Qumran community, despite its extremism, was similarly tolerated by the religious and political authorities).

5.40–42   The rounding off effect of these three verses is noteworthy. (1) The high priestly opposition (5.40) is reduced to repetition of the old threats, already effectively answered in the summary speech of 4.29–32, and to arbitrary wielding of judicial power (not at all uncharacteristic of the times). The flogging would presumably consist of forty strokes less one (cf. II Cor. 11.24), a fearful but evidently quite frequent punishment.

(2) The centrality of 'the name of Jesus' (the principal theme of chs 3–4) is reiterated (5.40–41), and Jesus as the Messiah/Christ is presented as the sum and substance of their teaching and preaching ('proclaiming that the Messiah was Jesus' – 5.42). It is on this point that the identity of the new sect is focussed (see Introduction to ch. 3). Their enthusiasm and supreme confidence in this Jesus is indicated by their rejoicing even in suffering – a feature within

earliest Christianity noted elsewhere in the New Testament (Luke 6.22; Rom. 5.3; I Thess. 1.6; I Peter 1.6).

Not least, (3) the apostles retain their centre in the Temple (5.42). As the previous phase also ended in the Temple (Luke 24.53), so does the first phase of the new movement. It began in Jerusalem – and remained there throughout this whole first phase. The implication is that the support of Gamaliel has secured Jerusalem as their continuing base. The mention that teaching and preaching also took place 'at home' (as in 2.46) confirms that another locus of Christian identity is emerging. And the concluding mention of the apostles' continued allegiance to the Temple sets the stage for the next dramatic development (chs 6–7). But the final note struck by Luke in this opening section is that of continuity: it began in Jerusalem because hitherto that had been the symbol and the locus of the divine presence and purpose.

PART II
The Initial Expansion
6–12

With the characterization of the earliest Jerusalem church satisfactorily rounded off – not least its Jesus focus and Spirit empowerment, and the continuity symbolized by the Temple, despite the hostility of the Temple authorities – Luke was ready to describe the next phase of Christian beginnings. Here also the structure of this next major section of Luke's account is quite deliberate. It recounts the circumstances which resulted in the initial expansion of the Jesus movement out from the beginnings in Jerusalem and how the first stages in that expansion began to transform the self-understanding of the new movement which had so far prevailed. Particularly striking is the tension running through the ordering of events between continuity with Jerusalem and the programme of missionary outreach.

The initial point of continuity and hostility is again the Temple. Stephen, who emerges as a leading Hellenist, provokes a much fiercer reaction over his views on the Temple, which result in his summary execution (chs 6–7). It is the persecution following his death, not any deliberate policy of the Jerusalem church, which results in the first missionary move beyond Jerusalem. Here again, as with the judicial murder of Jesus (a regular motif in chs 1–5), the divine purpose overrules human malice to bring to effect the overarching divine plan (2.23; 4.28; 5.38–39).

The initial move into Samaria and in the conversion of the eunuch (ch. 8) continues the Temple theme, since it was dispute over the site of the Temple which was decisive in the schism between Jew and Samaritan, and since the eunuch was typical of those excluded from the Temple because of some defect. The narrow focus on the Temple which characterized chs 1–5 is now radically reversed to open up salvation precisely to those for whom the Temple marked disbarment rather than benefit. It is no coincidence that this double

75

episode of initial expansion also marks a decisive step forward in the programme of 1.8, not only into Samaria, but also already, by implication, to one end of the earth (Ethiopia).

Into the midst of what probably was a continuous Hellenist source (chs 6–8, 11.19–30) Luke has inserted two episodes – Paul's conversion (9.1–31) and the conversion of Cornelius (10.1–11.18). The space he devotes to both (with two further accounts of Paul's conversion in chs 22 and 26, and the Cornelius episode not only narrated twice but also cited in 15.7–9) shows just how important they were for Luke and how pivotal is their function in Luke's portrayal of earliest Christian expansion.

Paul's conversion is given primacy – not only because it followed directly from the persecution which arose out of the Stephen affair, but also because it prepares for the dominant role which Luke will give to Paul in the second half of Acts. The conversion of the great missionary to the Gentiles is recounted before any real breakthrough to the Gentiles is described. The conversion of Paul, in other words, is the headline under which the subsequent expansion into Gentile territory takes place. For all that Peter supervised the first Gentile conversion, it is Paul who is the dominant factor in what follows.

It was equally important for Luke, however, that the conversion of Cornelius (10.1–11.18) should be recounted before the breakthrough at Antioch (11.19–26). It is this which enables him to attribute not only the evangelism of Judaea to Peter (9.32–43) but also the crucial first acceptance of a Gentile without requiring circumcision. In this way Luke is able to maintain the strongest link between the beginnings in Jerusalem and the critical step which validated the subsequent massive expansion of the Jesus movement beyond the land of Israel. It is Peter's precedent which validates Paul's subsequent revolutionary ministry.

The second phase (chs 6–12) is rounded off by an astonishingly brief account of the breakthrough at Antioch (11.19–21) – astonishing in comparison with the space given to the Cornelius episode – in which the stronger concern seems to be to ensure that the Antioch church cannot be seen as independent of the Jerusalem church (11.22–30). It is presumably this concern to maintain Jerusalem as the vital symbol and medium of continuity which also motivated Luke to return his narrative to Jerusalem (ch. 12) before devoting more or less exclusive attention to Paul (chs 13–28). That the episode ends with Peter himself departing from Jerusalem (12.17) is a signal that the centre of gravity in the Christian mission was beginning to shift

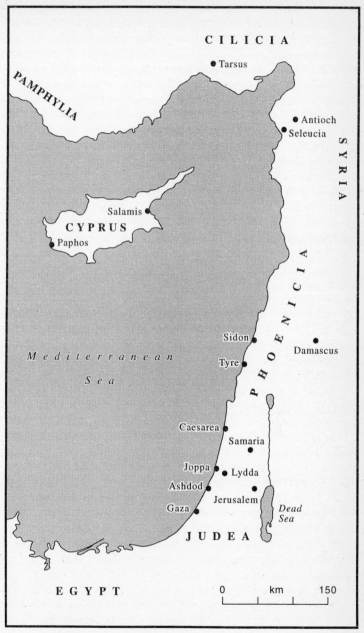

1: Earliest Christian Expansion

from Jerusalem. What began in Jerusalem can now no longer be contained within the terms which Jerusalem historically represented.

Within these episodes the other key identifying marks maintain their prominence. Jesus remains the focus of the preaching: his rejection as the climax of Stephen's speech (7.52), his place at the right hand of God in Stephen's vision (7.56), his name proclaimed (8.5, 12; 9.15–16, 27–28; 10.43). And the reception of the Spirit as the crucial mark of divine acceptance is given particular prominence in the two decisive breakthroughs, to the Samaritans and to the Gentile Cornelius (8.14–17; 10.44–48; 11.15–18). Perhaps most striking of all, however, is the way in which the issues which help define identity broaden out from from the intra-Jewish one of the Temple (chs 6–8) to issues of Jewish and Gentile relationship (chs 10–11) and the encounter between the Jewish-Christian understanding of God and that of the non-Jewish world (8.4–24; 10.25–26), with the importance of the latter reinforced by the final episode of the section (12.20–23).

The Stephen Affair
6.1–15

With chapter 6 the mood abruptly changes as Luke introduces the first note of serious discord into the history of the Jerusalem church. The tragic affair of Ananias and Sapphira (5.1–11) had been of a different order – to show how the holy, if abused, becomes a power of destruction rather than of salvation. But now the idyll of the holy congregation begins to come down to earth with the opening report of Hebrew failings and Hellenist complaints regarding a breakdown in the administration of the common fund. Luke introduces the report abruptly to signal that a new phase in his history of Christian beginnings is being opened up.

In fact, the introduction of the Hellenists begins a sequence which runs through ch. 8 and seems to be picked up again in 11.19. Almost certainly Luke has been able to draw on a more or less coherent source for these chapters – perhaps the account of their own origins told by the church at Antioch. The source indicated that decisive developments in the earliest outreach of the new movement were to be attributed to the group from which both Stephen and Philip came, that is, almost certainly, those he calls the Hellenists. It was knowledge of those developments which no doubt caused Luke to frame his table of contents as he did in 1.8 ('in all Judaea and Samaria').

Of course it suited Luke's purpose to be able to attribute these developments to the Hellenists who were subsequently expelled from Jerusalem (8.4; 11.19). It was important for him that the expansion of Christianity was not rooted elsewhere – in some mission emanating from groups in Galilee, for example, as some have wanted to argue. It began in Jerusalem, and the 'it' in this case included the dramatic emergence of Gentile churches over the next three decades. But there is no reason to doubt that the source Luke drew on embodied a fair memory of what had actually happened, and that it was indeed the Hellenists who were responsible for the first real outreach beyond Jerusalem.

This becomes all the more likely when we realize that the account

79

of the Hellenists does not fit entirely easily within Luke's scheme of things. In particular, it is doubtful whether Luke has indicated the full extent of the discord noted in 6.1. The circumstances narrated hint at dimensions to the complaints of which Luke says nothing. And we know from his complete silence on other serious tensions within the early Gentile mission (of which we learn in passages like Gal. 2.11–14 and II Cor. 10–13) that Luke was ready to draw a curtain over what he presumably regarded as less creditable episodes within earliest Christianity. The emergence of the Hellenist seven (6.3–6) also fits awkwardly with the exclusive focus he has so far put upon the apostles. And the fact that Stephen criticizes the Temple (6.13–14) runs counter to the positive symbolic role Luke otherwise attributes to the Temple. As we proceed we shall also notice several linguistic indications that Luke was drawing on a source – 'the disciples' (6.1), 'the twelve' (6.2), 'full of the Spirit' (6.3), and so on.

In short, the brevity of Luke's account in 6.1–6 probably indicates that the Hellenists were too important a factor in the earliest movement's expansion for Luke to ignore them, and that the circumstances of their emergence as a distinct force within Christian beginnings had to be told even if the circumstances were not entirely to the new sect's credit and even though the veil could not be drawn completely over the circumstances.

The emergence of the Hellenists
6.1–7

Luke has an odd habit of introducing absolutely vital information without warning and without explanation (cf. 11.20). Here he suddenly confronts his readers with 'the Hellenists', without any indication whatsoever of who they were and why they were so called. It may be, of course, that he could assume his readers' familiarity with 'the Hellenists', or that the name itself would be self-explanatory. Or his silence on the point could be a further reflection of his own somewhat ambivalent attitude towards them. But given their evidently crucial role in what follows it is very frustrating for the modern reader to be left so much in the dark. Some detective work is called for, which, even on the basis of the minimal information provided by Luke, uncovers some fascinating inferences and possible corollaries still relevent to today.

6.1 Once again, there is no time scale indicated, but such measurement of time as we can achieve suggests that the problems referred to could easily have arisen within the first year of the new movement's existence. Certainly if there was anything like the growth indicated in 4.4 and 5.14, and a realistic attempt to operate a common fund to support the poorer members of the sect, then the numbers must quickly have made almost impossible demands upon the common fund. This indeed is precisely what the opening clause indicates. There was, presumably, a more established system of poor relief within Jerusalem for all poor, but perhaps it was already a point of principle that those who had aligned themselves with the new movement should look to it for support.

For the first time the title 'the disciples' is used, its use perhaps indicating that it was initially a self-description within Hellenist circles (6.1, 2, 7; 9.1, 10, 19, 25–26; 11.26).

All we know about 'the Hellenists' is given by their name. The name 'Hellenist' itself denotes one who speaks Greek. The fact that the contrasting name is 'Hebrews' also focusses attention on language as the key identifying characteristic. For the only reason why a group should be identified as 'Hebrews' is that, in contrast to the 'Greek speakers', they spoke Hebrew, or its contemporary vernacular equivalent, Aramaic (cf. 21.40 and 22.2). But since Greek was the international language of the day, and since we know that Greek was widely used in Israel, not least in Jerusalem (about a third of ossuary inscriptions from this period found in Jerusalem are written in Greek), the probable distinction is between those who used Aramaic as their daily language (but could understand at least some Greek) and those who could speak effectively only Greek. The two groups, then, were called 'the Greek-speakers' and 'the Aramaic speakers'.

This basic deduction, however, leads unavoidably to a second deduction. For language is a vehicle of culture. And anyone who functions in a single or predominant language is almost certainly a product of the culture which that language embodies. Someone who functions in Welsh or Urdu in a British town or city will most certainly be shaped in greater or less degree by a Welsh or Pakistani/north Indian culture. The inevitable inference, then, is that the Hellenists were a language and culture sub-group within Jerusalem (a key point ignored by Hill 22–24).

It also follows, almost immediately, that they must have come from abroad. That is to say, they were Jews from the diaspora, who had needed only Greek for work and life, though possibly also the language of their place of residence (cf. 2.6, 11). In other words, the larger Hellenist community in Jerusalem was made up of those who had returned from the diaspora to settle in Jerusalem (cf. 2.5; 9.29). 6.9 provides confirmation of this, since it speaks of a synagogue attended by Jews from different parts of the daispora. We can assume that Greek was the language of communication, study and prayer there.

We should also recall that the history of the Maccabean period must have left a residue of suspicion among devout Torah Jews of such Greek speakers. For it had been the Hellenizers, those who wanted to abandon Jewish distinctives (circumcision, food laws, prescribed sacrifices in the Temple), who had precipitated the crisis which led to the Maccabean revolt (see I Macc. 1–2). Whether such suspicion played any part in the Stephen affair we cannot say, but the fact that the crisis here too focussed on the Temple may be significant.

At all events, it would appear that a significant number of the larger Hellenist group in Jerusalem had responded to the earliest preaching of the first believers and had become a significant group within the Jerusalem church. We should note in passing that their inability to function in any other language than Greek must mean that the Jesus tradition was already being put into Greek for their benefit. They formed a coherent group within the church: they could be identified as 'the Hellenists'; though to speak of them as a 'party' or faction as such goes beyond the evidence; and there was an extended family concern for 'their widows'. Since girls could be married quite young, often to older husbands, it was inevitable that there should be a high proportion of widows in any community (cf. 9.39–41; I Tim. 5.9–16). On traditional Jewish concern for widows see on 3.2–5; in the New Testament cf. James 1.27.

Given all the background indicated above, one wonders whether there was some element of tension between the Hebrews and the Hellenists within the young Christian community: such language differences often cause misunderstanding; 'Hebrews' may carry a note of nationalist resistence to Hellenistic influences (cf. Phil. 3.5); and why should the Hellenist widows, and apparently they alone, suffer from the inefficiencies of the administration of the common fund (the imperfect tense indicates a persisting state of affairs)?

6.2–4   For the only time in Acts 'the apostles' are called 'the twelve', a fact probably indicative of Luke's use of a source (cf. I Cor. 15.5; see also Introduction to 1.15–26). Their primary (though not exclusive) role is indicated as the preaching of the word (see on 4.4), and prayer (6.4), an emphasis characteristic of Luke (see on 1.14). Nothing yet indicates a sense of calling to take the word beyond Jerusalem. Ironically, it will be some of those chosen to 'wait at tables' who will do that.

We see here the first clear recognition of different kinds of ministry, of a ministry of word (preaching) and a ministry to basic human need (food and shelter). Also of different people set apart for such different ministries; the apostles could not do everything. Consequently it is also possible to see here the first steps towards a diaconal ministry. But we should also note that the term 'deacon' is not used, and that the related noun (*diakonia*) is used both of the administration of the common fund and of the ministry of the word (6.1, 4).

The men chosen are to be 'full of the Spirit and of wisdom'. Both terms occur only in the 'Hellenist section' of Luke's narrative ('full of the Spirit' – 6.3, 5; 7.55; 11.24; 'wisdom' – 6.3, 10; 7.10, 22) – again suggesting that Luke's use here is drawn from a Hellenist source. The contrast with Luke's usual verbal phrase ('filled with the Spirit' for a particular occasion) may also suggest that the Hellenist source had a concept of a more settled level of inspiration (contrast 4.8 with 7.55). The full phrase certainly envisages one whose inspiration, insight and discernment was exceptionally well matured. There are echoes in all this of Num. 11.16–30 and 27.16–23 and possibly also Ex. 31.3 and 35.31.

6.5 Who were the seven? All their names are Greek, which suggests they were all Hellenists. The deduction is by no means certain: some of Jesus' own disciples also had Greek names (Andrew and Philip). But the sequel (chs 6–8) seems to indicate that Stephen and Philip were Hellenists. The last of the seven, Nicolaus, was a proselyte, that is, a Gentile who had converted to Judaism. And the substantial evidence of names used in Israel (from inscriptions and other texts) shows that only two of the names were familiar names within Israel (Philip and Nicanor). So it is a fair deduction that the seven were indeed all Hellenists.

In which case, we can probably make a further deduction. Those who spoke only Greek would presumably have met separately from the Aramaic speakers, in Greek-speaking homes (cf. 2.46; 5.42).

Consequently, the seven may have been the leaders of the Hellenist house churches. It could be, indeed, that the choice of just seven indicates that there were seven Greek-speaking house churches. Which would also mean that the seven were seen as representative leaders of the Hellenist believers, analogous to the leadership, provided by the twelve, of the church as a whole; hence they can be called 'the seven' (21.8) in parallel or some equivalence to 'the twelve' (6.2). This would also help explain how it was that those appointed as table-waiters became such vigorous leaders in evangelism (Stephen and Philip).

At all events, if only Hellenists were chosen, just as only the Hellenist widows had been neglected, then the suggestion of a church already marked by two distinct groups is strong. Diversity, in language and culture, and presumably in social composition too, was part of the first church more or less from the start. There was never a time when the church did not know the tensions which come from diversity of culture and viewpoint and defects in organization!

6.6 If the episode foreshadows the diversity of ministries within the future church, then this first example of laying on of hands for ministry in Acts presumably foreshadows the future rite of ordination (cf. I Tim. 4.14). As such it was itself foreshadowed by precedents from the history of Israel (particularly Num. 27.22–23; Deut. 34.9). To be noted here, then is the odd fact that the Greek taken in its most obvious sense, indicates that it was the crowd of disciples, rather than the apostles, who laid their hands on the seven. On balance, we should probably assume that Luke has simply expressed himself in too casual a fashion, and that he meant his readers to understand that it was the apostles who laid on hands. But the possible echo of Num. 8.10 (the people lay their hands on the Levites) does leave the question much more open than is usually assumed by translators (Barrett 315–16 insists strongly on the Greek being taken in its most natural sense).

6.7 Luke inserts another brief summary to indicate the passing of time. 'The word of God' (see on 4.4) is used for the first time as the subject of the action, as though it was a living being, the formula expressing the sense of the vitality of the movement and foreshadowing the still greater growth to come (12.24; similarly 13.49 and 19.20). The phrase 'obedient to the faith' has a Pauline ring (cf. Rom. 1.5).

This fourth indication of rapid expansion (2.41, 47; 4.4; 5.14) explicitly mentions many priests joining the disciples. The note is striking, given the hostility attributed to them in the only other reference to priests (4.1). That a good number among the lower ranks of priests should be attracted to a vibrant and expanding sect is quite understandable (at this time there were probably about 8,000 priests in Israel). But the mention of this fact here is obviously deliberate on Luke's part. On the one hand it narrows the hostility against the disciples to the high priests and their supporters (5.17, 21, 27). But it also stands in immediate contrast to the hostility against Stephen about to be expressed in reference to the Temple (6.13–14). 6.7, in other words, stands as the highwater mark of early success within Jerusalem (only to be compared to 21.20). This reference to priests joining the disciples is Luke's way of indicating that prior to Stephen the continuity of the new movement with the Israel of old, as focussed above all in the Temple, was unbroken.

He speaks against this holy place
6.8–15

The preaching of Peter had called no vital principle of Israel's religion or heritage in question. Despite the high priest and his entourage being given the most prominent role in the opposition to the apostles, their grounds of complaint were insufficient to give them real leverage against the new church (chs 4–5). On the contrary, the support of the many priests, just mentioned (6.7), indicates a movement wholly in accord with Israel's central traditions. Now, however, a major disruptive factor is introduced – the charge against Stephen that he spoke against the Law and the Temple. In fact, as will become clear, the charge focusses on the Temple. What Luke does here, then, is to set in contrast Stephen, as the representative of the holy congregation – his sanctity is repeatedly emphasized (6.8, 10, 15) – and the Temple, 'this holy place' (6.13), in which Israel's understanding of Moses and God had hitherto focussed. How this will work out for the history of Christianity will be the subject of the following chapters.

6.8   Luke signals that Stephen is to be seen as the spokesman for God, embodiment of his grace and power, worker of the signs and wonders which manifest God's approval, no less than the apostles

(2.43; 4.30; 5.12). What time this left for administration of the common fund Luke does not indicate.

6.9   Those referred to here will be the larger group of Hellenists (9.29) who had returned to Jerusalem from the places mentioned. Probably only one synagogue (for Greek-speaking Jews resident in Jerusalem) was in mind (though the Greek could refer to more; cf. 24.12). There is archaeological evidence of a synagogue in Jerusalem founded by one Theodotus for the benefit of Jews who came from abroad, but the age of the inscription is disputed (see Winter 4.192–200, 204–6). The 'Freedmen' ('Libertini', a Latin term) was probably the name used for the descendants of those who had been taken to Rome as slaves in 61 BC, following the conquest of Jerusalem by Pompey, and subsequently freed (Philo, *Embassy to Gaius* 155, provides this information). Slaves were regularly manumitted (freed) after a period of service. There were substantial Jewish populations in Cyrene and Alexandria (we later hear of believers from both areas – 11.20 and 18.24). Paul came from Cilicia and Asia was a major focus of his mission.

In the light of the accusations against Stephen (6.13–14) we can guess at the reason for their hostility to Stephen's message. The reason why there were Hellenists in Jerusalem in the first place is because, as devout Jews, they had wished to return, most of them, presumably, to retire in Jerusalem. The reason would be, of course, to be near the Temple. Still today Jews, Christians and Muslims want to be buried in the Holy City, and when the Temple still stood, its presence would have exercised a powerful magnetic effect for many diaspora Jews. But now, one of their number, perhaps a younger member of a diaspora family, was preaching in such a way as to call into question the whole reason for their existence in Jerusalem. We can well imagine that religious fervour and economic uncertainty (a potent combination) generated a strong reaction to such a proclamation.

6.10–14   Attribution of the charge to false witnesses is an obvious way to devalue or undercut the opposition to Stephen (cf. Pss. 27.12; 35.11; Prov. 24.28; the classic case was the tale of Naboth's vineyard – I Kings 21). But one can well imagine that a message which combined defence of Jesus with critique of the Temple would create all sorts of misunderstanding on the part of other devout Hellenists. For Luke it was evidently the latter which turned the people from support (as in 5.13, 26) to the hostility of 6.12. Luke envisages a council convened by the high priest (6.12), but nothing more regular than that (see on 4.5–6), and, on this occasion, with a crowd of petitioners from the Hellenist synagogue(s) also present.

'Blasphemous words against Moses and God' (6.11). We should not look for a reasoned exposition of what amounted to blasphemy here: technically blasphemy means insulting or reviling the divine name; but Josephus, *Jewish War* 2.145 also speaks of blasphemy against Moses. At any rate, the language used here sounds like an over-the-top reaction of someone whose most cherished conviction had been called in question (though see on 7.2 and 56). Any criticism of something so fundamental (as the Temple) to a religion in which one had invested one's whole life would sound like a criticism of the whole. There are no passions like religious passions, no charges so exaggerated and intemperate as made by those whose deepest religious sensibilities have been wounded.

The charge becomes more explicit in 6.13: 'he speaks against (this) holy place and the law'. If the speech of ch. 7 answers to the charge, as seems likely (see Introduction to 7.1–53), then the charge actually focusses on what Stephen was saying about the Temple (the 'holy place', as in Ps. 24.3). The law comes in as a corollary, since so much of the law had to do with the proper functioning of the Temple. The same applies to 'the customs of Moses' in 6.14. But one of the following speech's points in defence will be that Stephen was in fact not hostile to the law, or Moses (as many commentators still assume), still less to God.

The most striking part of the charge against Stephen is given in its third version: 'Jesus the Nazarene will destroy this place . . .' (6.14). Here it is confirmed that Jesus stood at the heart of Stephen's message (even though nothing of that had been said in 6.8–10). More to the point, the charge echoes the (similarly false) charge brought against Jesus, according to Mark 14.57–58. It is almost certain that Jesus was remembered as having said something about the destruction of the Temple: although Mark indicates that the charge as given in Mark 14.58 was false, he himself had already recorded Jesus as talking about the Temple's future destruction (Mark 13.2); and John 2.19 attributes a saying to Jesus very like that with which Jesus was charged in Mark 14.58. It is very likely, then, that some talk of the destruction of the Temple (and its rebuilding) was a feature of Jesus' teaching which Stephen had taken up (see also on 7.46–47), and which provoked a violent reaction from the Hellenists for whom the

Temple was the centre of their religion and being, the sole reason for their return to and continuing presence in Jerusalem.

What the precise form of Jesus' teaching on this point was we can no longer be certain. Nor can we know the form of Jesus' teaching that Stephen may have used or what he drew from it (but cf. Introduction to ch. 7.1–53). One plausible solution is that Jesus foresaw or was understood to foresee the replacement of the Temple by the community gathered round the twelve – somewhat as the Qumran community saw itself as a priestly community fulfilling the role which the (for them) discredited Temple could not fulfil. Something of this may be hinted at in the talk of the three leading apostles as 'pillars' in Gal. 2.9 – that is, pillars in the Temple of God (cf. Rev. 3.12). But that would have been enough to bring the scorn and wrath upon Stephen of those who had invested savings and life in the significance of the Jerusalem Temple itself.

One odd feature is that Luke omitted the charge against Jesus (Mark 14.58) from his version of the trial of Jesus. This is odd, since Luke elsewhere tries to bring out points of parallel between Jesus and the heroes of his Acts (so later in the death of Stephen – see on 7.60). What is operative here, however, is another factor in Luke's two-volume record, and one which shows that he had the second already in mind when he wrote the first. At several points he omits episodes in his Gospel because he evidently wanted to delay the break which they signified until the second volume. This is the first. The break with the Temple implied in the word of Jesus first appears only on the lips of Stephen (see further Introduction §3). The editing here, then, is not motivated by the desire to draw a parallel between the death of Jesus and that of Stephen. It is motivated rather by Luke's attempt to portray the redefining of the Jesus movement's relation to Israel's traditionally key points of identity in a carefully ordered sequence spanning a significant period – with the corollary that prior to that redefining, the new sect's continuity with Israel's heritage had been unquestioned and unbroken.

6.15   The allusion here is to the gloriously bright appearance of angelic messengers typical in well-known visions of the time (e.g. Ezek. 8.2; Dan. 10.5–6). Perhaps even more so to Moses' face shining after his encounter with God on Sinai and his regular encounter with God thereafter (Ex. 34.29–35). Either way the implication is the same: Stephen, in his testimony before the council, speaks for God, as had Moses before and his angelic messengers since.

Stephen's Defence and Martyrdom
7.1–60

Stephen's defence
7.1–53

How does a people achieve and maintain its identity and self-understanding? It tells its story. The story, particularly of its beginnings, says what it is, how it is constituted, what it stands for. Virgil's *Aeneid* did this for the Rome of Augustus. The story of Muhammad plays the same role for Islam. The account of the pilgrim fathers and the declaration of independence have the same significance for the United States of America. And so too for Israel. The telling and retelling of the story of the patriarchs, the exodus and the wilderness wanderings constitutes Israel. That is why so much of the Torah (the Law) is in the form of story, why the principal feast of Passover is actually a reliving of the story of the foundation event of exodus. Recognition of this fact is vital to a proper understanding of Stephen's speech in Acts 7. Some have thought it a rather dull rehearsal of Israel's early history. They fail to appreciate the power of the story of origins.

The key to understanding Stephen's speech, then, is to note the way Israel's story is told by the speech – where it concentrates, what it adds or omits. Since the story has such power to express and define Israel's identity (so already Deut. 6.20–24 and 26.5–9) a careful retelling can reinforce that identity or reshape that identity. Thus, for example, the retelling of Neh. 9.6–31 encourages a proper sense of penitence before the covenant God, and the retellings of Pss. 105 and 106 recreate a spirit of devotion to the covenant God. The retelling by the book of *Jubilees* (written about 150 BC) reinforces a strict interpretation of the Law and abhorrence of Gentile practices. And the retelling in visionary guise in the dream visions of *I Enoch* 83–90 (some time before *Jubilees*) encourages a sense of trust in the overarching and climactic purpose of God. So with the retelling of Acts 7. A little analysis indicates a double theme.

(1) The rejection of God's servants – Joseph (7.9), Moses (7.23–29, 35, 39) and the prophets (7.52) – finds its climax in the rejection of (Jesus) the Righteous One (7.52). This is fully in line with the repeated emphasis of the earlier speeches (2.23; 3.13–15; 4.10; 5.30). In particular, the 'but God' of 7.9 echoes the 'but God' of 2.24. And the emphasis on the hope of a prophet like Moses (7.37) echoes the same hope in 3.22–23. On this point Stephen has said nothing worse or more challenging than Peter and John before him. More provocative, however, is the second theme woven into the first and given more prominence.

(2) The rejection of the Temple as necessary to guarantee God's presence. There are several striking features of the speech here. (*a*) The bulk of the speech focusses on the period prior to the entry into the promised land and the building of the Temple (7.2–46). In the course of the retelling the emphasis is made repeatedly: God was with them, outside the promised land. He appeared to Abraham in Mesopotamia (7.2). Abraham himself had no inheritance in the land (7.5). God was with Joseph in Egypt (7.9). God appeared to Moses at Mount Sinai, on holy land far from the promised land (7.30–33), and gave the congregation (*ekklesia*, 'church') in the wilderness living oracles (7.38). The implication of this telling of Israel's story is clear: promised land or sacred site is not necessary to ensure the presence of God with his people.

(*b*) Conversely, a direct line is drawn from the sin of the golden calf at Sinai (7.41) to the worship of the host of heaven (7.42) to which Amos attributed the Babylonian exile (7.42–43). These two episodes were regarded within Israel as the two lowest points of Israel's story, the nadir of Israel's failures. Stephen's speech in effect ignores all the history of the settlement in Canaan and the monarchy and sums up the span of Israel's intervening history by these two nadir points. Israel's worship has always been flawed.

(*c*) These two points, the one more implicit, the other almost explicit, are summed up in the penultimate paragraph (7.44–50). The period of the wilderness, and of God's presence with them in the wilderness, was epitomized in the tent of testimony, which had been made in accordance with the heavenly blueprint (7.44). That focus for divine presence had continued right through the reign of Israel's greatest king, David (7.45–46). The subsequent building of the Temple by Solomon (7.47) was fundamentally misconceived, or embodied a false perception of God (7.48–50). Particularly noticeable here is the way in which the Temple is described in more or less the same terms as those used for the golden calf in 7.41 (7.41 – 'the works of their hands'; 7.48 – 'made with hands'). The implied criticism is clear: the attitude of Stephen's accusers to the Temple was little short of idolatrous.

In the final climactic sentence the two themes come together: their failure to acknowledge Jesus is of a piece with their idolatrous attitude to the Temple. Far from being faithful to their law, their misconception of both Temple and Christ was a failure both to keep the law and to hear the Holy Spirit.

This is the retelling of Israel's story which Stephen's speech expresses. The Holy Spirit and Christ, appearing at the climactic point (7.51–52), reinforce Luke's repeated emphasis that these two are the central features of the new Christian sect (see Introduction §5(2) and (3)). The sovereign purpose of God directing affairs is a still more constant theme (7.2, 6–7, 9, 17, 25, 32, 35, 37, 42, 45–46). But now in addition, or in contrast, the continuity which the Temple had provided is radically questioned and the line of continuity begins to be redefined – particularly in terms of a God who is known to his people in lands afar and without dependence on the holy place of the Temple as such. Not only so, but there seems to be something of a recoil from the continued devotion which the first believers had continued to pay through and by attending the Temple. The Temple is presented, not least by contrast to the mobile tent, as a serious hindrance and embodiment of a false perception of God. The way is thus prepared for the next phase in the Christian mission (ch. 8), itself occasioned by the expulsion of the followers of Stephen from Jerusalem.

So far as the theology of the speech is concerned, a final point is worth noting. For all that the speech seems to criticize the Temple, it does not criticize the law. Moses is presented as the hero of Israel's story: nearly half the speech is devoted to him. The promise to Abraham was fulfilled in the time of Moses (7.17). Moses is presented as one specially favoured by God (7.20, 35), the prophet pattern for the Christ (7.37). It was an angel that spoke with him on Mount Sinai; the law he received there is described as 'living oracles' (7.38). The law was not at issue between Stephen and his accusers; their failure was not devotion to the law, but failure to keep it (7.52–53). In short, so far as Luke was concerned, there was no breach over the law at this stage. That would come later (ch. 15).

Where did Luke get this speech from? Its rendering in Greek is crucial to the argument (see on 7.38, 43 and 45), and it must be doubted that the whole hearing was conducted in Greek. So it is hardly likely that the whole speech as such was derived from some memory or record of the proceedings. Moreover, as Richards among others has shown, Luke has certainly put it into his own words. Yet, at the same time, the speech is hardly Luke's own. (1) Its content is unique in Acts, it is much longer than his usual speeches, it is hardly overtly Christian till the end, and even then it lacks the usual call for repentance. (2) It contains features which read like a somewhat unorthodox account of Israel's history – particularly the burial of Abraham, Isaac and Jacob in Shechem (Samaria) rather than in Hebron, as Israel's official history recorded (7.16); see also 7.32. (3) The lack of any hint of anxiety over circumcision (7.8) reflects a period prior to Paul. (4) And not least, the denunciation of the Temple in 7.48 runs quite counter to Luke's otherwise consistently positive appraisal of the Temple (Luke 1.8–23; 2.22–38, 41–50; 24.53; Acts 2.46; 3.1; 5.42). The best explanation is probably that Luke was able to use a Hellenist source, perhaps a Hellenist tract, which expressed a Hellenist view of Israel's history and of the Temple in particular. And since Stephen had been a leading Hellenist and had suffered martyrdom for his attitude to 'the holy place', that was ground enough for the speech to be regarded as representative of the views which had brought about Stephen's death.

7.1   The charge against Stephen is presented as a formal complaint before the council (6.12) with the high priest presiding. The scene is set for confrontation between the old order and the new.

(a) *The Patriarchs* – 7.2–16

7.2 'The God of glory' is an old title (Ps. 29.3). But here its function as the headline of the speech is twofold: to emphasize the transcendence of the God of Israel; and to provide an inclusio or bracket with 7.55. Stephen saw the glory of God (7.55) to which he bore testimony. That it is a right understanding of God which was ultimately at stake is implicit, and gives more weight to the first formulation of the charge against Stephen (6.11).

Abraham is important in the Acts speeches (3.13, 25; 13.26). It is important that Stephen can call him 'our father' (so repeatedly 7.11–12, 15, 38–39, 44–45). The claims made by the speech are made by one standing within a common Jewish heritage (contrast 7.51–52).

7.3 = Gen. 12.1.

7.4 is a summary of Gen. 11.31 and 12.5.

7.5 The emphasis that Abraham himself had no inheritance in the land, though possibly echoing Deut. 2.5, was not properly speaking part of the tradition. Thus Israel's defining story is given its first twist. The use of Gen. 17.8 ('to you and to your seed after you') simply sharpens the assertion made in the first half of the verse.

7.6–7 is a combination of Gen. 15.13–14 and Ex. 3.12. Notable is the way in which the speech passes over the other elements in the promise to Abraham. The promise of seed (Gen. 15.5 etc.) is alluded to in passing in 7.5. And the promise of blessing to the nations, which might have given a different twist to the story (see on 3.25) is ignored. 'In this place' echoes the charge of 6.13–14.

7.8 Very striking is the way the covenant with Abraham is described as 'the covenant of circumcision'. This catches an authentic note of Jewish identity, since circumcision was so much part and parcel of it (Gen. 17.9–14). To be noted is the absence of any hint that circumcision might be an issue (contrast 15.1, and the importance given to circumcision at this point in the retelling of the story in *Jubilees* 15.25–34).

The phase of patriarchal history, through Isaac and Jacob (Gen. 25–36), is jumped over as being of little significance for this retelling. There are similar abbreviations in other retellings of Israel's history of the time.

7.9 The jealousy of the patriarchs (Gen. 37.11) was a subject of considerable reflection in the Jewish references to this episode (see e.g. Philo, *On Joseph* 5, 17 and *Testament of Simeon*). Here it echoes that of the high priest and those with him in 5.17. 'But God was with him' draws on Gen. 39.2–3.

7.10 draws on Gen. 39.21, 41.43, 46 and 45.8 (cf. Ps. 105.21).

7.11–15 summarizes the familiar story from Gen. 41.53–47.28, without embellishment. The recorded facts contributed to the theme quite well enough as they were. The numbers are a close enough match to Gen. 46.27 and Ex. 1.5.

7.16 According to Gen. 49.30–31 and 50.13 the place of burial of the patriarchs was at Machpelah, that is modern Hebron. Possibly there has been some confusion with Gen. 33.19 correlated with the record of Joseph's burial at Shechem in Josh. 24.32. Alternatively, the speech here may be following a variant tradition of the Samaritans, which claimed that the sacred burial site was Shechem (in Samaria), and which may in turn suggest that the speech or tract was shaped by Samaritan tradition subsequent to Philip's successful mission there.

(b) *Moses – 7.17–43*

7.17 'The time of promise' is presumably a reference back to 7.7. The growth of Israel as a people is not here regarded as part of the promise (again Gen. 15.5 plays no part), but draws on Gen. 47.27 and Ex. 1.7.

7.18 = Ex. 1.8.

7.19 summarizes Ex. 1.9–11, 15–16, 22.

7.20 elaborates Ex. 2.2 slightly; Moses was not only 'a fine child' (cf. Heb. 11.23) but 'beautiful before God'.

7.20–21 summarizes the story of Ex. 2.2–10.

7.22 has no parallel in Exodus but represents well the sort of glorification of Moses which was a feature of Jewish apologetic in that period. That he was 'a powerful speaker' runs counter to Ex. 4.10–16.

7.23–29 retells the events of Ex. 2.11–15, before summarizing his family history (drawn from Ex. 2.22 and 18.3). One addition is the mention of Moses' age – 40 years. The other is 7.25; the storyteller can tell his story with hindsight of what was to come. In this way Moses is given the further credit of being fore-sighted. Like Jesus (4.12) Moses brought 'salvation' (7.25). 7.27–28 = Ex. 2.14.

7.30–34 is a retelling of Ex. 3.1–10. Again the extra information about the passage of a further forty years is added. 7.32 = Ex. 3.6, though the plural 'your fathers' is in accord with the Samaritan Pentateuch rather than the Hebrew and LXX ('your father'). There is a slight re-ordering of the details with 7.32–34 following the order Ex. 3.6, 5, 7–8. 7.33–34 = Ex. 3.7–8, 10.

7.35 is another variation. A recap of 7.27, 7.35a effectively reinforces the motif of prophet rejection. In the same way, the second half of the verse, recaping the previous paragraph (7.30–34) emphasizes the divine and revelatory character of Moses' commission. The title, 'ruler and deliverer' serves as an echoing variation of the titles of Jesus in Acts 5.31 (cf. also Luke 24.21).

7.36 'Signs and wonders' were a marked feature of Moses' rescue of his people (particularly Ex. 7.3; cf. Ps. 105.27) and a regular feature of retellings of the Moses story (e.g. *Jubilees* 48.4, 12). Quite possibly this is the source of one of Luke's own favourite phrases (see on 2.22). The inference for the reader, of course, is that the first believers were as much attested by God as Moses had been.

7.37 = Deut. 18.15 – the prophecy already cited in Peter's second speech (3.22). Again the inference is clear: as Moses had been rejected by their fathers (7.35), so the prophet like Moses had been rejected by them.

7.38 The repeated 'this one' keeps the focus on Moses. The charge is building up: those listening to Stephen have been unfaithful to their own greatest hero. The points are reinforced. Moses was part of 'the congregation or church' (same word, *ekklesia*) in the wilderness (Deut. 9.10; 18.16; 23.1). Again the implication is obvious: that Moses belongs more with the Jerusalem church (5.11), whereas Stephen's opponents belong more with those who rejected Moses. That Moses was angelically inspired is emphasized for the third time (7.30, 35, 38; as again 7.53). And the law that he received is described as 'living oracles', that is, oracles which determine their lives (cf. Deut. 30.15–20; 32.47). As elsewhere in both Jewish and Christian tradition, the participation of angels in the giving of the law is a wholly positive motif (7.53; Deut. 33.2 LXX; *Jubilees* 1.29–2.1; Heb. 2.2; cf. Gal. 3.19).

This verse more than any other should make the positive claim of the speech clear: there is no critique of Moses here, no rejection of his law; on the contrary, a bid is being clearly made that the speaker is in closer continuity with Moses than his hearers ('living oracles to give to us'). Thus the retelling of the same story can constitute a bid for the identity embodied in the story.

7.39 represents the repeated complaints of the people in the wilderness (particularly Num. 14.3), though in this form the complaints came later than the sin of the golden calf.

7.40 = Ex. 32.23.

7.41 summarizes Ex. 32.4, 6 and 8. This would not be regarded as an unjustified attack on Israel's ancestors since the sin of the golden calf was generally regarded within Jewish writings as the national equivalent to the sin of Adam. Not least, it was regarded as archetypal of Gentile sins, the sin of idolatry inextricably linked with unacceptable sexual license. This latter aspect (implied in Ex. 32.6) is not picked up here (contrast e.g. Wisd. 14.12–27; Rom. 1.24–25; I Cor. 10.7–8). Attention is focussed solely on the aspect of idolatry. It is this aspect which is heightened by speaking of the golden calf as 'the works of their hands' (probably echoing classic condemnations of idolatry in Deut. 4.28, Ps. 115.4 and Jer. 1.16; see also on 17.29). This contrasts sharply with the law, received from angels (7.38), and foreshadows the characterization of the Temple in 7.48 in similar terms (see on 7.48). The implication once again is that the people addressed by Stephen have more in common with the idolaters of Ex. 32 than with Moses the law-giver.

7.42–43 is the most astonishing jump in the speech, since it takes the link provided by Amos 5.25, and associates the idolatry of the golden calf immediately with the worship of the star gods and planetary powers to which Amos and Jeremiah after him attributed Israel's exile (Jer. 7.18; 19.13). A direct link is drawn between the golden calf apostasy and the apostasy which spelled the end of Israel as an independent state, and all that intervened is ignored. 7.42b–43 = Amos 5.25–27 LXX, with 'beyond Damascus' replaced by 'beyond Babylon'.

(c) *Tent and Temple* – 7.44–50

7.44 switches back to the earlier period of Israel's story, in order to focus the primary issue at stake more sharply on the Temple itself. It recalls that the concomitant of the law as given by angels in the wilderness was the tent of testimony – the name derived from Ex. 27.21 etc. It was for the fathers in the wilderness, the true focus of encounter with God in sharpest possible contrast to the golden calf. Most striking of all, it had been made in accordance with the pattern shown to Moses on the Mount (Ex. 25.40). Here the speech picks up one of the more intriguing verses in Exodus, indicating as it does that Moses saw a divinely prepared blueprint (in heaven?) of the tent. The verse fed directly into the apocalyptic idea that God's plans for the future had all been already drawn up in heaven and it gave similar scope to Hebrews' own distinctive reworking of the theme (Heb. 8.5). Here the point is simply to highlight the contrast between the tent of testimony and 'the works of human hands'.

7.45 recalls that the tent continued with the people not only throughout the wilderness period, but on into the promised land – alluding first to Josh. 3.14 and 18.1 and then to Josh. 23.9 and 24.18. It will hardly be accidental that 'Joshua' in Greek is rendered as 'Jesus' – no more so than the description of the assembly in the wilderness as 'church' in 7.38. Jesus and the heavenly patterned tent go together.

7.46–47 This state of affairs remained all through the period of settlement. The great king David had indeed wanted to build a dwelling place for the God of Jacob (cf. Ps. 132.5) but had been prevented, though he had also been given the assurance that his son Solomon would do so (II Sam. 7.1–13; I Chron. 17.1–15). This promise (II Sam. 7.13–14; I Chron. 17.11–14) was very much at the heart of Israel's self-understanding as a dynasty under God, and became central also in the eschatological hope of a restored or renewed temple (see particularly the Qumran text 4QFlorilegium 1.10ff.). It probably underlay the line of questioning at Jesus' trial (Mark 14.58–61 paralleling II Sam. 7.13–14 – the Son of David who would build the Temple and be called God's Son). And it may therefore have been a factor in Stephen's own reassessment of the relation between the new Jesus and the Temple (see also 2.29–32 and 13.20–22).

In 7.46 the best attested text actually speaks of 'a dwelling for the house (not God) of Jacob', that is, presumably, a dwelling to be used as a temple for the God of Jacob's house.

7.48 is the highpoint of the speech in so far as it is directed against the Temple. Of course it was no new thought that a humanly built house could hardly contain the Most High God (a traditional Jewish title for the one God within a polytheistic context). Solomon himself had said as much in his dedication of the first Temple (I Kings 8.27). What transformed that properly devotional thought into a searing insult was the use of the adjective 'made with hands'. For this adjective in the Greek scriptures was used more or less exclusively for an idol – 'the thing made with hands' (Lev. 26.1, 30; Isa. 2.18; 10.11 etc.; Dan. 5.4, 23; Judith 8.18; Wisd. 14.8). Consequently, for a Greek-speaking Jew to use precisely this word of the Temple was in effect to denounce the Temple as itself an idol (a point usually missed by commentators). The history of Israel's own idolatry is thereby shown to extend from the golden calf, 'the works of their hands' (7.41), not simply to the worship of the planetary powers (7.42–43), but also to their devotion to the Temple itself!

7.49–50 The point is driven home by citation of one of the prophetical oracles most critical of abuse of the Temple cult (Isa. 66.1–2; see also 66.3–4). Of course many prophets warned against such abuse and did not thereby denounce the cult as such (e.g. Isa. 1.12–17; Jer. 7; Hos. 6.6; Micah 6.6–8). But linked as this one is to the denunciation of 7.48, it sounds like a justification and extention of that denunciation.

(d) *Final denunciation – 7.51–53*

7.51 The final paragraph quickly rounds off the speech. The rehearsal of Israel's disobedience and failures, clearly intended to evoke a proper sense of humility and penitence, is a feature of several of the retellings of Israel's story (Neh. 9.16–17, 26–37; Ps. 106.13–43). Here in particular, the denunciation echoes the Lord's denunciation of the

Israelites for their golden calf apostasy (Ex. 33.3, 5), other pleas for obedience to go more than skin deep (Lev. 26.41; Deut. 10.16; Jer. 4.4; 6.10), and the description of Isa. 63.10, and is thus as harsh and unrelenting as can be imagined (though quite closely parallel to Neh. 16–17, 26, 29–30). The line of apostasy from golden calf, through worship of the planetary powers to the Temple is unbroken – like fathers, like children.

7.52 The other charge, rejection of God's prophets, is tied in. Persecution and murder of those who spoke for God has been as unremitting as their apostasy. The betrayal and murder of God's Righteous One (Jesus – see 3.14) is simply the climax of Israel's history of rejection (similarly Luke 11.47–51).

7.53 All this despite the fact that they were custodians of the law given by angels (see on 7.38), which they failed to keep. Their failure is complete.

The denunciation is horrific in its unrelieved attack. Although placed in the mouth of a Jew, to many it sounds to be anti-Jewish. The charge has to be softened, however, since such polemic was not altogether uncommon within Judaism. In fact it echoed some of the scriptures' own summary of Israel's failure (I Kings 19.10, 14; II Chron. 36.16; Neh. 9.26). And we know from the Jewish writings of the period that polemic, invective and vilification could be still more severe between Jewish factions (cf. 1QS 2.4–10!), including accusations of profanation of the Temple by the priests themselves (e.g. *Psalms of Solomon* 1.8; 2.3; 8.12). These were much more forthright and outspoken days than our own more sensitized speech, made cautious by libel laws! Nevertheless, the fierceness of the polemic here remains unnerving and probably reflects the depth of passion stirred by the controversy over the continuing status of the Temple in these very early days of the new movement.

Stephen's martyrdom
7.54–60

The story is told with great dramatic effect, particularly the repeated contrast between the unreasoning anger of the audience (7.54 and 57) and the totally calm, enraptured Stephen (7.55–56, 59–60). Most striking is the way the martyrdom of Stephen is deliberately modelled on the death of Jesus. (*a*) The rejection of the prophets which climaxed in the rejection of the Righteous One (7.52) is continued in the frenzied rejection of Stephen himself (7.57–58). (*b*) Stephen in his final utterance before the council, 'full of the Holy Spirit', identifies himself with Jesus as the Son of Man at God's right hand, vindicated after his suffering (7.55–56). (*c*) His final utterances are prayers (7.59–60) which echo those attributed to Jesus in Luke 23.34 and 46.

Despite such editorial shaping, the story itself is probably based on sound tradition. (1) We are well enough aware today of the way in which zealots for a religious cause can be roused to the fiercest passions, not least in a crowd and particularly when their sensibilities are triggered or cherished self-defining beliefs are challenged. (2) The designation of Jesus as 'the Son of Man' (7.56) is wholly exceptional outside the Gospel tradition. It is not plausible to envisage Luke as introducing it here of his own design when he shows no interest in it anywhere else in Acts. It seems rather to be another case (as in 3.14 and 5.31) where Luke has been able to draw on tradition of an early usage which failed to become established. (3) Also to be noted is the fact that the exalted Jesus is distinguished from the glory of God (in contrast to John 12.41). We are not yet into developed christological reflection. As in the echo of Isa. 52.13 in Acts 3.13, the thought is still the basic one of the suffering Jesus having been vindicated by God. (4) Even the final prayer of Stephen may have been the martyr's own dying impulse to show the same concern for his executioners as had Jesus (though see on 7.60).

7.54   As in 7.51, the language echoes scriptural language, here particularly the language of Pss. 35.16 and 37.12 (the impious and wicked who grind their teeth at the righteous and seek to put them to death), perhaps indicating that the same hand has shaped both sections.

7.55   Other stories of martyrs focus on the martyr's resoluteness under suffering (as in II Macc. 7). Here the point being made is that Stephen shares the privilege of prophets and visionaries, and not least that of Moses himself, in that he sees the glory of God (e.g. Ex. 33.18–22; Isa. 6.1–4; Ezek. 1.28), the glory that appeared also to Abraham (Acts 7.2). Stephen stands wholly in line with patriarch, law-giving Moses and prophet. This, of course, is the storyteller's claim; he does not think of the vision as being perceived by the rest of those present. On Stephen being 'full of the Spirit' see 6.3.

He also sees Jesus standing on God's right. The claim has already been made in 2.33–34 and 5.31, though usually the thought is of Jesus sitting on God's right (in accord with Ps. 110.1; so also in Luke 22.69). The reason why Jesus should be depicted as standing is unclear, possibly to speak on behalf of or even to welcome his dying disciple.

7.56   The claim is repeated, spoken out by Stephen himself. To see the heavens opened and their otherwise hidden secrets revealed is the privilege of the apocalyptic visionary (apocalypse = unveiling, revelation) (cf. 10.11 and Rev. 4.1 and 19.11).

The status of Jesus is enhanced by designating him 'the Son of Man'. As a title of Jesus, apart from the present verse, it appears only in the Gospels and always, in effect, on Jesus' own lips. The inference is unavoidable that the phrase was Jesus' own usage, in self-designation, and that this pattern of usage was reflected and respected in the early churches' own christological reflection. The occurrence here, then, is truly unique. Most likely it reflects (*a*) the influence of the Dan. 7.13–14 vision, where the 'one like a son of man' represents the saints of the Most High in their vindication after terrible suffering, and (*b*) the influence of its use in the recollection of Jesus' own trial (Luke 22.69). Given the repeated mention of Jesus standing on God's right, we may say that as the man-like figure of Dan. 7 represents the suffering saints of Israel now vindicated, so Jesus stands for (the ambiguity is deliberate) the dying Stephen and the new saints for whom he speaks.

7.57   Again the vivid quality of Luke's storytelling is evident (cf. 19.29). One of his favourite words to describe early Christian unity (1.14; 2.46; 4.24; 5.12) is now used to describe the single mind of the crowd's implacable hostility (perhaps in echo of Job 16.10). The psychological dynamic of an enraged crowd is well captured here. We are to presume that their rage was occasioned by the depiction of Stephen's rejected leader as having been given the most exalted place beside God (though the equivalent account of Luke 22.69–71 is remarkably restrained in comparison).

7.58   All semblance of judicial process is swept away in the zealous indignation at the thought of a crucified man given the highest place of honour beside God. Mob psychology takes over (presumably the Hellenists who had brought the charges and their supporters are primarily in view). We may compare the outbursts of zeal recounted by Josephus when insult to the Temple was envisaged – a whole people willing to lay down their lives rather than allow images of the emperor to be brought into Jerusalem (*Jewish War* 2.169–74, 197–8). Stoning would be the appropriate penalty for blasphemy (Lev. 24.11–16), and should take place outside the city (cf. Num. 15.35–36), though the execution here is not presented as a legally justified act. If the council or hearing had taken place in the vicinity of the Temple, the city gate used would presumably have been the one leading into the Kidron valley. For witnesses cf. Deut. 17.1–7. Saul is mentioned with a view to his future prominence (see on 8.3).

7.59–60   The two prayers are similar to those attributed to Jesus in Luke 23.46 and 23.34 (though the latter is actually omitted by the most important textual witnesses). Stephen is identified with Jesus in his prophet-like rejection, his martyr-like suffering, his calm trust in the face of death and in his readiness to forgive his enemies. The 'Lord' in both cases is Jesus (see on 2.21). Death as a 'falling asleep' is a common metaphor (e.g. 13.36; John 11.11; I Cor. 15.6, 51; I Thess. 4.14–15).

In Samaria and to the End of the Earth
8.1–40

The principal object of this chapter is to show how the first major expansion of those who followed the Way of the Nazarene came about. The initial expansion in 'all Judaea' (1.8) is not regarded as something separate from the beginnings in Jerusalem itself; hence it can be simply alluded to in 5.16 and presupposed in 9.31. So the first real expansion is into Samaria. And the story of the Ethiopian eunuch immediately thereafter foreshadows the final 'to the end of the earth' phase, just as had the presence of representatives of 'every nation under heaven' at Pentecost itself (1.5).

In recounting these events Luke maintains his emphasis on the same twin identifying features of the new movement. Philip's success comes through his preaching the good news of the name of Jesus Christ and the Samaritans being baptized in the same name (8.12, 16), and again with the eunuch through preaching to him the good news of Jesus (8.35). The central importance of the Spirit to Christian identity is emphasized by means of the surprising story of Samaritans who have believed and been baptized and yet still lack the Spirit, so that it becomes a matter of first importance that Peter and John come down from Jerusalem to remedy the critical defect (8.14–17).

So far as continuity through Jerusalem with the past is concerned, it is no accident that the underlying motif of turning away from the Temple is extended. The Samaritans had broken with Jerusalem over the Temple (Gerizim or Jerusalem). The eunuch was excluded from the Temple as one who was physically maimed. The implicit point then, obvious to anyone who knew Jewish history, is that the expanding movement, driven out from Jerusalem because of Stephen's criticism of the Temple, surmounts such disablements. The hiccup over the reception of the Samaritans, which may itself reflect the depth of the hostility between Jew and Samaritan, makes their reception of the Spirit all the more emphatic. The Spirit proves integrative where the Temple had been divisive. The fact that the Spirit comes through Peter and John from Jerusalem underscores the point that continuity has been re-stablished, the breach healed. Likewise with the eunuch. 'What hinders?' he asks (8.37). So far as the Temple had been concerned, the answer was: his physical condition. But for baptism (and, by implication, also the Spirit): nothing.

In the Samaritan episode the encounter with Simon allows another important Lukan emphasis to emerge fully into the light. Not simply that God is the director bringing about and supervising the crucial action unfolding. But also that integral to the message itself is a right understanding of God and of how God's power is accessed (8.9–10, 18–24). Whereas the Temple had proved the major confrontational issue within Israel, as soon as the mission begins to move into Gentile territory it is God as such who becomes a central issue of confrontation with wider religious and philosophic thought.

Equally striking, as noted by Spencer, is the degree to which Luke was willing to portray Philip as the forerunner or trailblazer of Peter – not only in preaching in Samaria (8.4–25), but also in the breakthrough to a Gentile (8.26–39; cf. 10.1–11.18), and even in preaching along the coastal plain (8.40; cf. 9.32–43).

With Luke able to make so much of these episodes to advance his own concerns, how much of all this is historical? (1) We can be confident that the initial Christian expansion was caught up in persecution, indeed, in some measure at least, was the result of persecution. The self-testimony of Paul, himself the great persecutor, provides substantial independent confirmation on this point (e.g. Gal. 1.13, 23). (2) Luke may have known Philip personally (21.8). (3) There are other indications in Christian sources that there was an early breakthrough in Samaria (cf. John 4.1–42; Matt. 10.5). (4) Luke certainly makes use of the surprising gap between baptism and the coming of the Spirit (8.12, 16), but would Luke himself, on his own initiative, have introduced such a striking departure from the normal order of salvation he himself had laid out in 2.38? (5) Likewise in the encounter between Peter and Simon. We know of Simon from other sources, as himself a founder of an important, probably syncretistic religious movement, known subsequently as the Simonians. Had Luke wished to create a decisive victory of Peter over Simon (Christianity over the followers of Simon), one would have expected something more conclusive. (6) The account of the eunuch is added on rather awkwardly, hinting at 'to the end of the world', arguably the first full Gentile conversion (despite the care Luke takes to give

that honour to Peter – chs 10–11), but all left rather vague, not leading anywhere and not followed up. The implication must be that
Luke told the story here simply because it came to him with the
tradition about Philip's evangelistic efforts (including the reference
to Azotus in 8.40).

The persecution sparked off by Stephen's martyrdom
8.1–3

In this further summary passage it is clearly Luke's intention to
make two points. First, that the apostles were spared the initial persecution (8.1). The point here must be that the apostles, by remaining
in Jerusalem when all the rest of the church had been scattered,
maintained the continuity of the new movement with Jerusalem and
its beginnings there. Secondly, Saul was not only present at and
consenting to Stephen's death, but at once became a leader of the
persecution (8.3). In this way a link is forged between Stephen and
Saul, with the latter in effect soon to step into Stephen's shoes,
extending Stephen's proclamation of God's presence and activity
outside the holy land.

These two points, however, raise two important historical questions. (*a*) Could it indeed be the case that the persecution ignored the
leaders of the movement being persecuted? Such a claim beggars the
imagination. That just the apostles should escape speaks more of
ecclesiastical respect than of policies of repression as practised the
world over. The usual solution to this conundrum (e.g. Wilson,
Gentiles ch. 5) is that the persecution was directed by Hellenists
against Hellenists. This fits with the clear implication of the initial
rejection of Stephen (6.9–12) and with the fact that the leading
figures among those scattered by the persecution all seem to have
been Hellenists or diaspora Jews (8.4; 11.20). It also makes sense of
the fact that the chief persecutor ('the one who persecutes us' – Gal.
1.23; cf. Acts 9.21), Saul/Paul, was himself a diaspora Jew.

In this case, then, it would appear that Luke wanted to cloak the
degree of disagreement and even division which the Stephen affair
seems to have exacerbated within the first church. Some degree of
tension had been evident in the initial breakdown of the food distribution system (see on 6.1). The critique of a Temple-focussed
devotion, however it may have been expressed by Stephen, would

have been a critique also of his fellow believers' continued loyalty to the Temple. And the absence of any explicit indication of the church's support for Stephen, in his trial or even in his burial (see on 8.2), may further suggest that Stephen was in some measure disowned by his fellow-believers. In short, Luke's silence or ambivalence at this point may be his way of drawing a veil over an initial division between more traditionalist Galileans and local Jews (still focussed on the Temple and unquestioning of the customs) and a body of diaspora believers whose views are represented in the speech of Acts 7. By indicating that only the apostles were exempt Luke both achieves this end and re-emphasizes the importance of the apostles.

(b) Was Saul/Paul involved in the persecution from the first? The difficulty here is that Paul's own account of his motivation ('zeal' – Phil. 3.6; Gal. 1.13–14) suggests that his efforts were directed against those he saw to be infringing Israel's unique status before God and separateness from the nations (see on 21.20). This must mean that it was directed against those who first took the gospel to Gentiles, that is, against Hellenists (11.20). Which fits with the picture of Acts 9: a mission against diaspora Jews in Damascus, and, after his conversion, disputes with Hellenists (9.29). Also with Paul's own account that he was unknown to the churches in Judaea (Gal. 1.22), since, presumably, his persecution was directed against other than Judaean believers.

The problem, then, is that such outreach to Gentiles did not take place till a later stage (11.20, according to Luke). So what stirred up Paul's furious passion, according to his own account, had not yet happened. The solution may be, of course, that Saul/Paul was caught up in an initial reaction against the Hellenists, and had possibly even been one of the Jews from Cilicia who disputed with Stephen in 6.9. In which case, it would be some time later, when some Hellenists became even more threatening of Israel's distinctive status before God, that he became a man of 'zeal' (see again on 21.20), another Phinehas protecting Israel's boundaries.

The account here, therefore, may be another example of Luke's foreshortening, or telescoping of events (see Introductions to ch. 1(2) [p.3], ch. 9 [p.118], ch. 15 [p.187], and 17.1–15, and on 11.29–30, 14.23 and 15.33–35). The result is a simplification or tidying up of what were, historically, more complex or messy events, and a bringing together of developments which spanned a longer time frame. It was a quite acceptable tactic for an ancient historian and the fact that it leaves modern readers rather confused on details, which they regard as more important than did Luke, should not diminish our respect for his skill as an ancient historian and for the broad picture which he paints.

8.1 Modern translations include the opening sentence (Saul's approval of Stephen's execution) with the previous chapter. But those who made the chapter divisions had the right instinct. The focus now switches to Saul, and the mention of Saul here foreshadows the dominant role he will soon play in the narrative. So the first time Saul appears as subject of the sentence marks a new phase in Luke's story.

Given the extremes of religious passion such as must have been involved in the execution of Stephen, it would hardly be surprising that it resulted in a more widespread attack on those deemed to be associates of or sympathizers with Stephen. We need not assume that only diaspora Jews were thus scattered, though Greek-only speakers would have been more easily identifiable if the persecution was in any degree systematic. On the oddness of only the apostles being exempt from the persecution see Introduction to this section. The mention of Judaea and Samaria echoes 1.8, suggesting that this is how the plan of evangelization unfolded.

8.2 Who were 'the devout men' who buried Stephen? The implication is that they were pious Jews who would regard the burial of an executed or unclaimed corpse as an act of piety (cf. Luke 23.50). Luke makes no attempt to indicate that they were believers. And inserting the account as he does, after the report of the church being scattered by persecution, suggests that he did not expect his readers to identify them as Christians. We might of course ask, Why not the apostles? Here again it is hard to avoid the impression that Stephen had been left to stew in his own juice, and that none of the believers so respected by the people felt able to stand with him at the last.

8.3 The fierceness of the language here ('was ravaging the church'; cf. II Chron. 16.10 and Ps. 80.13) matches the fierceness of Paul's own recollection (Gal. 1.13; cf. Acts 9.21; 22.4; 26.10–11). In earliest Christian memory Saul the persecutor assumed almost demonic proportions. Here also, in ironic indication of the new form of church which was emerging, the persecution is directed against 'house after house'.

The first outreach and the first encounter with Gentile understanding of God
8.4–25

In the Samaritan episode two themes overlap and interact. (*a*) One is the outreach to Samaria, thus launching the next phase of the programme outlined in 1.8. The outreach is unique in that Philip's otherwise highly successful evangelism fails to secure the crucial mark of post-Pentecostal discipleship – the gift of the Spirit. The defect, however, is remedied immediately by the apostles commissioning Peter and John to minister to the Samaritan converts. Presumably Luke understood that the exceptional course of events were God's way of dealing with exceptional circumstances – that is, of healing the generations-old hostility between Jew and Samaritan. It is only by the (Jewish) apostles (still) in Jerusalem validating (through Peter and John) the acceptance of the Samaritans that the Spirit comes upon them. Thus the centrality both of the Jerusalem based apostles in ensuring continuity, and of the reception of the Spirit in clinching the Samaritans' converts the new movement is ensured by Luke.

(*b*) The other, which is thoroughly interwoven with the first (8.9–13, 18–24), is the first encounter with non-Jewish theology, or, more precisely, of near-Jewish religion corrupted by syncretistic elements (8.10). Simon's mission had rivalled that of Philip, but this was attributed to Simon's magic and to his portrayal of himself as a manifestation of divine power (8.9–11). The defeat of Simon, both by his submission to Philip (8.13) and then by his humiliation at the hands of Peter (8.20–23), is still more a defeat for such false ideas of God ('the power of God') by the true ministers of God who bring the kingdom, the word and the gift of God (8.12, 14, 20).

8.4 'The word' to which the apostles had seen themselves as dedicated (6.5) is more effectively spread by 'those scattered'. Here as before God supervenes upon human contriving and disaster to advance his purpose.

8.5 Philip's being picked out implies that he was not far behind Stephen in leadership ability and initiative among 'the seven' (6.5). Why he went to Samaria Luke does not say. The hostility between Judaea and Samaria, going back to the post-exilic period (Ezra 4), would probably be well known (the Jewish king, John Hyrcanus, had destroyed the Samaritan Temple at Shechem in 128 BC) and pre-

107

sumably was a factor (see on 7.16). Presumably also, on a broader theological perspective, we are to assume that Philip shared the attitude of the speech in ch. 7 – that God, his presence or his message, is not confined to holy land or holy place. The city itself is not identified, but if the text reads 'the city of Samaria', then presumably the capital city (Sebaste) is meant, though in view of the overtones just indicated it could be Shechem itself.

He preached to them 'the Christ'. We know from later sources of a Samaritan Messianic figure (Taheb), an expectation based on Deut. 18.18. So this could have been a calculated strategy on Philip's part (cf. 7.37). By linking the Jewish hope as fulfilled in Jesus with that of the Samaritans an effective evangelistic bridge would be established. Of course, the point would be that any such Samaritan hope needed to be redefined in the light of Jesus, as much as the Jewish messianic hope had been for the first believers.

8.6–8   The preaching is accompanied by miracles of exorcism and healing. As elsewhere in Acts, Luke presents such 'signs' (not his usual 'signs and wonders') as faith inducing, though he takes care here to indicate that the Samaritan response was occasioned both by what they heard and by what they saw. The 'loud cries' should be regarded not just as a literary stereotype (Luke 4.33; 8.28; but also 23.46), since they seem to be a regular feature wherever exorcism is practised. Somewhat surprisingly, the mention of 'much joy' (8.8) *precedes* the account of the Samaritans' actual conversion. Luke's account reflects the communal excitement which such a mission would cause rather than a narrow dogma that only believers experience joy!

8.9   Simon is one of the most interesting figures of the ancient world. In the second century the Christian apologist Justin Martyr, himself from Samaria, names Simon's home town as Gitta and reports that his people venerated Simon as the supreme God (*Apology* 1.26.3). That may be an exaggeration, but other second- and third-century sources (see e.g. Lüdemann 98–102 and Barrett 405–7) identify Simon as the founder of the Simonian gnostics, and that claim may be ultimately sound (see on 8.9b–10). How much of this may be reflected in Luke's narrative it is now impossible to say. That there was an encounter between the historical Simon and early Christian missionaries is entirely possible. Of course the outcome is told from a Christian perspective.

This is the first of several encounters with magic in Acts (also 13.6–11; 16.16–18; 19.18–19). We should not assume that 'magic' had a consistently bad image in the ancient world. Philo speaks of 'true magic . . . a fit object for reverence and ambition' (*Special Laws* 3.100). Even within the New Testament 'the three wise men' who visit the child Jesus are actually 'magi' (there in the sense of astrologers), the same term used in Acts 13.6–8. But in Acts 'magic' is presented as another and an inferior or false view of God. The implication is that 'magic' tries to manipulate the divine by use of special formulae and techniques (8.19) which could be written down in books, learned and used by would-be practitioners (19.13, 18–19). The Christian practice, of laying on hands or exorcism, may look very much the same, and indeed have a very similar effect (cf. 8.9–11 with 8.6, 8 and 13), but one of Luke's primary concerns in relating the episodes of 8.17–24 and 19.13–16 is to make clear the difference (see further Garrett).

8.9b–10   The title attributed to Simon ('The Great Power') has an authentic ring. In a monotheistic system 'the power' could stand for God (as in Mark 14.62). At this period, however, there was considerable speculation about how God, or the Most High God interacted with the world and with humanity. Philo, the Jewish philosopher from Alexandria, shows how a sophisticated monotheism could use language of the 'powers' to describe the diverse ways in which the divine impacted on the earthly and human (rather like the idea of divine Wisdom, or even the Spirit within wider Judaism). But to envisage a system of powers, of which one could be called 'Great', may reflect an early example of what became characteristic of Gnostic systems in the following centuries, where intermediate figures of decreasing divinity help explain the manifest gulf between the divine and the human. Luke takes some care to distinguish Simon's own claim for himself ('saying that he was someone great') from the popular opinion of him, that he was some sort of manifestation or embodiment of 'the Great Power'.

8.11   The repeated note of the eager attention of the Samaritans to Simon (8.10–11) is no doubt deliberate: it re-emphasizes that Simon had been as successful as Philip (8.6 – same word). What distinguishes the two has yet to be revealed. Likewise Luke repeats mention of the Samaritans' amazement at Simon's magical powers, adding that this had been the case for a long time (8.9, 11 – same word as used in 2.7 and 12). This is to set the scene for the report of

Simon himself being 'amazed' (same word) at Philip's exploits (8.13). Again the distinguishing feature, that which makes the difference, has yet to be revealed.

8.12   Luke uses two phrases to indicate that Philip's preaching was wholly in accord with the gospel as preached elsewhere in Acts: he preached the good news of the kingdom of God (cf. 19.8; 20.25; 28.23, 31; see on 1.3) and of the name of Jesus Christ (see Introduction to ch. 3 and on 3.6). The continuity with Jesus' own ministry is also underlined (cf. Luke 4.43; 8.1; 9.2, 11; 11.20; etc.). Likewise there is no hint that Philip acted wrongly in baptizing the Samarians, that is, baptizing them 'in the name of the Lord Jesus' (8.16). However, the intermediate step, they 'believed Philip', is an unusual formulation. Normally Luke would say 'they believed (on/in) the Lord/God' (5.14; 9.42; 10.43; 11.17; 16.31, 34; 18.8). That faith was directed to Philip is exceptional and may be Luke's way of signalling that all was not right with the Samaritans' response. Either way the point will be that the decisive mark of differentiation has yet to be described.

8.13   Simon's belief (presumably the same order as that of the Samaritans?) and baptism are described separately, and the impression is given that he was a whole-hearted convert, devoted to Philip. Simon's astonishment at Philip's 'signs and great miracles' indicates an initial victory over one who had astonished others, hints at the distinction between 'signs' and magic, and prepares for the denouement in the following paragraph. Although Philip now disappears from the action (he might simply have moved on), there is no suggestion of criticism of Philip in what follows; otherwise Luke would hardly have gone on to relate his subsequent solo ministry to the eunuch without similar corroboration.

8.14   No hint is given that the apostles might have found the news from Samaria to be surprising: they just accept that Samaria had received the word of God (cf. 11.1). But their decision to send Peter and John indicates some concern. This is the last mention of John, who disappears hereafter, even as Peter's silent partner (12.2 is no exception).

8.15–16   The fact that the sentence runs on without a break presumably implies that this was why they were sent. In other words, the report to Jerusalem had informed the Jerusalem leadership that no indications of the Spirit falling upon the baptized Samaritans had been witnessed. 'They had only been baptized in the name of the Lord Jesus'. The formulation clearly indicates that whatever had gone before had been insufficient. Whether the rationale is that the Samaritans' faith fell short of full commitment to the Lord (8.12), or that baptism even 'in the name of the Lord Jesus' was in itself not enough, Luke's point is clear: it was the reception of the Spirit ('the gift of God' – 8.20) which mattered above all else; Luke's account does not allow us to envisage either an earlier silent coming of the Spirit at their baptism or that Luke had in mind only a supplementary coming of the Spirit here; (see my *Baptism* ch. 5). Luke knows of no silent comings of the Spirit! Only the manifestation that God had accepted them by giving them the Spirit (cf. 10.44–47; 11.17–18; 15.8–9) could validate the major step forward. Only that could break down the barriers which had divided Jew and Samaritan (not least, dispute regarding the Temple). Only the shared participation in the Spirit (cf. 2.42) could make these representatives of divided peoples into one church. What makes the difference, be it noted, is not ecclesiastical formality but divine attestation (as still more emphatically in 10.44–48).

8.17   The precise relation between the laying on of hands and the coming of the Spirit is unclear. 8.18 uses the phrase 'through the laying on of the apostles' hands', but Luke is about to contrast that with Simon's magical conception of the act (8.19). The point is partly theological: the fact that the Spirit comes through the ministry of the apostles ensures the continuity with Jerusalem and with the beginnings in Jerusalem; this remains a fundamental factor in Christian identity. But if the detail is also historical (and would Luke have created such a dichotomy between baptism and the gift of the Spirit on his own initiative?), then presumably psychological factors arising out of the long schism between Judaea and Samaria were also a factor.

8.18–19   The story switches back to Simon, but with the reception of the Spirit still as the focal point, the implication being that Simon himself had not received the Spirit. What Simon saw would presumably have been the sort of manifestations which Luke elsewhere attributes to the gift of the Spirit (2.4; 10.46; 19.6; cf. I Cor. 1.4–5; Gal. 3.5). But he saw the whole proceeding still as a magician – a power to transform individuals by laying hands on them, a technique to be bought and learned and thus added to his stock of spells and incantations. The contrast is as sharp as that in 19.11–16. In this transition from one point to another, 'the gift of God' (8.20), which was the means and focal point of unity between Jewish and Samaritan believer, becomes also the point which differentiates Jewish and Samaritan believer from Samaritan magician.

8.20   'Peter's meaning is "To hell with you and your money!"' (Haenchen 304). It is this verse which provides the name 'simony', the attempt to buy ecclesiastical office or power by bribery or payment of a fee. It is typical of such later regularization of stories like this that the term should refer to ecclesiastical office rather than to the dynamic and unpredictable (as this episode shows) power of the Spirit.

8.21–24   The denunciation of Simon is emphatic and draws on a sequence of scriptural passages. 'No part or share in this matter' (or word – same term) may echo Deut. 12.12 and 14.27, 29 (cf. also Neh. 2.20). But unlike the Levites referred to in these passages, it is not a special commission from God which excludes Simon but his own attempt to manipulate God. His 'heart not straight before God' is a close echo of Ps. 78.37. And 'the gall of bitterness' (8.23) echoes Deut. 29.18. Whether Luke hereby wished to portray Simon as an apostate (another cautionary tale like that of Ananias and Sapphira in 5.1–11) or as a counterfeit from the first remains unclear. Luke does not say that he received the Spirit but indicates rather that he saw it simply as a form of magic power; yet he had 'believed' and been baptized. Again, he was still in the chains of wickedness (8.23); yet Peter encourages him to repent and pray to the Lord (here probably God). Presumably it is intentional on Luke's part that he leaves the question unresolved (8.24). No divine judgment, as in 5.5 and 10, or indeed in the parallel episodes of 13.11 and 19.15–16, brings the episode to a close. Simon remains an ambivalent figure, somewhat like Esau of old (cf. Heb. 12.15–17). What this tells us about any competition between Luke's church and any Simonians of his own day is obscure, except that he leaves the door open for them (8.22, 24).

8.25   The return through Samaria both consolidates the Samaritan mission and leaves the apostles once again back in Jerusalem. The double formula ('testified and spoke the word of the Lord') maintains Luke's double emphasis on witness bearing (2.40; 10.42; 18.5; 20.21–24; 23.11; 28.23; see also on 1.8) and on 'the word' as a summary of the gospel (see on 4.4). For the first time Luke varies his more usual formula, 'the word of God', by speaking of 'the word of the Lord' (here again probably God); but see again on 4.4.

The Ethiopian eunuch
8.26–40

The point of this episode lies in the double designation of its central figure in 8.27 (see particularly Spencer). Like the Samaritans he represents a half-way house between a movement still completely within Judaism, in the first five chapters, and the later mission of Paul to the Gentiles. As the Samaritans were an offshoot from an earlier phase, before the religion of Israel became 'Judaism' proper, so an Ethiopian who went up to Jerusalem to worship (8.27) represented those members of other nationalities who attached themselves to Israel out of admiration for the character of its religion and who were received sympathetically by Judaism.

But as with the Samaritans, who had broken with Israel over the centralization of cultic worship in Jerusalem, so the Ethiopian eunuch represented those close to Israel, but still disadvantaged in relation to its central symbol, the Temple. It was not his race or colour that made the difference; they mattered not at all where the devout proselyte was concerned. It was the fact that he was a *eunuch* and thus debarred from entering 'the assembly (church – same word) of the Lord' (Deut. 23.1); that is what made all the difference. He had gone up to Jerusalem to worship, but had been unable to enter the Temple to do so. The vision of Isa. 56.3–5 had not yet been realized. It was as he was returning (8.28) that he found an acceptance into the messianic church of the Lord hitherto denied him. The good news of Jesus has replaced the Temple as the expression of the openness of God's acceptance.

8.26 'An angel of the Lord' is one of Luke's shorthand ways of representing divine guidance or intervention (5.19; 10.3; 12.7; 27.23). The divine initiative is a feature of the story (8.26, 29, 39). Mission in Acts is always at the urging or ordering of God.

The description of the road from Jerusalem to Gaza is puzzling; it was certainly not desert, which only begins after Gaza. Has Luke or his tradition become a little confused on geographical details?

8.27–28   Ethiopia (or Nubia), whose territory bordered Egypt to the south (Ezek. 29.10), represented the limit of common geographical knowledge. Isa. 11.11–12 seems to regard it as one of 'the corners of the earth' (cf. Zeph. 3.10), and Ethiopians were regarded by Homer as the 'last of men'. So the Ethiopian here may be presented as precursor of the gospel reaching to the 'end (last) of the earth' (1.8). 'Candace' may not be a personal name but a title for the reigning matriarch (another slight misunderstanding by Luke or by his tradition). Eunuchs were often employed in high positions of responsibility – not least in service of royal women.

He had come to worship. As a eunuch he could not be circumcised, and therefore not become a proselyte. However ardent his desire to worship in the Temple, it could not be realized, since he was both a Gentile and a eunuch (Deut. 23.1). He evidently belonged, however, to a considerable number of Gentile sympathizers (see on 10.2). His degree of commitment had been shown by his journey. His degree of enthusiasm was shown by his purchase of a no doubt expensive scroll, evidently written in Greek.

8.29   Now it is the Spirit that prompts Philip. Did Luke envisage a different mode of divine communication (angelic prompting often/usually involved some visionary element; cf. 10.3; 12.7; 27.23)?

8.30–34   The passage read aloud (as was the custom of the time) is from Isa. 53.7–8, a passage (Isa. 52.13–53.12) already alluded to in 3.13. Here it is even more striking that the theme drawn from the Isaiah passage is not that of vicarious suffering (as in Rom. 4.24–25 and I Peter 2.24), but that of humiliation and suffering (the quotation stops just before the last line of 53.8), prior, presumably, to vindication (as in 3.13–15). The eunuch's uncertainty as to the passage's reference matches the puzzlement of commentators probably from the first, though fortunately the notorious obscurity of the Hebrew and divergent Greek of 8.33 does not affect the point here.

8.35   Philip's confidence that he has the hermeneutical key to the uncertain reference of the passage presumably reflects the light which the passage shed on earliest Christian attempts to make sense of what had happened to Jesus. 'He preached to him Jesus.' Since

Philip was hardly carrying round with him bulky scrolls of the prophets (though possibly the eunuch may have had others with him) we are to suppose his exposition was all from memory of the relevant scriptures.

8.36–38   We are presumably to assume that Philip's exposition included reference to baptism in the name of Jesus (cf. 2.38). The Ethiopian's response (8.36) is consistent with what we read throughout Acts. Baptism is itself the act of commitment to the gospel and to the one preached in it. The absence of hindrance contrasts with the hindrance on his participation (as a eunuch) in the people assembled for worship in the Temple (Deut. 23.1). The Spirit discounts such rules and regulations. The fact that the Ethiopian had no church to return to was itself no bar.

Later scribes probably felt some unease at the casual briefness of Luke's narrative and added verse 37 (a 'Western' addition not in the best manuscripts). But the addition, while formalizing the act of confession as part of baptism, does not modify the fact that baptism was administered so promptly without any testing of faith or further instruction.

Luke envisages a pool or even a stream (the route ran along the coastal strip) or possibly a small oasis (if he thought of it as a desert road – 8.26), though such details do not trouble him. His description (going down into the water) allows as much for a pouring or sprinkling as for immersion.

8.39–40   Luke presumably envisaged an actual physical transportation. So at least his language suggests: 'snatched away' is used of transportation to heaven in II Cor. 12.2,4 and I Thess. 4.17; and 'was found' implies an element of unexpectedness. But the language could also simply underline the abruptness of the disengagement and the fact that all Philip did was under inspiration. Luke may have had in mind I Kings 18.12 and II Kings 2.16 which envisage similar sudden transportation (of Elijah) attributed to the Spirit (cf. also Ezek. 11.24).

The eunuch returns to Ethiopia. The 'rejoicing' here is that of full and unhindered acceptance (in contrast to 8.8), though Luke does not stay to make the point very plain. In contrast to the preceding episode, there is no hint that the Spirit failed to come upon the eunuch (later scribes insert such a coming), nor any question of an incompleteness of baptism, nor any suggestion of any need for completion of an unfinished process by apostles. It was evidently not Luke's intention to disparage Philip's ministry as ineffective at the crucial point. Having shown that the outreach to Samaria maintained the continuity with Jerusalem's beginnings he felt no need to do anything similar here. Presumably he did not want to continue the story anyway, even if he knew of its continuation. For the decisive breakthrough into lands afar was still to come. He was content to leave the hint that here was an influential believer already able to take the good news to one end of the earth. We have no other evidence of a church in Ethiopia so early, but the Ethiopian church was to make a significant impact in subsequent centuries. How much might have been due to the eunuch remains hidden in the memory of God.

Philip reappears at Azotus (ancient Ashdod), twenty miles to the north of Gaza, presumably a detail derived from the Philip tradition. He then moves to Caesarea, the Roman capital of Judaea (23.33–35; 25.6), a further fifty-five miles to the north, as the narrative prepares for another major transition point. 'All the towns' would include Jewish settlements (cf. 9.32, 36), so it may be significant that Luke mentions only two Hellenistic cities. It is at Caesarea that Philip briefly reappears in the narrative in 21.8.

The Conversion of Saul and Peter's Mission in the Judaean Coastal Plain
9.1–43

Luke now interrupts the account of Hellenist expansion (he will resume it in 11.19) to swing the spotlight of his narrative on to Saul. Since the whole of the second half of his book will be devoted to Saul/Paul, Luke clearly regarded the episode of Saul's conversion as one of, if not the most significant event in the beginnings of Christianity. Hence the exceptional prominence he gives to it by recounting the story no less than three times (9.1–19; 22.3–21; 26.4–23).

The three accounts vary in detail, sometimes quite markedly. For example, it is unclear how Saul's companions were affected: did they all fall to the ground (26.14) or only Saul (9.4, 7)? Did they hear the voice of Jesus (9.7) or not (22.9)? Ananias has considerable prominence in chs 9 and 22 but does not appear in ch. 26. And the commission to the Gentiles comes once on the road itself (26.16–18), once through Ananias (9.15–17), and once later on in Jerusalem (22.21). The point of significance, however, is that all three variant traditions are used by one and the same author. Luke himself evidently saw no inconsistency in retelling the same story in such diverse terms. This tells us something about what a responsible historian like Luke saw as good practice. And it should caution us against making too much of such variations when they appear in different documents (e.g. different Gospels), whether in terms of historical accuracy or in terms of their theological significance. Most of what we have here are the variations which a good storyteller introduces to maintain interest in his story despite its repeated telling.

What is important, both historically and theologically, is that all three accounts centre on the encounter between Saul and the Jesus who appears to him (9.4–6; 22.7–10; 26.14–16) and climax in Saul's

117

commissioning to take the gospel to the Gentiles (9.15–16; 22.15, 21; 26.16–18, 23). These are clearly the points on which Luke wished his readers to concentrate. The fact that Paul himself gives equal emphasis to just these two points (I Cor. 9.1–2; 15.8–10; Gal. 1.13–16) shows that Luke and Paul were at one in their assessment of his conversion and its importance. We can also be confident that Luke owes this central thrust of his account to good sources, probably Paul himself.

At the same time Luke attends to his own concerns. In particular, he did not hesitate to exclude emphases dear to Paul's own heart and to tell his story in a way that runs somewhat counter to Paul's own recollection. Thus, he avoids describing Saul as an 'apostle' as a result of this encounter – an emphasis central to Paul's assessment of it (as again I Cor. 9.1–2, 15.8–10 and Gal. 1.1, 12, 15–16 demonstrate). In contrast, Luke's earlier definition of the qualifications of an 'apostle' (1.21–25) would seem to exclude Saul/Paul (see also on 14.4). Similarly, his restriction of resurrection appearances to the forty days after Jesus' resurrection (1.1–11) would seem to dispute Paul's claim that he too belonged to the circle of resurrection witnesses, even if he only just made it (I Cor. 15.5–8; see also Introduction to ch. 1(2)).

In some ways more striking is the implication of 9.23–30, that Saul went up to Jerusalem relatively soon after his conversion ('after some time', or even 'after many days') and was there introduced to the apostles. In contrast, Paul almost falls over himself to deny that he went up to Jerusalem so soon after his conversion. No less than three years transpired before he did so, and even then he visited only Peter and saw none of the other apostles (Gal. 1.17–20). Of course, this may be a further example of Luke's telescoping or collapsing into briefer compass events which had actually been separated by some time (see Introduction to 8.1–3). But the contrast here is so sharp that it raises a double suspicion: that Paul was writing to dispute just the sort of account of his conversion and its aftermath as we find in Acts; and that Luke has chosen to follow the version which downplays the independence from Jerusalem on which Paul had found it necessary to insist. This would certainly fit with Luke's eirenic concern to demonstrate the unity of the movement in its earliest days.

The final section of the chapter, on Peter's ministry along the coastline of Judaea (9.32–43), is presumably drawn from early memories of the mission associated with the name of Peter (cf. Gal. 2.7–9). Again, however, it enables Luke to display his evenhandedness: that the chief hero of the first half of his history (Peter) was not immediately eclipsed by the hero of the second half (Paul). So, in particular, he is able to recall a raising from the dead (9.40–41) to parallel Paul's later feat of the same kind (20.9–10). More to the immediate point, these brief recollections prepare the way for the next central episode (the conversion of Cornelius), the triple reference to which (chs 10, 11 and 15) marks it out in Luke's estimate as the only event to rival Paul's conversion in importance for earliest Christianity.

The conversion of Saul
9.1–22

Given the emphasis which both Luke and Paul put upon the event, the question has often been asked in recent years: should this episode be called Paul's conversion or Paul's commissioning?

The question arises, since the term 'conversion' in its common usage (conversion from no religion to religion, or from one religion to another) is inappropriate here. Neither Luke nor Paul saw the new movement as a new religion. It was not simply a continuation of Judaism, certainly not as Judaism was understood by the high priest, or (Paul would say) as Judaism had been understood by himself when he was a zealous Pharisee (Gal. 1.13–14). But it was a continuation of the religion of Israel. In all Luke's (and Paul's) concern to clarify the identity of the Jesus sect, continuity with Israel's own identity as embodied in its scriptures, its belief in the one sovereign God, and its heritage of faith and devotion was fundamental. So what happened to Paul on the Damascus road was not a renunciation of that identity and heritage. On the contrary, both would say that it was an awakening to the responsibility which had always been Israel's – to be a blessing to the families of the earth (3.25), to be a light to the nations (13.47; 26.17–18). Hence, the emphasis in the accounts is more on a prophetic calling or commissioning, as in Isa. 42.7 (cited or echoed in both the previous references), or in Isa. 49.1, 6 (echoed in 26.23 and Gal. 1.15–16).

Yet, at the same time, we can hardly avoid describing what happened to Saul on the Damascus road as a 'conversion'. For conversion it was in the basic sense of the term – a complete turn around to go in precisely the opposite direction. And the account in Acts implies the sort of inner trauma and transformation which has properly made the Damascus road encounter a (if not the) classic example of sudden conversion.

Historical and theological accuracy would best be served, therefore, if we speak of a conversion from one sect of first-century Judaism to another (on the term 'sect' see Introduction to chs 1–5(6) [p.2] and on 5.17); that is, conversion from a mainline sect (Pharisees) which wished to reinforce Israel's separation from the Gentile world, to a sect which, in the light of its experience of Jesus and the Spirit, was coming to understand Israel's commission as a 'light to the nations' to be its own.

Luke dates the event in direct sequence from the initial persecution consequent upon Stephen's martyrdom. Even though there is reason to believe that more had happened between Stephen's death and Saul's conversion (see again Introduction to 8.1–3), nevertheless it is likely that Paul was converted within two or three years or less of Jesus' crucifixion. Apart from anything else, the sequence of apostle-making resurrection appearances did come to an end (I Cor. 15.8 – 'last of all'). For Paul's claim to be accepted it must have followed quite closely upon those which had preceded. Most telling, however, is Paul's own account (Gal. 1.18; 2.1) that a period of fourteen to seventeen years elapsed between his conversion and the Jerusalem council (usually dated to the late 40s).

9.1–2 We have already noted the historical issues relating to Luke's account of Saul's early involvement in the persecution following Stephen's martyrdom (see Introduction to 8.1–3). The information, surprising to the reader, that a significant number of those scattered from Jerusalem had established themselves in Gentile territory (in some contrast to 8.1) is a reminder that Luke's account cuts corners. But we should also note the recurrence of the description 'disciples' (as in 6.1–2, 7; also 9.10, 19, 25, 26, 36, 38), and the first occurrence of the title of the new movement as 'the Way' (cf. 19.9, 23; 22.4; 24.14, 22). Both of these Luke probably derived from tradition. The latter was also used in self reference at Qumran (1QS 9.17–18; 10.21; CD 1.13; 2.6), for whom, curiously enough, Damascus had also been an early centre of exile (CD 6.5, 19). We know from Josephus (*Jewish War* 2.561) that a large Jewish minority population lived there.

It is usually assumed that the high priest's writ would not have been recognized as running beyond Jerusalem or Judaea. On the other hand, he was the leading political as well as religious figure within Judaea. Diaspora communities in effect acknowledged his authority in the devotion of their regular payment of the Temple tax (the Roman authorities made exceptional provision in this respect). And since the Temple also served as a bank it could even be the case that some of the scattered Hellenists had had to abandon their deposits, giving the high priest some leverage over diaspora communities not so far distant. So it is quite possible to conceive of some sort of authorization or letter of introduction from the high priest lying behind Saul's mission to Damascus (cf. 9.14; II Cor. 3.1; and earlier I Macc. 15.15–24). Whether such authorization could have stretched to bringing members of the Way back to Jerusalem in penal custody is probably another question. On the other hand, synagogues did have the right to administer corporal punishment (II Cor. 11.24), and Paul himself did recall his persecution to have been exceedingly fierce (Gal. 1.13).

9.3   Paul nowhere indicates where his conversion took place, but the claim that it took place near Damascus is consistent throughout all the Acts accounts, and it is probably confirmed by Paul's reference to Damascus in Gal. 1.17. That the encounter itself was one of blinding light is probably recalled by Paul in II Cor. 4.4–6, though it is also a common feature of heavenly visions (see on 6.15 and 7.55). The persecutor is converted by the same vision as that enjoyed by the persecuted (7.55–56).

9.4–6   In each of the three accounts the brief exchange between Saul and the exalted Jesus is word for word: 'Saul, Saul, why do you persecute me?' 'Who are you, sir?' 'I am Jesus (the Nazarene), whom you are persecuting; rise . . .' (22.7–10; 26.14–16). This gives a good illustration of how stories would be told, then as now. The core of the story is preserved, maintained with almost rigorous consistency, while the supporting details can be treated with greater flexibility, as circumstances may demand. We can well, and quite fairly imagine that the exchange had been burned into Saul's memory, and so from the first was fixed in the tradition by which the event of the great persecutor's conversion was retold and celebrated among the churches (cf. Gal. 1.23).

The christological implications of the exchange are not entirely clear. Saul at first simply hears an unidentified voice addressing him. He naturally asks the figure bathed or hidden in blinding light who he is; the address, usually translated 'Lord', can also be a polite form

121

of address to a superior ('sir'), but here to a glorious heavenly being (cf. 10.4, 14). Only then does the voice identify itself: 'I am Jesus (22.8 adds 'the Nazarene') whom you are persecuting.' Presumably only then did Saul begin to grasp the significance of the encounter: that the glorious figure was none other than Jesus; and so, conversely, Jesus had the status of someone clothed in divine glory (so we may deduce also from II Cor. 4.4–6). How quickly all these corollaries became clear to him, Luke does not say at this point, but see 9.20 and 22.

It has been suggested that the personal identification implied in the words between Jesus and his persecuted followers ('Why do you persecute me?') provided the basis for Paul's later theology of the church as the body of Christ. But that may be pressing the language too hard (cf. Matt. 25.40, 45). On the other hand, the question suggests that it was personal hostility towards Jesus himself, presumably because of the claims made for him, which was the chief motivation for Saul's persecution.

9.7–9   The shock to Saul's companions and the severe trauma into which the experience threw Saul are vividly narrated. We should not assume that they were a troop of soldiers accompanying Saul, as has often been represented (the high priest would not have had so much authority). They were probably just travellers who found greater security (and companionship) in making the journey together. The contrast between Saul's previous power and now his helplessness (9.8) would hardly be missed by the good storyteller (cf. II Macc. 3.27–29). The fasting implies holding oneself in disciplined readiness for further revelation (e.g. Ex. 34.28; Dan. 10.2–3).

9.10–14   This is the first of the visions which Luke will recall over these next crucial chapters as authenticating radical departures (also 10.3–7, 10–17; 11.5–10), all making the point that these unexpected changes of course were fully authenticated from on high (cf. 2.17). That Saul was praying and had also seen a vision serves to authenticate Ananias' vision (similarly in 10.3–6 and 10–16). 'The Lord' here is clearly Jesus (9.15 puts the point beyond dispute). In what follows Jesus as Lord exercises a sovereignty elsewhere attributed only to God (9.15 – 'my chosen instrument').

Ananias appears only here and in the second account, where he receives a more fulsome description (22.12). He is not represented as a refugee from Jerusalem, so presumably he was a local diaspora

Jew. The name itself, and the details of Saul's lodging (9.11) must come from Luke's tradition. Another new name for the followers of Jesus also appears, no doubt also from the tradition, since Luke makes little use of it on his own account – 'your saints' (9.13, 32, 41; 26.10). That such a title could be used so early (Paul also uses it with particular reference to the Jerusalem church – Rom. 15.25–26; I Cor. 16.1; II Cor. 8.4; 9.1, 12) indicates a conscious claim on the part of the first believers to belong to or even represent the people set apart by God to be his own (e.g. Pss. 16.3; 34.9; Isa. 4.3; Dan. 7.18). 'Those who call upon his name' (9.14) recalls 2.21 and the importance of Jesus' name as an early mark of identity for the first believers (see Introduction to ch. 3 [p.38]).

9.15–16   This is the first of the three versions of Saul's commissioning which Luke gives us in his three accounts. Striking once again is the prominence Luke gives to the name – Saul's mission will be to carry Jesus' name before various audiences and to suffer for the sake of the name (cf. 5.41), a double emphasis thoroughly Pauline in character (see e.g. Phil. 1.29). As in chs 3–4, the name of Jesus continues to be a central identifying factor for the new movement and for its mission, the mission itself being an increasingly integral part of its identity.

The order, Gentiles, kings and sons of Israel, certainly reflects something of the subsequent course of Paul's mission (cf. 25.13, 23; 26.1; 27.24; see Introduction to chs 21–28 [pp.277f.]). But the addition of the third item is a clear indication that Luke did not see Saul's mission as mission to Gentiles as against Jews, far less to Gentiles in rejection of his fellow Jews (see Introduction §5(4)).

9.17   Ananias addresses Saul as 'Brother'. Since the vocative is usually used in Acts as 'fellow Jew' (2.29; 3.17; etc.), but also as 'fellow believer' (1.16; see further on 1.15), it is not clear what its significance is here – that is, whether Ananias was accepting Saul as already committed to the cause of the Lord Jesus.

The actions of Ananias do not match the commission recorded in 9.11. But this is precisely the sort of complementary variation which keeps a repeated story fresh for the listener (note the further variation in 22.16). Luke naturally assumed that a primary objective of Ananias would be for Saul to be filled with the Holy Spirit. The Spirit is so much the mark of the disciple for Luke, it could hardly be otherwise. But since Ananias himself belonged to an enthusiastic sect marked by its reception of the Spirit, it would be equally natural for Ananias himself to have seen this as his role also. It is to be noted that Luke makes no attempt here to represent Ananias as a representative of Jerusalem or as ineffective as Philip had been in the previous chapter in dealing with the Samaritans. The Spirit's filling is at the initiative of the Spirit, not under the control of the apostles. On this point at least, Luke's account accords with the mind and memory of Paul (Gal. 1.1, 12).

9.18   The healing echoes that of Tobit in Tobit 11.10–13. Luke leaves it unclear whether the laying on of Ananias' hands secured both the healing and the Spirit. We cannot assume that he intended his readers to infer that the Spirit's filling preceded baptism. But neither can we assume that he subsumed Saul's reception of the Spirit under the note of his being baptized. Luke has simply not made the point clear. The relationship of baptism and Spirit was dealt with sufficiently in the two surrounding incidents (8.14–17 and 10.44–48). Nothing is said of Saul's being given instruction, though he must have received traditions like I Cor. 15.3–7 at some very early stage. Nor that Saul 'repented' his previous actions (unless it is implied in Saul's fasting in 9.9), even though such repentance was regularly called for in the earliest preaching (2.38, etc.). Again the variation in Luke's account is partly artistic in motivation, but also partly refusal to be bound by any stereotyped process of 'reception of converts'.

9.20–22   Luke emphasizes the immediacy of Saul's commitment to his calling. As regularly thereafter, Saul uses the synagogues as his platform (see on 13.5).

His message is summed up in a new way: 'he proclaimed Jesus, saying "He is the Son of God"'. This may reflect a more Hellenist emphasis: 'Son of God' was a more meaningful title in Greek speaking circles than 'Messiah' (but note also 9.22). God's 'Son' is the title used in what is generally regarded as typical of Paul's early preaching in the wider Greek world (I Thess. 1.9–10; cf. Acts 13.33; Rom. 1.3–4). But the usage belongs to earliest Christian perception of Jesus as well. It may be rooted in Jesus' own remembered prayer address to God as 'Abba' (Rom. 8.15 and Gal. 4.6). And given the previous degree of interest in the Temple (chs 6–8) it is worth recalling that the 'son of God' title was also bound up with the Nathan prophecy of II Sam. 7.13–14 (see on 7.46–47). At the same time the modern reader should remember that the title did not have such exclusive focus on Jesus or embody such a high christology as it came to bear in the course of Christian controversy over the next four centuries. At this stage it could simply signify one highly or specially favoured by God. It was not a case of the title bestowing on Jesus a significance he would not otherwise have had. Rather it was Jesus' significance which gave the title its importance within Christianity.

The other aspect of or way of summarizing Saul's preaching is the more familiar 'demonstration' that Jesus was the Christ (cf. 5.42; 17.3; 18.5, 28). Here Luke takes the opportunity immediately to confirm that the apostle to the Gentiles was as much concerned to persuade his fellow Jews. This may be the first time (9.22) that the absolute '(the) Jews' is used by Luke (though the definite article is lacking in the best manuscripts). The usage becomes more prominent in the course of Luke's description of Paul's mission (13.5, 45, 50; 14.1–5 19; etc.), and has been cited in evidence that Luke is anti-Jewish and presents Christianity as completely other than and consistently opposed by 'the Jews'. So it is worth noting that the reference here is to '(the) Jews who lived in Damascus', a wholly natural, not to say unavoidable way of describing a large swell of opinion among a single ethnic group within a city. At the same time, however, the clear implication is that the Hellenist Jews who believed Jesus to be the Christ were a small minority within the Jewish community.

The initial opposition to Saul
9.23–31

Luke's concern in this brief section is to link Saul to Jerusalem and then to show how it was that, although commissioned to take the gospel to the Gentiles (9.15), a gap of some time intervened before he did so. All this is necessary since, having recounted Saul's conversion at this stage, Luke has still to describe the breakthrough to the Gentiles in Antioch by unknown Hellenists (11.19–20), and prior to that the breakthrough at Caesarea by the leading apostle, Peter, himself (10.1–11.18).

So far as historical detail is concerned, there is some inconsistency between Luke's account of Saul's preaching in Damascus (9.20–22) and Paul's own recollection that he went away to Arabia before returning to Damascus (Gal. 1.17), though Paul does not say he spent all three years prior to his visit to Jerusalem in Arabia. And we have already noted that the terms of Saul's visit to Jerusalem seem to be in some dispute between Luke and Paul (see Introduction to ch. 9 [pp.117f.]). On the other hand, the record of Paul's escape from Damascus by basket is common to both (9.25; II Cor. 11.32–33), and Luke's conclusion that Saul returned to Tarsus is consistent with Gal. 1.21. In short, we may simply have to accept that we are confronted with two rather tendentious readings of the same basic data, Paul emphasizing his independence from the Jerusalem apostles, Luke emphasizing his acceptance by them (clearly implied in 9.28).

9.23–25   'The Jews' are presumably the Jews just mentioned (again a quite natural usage), that is '(some of the) Jews who lived in Damascus'. But the phrase has an ominous ring and has helped feed the view that Luke did set 'the Jews' consistently in opposition to Paul. The plot here parallels the later plot in 23.12–30. Paul's ministry begins and ends enshrouded in hostility. The circumstances occasioning the escape are recorded differently in II Cor. 11.32–33 (King Aretas was attempting to seize Paul). The two accounts could be complementary (the king responding to unrest within or complaints from the important Jewish community). But Luke may be cloaking more serious opposition to Saul (the reasons we do not know), or may have chosen to focus only on the opposition from within the Jewish community of Damascus. Unusually here Luke speaks of 'his (that is, Saul's) disciples'. Does he mean that Saul had been very successful in his preaching, or has he simply expressed himself casually – Saul's fellow disciples?

9.26–27   The suspicion of Saul would have been entirely understandable given his record and reputation as a persecutor, even if it runs counter to Paul's own clear recollection in Gal. 1.18–20. The role attributed to Barnabas, however, is entirely consistent with his character (4.36), the memory of him as a bridge between the Jerusalem leadership and the Hellenists (11.22–24), and his later association with Saul/Paul (chs 13–14; see further on 4.36–37). Barnabas' description of Saul's Damascus preaching as 'in the name of Jesus' clearly signals that Saul meets one of the key identity markers of the new movement (similarly Luke in 9.28–29).

9.28–29   Again Luke makes a point of showing that Saul, the apostle to the Gentiles, began by preaching to his fellow Jews, and at the

126

heart of Jewish religion and tradition. The claim should not be dismissed out of hand, since Paul himself seems to recollect some such preaching in Rom. 15.19. Its boldness, as well as preaching in the name of the Lord, identifies him firmly with the group who prayed the prayer of 4.29–30. In a similar way, the opposition from the Hellenists, who had brought about Stephen's death (cf. 6.9–14), also identifies him with Stephen, that is, with those whom he had persecuted. 'Our former persecutor now preaches the faith which once he tried to destroy' (Gal. 1.23). The reported rejection (9.23, 29) of Saul by Jews (but Luke does not say 'Jews' here) sets a pattern to be regularly repeated in Paul's later missionary work (see Introductions to chs 13–15 and 16–20).

9.30 For the first time since 1.15 the followers of Jesus are again called 'brothers' (see on 1.15; why not 'the apostles'?). According to 22.3, Tarsus, chief political and cultural centre of Cilicia, was Saul's home city. It would make sense for someone who had suffered such trauma and consequent total readjustment to withdraw from the area of severest friction. Paul's own account of the period indicates a time of very fruitful evangelism (Gal. 1.21; 2.7–9).

9.31 The scattering of persecuted Hellenists into Judaea (8.1) had borne fruit. The 'church' (Luke uses the singular to embrace a number of groups of disciples across the single territory of ancient Israel) had also extended to Galilee. Luke's account of Christian expansion inevitably had to be selective. But it is slightly surprising that he gave no space to a description of the initial expansion into 'all Judaea' since it was part of his own itemized programme (1.8). It is also something of a puzzle why church groups in Galilee receive no further mention. Luke's silence has raised some suspicion regarding his motives: that Galilee may have been an alternative centre for Christian growth (led by disciples of Jesus who did not go to Jerusalem). But had there been such an alternative centre Luke would certainly have wanted to give some account of how it was absorbed into the Jerusalem centred mission (as he has in 8.14–17 and 11.22–24; cf. 18.24–19.7). The silence over Galilee is only a more extreme example of the relative silence over Judaea, and is adequately explained if such groups as there were in Galilee were few and of little influence.

The brief summary of Christian consolidation is the continuation of Luke's technique of summarizing developments between significant episodes (see on 13.49). 'The fear of the Lord' is the traditional language of piety (Ps. 34.11; Prov. 1.29) but here carries some of the numinous overtones of the earlier references (2.43; 5.5, 11). Luke may deliberately have left it ambiguous whether 'the Lord' is God or Christ (cf. 2.21), allowing further reminder of the two clearest marks of Christian identity, the Lord and the Spirit. 'The encouragement of the Holy Spirit' is an important reminder that Luke's understanding of the Spirit was not all in terms of speaking in tongues and inspiration. 'Encouragement/comfort' is one of the functions of the Spirit which all the principal New Testament writers prized (John 14.26; 15.26; Rom. 12.8; I Cor. 14.3). The overall impression is of a period of relative peace, consolidation and steady growth.

Peter's mission along the Judaean coastal plain
9.32–43

In a deliberate attempt at evenhandedness between Paul and Peter, Luke swings the spotlight back on to Peter. He has shown Peter as initially drawn from Jerusalem to investigate unexpected developments in Samaria (8.14–17), but then taking the opportunity for further preaching in Samaria, albeit on the way back to Jerusalem (8.25). The account which follows here is somewhat similar, in that Peter is shown as moving about among the local groupings of believers ('saints' – 9.32, 41). He has not yet taken the plunge or caught up with Philip in readiness to engage in pioneer missionary work (were 'the saints' converts of Philip? – 8.40). That it took a considerable jolt to his theology and self-understanding before he was prepared to do so is the chief burden of the Cornelius episode (10.1–11.18). This probably reflects fairly accurately the serious qualms and hesitation which many of the first Jerusalem based believers experienced as they contemplated the possibility that their movement was beginning to break through the boundaries which in Jewish perspective God had established to mark out the difference and distictiveness of their religion (their set-apartness to God). It also probably signals that Peter himself was beginning a broadening process which was to take him away from Jerusalem (on mission among fellow Jews – Gal. 2.7–9), leaving James and the more traditionalist element in control there (see on 12.17).

9.32–35   The details of the names of the paralysed man (Aeneas, another Greek name for a Jew) and the local towns (Lydda and Sharon) surely indicate a well-rooted memory on which Luke has been able to draw. We may also observe that the healing is not particularly spectacular (afflicted for eight years; contrast 3.2). And the formula used by Peter is unparalleled – 'Jesus Christ heals you' (but to the same effect as 3.6). Luke does not seem to have made any attempt to draw out parallels here, except briefly with the mission of Philip (8.7). The effect of the cure (9.35) is consistent both with what might have been expected and with Luke's consistent emphasis on the faith-generating effect of miracles. 'All the residents' means all Jews, since the towns were Jewish. 'Turned to the Lord' (note again the ambiguity) becomes one of Luke's principal ways of describing conversion (11.21; cf. 14.15; 15.19; 26.18, 20).

9.36–42   This story too is assuredly rooted in good historical memory, as the mention of both name and location (Joppa was about ten miles northwest of Lydda), and probably also the vivid account of Tabitha's reputation and the details of the arrangements made following her death all attest. The details of the raising of Tabitha by Peter may, however, be a little more contrived. They echo the account of the raising of Jairus' daughter in the Gospel at two points: the expulsion of the crowd (Luke 8.51) and the formula used (personal address and the command to arise – Luke 8.54); still more closely the Markan account (Mark 5.40–41); and more distantly the accounts of similar recallings to life attributed to Elijah and Elisha (I Kings 17.17–24; II Kings 4.32–37). On the other hand the verbs used in the raising formula are different (Luke here, as in 9.34, uses the verb which elsewhere describes Jesus' resurrection), and Luke's failure to mention 'calling upon Jesus or the name of Jesus', more typical of his own healing accounts, may equally suggest he was also drawing on tradition at this point. Whatever the actual condition of Tabitha, which we have no way now of checking, it was no doubt the widespread understanding of those closest to the event that she had been raised from the dead.

By way of variation on the preceding episode Luke describes the impact of the healing this time using his favourite 'believed on the Lord' (as in 11.17; 16.31; 22.19). 'Turning to' (9.35) and 'believing on' (9.42) are complementary descriptions of the turn around of life which commitment to the Lord involves.

9.43   The final verse prepares for the spectacular next step, to be recounted immediately (ch. 10). But the description of Peter's host as 'a tanner' may be significant. The smell associated with tanning made the job not only unpleasant but its practitioners unacceptable among those who regarded cultic purity as something to be maintained as far as possible (a tanner's very work involved constant touching the skins of dead bodies). Does the mention of this fact indicate that Peter was already moving away from his previously Temple-centred focus of worship and ministry (5.42)? This is probably more likely than that Luke expected his readers to pick up such significance from the bare mention here.

The Conversion of Peter and the Acceptance of Cornelius
10.1–48

Chapter 10 begins the second major insertion into the history of Hellenist Christian expansion, which had begun with ch. 8. Chapter 9 had interrupted it to ensure that the conversion of Saul was given due and early prominence. But now an even lengthier insertion is made (10.1–11.18). The object is plain: to demonstrate that the first breakthrough of the gospel to the Gentiles, or at least the first breakthrough recognized by the Jerusalem church (so the conversion of the Ethiopian eunuch in 8.26–40 does not count), was led by Peter himself.

The decisive proof recited is twofold. First the interlocking visions of Cornelius and of Peter (10.1–23), both recalled again in the following verses (10.30–32; 11.5–10). As in the case of Ananias (9.10–12), it is the double testimony of divine approval given by the complementary visions which puts the issue beyond doubt: God approves and wills the next step. In Peter's case the significance of the vision is, exceptionally, confirmed by the prompting of the Spirit – again twice told (10.19–20; 11.11–12). Secondly, the unexpected outpouring of the Spirit on Cornelius and his companions, again rehearsed twice for double effect (10.44–47; 11.15–17). The former secures Peter's complete acceptance of Cornelius (10.47–48), the latter that of the Jerusalem apostles and brothers (11.18).

So far as the critical identifying marks of the church are concerned (Jesus and the Spirit), the first phase (the visions) is really a precursor. In it Jesus does not feature: the 'Lord' addressed in 10.4 and referred to in 10.33 is identified as an angel; and the 'Lord' addressed in 10.14 is an unidentified voice. That preliminary stage is about bridging the sharp division between Jew and Gentile, not yet the division between believer and non-believer. Only in Peter's speech does the focus swing to Jesus himself (now identified as 'Lord of all'

– 10.36). Thus it is that the coming of the Spirit is associated with the preaching for commitment focussed in this Jesus and the promise of forgiveness offered through his name (10.43). The primary marks of discipleship are reaffirmed: Jesus and the Spirit.

It is important to grasp that the first part in the process is the conversion of Peter himself and that it comes in two stages. There is the initial reluctance of a devout Jew to associate with a Gentile. The revelation which Peter receives and the new conviction which comes to him was neither so dramatic nor so traumatic as in the case of Saul (ch. 9). But it was every bit as much a conversion as in Saul's case – a conversion from traditional and deeply rooted convictions which had completely governed his life till that moment (10.14–15, 28). He was then ready, as not before, to preach the good news of Jesus to this Gentile. The fact that it took the further event of the Spirit's coming upon Cornelius in such an unexpected, unprecedented way to complete Peter's conversion indicates Luke's appreciation of just how major a transformation had taken place in Peter and how epochal a step was being taken by the new movement.

As usual we must ask how much of all this was contrived by Luke and how much is well rooted in history. And as usual the answer is a bit of both.

First, the evidence of Luke's shaping of the record is clear. We need mention only the two most striking points. (1) It is quite likely that the first breakthrough, in chronological sequence, happened at Antioch (11.19–24), not forgetting the conversion of the Ethiopian eunuch (8.26–39). The problem was that Jerusalem's relation to these (earlier) developments was a good deal less clear. For Luke, then, the decisive breakthrough was that in which Peter was personally involved, the one which Peter himself made. It was crucial, for Luke, that not only had the unheard of step of accepting (eating with) and baptizing an uncircumcised Gentile been taken by the leading apostle (10.1–48). But also that Peter had been able to convince his Jerusalem colleagues by recounting the clear evidence of divine approval which had first convinced him (11.1–18). Only so could Luke demonstrate to his readers that this decisive breakthrough into a whole new dimension for the Jesus movement was in full continuity with all that had gone before.

(2) Luke has delayed any confrontation over the question of clean and unclean till this point. In Mark's Gospel the issue is already confronted by Jesus and the challenge to Jewish tradition sharply posed by Jesus in Mark 7.1–23. But Luke has completely omitted that

passage from his own Gospel – part of, and quite probably the principal reason for the so-called 'great omission' (Mark 6.45 to 8.13/26) Luke made in his use of Mark as a primary source. We have seen him use this technique before, in his delay of the charge of destroying the Temple from the trial of Jesus until the accusation against Stephen (see on 6.14). So here, Luke had evidently decided that the proper place in his two-volume account for the issue to be confronted was in the Peter/Cornelius episode. He did this, presumably, partly out of a concern for an orderly account, but also partly in order to show that the questioning of Judaism's traditional identity markers did not seriously begin until the new movement was already well launched and even then only at the undeniable insistence of God's direction. In this way he avoids the problem posed when Mark 7.1–23 is juxtaposed with Acts 10.14, but sharpens the historical question: if Jesus had indeed spoken as he did in Mark 7.15, 18–19 (with the implication Mark himself draws in 7.19), and had acted in accord with that teaching, how could Peter say he himself had never contemplated the eating of unclean food?

On the basis of such considerations some have assumed that the story is more or less wholly contrived: a rather obscure episode briefly recalled from Peter's early missionary work has been taken over by Luke and elaborated into a major event whose significance was recognized from the first (see e.g. the review by Haenchen 355–7).

Secondly, however, there is more to be said for the historical value of Luke's tradition. (*a*) Peter's hesitation on the subject of Jew/Gentile relations is attested also by Paul (Gal. 2.11–12). If Peter was so reluctant to maintain table fellowship with Gentile believers, even after the Gentile mission had been given formal approval (Gal. 2.7–9), it is very likely that his reluctance at an earlier date was even more marked. At the same time, the tendentiousness of Mark's account in Mark 7.15–19 should also be recognized (contrast the Matthean parallel – Matt. 15.11–17), and probably reflects the sharper focus which the Gentile mission brought to Mark's retelling of the tradition. So Luke may well be representing in Acts 10.14 the genuine reluctance which Peter had displayed on this question, a reluctance which had not been challenged until the question of Gentile acceptability was first raised for him personally.

(*b*) It is unlikely that Luke would have invented on his own novellistic initiative the sequence narrated in 10.44–48. Such a departure (Spirit preceding baptism) from the normal pattern (baptism and Spirit – 2.38) would have made Cornelius into a precedent uncomfortable for the ecclesiology of Luke's day. It is more likely, given the enthusiastic character of the new sect, that some early preaching of Peter was attended by charismatic manifestations of the Spirit's presence from Gentile members of the audience; as a Godfearer (10.2), Cornelius would probably have participated in many Jewish gatherings. Such divine attestation is implied in the brief allusion to Peter's ministry to the circumcised in Gal. 2.8. But if that was indeed what happened, then the event had a significance which Peter could not have failed to recognize: the Spirit had fallen on Gentiles, 'even on Gentiles' (10.45), just as it had upon the first disciples at Pentecost (11.15); God had given to Gentiles the same gift as they had received when they had believed in the Lord Jesus Christ (11.17). The conclusion, for a sect which valued such manifestations, was unavoidable. God had accepted them; how could Peter and the other believers obstruct God's clearly signalled will (11.17)?

In other words, whenever it took place (and it must have been early), the event of Cornelius' acceptance by Peter marked a step forward of momentous significance, which can hardly have been ignored at the time. All that Luke seems to have done, therefore, is to bring it into even sharper prominence, and by interposing it before the account of the Hellenists' mission in Antioch, to have ensured that the strongest precedent (acceptance of Gentile Cornelius by apostle Peter and Jerusalem church) is given the full glare of attention on centre stage. The basic story itself may have come to Luke together with the traditions lying behind 9.32–43, perhaps part of the founding tradition preserved by the church in Caesarea.

The conversion of Peter
10.1–29

The care with which Luke narrates the story is telling. The detail is painstaking. No doubt must be left that this initial step was at God's direct bidding. By way of contrast, we may compare the relatively brief record of other events of potentially comparable significance (8.5–8, 12–13; 11.19–21).

The narrative runs unbroken through the whole chapter. But two stages are clearly distinct. First, Peter's recognition that God does not make distinctions between human beings in general as to their acceptability or unacceptability on grounds of their basic identity (ethnic, social or religious). And secondly, Peter's preaching to Cornelius on the basis of that recognition, with the further consequence of God's visible acceptance of Cornelius and his companions as such. The climax of the first stage comes in Peter's initial address to Cornelius (10.28–29). So it is fitting to make the break in the chapter at this point, with 10.30–35 recapitulating the basis for the sermon proper (10.36–43).

10.1   The name, Cornelius, was no doubt part of the tradition which came to Luke. He is clearly understood to have been a Gentile (10.35, 45; 11.1). Since the Roman army recruited widely from nations within the Roman Empire we do not know what nationality he was, though 'the Italian Cohort' was presumably made up originally of Italians. He is located in the Roman administrative capital (Caesarea), and the implication is that he was still a serving officer, with soldiers at his command (10.7). It is true that we lack any record of the Italian Cohort being stationed in Caesarea (but our records are hardly complete). And it would be unlikely for Roman troops to be stationed in Caesarea during the reign of Herod Agrippa (cf. 12.20–23). However, the possibility cannot be excluded that Cornelius had retired from the army and settled in Caesarea (in its own interests the Roman army's terms of settlement for its veterans could be generous). The soldier of 10.7, notably described also as 'devout', may have been a favoured subordinate who had chosen to retire with him.

10.2   The description of Cornelius emphasizes his piety. The terms used indicate that he was one of many Gentiles attracted to Judaism (was that why he settled in Caesarea?). He feared God and prayed constantly to him. Coming from Luke's pen this must mean the God of Israel. Cornelius already believed Israel's God to be the one true God. And he gave many alms to the people – a characteristic mark of Jewish piety (see on 3.2–5; cf. Matt. 6.2–6). This impression is confirmed by the additional information of 10.22: Cornelius is further described as a 'just/upright' man (cf. Luke 1.6; 2.25; 23.50), 'well spoken of by the whole Jewish nation'. Cornelius is one of Luke's good centurions (Luke 7.5; Acts 27.43). By thus demonstrating his openness to and membership of the new movement Luke can advance the further objective of showing the growing sect to have been on good terms with the Roman authorities.

Has Luke exaggerated the degree of Cornelius' closeness already to the religion of Israel, in order to diminish the gulf which Peter was about to cross, in order to make the crossing that much less threatening to Jewish traditionalists? Not necessarily. We have many records of other Gentiles who were attracted to Judaism, and who 'judaized' in some measure (that is, followed a distinctively Jewish way of life), without going all the way to become proselytes (that is, without being circumcised; see e.g. Josephus, *Jewish War* 2.462–3; 7.45; *Against Apion* 2.282). Judaism did not seek out such (it was not a missionary religion, though some misread Matt. 23.15 on this point) but was very willing to welcome such sympathizers at gatherings for prayer and Torah reading and at festivals. Such Gentile sympathizers are usually called 'God-fearers', which is quite appropriate so long as we do not assume that it was a formal title but simply denotes a dominant attitude of piety (as in 10.2, 22, 35; also 13.16, 26, 50; 16.14; 17.4, 17; 18.7).

Cornelius' house, included within the description of 'God-fearing', presumably includes his household retainers. The presence of 'relatives' (wife and children?) is indicated in 10.24 (see also on 11.14).

10.3   The timing will not be coincidental. The ninth hour was the time of the evening sacrifice in the Temple and the appropriate time for evening prayer (see on 3.1). So the vision is like that with which Luke began his first volume (Luke 1.10–11; cf. also 8.26 and 27.23).

10.4   As earlier in Luke's account (2.43; 5.5, 11), the mention of 'fear' (here in stronger form, 'terrified') conveys the note of numinous awe (the word is used in Luke 24.5 and 37; see Introduction to 5.1–11). The fact that the angel is addressed as 'Lord' is a reminder of how flexible the title was; as in 9.5 a glorious heavenly visitation calls forth an address of due respect and humility. Worth noting is the combination of 'prayers and alms'. It was the roundedness of Cornelius' piety which commended him to God. Luke's use of scriptural language at this point (e.g. Lev. 2.2, 9, 16; 6.15) is certainly deliberate.

10.5–8   The care with which details are recounted gives the whole account a weight and gravitas commensurate with its importance.

10.9–10   Peter likewise is shown as praying – at midday, an additional (third) hour of prayer (cf. Ps. 55.17; Dan. 6.10), or simply an opportunity for prayer? Is the implication of verse 10 that he had finished his prayer before he fell into a trance, or that he fell asleep while praying? The latter would certainly add a very human touch. Luke is also happy to imply that the subject of the vision was conditioned by Peter's feelings of hunger. He thus implicitly recognizes the physiological/psychological mechanism involved in visions. Nor does he hesitate to describe the vision as 'ecstatic' (literally, 'ecstasy came upon him').

10.11–13   It is not stated explicitly, but in the vision the animals in the sheet obviously include those regarded as unclean in Jewish law, particularly the reptiles (see Lev. 11.1–47). The command to 'kill and eat', without any further discrimination, would be regarded as reprehensible for a devout Jew. As in a dream, Peter knows, as part of the vision itself, what animals the command refers to (possibly a historical reminiscence).

10.14   Peter's reaction is strong: 'Certainly not, Lord!' He refuses and implicitly rebukes the heavenly visitation (once again 'Lord' is not necessarily Jesus or God as such; cf. 10.4). Equally strong is the self-testimony which follows: 'I have never eaten anything common or unclean' (using both words commonly used to denote 'unclean' foods – cf. 10.15; 11.19; Rom. 14.14, 20). The emphatic denial is repeated in 11.8 and reflected in 10.28.

Peter here is portrayed as through and through loyal to his ancestral traditions. Observation of the laws of clean and unclean foods had become a distinctive identifying mark of the Judaism which defined itself by its opposition to Hellenistic/Gentile influences (I Macc. 1.62–63). The heroes and heroines of Israel's popular tales of the period demonstrated their loyalty to their people and religion by refusing to eat the food of Gentiles (e.g. Dan. 1.8–16; Tobit 1.10–13; Additions to Esther 14.17). Both Pharisees and still more the Essenes were noted for the strictness with which they protected the purity of the meal table by their various halakoth (rulings on less clearly defined laws). And the subsequent tensions within the Christian communities of Antioch, Corinth and Rome show just how important dietary rules continued to be for the self-identity of many Jewish Christians (Gal. 2.11–14; I Cor. 8; Rom. 14).

It is important, then, for the modern reader to appreciate that the issue was not a minor matter of insignificant dietary fads. It lay at the heart of Jewish identity (see also on 10.28). What was at stake was the character of the new movement as a Jewish movement and the process of identity transformation. Was it to be still loyal to the now traditionally distinctive features of the covenant people? Was it to be loyal to the principles and practices for which martyrs had died and heroes and heroines had been willing to sacrifice everything? Hitherto Peter and his brother apostles and believers in Jerusalem would have assumed the answer was Yes (10.14; 11.3; cf. Gal. 2.12–13). Now he is faced with one of the most radical rethinks of religious principle imaginable. That is why Luke gives the episode such prominence and tells the story with such care.

10.15–16   The challenge to traditional practice is as sharp as could be: 'What *God* has made clean (cf. Lev. 13.6, 13, 17; Mark 7.19), you must not call unclean' (playing on the same two words). This is the moment when new religions or sects are born – when what has hitherto been taken for granted as a fundamental and defining principle is called in question, and the question is heard as the voice of God. Lest there be any doubt in Peter's or the reader's mind Luke notes that the revelation was repeated three times.

10.17–23   No wonder Peter was perplexed: how should one evaluate a dream or vision which cuts so radically across long established principles and traditions? The answer is given by the double confirmation. (*a*) The Spirit tells him (gives him the clear conviction – cf. 13.2 and 16.6) that he should go with the messengers just arrived; the coincidence of his vision and their arrival can hardly be accidental. (*b*) And the request of the three men reports Cornelius' complementary vision. The conclusion is obvious: Peter's vision of ancient uncleanness nullified by God himself must refer to this God-fearing Gentile who was calling for him at angelic command. To be noted is the fact that angel and Spirit can be equally and variously described as the voice of God (cf. 10.5–6 with 10.20).

10.24–26   The initial meeting allows Luke to reinforce one of his constant themes in the various encounters he relates between Jewish/Christian missionaries and pagan ideas of God (particularly 14.11–18; 17.22–31). Cornelius makes the mistake of kneeling before Peter and reverencing him; the latter verb can denote simply (oriental) respect, but in Luke's vocabulary it has more the connotation of 'worship' (Luke 4.7–8; Acts 7.43; 8.27; 24.11). Peter corrects

138

him: there should be no confusion between God and a mere human being.

10.27–29   This is the climax to the first half of the chapter. The importance of the lesson learned is drawn out clearly. Peter is in process of breaching a fundamental guiding principle of Jewish communal living: that Jews should keep themselves separate from Gentiles. Of course the practice was not quite so cut and dried, otherwise there could have been no business or social relationships whatsoever between Jews and Gentiles, whether in Israel itself (where many Gentiles had settled – the 'resident aliens' of the Old Testament), or in the diaspora (where Jews were in the minority). Josephus, for example, observes that in Syria many judaizing Gentiles had become 'mixed up' (literally) with the Jews (*Jewish War* 2.463). And the Jews of Caesarea who commended Cornelius so highly (10.22) must have had some association with him. But the principle was nevertheless a basic item of Jewish identity – the fundamental conviction that Israel as a nation had been chosen by God and therefore was required to keep itself separate from other nations to maintain its holiness before the Lord (e.g. Lev. 20.24–26; Ezra 10.11; *Letter of Aristeas* 139–142; Philo, *Life of Moses* 1.278). And the testing point again and again was the meal table, the main expression of hospitality or friendship and the principal occasion for the transmission of impurity (hence the assumption and accusation of 11.3; cf. Luke 7.34; 15.1–2; 19.7; Gal. 2.11–14).

The point is, then, that Peter has recognized the close correlation of the clean/unclean food laws and the separateness of Jew and Gentile (it was clearly spelled out in Lev. 20.24–26). But, more to the point, he has recognized the significance of his vision. As the law of clean and unclean served to embody and defend Israel's separateness, so its abolition meant that the time of Israel's holding itself separate from the nations was over. If no animal was by nature unclean, then neither could any human being as such be so designated. Peter was now free to deal with Cornelius as he would have dealt with any fellow Jew.

In short, the gulf which Peter had had to cross was not one between God and humanity (hence Luke's emphasis on Cornelius' piety) but one between Jew and Gentile. The breakdown of the ethnic/religious boundary round Israel was indispensable and integral to the breakthrough of the gospel to the nations at large. The success of God's plan for 'all the families of the earth' (3.25) involved a redefinition of

Israel's own identity in so far as it was defined by separation from Gentiles. It was this process of redefinition in which Peter found himself. The process is not yet complete even today, but remains equally fundamental to Christian self-understanding and a primary topic in Jewish/Christian relations (see also Introduction to 28.23–31).

The acceptability of Cornelius; Peter's third sermon
10.30–43

The story is only half told. What has happened so far has been the removal of the barrier which had prevented Peter from even conceiving of the possibility that the gospel might be for a Gentile. Now Peter is free to offer the gospel to Gentile Cornelius as he had to Jerusalem residents. The fuller, climactic manifestation of God's purpose in Christ can now be opened to Gentiles for their participation in it if they so desire.

This second half of the story falls into two parts – the speech of Peter and the pouring out of the Spirit on Cornelius and his companions.

The speech as usual is a fine Lukan cameo; it would take little more than a minute to deliver. 10.44 suggests, and 11.15 states explicitly, that the speech had hardly started when the Spirit intervened. But as usual with the Lukan speech cameos, this one is a nicely rounded whole, where nothing more needs to be said (cf. 22.22; 26.24).

The structure is clear enough. The main body of the speech (10.36–43) is built round four Old Testament allusions (Ps. 107.20; Isa. 52.7; Isa. 61.1; Deut. 21.22), followed by the now familiar rehearsal of Jesus' death and resurrection, and an implicit call for belief and promise of forgiveness. It contains the same Lukan, but also possibly older features: Jewish responsibility for Jesus' execution (10.39); the theme of witness thrice repeated (10.39, 41, 43); the resurrection as something 'manifest' (10.40, 41); the mention of Jesus' name (10.43); but now also a more distant, less urgent eschatology (10.42), suggestive of a longer time perspective.

But again, as usual, there are primitive features: Israel-centredness (10.36, 42); 'you know', perhaps implying a Judaean audience (10.36); the setting of John the Baptist and his baptism at the beginning and the description of the ministry of Jesus of Nazareth

(10.37–38); the primitive christology of 10.38 and 42; the suffering-reversal theme (10.39–40); and the degree to which the speech has been moulded round the Old Testament allusions. In addition, 10.34–35 look like an introduction added to already existing material to fit it to the context: the jump from 10.35 to 36 is rather abrupt. It is possible, indeed, that verses 34–35 and 43 have been added to an already fairly coherent torso.

One plausible hypothesis which takes the above details into account is that Luke has moulded his cameo on some tradition of preaching to God-fearers. This would explain the slight tension between the more traditional formulations and the more universal dimension evident in 10.34–35, 36c, 39 ('the country of the Jews') and 43 ('all who believe').

10.30–33 retells the story of Cornelius' vision, for emphasis, but also building up the dramatic 'feel' of the story towards its climax. The detail of the angel's clothing has been added (10.30) to provide some variety. The final verse is a mixture of familiar courtesy ('you have been kind enough to come') and Old Testament solemnity ('met here in the presence of God'). The terms are no doubt Luke's, but the tone well expresses the character of Cornelius as so far depicted.

10.34–35 summarizes the principal lesson that Peter has learned from his recent revelatory experience. He has realized that the statement of God's impartiality, as in Deut. 10.17 and II Chron. 19.7, extends to his regard for Gentile as well as Jew. This becomes a repeated emphasis within earliest Christian thought (Rom. 2.11), particularly in inculcating a due sense of ethical responsibility (Eph. 6.9; Col. 3.25; James 2.1, 9; I Peter 1.17).

To the impartial God, what makes a person acceptable is not a matter of ethnic heritage or nationality, but reverence of God and doing what is right. The insight, of course, stands in some tension with the axiom of Israel's election, but Peter was not the first, nor was he the last to give voice to it within Judaism (already in Amos 9.7; Jonah; Matt. 3.8–9). So this is the language of the liberated Jew, willing now to recognize that the God-fearer (see on 10.2), the one who fears God, is as acceptable to God as the Jew (cf. Deut. 10.12; Ps. 2.11; Prov. 1.7; Mal. 4.2), without meeting any further stipulation of the law (circumcision in particular). The national boundary round Israel which had hitherto functioned also as a religious boundary is

141

no longer relevant 'in the presence of God'. In other words, the God-fearing Gentile is as ready to receive the blessing which comes through the name of Jesus and the Spirit of God as the God-fearing Jew.

Was Cornelius 'acceptable' to God or already 'accepted' by him? The Greek could have either meaning. The key is the recognition that 'fearing God' and 'doing what is right' (literally 'working righteousness') are classic expressions of what is expected of God's people, of what membership of God's covenant involves (cf. particularly Ps. 15.2). The issue then which Peter has confronted is this: if a Gentile displays the spirituality characteristically expected of the devout member of God's people, how can it be doubted that he is acceptable to God. For Luke (and Peter) the test of whether 'acceptable' means 'accepted' will be the gift of the Spirit to Cornelius.

10.36   begins awkwardly – literally, 'As for the word which he sent . . .'. Is this where Luke begins to incorporate pre-formed material? At any rate, the language is clearly built round one or two deliberate scriptural allusions. First, Ps. 107.20 – 'he sent out his word and healed them'. Secondly, less clearly, Isa. 52.7 – '. . . those who preach peace'. Both may well belong to an early arsenal of Christian texts: Ps. 107.20 is echoed again in 13.26, and Isa. 52.7 is cited in Rom. 10.15 as part of a catena of texts.

Noticeable is the fact that both texts seem to have Israel primarily in view as beneficiaries. To Ps. 107.20 is added the phrase 'sent to the sons of Israel'. And in Isa. 52.7 the proclamation is to Zion as such. This brings out still more the tension implicit in 10.34–35. It is the same tension as we already noted in 2.39, 3.25 and 4.10, 12. A blessing focussed *on* Israel is becoming a blessing channelled *through* Israel. The identity of the people of promise is being broadened beyond the boundaries of Israel. This is the reconfiguration in Peter's self-understanding which Luke intended the whole episode to express.

The tension is heightened still more by the phrase, 'He is Lord of all'. It was a tension bound up in Israel's own monotheism: if God is one, then he is God of all peoples, of Gentile as well as Jew (Paul exploited this tension to good effect in Rom. 3.29–30). But the 'Lord' here, once again, is clearly Jesus (cf. 2.21,36; Rom. 10.12–13). Peter seems to be saying two things to Cornelius here. First, the Lord God who had commanded Cornelius (10.33), had shared his Lordship with Jesus Christ (the point already made in 2.21, 34–36). Secondly, this Lordship of Christ had brought home to Peter that the Lordship of God extended over all, Gentile as well as Jew. In this phrase, then, is encapsulated the redefinition of God as well as of his purpose which, within a few decades, was to pull Christianity apart from the Judaism which shared its common heritage.

10.37–38   This rehearsal of Jesus' ministry is unique in the sermons of Acts and bears several marks of very old tradition. (1) Particularly noticeable, again, is that the beginning of the gospel is linked with the Baptist (cf. 1.22; 13.24). Here almost certainly we see the traditional gospel format (as subsequently in Mark) being already fixed. (2) Jesus is identified as 'the one from Nazareth', still needing to be identified, a more weighty title not yet assumed. (3) God anointed him with the Spirit and power. He is presented as an inspired prophet. This contains the speech's third scriptural echo – Isa. 61.1. Luke made much of this passage in the construction of his own Gospel (Luke 4.17–21), but it was already implicit in the traditions he himself had been able to draw on, and may indeed have represented Jesus' own self-understanding (Luke 6.20; 7.22). (4) Jesus' ministry of healing is described in restrained terms (good deeds and exorcisms), his success again attributed to the fact that 'God was with him' (cf. 2.22; 7.9). The description is one which might have come from the mouth of any sympathetic observer of Jesus' ministry. The juxtaposition of this very moderate portrayal of Jesus with the final confessional claim of verse 36 is striking.

10.39–41   The emphases here are more characteristic of the Acts sermons, but also contain primitive features. There is a double emphasis on the role of witness (10.39, 41) – both of Jesus' ministry (cf. 1.21–22) and of Jesus' resurrection (see on 1.8) – with reference to 'the country of the Jews' recalling that the speech is addressed to a Gentile audience. There is the usual accusation of Jewish responsibility for Jesus' death (see on 2.23) and the usual 'but God' vindicatory response (see on 2.24). 'Hanged on a tree' (10.39; as in 5.30) brings in the fourth scriptural allusion (Deut. 21.22). 'On the third day' (10.40) is unparalleled in Acts, but is already enshrined in the early confessional formula received by Paul after his conversion (I Cor. 15.4). The recollection that the resurrected Jesus ate and drank with his disciples (10.41) is more distinctively Lukan (see on 1.4).

10.42   For a third time the role of those favoured with a resurrection appearance as witnesses is emphasized. 'To the people' expresses the same Israel-focussed view and resultant tension as 3.25–26. Jesus 'ordained by God' is a consistent feature of the early proclamation (3.20; 17.31).

That Jesus had been appointed 'judge of the living and the dead' is a new feature. It could be early: that God had chosen to give others share in his role as final judge is reflected in Jewish speculation of the period in regard to such great heroes as Enoch and Abel, as well as in very early Christian tradition (Luke 22.30; I Cor. 6.2); and the identification of Jesus with the man-like figure of the vision of Dan. 7.13–14 would have reinforced the link in the case of Jesus. On the other hand, the formulation is remarkably lacking in any sense of urgency (so also 17.31; contrast 3.19–20), and reads more like a doctrine of the last things framed in the light of Jesus' return having been much delayed (but cf. I Peter 4.5 and II Tim. 4.1).

10.43   This may be Luke's own rounding off of the speech. The emphasis on prophets bearing witness is a constant theme of the speeches, and reflects also Luke 24.25–27, 44–48. Passages in mind could be Isa. 33.24, 55.7 and/or Jer. 31.34. The call for repentance is lacking, since it refers usually to responsibility for the death of the Christ. But it is replaced by a call for belief, with the Pauline emphasis on 'all who believe' again underlining the tension with 'the people' of verse 42 (as again in 3.25–26). The phrase is a further variation on Luke's belief formulae: here believe in (or into) him, giving more the force of commitment to the person named (such as would normally be expressed in baptism). To this invitation is attached the promise of forgiveness of (presumably a much wider range of unspecified) sins. 'Through his name' is the characteristic emphasis of 2.38 and 4.12.

The acceptance of Cornelius: the Gentile Pentecost
10.44–48

The speech has brought the Jesus identity marker to full expression: 'He is Lord of all', 'anointed with the Holy Spirit and with power', 'God was with him', 'God raised him from the dead', 'ordained to be judge of the living and the dead', 'believe in him and receive forgiveness through his name'. Now the final paragraph does the same for the Spirit, and in a dramatic mode whose significance for such a Spirit sect was inescapable (10.44–48). Here again the primacy of the Spirit as the mark of God's acceptance is plain beyond dispute. The implication is clearly that Cornelius has believed (10.43; so explicitly in 11.17 and 15.7, 9). The coming of the Spirit awaits no human regulation or ordering. At the same time, baptism in the name of Jesus Christ is not dispensed with. In fact, it will not be accidental that the repeated emphases on Cornelius' reception of the Spirit (10.44–47) are bracketed by the double reference to the name of Jesus (10.43, 48). The two primary identity markers of the new movement are interdependent. And thus Cornelius moves from being acceptable to be accepted and the decisive breakthrough of God's blessing to the nations has taken place.

10.44   Luke goes out of his way to heighten the drama. Peter was still speaking (though the sermon was in effect complete). What happened, then, was wholly of God's doing. At the same time, the characteristic Christian order of salvation has been safeguarded by 10.43: the Spirit 'fell upon all who were hearing the word', that is, those who heard with assent, who believed in the one proclaimed in the word. The fundamental junction point in divine human encounter continues to be faith in him and the gift of the Spirit (11.17). The acceptability of the God-fearer to the God of Israel becomes the acceptance of the anyone who believes in God through Jesus.

10.45   Those with Peter are described as 'the faithful' rather than as 'believers' – literally, 'the faithful from circumcision'. Thereby Luke signals that they represent that portion of the church which continued to regard circumcision as the most distinctive feature of the covenant people (cf. 7.8), and who would thus be most convinced that the fundamental separation between Jew and Gentile marked by circumcision had to be maintained (cf. 11.2; 15.1, 5); Paul indeed could distinguish Jews and Gentiles simply as 'the circumcision'/'the uncircumcision' (Rom. 2.25–26; Gal. 2.7). 'Those of the circumcision' were faithful, loyal to Israel's basic calling to be holy and separate, eager to maintain its identity markers and boundaries. The fact that even they were convinced of the Spirit's coming upon the Caesarean Gentiles meant that the fact of the outpoured Spirit was beyond question.

10.46   A particular feature of these three verses (10.44–46) is the emphasis on the visible impact of the Spirit. The Spirit 'fell upon' them (as in 8.16); something 'hit' them; there was a visible impact of invisible power. The effect was so obvious that those with Peter could not deny or doubt it. The particular evidence mentioned is their speaking in tongues and extolling God. The double echo of the experience and event of Pentecost ('poured out' – 2.17–18, 33 and 10.45; speaking in tongues and saying great things of God – 2.4, 11 and 10.46) is obviously deliberate. What happened to Cornelius and his companions was manifestly no different from what had happened to the first disciples on the day of Pentecost. How could 'the faithful from circumcision' affirm the one and deny the other? They couldn't.

10.47–48   It is Peter himself who draws the inevitable conclusion. God has so clearly accepted them; the parallel with Pentecost is reiterated ('just as we did'). So how can we refuse them? This could not be dismissed as arbitrary or mindless ecstasy. God's hand in it all was beyond dispute. The fourth supernatural sign, following the two visions and the Spirit's prompting, left the matter in no doubt. The question is the same as that posed by the eunuch in 8.37: who can forbid what God has so clearly ratified? And the answer is the same: no one. Peter apparently does not carry out the baptisms himself.

The order here is exceptional. The Spirit precedes baptism. God had to give so clear an indication of his will otherwise even Peter might have hesitated to take such a step in the case of Gentiles without first requiring them to be circumcised. At the same time, the already bestowal of the Spirit does not lead Peter to the conclusion that baptism can be dispensed with. Baptism 'in the name of Jesus Christ' closes the circle already drawn with the proclamation of belief in him and of forgiveness of sins in his name and the outpouring of the Spirit. Where the gift of the Spirit had ratified God's acceptance of Cornelius now the church of Jews and circumcised must ratify their acceptance of these Gentiles by baptism. As usual the baptism proceeds at once, without further instruction or delay. A final sentence indicates the extent of their acceptance: these faithful circumcised accept hospitality of guest friendship and table fellowship for some days.

Peter's Action Ratified and Confirmation of the Breakthrough at Antioch
11.1–30

Whereas ch. 10 was primarily about the conversion of Peter, ch. 11 is primarily about the way in which the Jerusalem church came to accept the astonishing turn of events which Peter narrated, with the report of the (prior?) events at Antioch added on as it were in the backwash, as a kind of corollary. Here again Luke shows his awareness of how fundamental was the transformation in Christian understanding which he was recording. It took massive and repeated intervention by God before Peter was able to accept Cornelius, even Cornelius the God-fearing Gentile, who had already judaized almost all the way to proselyte status (10.2). But now Luke has to ensure that not just Peter but also the (other) apostles and the mother church at Jerusalem are seen to stand with Peter in this momentous advance. And once again, it is the clear evidence of the Spirit's coming upon Cornelius and the manifest parallel with Pentecost which proves decisive (11.15–18).

In contrast, the breakthrough at Antioch, narrated as the immediate sequel to the Jerusalem church's acceptance of the conversion of Cornelius, is treated in a quite cursory manner. Only the bare details are provided, emphasizing the Lord Jesus as the focus of the preaching and the Lord's hand in its success (11.20–21). But the focus quickly swings to the Jerusalem church's sending of Barnabas to monitor what was happening (11.22–24). Barnabas' mission in turn becomes the occasion for the reintroduction of Saul/Paul (11.25–26). However, the sequence cannot be rounded off without some reference back to Jerusalem, achieved by using the report of the famine relief visit to Jerusalem of Barnabas and also Saul (11.27–30). In this way the circle is complete. Not only the decisive breakthrough at Caesarea is accepted by the Jerusalem church, but also the continuity between Jerusalem and the other developments at

Antioch is secured. The beginning of the outreach to the Gentiles had been accomplished without serious strain or division.

Jerusalem accepts Peter and his acceptance of Cornelius
11.1–18

It is important to appreciate that 11.1–18 is not simply a storyteller's self-indulgence in repeating a dramatic tale. The retelling serves a different purpose. It is as much about the acceptance of Peter as it is about the acceptance of Cornelius and what he represented. The second account of the events which climaxed in Cornelius being baptized in the Spirit (11.4–17) are presented as Peter's defence of his own conduct (11.3). And the charge levelled against him is not that he had baptized uncircumcised Gentiles, but that he had *eaten* with them (11.3). It was Peter's initial action of acceptance, as a Jew of a Gentile, which was the primary issue. Thus the second account of the epochal event reflects the two stages of the first account. As the first account hung on the conversion of Peter, on the breakthrough of Jewish separateness from other nations, on the abandonment of the presumption that non-Jews *per se* are unacceptable to God, so the second account hangs on the Jerusalem apostles' acceptance of Peter in his new conviction and consequent action. Once again Luke underlines just how important were not only the events at Caesarea themselves, but also the acceptance of them by the Jerusalem apostles. Thus the unity of the new movement and its continuity with its previous heritage, even through the process of transformation of previously cherished and fundamental beliefs, is maintained.

If the basic outline of the events narrated in ch. 10 was derived from early memories of the church at Caesarea, then the event must have occasioned the sort of misgivings as are expressed in 11.3. It follows also that Peter's unexpected initiative in this case would have had to gain wider acceptance within the Jerusalem church. Whether that approval was of an exception to the rule or of a principle of more universal significance would probably have been unclear in the event. So it is not surprising that the issue arises again in 15.1, 5. Luke himself concludes the retelling with a clear indication that a crucial precedent had been recognized (11.18). But no doubt there were others among the apostles and brothers who saw it only as an exception.

11.1   As usual with these initial breakthroughs, Luke makes a point of noting that the news came back to Jerusalem (cf. 8.14; 11.22). It was always his concern that they should not be seen as any kind of breakaway from Jerusalem, since the unity of the new movement and its continuity with the heritage represented by Jerusalem was fundamental to his understanding and portrayal of Christianity. Luke mentions both apostles and brothers, the one denoting the Jerusalem church's leadership, the other its membership at large. As was customary then (as indeed until recently) 'brothers' would be understood to refer to women as well as men.

11.2   Newer translations rightly avoid the older rendering 'the circumcision party', as though Luke intended to indicate a well defined faction already operative in the Jerusalem church. More accurate are REB ('those who were of Jewish birth') or NIV and NRSV ('the circumcised believers'). The clear implication of Luke's wording, however, is that their circumcised state was fundamental to their identity – hence, literally, 'those of/from circumcision'. They were some of 'the apostles and the brothers' but not necessarily all of 'the circumcision' (cf. 10.45). They should not be demonized or caricatured: Peter had shared their viewpoint and only been changed by extraordinary signs of God's will!

11.3   The point is made still more sharply by their accusatory statement, 'You went into the house of uncircumcised men and ate with them!' (NIV; cf. REB, JB) or question, 'Why did you . . .?' (NRSV). It was not that they doubted Cornelius' reception of the word. It was not that they thought Peter wrong to baptize them. The issue rather was one raised by the characteristic assumption of Jewish piety and by their loyalty to God and to his choice of Israel. These were people who understood their religious identity and duty to include separateness from Gentiles. Consequently their criticism of Peter is twofold: he had gone into the house of an uncircumcised person; and he had eaten with him. In both cases the underlying rationale is the logic of religious purity: it could not be assumed that Gentile households and meal tables (even those of God-fearers) would observe the laws of clean and unclean; they might well be tainted by idolatry. They should therefore be avoided in principle (note again Lev. 20.24–26). How could Peter now (10.14!) have ignored this basic axiom of traditional Judaism?

11.4–14   The story is told again, this time with Peter himself in central focus, and more vividly in consequence. The fact that it was an ecstatic vision ('in a trance') is repeated (10.10; 11.5). There is some stylistic variation in the description of the vision itself (cf. 11.6 with 10.12, and 11.10 with 10.16). As often in such storytelling the key words are repeated exactly (10.13, 15; 11.7, 9). There is some variation in Peter's response (11.8), but the key words are the same ('common', 'unclean', 'never'); there may be some unconscious influence from Ezek. 4.14. In 11.11 'at that very moment' heightens the dramatic coincidence of events, as at 10.17–18, and in 11.12 the Spirit's direction over and above the vision is again emphasized. The final verb of verse 12a can be translated either 'making no distinction', or 'without doubting' – an effective *double entendre*. The number of Peter's companions (six) is the sort of detail which can be held back from the first telling to help maintain interest in the second.

In some contrast, the recollection of Cornelius' vision is much briefer. Reference to 'the angel' presupposes an audience who already know the previous chapter. And 'a message by which you shall be saved' is another example of storyteller's license: Peter's ministry is introduced with reference to the result it produced. That Cornelius' household is included within the prospective salvation means that this will be first conversion and baptism of a household in Acts (see on 10.2; see also 16.15, 31–34 and 18.8). Whether it included those mentioned in 10.24 is unclear. But if so it would provide a good example of 'house' meaning extended family.

11.15   The two key points are made right away. First the abruptness and unlooked for character of the Spirit's falling upon Cornelius is exaggerated ('I had hardly begun . . .'). This was no human contrivance, but God taking affairs into his own hands. Secondly, what happened to Cornelius was just what had happened to us in the beginning (at Pentecost).

11.16   This second point is repeated for emphasis. The reference is back to 1.5, both for Peter's audience and for Luke's readers. As 1.5 directed the Baptist's (or Jesus') words forward to Pentecost, so 11.16 likewise identifies what happened at Caesarea by reference back to Pentecost. In both cases they had been baptized with the Holy Spirit. Implicit here is the theology correlated with 1.5: that this outpouring of the Spirit was in fulfilment of the promise of the father (Luke 24.49; Acts 1.4; 2.39). This was the stunning new development for the circumcised believers: that God was fulfilling what he had promised through his prophets to his people, but he was doing so also for Gentiles without their first becoming proselytes (cf. again 3.25).

As the next verse makes particularly clear, the metaphor of Spirit baptism at this point is a metaphor for God's initial acceptance, not for some second experience subsequent to conversion (cf. 11.14 – 'words by which you shall be saved'). At the same time, as I Cor. 12.13 makes still more clear, that initial acceptance was also understood to be an empowering for ministry within the body of Christ – an emphasis quite far removed from Luke's point here, even if it may be implicit in 10.46, and even more, earlier, in 1.5 and 8.

11.17   For the third time within three verses the same point is put: God has given these Gentiles the same gift; this can only mean that they are as much accepted by God as Peter's fellow Jews; how then could Peter resist (the same verb as in 8.37 and 10.47) God? Peter's self-defence is complete. Interestingly, baptism itself is not mentioned in this second telling. For that is not the point: it was the gift of the Spirit to uncircumcised men which settled the matter. It was the Spirit, not baptism which rendered circumcision irrelevant.

It is particularly striking here that Peter says: 'God gave them the same gift as he did to us when we believed on the Lord Jesus Christ.' (*a*) Peter assumes that Cornelius and his friends had made an act of faith/faith-commitment to the Jesus he had preached to them; the implication of 10.43–44 is confirmed (so also 15.7, 9). The nexus of the divine-human encounter is the openness of trust met by the openhandedness of God's gift. (*b*) But as the Gentile Pentecost presupposed a commitment of faith, so did the Jewish Pentecost. This is the most astonishing feature of Peter's words – 'as he did to us when we believed'. Pentecost in Jerusalem was as much a beginning as Pentecost in Caesarea. So much is the gift of the Spirit the clinching sign of God's acceptance of the initial commitment of faith, that Peter can even portray Pentecost as the time when he himself first believed. There could scarcely be clearer indication that for Luke the gift of the Spirit is the divine response to the act of faith commitment, the divine life outreached to meet and embrace the human turning to God (11.18).

Thus Luke re-emphasizes again that it is the Spirit which is the primary mark of divine acceptance and of discipleship. As with the Samaritan episode (8.14–17), the narrative builds to this as the climax, that which makes the decisive difference, that which identifies the new movement above all else. But even though it is Luke's emphasis, we need not doubt that the heart of Luke's account is firmly rooted in history and that it took such evident manifestations of the Spirit's presence to convince believers so deeply rooted in their Jewish traditions (cf. Gal. 2.8).

11.18   This is the climax to the double narrative of 10.1–11.18 – not only Peter's conversion (10.47–48), but the Jerusalem church's positive affirmation of what had happened. The verb used, 'fell silent', may signify continuing reservations, as in 21.14 (cf. 15.1, 5). But the proof of divine approval had been too overwhelming.

The description used, 'God gave repentance', echoes the same formula in 5.31. Only, where 5.31 celebrated repentance given to Israel, here God is glorified for giving the very same repentance to Gentiles – 'even to the Gentiles!'.

Interesting is the way Luke has scattered the various elements within the process of conversion-initiation across the double narrative – faith (10.43; 11.17), forgiveness (10.43), Spirit (10.44–47; 11.15–17), baptism (10.48), and only now repentance (11.18). It would be foolish to attempt a fine clinical analysis of their relation. The fact is that here Luke can sum up the whole process in the single phrase, 'repentance into life', from beginning to end, as it were, just as he had summed it up in 10.43 in terms of belief and forgiveness. There is no hard and fast 'order of salvation' indicated here which must be followed by all would-be evangelists. Rather the flexibility of language reflects the variety of ways, and often unexpected ways (as here) in which individuals come to God. It is the encounter between the open heart and the openhearted God which matters, however it comes about and however it may be expressed.

The breakthrough at Antioch likewise ratified
11.19–30

Luke now seems to revert to the same Hellenist source on the basis of which he had constructed chs 6–8. We may note, in particular, the way the description of Barnabas in 11.24 matches that of 6.5 and 7.55; also the repeated use of 'church' (8.1, 3; 11.22, 26; 13.1) and 'disciples' (6.1, 2, 7; 11.26, 29). Having inserted the two most momentous events for the early Christian expansion (the conversion of Saul, and the conversion of Peter and acceptance by Jerusalem), Luke returns to where he had left off, as the repetition of the wording used in introducing the Philip sequence (8.4) indicates. But unlike the attention given to these intervening episodes, the attention given here to the breakthrough at Antioch is minimal. In striking contrast, Luke narrates here no axiom-transforming visions, no perspective-transfiguring outpourings of the Spirit. At the same time, however, he ensures that the development, so pregnant with future potential (13.1–3), is still tied back into Jerusalem, first by the mission of Barnabas and then by the account of the famine relief visit from Antioch to Jerusalem.

The fact that the breakthrough at Antioch is described in the briefest of terms should not be taken to imply that Luke was unaware of its significance. On the contrary, the care he took in his account of the conversion of Cornelius (the conversion of Peter and the acceptance by the Jerusalem church) shows just how important he saw the initial acceptance of Gentiles to have been. Ironically, then, the playing down of the significance of the Antioch breakthrough attests Luke's appreciation of its importance. It was so important that it had to be securely interwoven into the history of the movement's steady expansion, and the revolutionary shift to the Gentiles validated beforehand by the critically scrutinized and divinely approved breakthrough at Caesarea.

In contrast it is probably significant that the one hint of Antioch's importance for the earliest mission which Luke retains is the fact that the believers were first called 'Christians' there (11.26). The significance is that the first quite distinctive title for members of the new movement is coined in Antioch. It is precisely Jewish believers preaching successfully to and forming one church with Gentiles which provides the model for the new and most distinctive identity of the Jesus sect.

11.19 As well as going into Judaea and Samaria (8.1), not to mention Galilee? (9.31), those scattered from Jerusalem by the wave of hostility to the Hellenist believers had also gone up the coast to Phoenicia, across the short stretch of sea to Cyprus, and not least to Antioch. Luke makes Antioch in Syria the climax of the account, since Antioch was the major city in the region, the old capital city of the Seleucid Empire, the headquarters of Rome's provincial government, and the third largest city in the Roman Empire (after Rome and Alexandria).

That they preached initially only to Jews (no definite article) makes sense. Antioch was a major centre of the Jewish diaspora. The theological point implied, however, is that the Hellenist believers represented by Stephen had not turned from their native faith, despite the criticism of the Temple indicated in the charge brought against Stephen, as expressed also in the speech attributed to him (ch. 7). They may have turned from the Temple, but they had by no means abandoned the synagogue as the natural focus for their own worship and for the exposition of their faith as Jews.

11.20   It is frustrating that Luke can be so specific – some Cypriots and Cyrenians – but only so specific. He mentions no names. The breakthrough at Antioch, even more momentous in its consequences than the breakthrough in Caesarea, is linked to no particular individual. So, often, it is the unsung heroes to whom the work of church and gospel owes its greatest human debts. The fact that the early leadership of the church at Antioch included Lucius of Cyrene and Barnabas of Cyprus (13.1) at least gives us enough confidence that the tradition is based on good first-hand information.

Luke obviously intended to recount a significant development in this verse. Precisely what he wrote, however, is confused by textual variants. Did he write 'Hellenists'? Then that would make the contrast with verse 19 something of a puzzle. Since the Hellenists in 6.1 and 9.29 were almost certainly Jews, the contrast with the 'Jews' of 11.19 (who presumably also functioned largely in Greek) would be lost. Most commentators therefore accept the other most frequent reading in the manuscripts – 'Greeks' – which does make an obvious contrast with the 'Jews' of verse 19 (cf. 14.1; 18.4; 19.10, 17; 20.21). 'Hellenists', we may assume, was inserted by early copyists attempting, consciously or unconsciously, to maintain consistency with the earlier references.

The point then, is that a decisive step was taken at Antioch, and, even in Luke's account, taken independent of Jerusalem and of any precedent like that recounted in 10.1–11.18. We may presume those preached to were God-fearers, Gentile sympathizers attracted to Judaism's ethos, its worship, festivals and moral standards. Josephus indicates that there were many such in Antioch (see on 10.2). We may also presume that at least the initial impact was made within the synagogue gatherings.

The absence of any comment over circumcision is surprising, but may have been excluded by Luke's abbreviation. Luke wanted to keep that controversy for later (ch. 15). It may also be that the more traditional Jewish believers ('those of the circumcision') were concentrated in the Jerusalem church and were unaware of the significance of developments in Antioch (Barnabas did not 'report back' for some time – 11.30). How these Gentiles who believed, turned to the Lord, and no doubt were baptized in the name of Jesus, were regarded by the Jews who did not so believe is also unknown. Possibly the anomaly of many God-fearing Gentiles attached to Antioch synagogues, while still unwilling to become proselytes, was simply expanded to embrace such Gentiles being regarded as full members of a particular Jewish sect. In such confusion and unclarity the most important step in earliest Christian history seems to have been taken.

11.21   At any rate, Luke was quite sure that the success in thus drawing in many new converts was the work of God (cf. 4.28, 30; 13.11). He uses a summary of success similar to 2.47, 4.4, 6.7 and 9.35 (see on 13.49). For the metaphor, 'the hand of the Lord', cf. I Sam. 5.6, 9 and II Sam. 3.12. Luke can vary the imagery he uses to describe divinely enabled success (cf. e.g. 2.47; 9.31; 11.23; 12.24).

11.22–24   The same procedure is followed as in 8.14–15 and 11.1–3. News of the unexpected development is brought to the church in Jerusalem. They have the wisdom to send Barnabas, himself both a Cypriot and a member of the Jerusalem church held in high standing (4.36–37), and one who shared the charismatic endowment of the Hellenist leadership (6.5; 11.24). Given the strength of the traditions regarding Barnabas (4.36–37 and 13.1) there is no reason to dispute this version of events.

Barnabas' open-hearted response ('he rejoiced') is in contrast to the negative reaction in Jerusalem (11.3). The success he saw is described not in terms of God's Spirit but in terms of 'the grace of God' – an anticipation of the Pauline use of the terms which characterizes the subsequent narratives (13.43; 14.26; 15.40; 20.24) and anticipates the reports which were later to convince the Jerusalem council (15.11; Gal. 2.9). It is in such instances that 'Spirit' and 'grace' become almost synonymous, the one denoting the power, the other the generosity of God's outreach and enabling to feeble humans. Characteristic of the new movement is that they should hold fast to the Lord (here no doubt Christ) with resolute hearts.

Another brief summary of expansion echoes that of 5.14. That two such summaries follow in such close succession (11.21, 24) is a reminder of just how compressed Luke's account of this major breakthrough is.

11.25–26 The Jerusalem-Antioch link represented by Barnabas now stretches to Tarsus to draw Saul back into play. When this happened we can no longer say. The evangelistic work during this period to which Paul briefly refers (Gal. 1.21–2.1) could have been carried out from either Tarsus (Cilicia) or Antioch (Syria). The implication of both Gal. 2.1 and of the succeeding narrative here, however, is that Saul/Paul functioned during that period as a teacher or representative or emissary of the Antioch church. The 'whole year' mentioned in verse 26, an unusual time note in the first half of Acts, covers only part of the period. The likelihood is that he spent a substantial time in Antioch, during which he emerged as one the leaders of the church there in his own right (13.1). That it was Barnabas who drew him back into the mainstream of developments is consistent with the early close association between the two attested by both Acts (chs 13–14) and Paul (Gal. 2.1–10; I Cor. 9.6).

The name 'Christians' was first used in Antioch. To be noted is the fact that it is a Latin formation – *Christiani* (like the *Herodiani* of Mark 3.6 and 12.13). That must mean that it was coined by the Roman authorities in Antioch; it next appears in situations of confrontation in 26.28, I Peter 4.16 and the second-century Roman historian Tacitus, *Annals* 15.44 (referring to those blamed for the great fire of Rome in 64). The Antiochene authorities presumably observed, through their agents, that there was a coherent and substantial grouping emerging within the penumbra of the Antioch synagogues, involving both Jews and Greeks. Evidently their sources were sufficiently good for them to recognize that this Jewish sect was characterized by its belief in Jesus the Christ and by living out lives in the name of this Christ. It was natural that they should be referred to, then, as the Christ-ones, 'Christians'. The name thus coined got about, and as so often with nicknames (e.g. 'the Moonies'), it stuck. It does not seem to have had political connotations or to carry a negative overtone; so the first Christians were not seen as a threat to the civil authorities. But neither should we assume (as many do) that the name was coined because of any perceived self-distancing from or opposition to 'Jews'. Like the 'Herodians', the 'Christians' may only have been perceived as a substantial faction within the larger Jewish constituency of Antioch.

11.27–30 The function of this final paragraph is to complete the circle drawn by Barnabas' mission from Jerusalem to Antioch, thence to Tarsus, and then back again to Antioch. In this way the expansion at Antioch remains linked firmly into the mother church at Jerusalem.

That prophetic activity was a feature of earliest Christianity, there can be no doubt (e.g. 13.1; 15.32; I Cor. 12.28–29; Eph. 4.11). That is to say, there were those who spoke out in Christian gatherings under the inspiration of the Spirit; Paul's directions on the subject give us a fair idea of the sort of thing that must often have happened in Christian assemblies (I Cor. 14). Likewise it is clear that there were wandering prophets who moved from one Christian gathering to another (attested subsequently in *Didache* 11.1–13.1). Agabus himself we meet again, still travelling, in 21.10 (when Luke himself was probably present).

Agabus' prediction of a great and universal famine is attributed by Luke to the Spirit. And though we know of a number of famines during the reign of Claudius (who ruled from 41–54), the best attestation is for a severe famine in Judaea itself round about 46–47 (Josephus, *Antiquities* 20.51–53 and 101; cf. 3.320–21). Why Luke thought of it as a universal famine is unclear (cf. the universal census of Luke 2.1). A universal famine would have been quite exceptional, and would have left the Antiochenes in as much of a plight as the Jerusalemites. Perhaps our sources are incomplete, or possibly Luke has exaggerated or simply made a slip. At any rate, the Greek implies that the prediction was of an imminent famine (not always brought out in translation); hence the otherwise puzzling immediate response of the Antioch church. But the whole episode is rather obscure.

11.29–30 Why the Antiochenes should jump to the conclusion that the Jerusalem church needed help is also unclear (unless Agabus did, after all, predict a famine in all the land, that is, of Judaea!). But we should observe that the practice of the common fund and of selling off capital (rather than simply contributing from income), as described in 2.45 and 4.34, could well have left the Jerusalem church in substantial impoverishment, little able (as Barnabas would know well) to cope with any famine. In Luke's account, Barnabas and Saul are sent by 'the disciples', that is as representatives of the Antioch church, to take the relief monies collected (literally 'service', as again in 12.25; cf. Rom. 15.31; II Cor. 8.4; 9.1, 12–13). They are sent to the

Judaean 'brothers', or more specifically to 'the elders', who now appear for the first time as a group of leaders in Jerusalem, but who play an important role thereafter (15.2–6, 22–23; 16.4). Why not 'the apostles'? Perhaps, for Luke, because 'the elders' had taken the role (administering the common fund) for which the seven had been elected (6.2–3).

All this may have bearing on the most puzzling feature of all. For Paul's own account of his relations with Jerusalem does not leave room for a visit to Jerusalem at this stage. Some argue that the visit of Gal. 2.1–10 must refer to this visit (the famine relief visit). But it is more likely that Gal. 2.1–10 is Paul's account of the Jerusalem conference described by Luke in Acts 15. It is difficult, therefore, to know what to make of this anomaly. Luke certainly uses the account to make secure and solid the links between Jerusalem and Antioch, so that when Antioch becomes the springboard for further advance it will not appear as a breakaway from the movement whose centre was still Jerusalem. But where did he get the tradition from? It can hardly be squared with Paul's insistence that he stayed away from Jerusalem for fourteen years, following his first visit. Any dissembling on Paul's part on this point would have undermined his whole argument in Gal. 1–2, an argument on which his rebuke and plea to the Galatians was based.

The simplest solution may be to see here another example of Luke's foreshortening or concertinaing events to bring into closer juxtaposition events which were more separate. Perhaps in this case he has brought forward that aspect of Paul's final visit to Jerusalem (ch. 21), since (apart from 24.17) he ignores the reason that Paul himself gave for it (to deliver the collection), just as he had omitted the issue of clean and unclean in Mark 7 and the accusation against Jesus at his trial (Mark 14.55–60) because he wanted to deal with them later (see further Introduction to 8.1–3). Alternatively, and if anything more likely, Acts 11.29–30 is a different version of the visit described more fully in ch. 15. That is, the embassy from Antioch in ch. 15 had a double function – to seek clarity on the issue of circumcision for Gentile believers and to bring famine relief to the impoverished believers in Jerusalem (cf. Gal. 2.10). It may therefore not be necessary to impugn the basic historical value of the tradition Luke uses here. Nevertheless, the difficulty of correlating Acts 11.29–30 with Gal. 1–2 in particular remains, and the scholarly discussion of this issue seems to be endless.

Update on Events in Jerusalem and Judaea
12.1–25

Luke is about to devote the whole of the second half of his book (more than half) to the missionary work of Paul, his subsequent arrest and the final journey to Rome in custody (chs 13–28). In that account the story will return to Jerusalem (chs 15; 21–23), but with Paul in the spotlight. It was important for the integrity of Luke's narrative, however, that he should round off the first half, in which the beginnings in Jerusalem and Peter's expanding mission were central, rather than let it simply peter out (as the transition at 11.19–26 would have allowed). The fact that the famine relief visit of Barnabas and Saul (11.29–30) provided the occasion for the switch back to Jerusalem will not be accidental. But Luke was hardly concerned to integrate the two, since, despite their presence in Jerusalem (12.25), neither Barnabas nor Saul feature in the intervening episodes.

The two episodes each mark the end of an epoch. In the first (12.1–17), the apostolic circle is broken (with the execution of James) and no attempt is made to close it again. 'The apostles' will feature again (in 15.2, 4, 6, 22–23 and 16.4), though always in the phrase 'the apostles and (the) elders'. The early ideal of a reconstituted Israel is being transformed into an organizational structure.

More important, this is the last time Peter himself will feature in the narrative and in Jerusalem, apart from 15.7–11, where he seems to be distinguished from 'the apostles and the elders' (15.6–7). The first episode, then, is Peter's own swansong in Jerusalem. It is not simply that Jerusalem becomes too dangerous for him, for Herod soon dies (12.20–23) and he does return for the Jerusalem council (ch. 15). The point seems to be, rather, that Peter himself is moving on. The missionary responsibility clearly indicated in Gal. 2.7–9, draws him away from Jerusalem as such. It is probably significant, then, that the first episode concludes with the enigmatic note: 'he went off to another place' (12.17). For in chs 6–12 the only other 'place' mentioned (apart from the burning bush – 7.33) has been the Temple (6.13–14; 7.7, 49). This sentence, then, makes an effective conclusion to a section (chs 6–12) which began with the Temple as an issue. The Temple ties which had previously bound the church to Jerusalem are now further loosened: Peter himself 'went off to another place'. The spectrum is opening out, with the Hellenists (and soon Paul) at one end, the Jerusalem apostles at the other, and Peter in the middle.

The second episode (12.18–23) also narrates the end of an epoch. For the death of Herod Agrippa marked the end of the Herodian line in the rule of Judaea. He was replaced by a series of inefficient procurators under whom events spiralled steadily downwards into the tragedy of the Jewish revolt twenty years later. Luke would be aware of this, though he does not indicate it in his narrative. What was important for him, rather, was that the death of Herod provided a classic example of the Gentile folly of confusing the human with the divine. This cautionary tale, therefore, can serve a double function: it can round off a section which began by denouncing human misconception of God's dwelling place (7.48–49) and continued with the encounter with Simon Magus (see Introduction to 8.4–25); and it provides the ideal preamble to the theme (human misconception of God) which will largely dominate the encounter of the gospel with pagan theism in the Pauline mission (particularly chs 14 and 17).

Peter's departure from Jerusalem
12.1–17

The account of Peter's release from jail is a classic example of supernatural intervention into human affairs. It stands in some contrast to the brief parallel account in 5.17–20 and the relatively modest account of Paul's release from prison in Philippi (16.25–28), another of the Peter/Paul matches. For in it Luke glories unreservedly in the supernatural character of the tale. Peter was guarded by four squads of soldiers (12.4); in the event he was sleeping between two soldiers, bound with chains, and with sentries at the gates (12.7); he could hardly have been more secure. And the angel which appeared was real, as was the angelic action on Peter's behalf; it was no mere vision (12.7–9). The heavy outer gate opened 'of its own accord' (12.10). The immediate sequel (12.12–17) conjures up a vivid picture and evidences the hand of a master storyteller.

There can be no doubt that Luke believed the account completely. His own unquestioning faith in the miraculous ('signs and wonders') and the tangible nature of the spiritual realm's impact on the physical is clearly manifest (cf. 2.4; 5.15; 8.17–18; 10.44–47; 19.6, 12). There would be as little point in questioning that faith in this instance as there would in questioning the miracles Bede attributed to Cuthbert. These were firm convictions held by those for whom the interface between the spiritual and the natural was much more immediate and perceptible. The convictions themselves tell us much about the higher energy spirituality of Christianity's earliest days. For such a spirituality the theological puzzle of why Peter should have been spared, and not James (had the church not prayed for James?), or why Peter should have been spared and not other Christian leaders of other ages in similar circumstances, is submerged in the wonder and rejoicing of open-hearted trust. Those who find the historical and theological problems still troubling can at least rejoice with those who so rejoice.

That being said, we should note possible indications of an underlying story – particularly the recollection that it happened at Passover (12.3–4), the fervent prayer (12.5, 12), and the hints in 12.9 and 11 that Peter dreamt it all. The comic sequel can also recall details of place and names (Mary and Rhoda). And following the execution of James it is very likely that Peter too was the object of Agrippa's malice and subsequently did have to slip away from Jerusalem at risk to his life. Beyond that, however, it would be hazardous to try to reconstruct 'what actually happened', enmeshed as any first-hand report now is in Luke's delight in the miraculous and skill as a storyteller.

12.1   The chief actor is now the king – Herod Agrippa I, son of Aristobulus and grandson of Herod the Great. He was a friend of the imperial family, having been brought up in Rome; it was customary to cement the bonds with conquered nations and to guarantee royal compliance by having their princes brought up in Rome. He had been given the tetrarchies of Philip and Lysanias (cf. Luke 3.1) and the title 'king' by Gaius Caligula in 37. In turn, Claudius, when he became Emperor, had added Judaea and Samaria, in 41, in effect restoring the kingdom of Herod the Great to its old boundaries.

Why he should have acted against the church is not said. But we do know from other sources that once established in power, Agrippa had set out to revive the fortunes of his people, lived a life of notable piety and was held in considerable respect by the Pharisees and the people. So a policy of repression against a recently formed sect held in some suspicion by the religious leaders of his people would make sense. That he could act with such arbitrary power (12.2–3) we can have no doubt. And that he did so in this case was no doubt all too clearly recalled by the Jerusalem church.

12.2   James, brother of John, was chosen, presumably to make an example. The implication, borne out by his being named with Peter and his brother John as a kind of inner circle (Mark 3.16–17; 5.37; 9.2; 14.33; Acts 1.13), is that he was recognizably one of the leaders of the new sect (contrast 8.1). That he was executed by a sword may indicate that the believers were now being regarded as a political threat. But all sorts of scenarios could lie behind these bare details. We need only envisage growing tensions between the believers and their fellow Jews (12.3). No one in higher authority would complain if the king engaged in some arbitrary despotism in regard to his own subjects.

12.3   Growing opposition is ascribed simply to 'the Jews'. This is odd, since those attacked were also Jews. Here we see again the tension which runs through Luke's portrayal of the new movement's identity. On the one hand, the new sect was in full continuity with Israel's hope and heritage. But on the other, there was a growing distinction between this movement and those with a more obvious claim to that heritage in national and religious terms. How else better to describe the latter than as 'the Jews'? Although it took the influx of Gentiles to bring that distinction to breaking point, Luke no doubt wished to maintain as much continuity as possible between the Jerusalem church and the expanding mission by indicating that the distinction and opposition from 'the Jews' was early on experienced also and even in Jerusalem itself (see on 9.22). The account at this point, however, is also consistent with the report (in the Mishnah, *Sota* 7.8) that Agrippa felt deeply the fact that he was not fully of Jewish lineage (Herod the Great having been an Idumaean); consequently, setting him over against 'the Jews' was quite appropriate.

12.4   Peter's arrest was remembered as having taken place at the time of Passover – probably a genuine memory rather than an attempt to draw out a parallel between Jesus and Peter (cf. Luke

22.1), since Luke makes little of the Passover timing of Jesus' actual arrest and execution. The prison, presumably, would have been the Antonia fortress which abutted the Temple platform.

12.5   The fervent prayer is also a typical Lukan interest (see on 1.14), but since it is part of though not integral to the amusingly told sequel (12.12), this detail too can probably be credited to memory of the occasion. It would be a natural reflex of a people for whom the curtain between heaven and earth was already very thin and for whom recourse to worship and prayer was a daily delight.

12.6–11   The story is told to bring out the wonder of it. It did not happen until the very last night possible (12.6). Soldiers, chains and doors proved no obstacle (12.6–10). There was a real angel, in the glow of heavenly illumination (see on 6.15) and in complete charge of events, who prods Peter into wakefulness and is as concerned for Peter's attire as for his deliverance.

There are possible hints that Peter's(?) own memory of the affair was exceedingly hazy, or indeed dream-like. 'He did not know that what was done by the angel was real, but thought he was seeing a vision' (12.9). He 'came to himself' once outside, the angel vanishing at the same time (12.10–11). But Luke himself had no doubts on the matter: it was real (12.9); and Peter drew the same conclusion (12.11).

The Lord in 12.7, 11 will be God who sent his angel (cf. 5.19; 7.35; 8.26; 10.3; 12.23; 27.23). That Peter should speak of 'the Jewish people' (12.11) is surprising; the perspective is more that of the story-teller for whom the movement represented by Peter had become clearly distinct from 'the people of the Jews' (see on 12.3).

12.12   The name of John Mark is given with a view to his part in the subsequent narrative (12.25; 13.13; 15.37–39), and as one well known among the churches subsequently (Col. 4.10; II Tim. 4.11; Philemon 24; I Peter 5.13). But the detail of the rather substantial house (outer gateway, maidservant, large enough for a gathering of 'many') and householder will certainly reflect knowledge of one of the earliest Jerusalem church's meeting houses and was presumably part of this tale from its first telling. From 12.17 we can deduce that none of the other apostles was present (in hiding?) and that ad hoc meetings for prayer without recognized leaders present were a natural expression of early Christian spirituality.

12.13–16   Whoever first told this story evidently had a sense of humour: Peter who has just walked through gates manned by soldiers is left standing at the door by a maid servant and has to keep knocking to gain attention (12.14, 16); and those inside dismiss the maid's story twice (12.15 – 'You are mad'; 'It is his angel') and are amazed when they at last open the door (12.16). So much for their confidence in the power of prayer! Would Luke have thus disparaged their faith by creating such details on his own initiative?

12.17   The heavenly actor is now identified as 'the Lord' – yet one more case where the 'Lord' retains an ambivalence which leaves the reader uncertain whether it is God (see on 12.7, 11) or the exalted Christ who is meant.

The James referred to will be James the brother of Jesus, who now emerges as the principal leader of the Jerusalem church (15.13; 21.18; Gal. 1.19; 2.9, 12). When he became a member of the church is never indicated (see on 1.14). In middle Eastern tradition rule usually passes to a brother rather than to a son. This presumably was a factor in James (as Jesus' brother) in effect succeeding Peter (and the brothers John and James?). But he certainly was a man of weight and influence (Gal. 2.9, 12). The New Testament letter of James is attributed to him, as well as other apocryphal writings, he is alluded to in the *Gospel of Thomas* 12, and he is a hero in the third-century *pseudo-Clementine* literature.

Peter then disappears from Jerusalem, and, apart from 15.7–11, from the story. This will have been, partly, presumably, because he had to withdraw from public activity; Herod's agents would operate throughout Judaea. But it also serves Luke's grand design. For though Peter evidently continued to engage in missionary work thereafter (Gal. 2.8; I Cor. 9.5), his departure 'to another place' in effect completes the action of the first half of Luke's second volume. If the event happened in as close proximity to Agrippa's death as the narrative (12.19–20) seems to imply, then we can date Peter's departure from Jerusalem fairly precisely to 44.

A cautionary end-note
12.18–25

With Peter no longer in the focus the story could move on at once to Saul/Paul. But Luke knew the history of Herod Agrippa's fearful end and it fitted well with one of his major purposes in the second half of his book. So he took the opportunity of this transition from the first to the second half to slip it in at this point. It also fitted neatly on to the end of his narrative of Peter's departure from Jerusalem, with verses 18–19 added in to make the link. Its starkness contrasts with the tension-relaxing humour of 12.12–17, and its message reinforces that of 12.6–11 (faithfulness delivered, pride punished), 'an angel of the Lord' being the agent of divine intervention on both occasions (12.7, 23).

The gruesome account of Herod's death is closely parallel to the account in Josephus, *Antiquities* 19.343–52. Both accounts place the event in Caesarea, on a public state occasion. Both refer to Herod's robes and agree that Herod was hailed as a god. Both report that he was then struck by a sudden illness and died in great pain. And both draw the appropriate lesson, that the words addressed to him ought to have been rebuked by him. There can be no doubt, then, that Luke was able to draw upon a widely retailed and moralistic account of the king's death. The divergences are such as we might expect to find in such multiple retellings. Luke's object, however, was not that of Josephus, and his much briefer account serves his more restricted object quite adequately.

That object is plain: Herod is a fearful warning to all who think they can somehow identify a human being with God. It was a theme already part of the initial outreach beyond Judaea to Samaria (8.9b–10) and further hinted at in the first proper encounter with a Gentile (10.25–26), and will become dominant in the subsequent narratives devoted to encounter between the new movement and paganism (chs 14 and 17). But since it is a point of confrontation occasioned by the new movement's heritage of monotheism, Israel's understanding of God, it is ironic, and no doubt purposely so in Luke's account, that the the first full denunciation of the fallacies of Gentile theism takes as its warning example the king of the Jews.

12.18–19   The account of Peter's departure is already complete, but the addition rounds off the story still more effectively, and allows the spotlight to remain on Agrippa. The balance of the story is now completely the reverse of that in 5.19–26. There the angelic rescue was retold with the greatest brevity, with the pace of the narrative then slowed for the perplexity of the Temple authorities to be savoured more fully. Here the object is to swing the spotlight back on to Agrippa, so little attention is given to the aftermath. The brusque brutality of the discipline for military inefficiency (the failed sentries 'led away', that is, almost certainly to execution), however, would be characteristic of the times.

The return to Caesarea is indicative of Agrippa's political strategy. Apart from anything else, it had been the Roman provincial capital, and the lines of communication to the other eastern Mediterranean cities and statelets would certainly be more efficient from there than from Jerusalem in its out of the way location amid the Judaean hills.

12.20   We have no other record of a delegation from Tyre and Sidon or of the anger which occasioned it, but the account is at least consistent with Josephus' reports that within his brief three-year reign Agrippa had begun to flex his political muscles, by attempting to strengthen Jerusalem's fortifications and by seeking to develop links with other client kings (*Antiquities* 19.326–7, 338–42). Here, however, Josephus reports that those attending the gathering were Agrippa's own officials and prominent citizens (*Antiquities* 19.343).

12.21   Unlike Josephus, Luke ignores the version which told how it was Herod's glorious apparel, the silver in it glittering in the sunlight, which provoked 'his flatterers' to address him as god (*Antiquities* 19.344). Luke's much briefer account, in contrast, suggests, less plausibly, that it was the oration given by Herod which provoked the crowd's acclaim.

12.22   In Luke it is 'the people' (NIV, NRSV), 'the populace' (REB) who hail Agrippa as god. The word here, however, is not the one used to denote 'the people of Israel, the Jews' (as in 12.11). It refers simply to the crowd gathered for the occasion (as in 17.5 and 19.30, 33). Thus Luke manages (12.20 and 22) to give the impression that the occasion was Gentile in character. The mistake made was a typically pagan one of failing to distinguish a man from God.

12.23   Characteristic of their different perspectives are the different accounts given of Agrippa's actual death by Josephus and Luke. Josephus refers it to 'fate' and describes how Agrippa saw an owl, 'harbinger ('angel/messenger') of woes', immediately prior to his fatal attack (*Antiquities* 19.346–7). Luke attributes Agrippa's death immediately to 'an angel of the Lord', and provides the reason in succinct terms: 'because he did not give God the glory'. God did not brook a man, least of all king of the Jews, claiming share of the glory which was God's alone. The literary and dramatic effect should not be missed, giving the chapter as a whole its unity: God struck down Agrippa in as summary fashion as Agrippa had struck down James (12.2).

The common features of the accounts of Josephus and Luke could suggest that Agrippa's death was caused by peritonitis or poison. Worms in the alimentary canal could have hastened his death. But Luke's concern is more to describe the death as an act of God: 'the angel of the Lord (= God)' was responsible, as in the much recalled deliverance of Jerusalem from the Assyrians (II Kings 19.35; Sir. 48.21; I Macc. 7.41). Even more to describe it as a warning sign, as in the case of other infamous kings, Antiochus, whose 'body swarmed with worms' (II Macc. 9.9), and Herod the Great (Josephus, *Antiquities* 17.168–70), not to mention the cases of Judas (1.18) and Ananias and Sapphira (5.5, 10). Thus perish all who set themselves against God. The prince of Tyre in particular should have served as a warning to any king, lest he say, 'I am god', when he was but a man and no god (Ezek. 28.2, 9).

12.24   is one of Luke's brief summaries (6.7; 9.31; 13.49; 19.20) which indicate the passage of time and function like a brief break between scenes in a play (see also on 13.49).

12.25   Luke did not forget that he had left Barnabas and Saul in Jerusalem (11.30). He could have recounted their return to Antioch before embarking on the Peter and Herod episodes (12.1–23), since the presence of Barnabas and Saul in Jerusalem during these episodes was irrelevent to them. But in artistic terms the return of Barnabas and Saul from Jerusalem to Antioch provides the hinge on which Luke's narrative swings from the first to the second half of his book. The reference to Mark provides a link still further forward into Part III (13.13; 15.37, 39).

PART III

The Mission from Antioch and the Jerusalem Council

13–15

As Luke turns his attention fully to Paul his task simplifies. He has done the hard work of securing the beginnings of the new movement in Jerusalem (chs 1–5) and in ensuring that the precedent(s) for mission to the Gentiles were clearly established (chs 10–11). The objective now can be relatively more straightforward: to narrate how, through the missionary work of Paul, the word spread throughout the north-eastern quadrant of the Mediterranean and was finally brought to Rome.

The initial task of this second half was to show how Saul emerged as the leading figure and became the prominent spokesman in the first mission from Antioch, and how this first major thrust into Gentile territory further afield 'opened the door of faith for the Gentiles' (14.27; alluding back to 13.8, 12, 48; 14.1, 9, 22–23), confronted the falsities of other religious practices (13.6–11; 14.11–18), and provoked Jewish opposition (13.6–8!, 50; 14.2, 4–5, 19). The pattern of Paul's missionary work is thus established, marked by his custom of going first to the synagogue (13.5, 14; 14.1), to reach both fellow Jews and Gentile proselytes and adherents (God-fearers). If the inclusion of speeches highlights important phases and aspects of Paul's mission, then we should note how Luke focusses first on mission to Jews (ch. 13) and then mission to Gentiles (ch. 14). In accord with the commission of 9.15, Paul is presented as missionary to both Jew and Gentile (see further Introduction §5(4)).

The second objective was evidently to show how the tensions which arose in the wake of this further outreach to Gentiles were resolved amicably and decisively for the future by a meeting in Jerusalem under the united agreement of the acknowledged leaders (ch. 15).

These events were presumably closer to home for Luke than those in the first half of his book. He probably had more first-hand reports to draw on, though, as before, he continued to reshape his traditions, to tell his story in his own language and to make his own points.

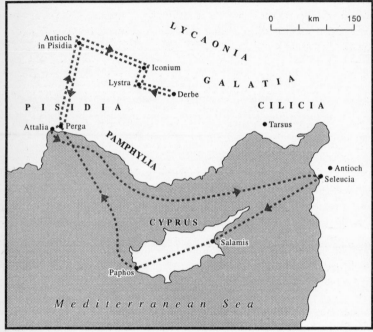

2: Paul's First Missionary Journey

The Mission from Antioch (1)
13.1–52

The route of the mission describes a semicircular sweep through the island of Cyprus and into the underbelly of modern Turkey. This first phase (ch. 13) allows Luke to advance some of his ongoing concerns. (1) Mission undertaken at the behest of and in the inspiration of the Spirit (13.2, 4, 9 and 52). (2) A further confrontation with and victory over magic (13.6–11). (3) The sympathy of Roman authorities (13.7, 12). (4) The synagogue as the obvious venue for initial mission (13.5, 14–15). (5) A sermon which emphasizes continuity of Jewish heritage and hope through Jesus (13.16–41). (6) The opposition from 'the Jews' (13.45, 50–51), with the consequent tension between Jewish obligation and Christian identity the more sharply highlighted (13.46–48). (7) The spread of the word and disciples full of joy and the Holy Spirit (13.49, 52).

Barnabas and Saul commissioned by the Spirit and the church at Antioch
13.1–3

It was important that the launch of the first planned mission into Gentile territory (at least according to Luke) be represented appropriately. Saul/Paul had already been forewarned of this mission and its consequences in 9.15–16. But now, rather like Peter in 10.17–20, the heavenly vision has to be confirmed by the Spirit's prompting (13.2, 4); and, again rather like Peter in 11.1–18, by the church's confirmation (13.3). Of these two, the most important, as always for Luke, is the clearly manifest will of the Spirit. But the latter is not unimportant. To put it another way, what follows is usually called 'the first missionary journey'. In fact, however, it is the only missionary journey as such which Saul/Paul undertakes (see

Introduction to chs 16–20 [pp.212f.]). And he does so with the full backing of the Antioch church, and as their missionary.

13.1   Here we have the first real insight into a form of organization and worship other than that in Jerusalem. There it appears to have been a mixture of ideal theology ('the twelve' representing a reconstituted Israel) and pragmatic reaction to developments (the appointment of 'the seven' in 6.1–6), with the emergence of James and 'the elders' (12.17; 11.30) foreshadowing a more settled structure – foreshadowing, we might say indeed, the emergence of a single figure leader (bishop) supported by a team of elders/deacons (cf. I Tim. 3.1–13 and 5.17–22). And the worship is represented as an evolving combination of attendance at the Temple and the teaching and fellowship, breaking of bread and prayers in members' homes (2.42, 46; 5.42; 12.12). But here we see a different pattern, a community characterized by a leadership of prophets and teachers. This certainly foreshadows the structure of the churches subsequently established by Paul (Rom. 12.6–9; I Cor. 12.28) and implies a more charismatic or more immediately Spirit-led organization and worship (as the next verse confirms; cf. I Cor. 14.26; I Thess. 5.19–22). It is not unimportant to observe that already within earliest Christianity there was such a diversity of structure and liturgy, and that the vigour of Paul's mission to the Gentiles grew immediately out of the spiritual vitality of the Antioch church.

That only 'prophets' and 'teachers' are mentioned may be significant (this is the only place in Acts where 'teachers' as such appear). The two together imply a balance necessary to the life of any church – an openness to new insight and development inspired by the Spirit (the role of the prophet), balanced by a loyalty to the tradition taught and interpreted (the role of the teacher). No other or higher figure of authority (apostle, elder) is mentioned. Since Luke elsewhere assumes the appointment of elders in the Pauline churches (14.23; 20.17) the portrayal here is hardly of his contriving and assuredly is derived from tradition.

The diversity of the leadership group is also noteworthy – Barnabas first mentioned (embodying the continuity with Jerusalem begun in 11.23–26), Simeon, probably a black man (Niger = 'black'), Lucius from Cyrene where there were strong Jewish colonies (cf. 2.10; 11.20), Manaen, a man who may have been brought up with Herod (Antipas) the tetrarch and/or had been his intimate friend (or courtier), and Saul. The Greek may imply that the first three were designated as the prophets and the last two as the teachers – if so, an interesting status for Saul/Paul in the light of his subsequent work (cf. Stephen and Philip in chs 6–8). That none of the names match those in 6.5 need not count as evidence against the view that the Antioch church was founded by Hellenists; in a rapidly developing mission new leadership would continually emerge.

13.2 The guidance from the Spirit came in the course of worship, presumably through a word of prophecy – that is, prophecy not just as a general exhortation but as a specific directive. The religious service was offered (a more accurate rendering than 'worship') to the Lord – once again the identity of 'the Lord' (God or Christ) being left unclear. That it was accompanied by fasting suggests both a sense of loss at the departure of Jesus (cf. Luke 5.34–35) and a disciplined seeking out the will of the Lord (cf. Neh. 1.4; Luke 2.37). The Spirit is represented in speaking in 'I' terms. Alternatively expressed, the 'I' of the prophecy is understood not as God or as the exalted Jesus speaking, but the Spirit – that is, of course, the Spirit as the mouth-piece of God and/or Jesus (cf. 16.7). But the corollaries of such language for Christian understanding of God were not yet being explored.

13.3 The other leaders evidently did not immediately obey the word of prophecy. There was further fasting and prayer. Already, in other words, we see a recognition that prophecy is not self-validating (it must be of God because it was spoken by a godly person under inspiration). Rather it must be tested and evaluated (as in I Thess. 5.19–22 and I Cor. 14.29–32). But once a common mind had been achieved the church acted.

As in 6.6, the laying on of hands here is in part recognition of an already manifested spiritual endowment and vocation, and in part commissioning to a particular work. In this case Barnabas and Saul are commissioned as missionaries of the church in Antioch – a longer term commissioning than in the case of Stephen (to waiting on table), but still a short term commission in the light of the subsequent developments in Paul's missionary work. This probably determines the sense in which Barnabas and Saul are subsequently designated as 'apostles', in some contrast to the apostolic status Paul insisted on for himself (see on 14.4 and 14).

Success in Cyprus
13.4–12

This first missionary outreach (Luke tells us nothing of any earlier missionary work of Saul in Arabia?, or in Syria and Cilicia, alluded to by Paul in Gal. 1.17, 21–23) is attended by immediate success: (1) the chief Roman official, proconsul no less, is first attracted, then converted by them; and (2) a further confrontation between the gospel and a corrupted form of Judaism and magic results in clear victory for the former, thus enhancing the parallel with Peter (cf. 8.18–24). Luke clearly regards these as the main outcome of this first missionary thrust. He does not stay to narrate any reaction from the Cypriot Jews or any other successes; oddly enough, the twin victories do not seem to have brought other conversions in their wake (contrast e.g. 19.17–20). Is this simply a case of Luke's reserve, that he wished to hurry on to the next episode? Or does it in fact indicate a striking lack of success in Cyprus (but cf. 15.39)? Or was he more restricted by the brevity of his sources than some allow? At any rate, it should be noted that Luke did not compose his narrative on simply repeated formulae or some standard pattern; his tradition may have been sketchy, but he almost certainly had some.

13.4   Note that the primary commissioning authority, it is repeated, is the Holy Spirit, not the Antioch church. Antioch lay some way up river (about fifteen or sixteen miles) from the mouth of the Orontes; Seleucia was its port. From there Cyprus was only about sixty miles distant. That Cyprus was the first target reflects the fact that Barnabas was still at this stage the leader of the missionary team – Cyprus being his native land (4.36) – the contacts already established between Cyprus and the church in Antioch (11.20), and possibly also the fact that many Jews had settled in Cyprus (cf. I Macc. 15.23).

13.5   The strategy is immediately established, the tense of the verb indicating a repeated practice: the word was preached in the synagogues ('of the Jews' being added, since for a non-Jewish reader 'synagogue' could mean simply 'meeting place'). It is represented as Paul's invariable strategy thereafter (13.14; 14.1; 16.13; 17.1, 10. 17; 18.4, 19; 19.8; 28.17, 23). Some have questioned whether Paul, the apostle to the Gentiles, would indeed have followed this practice. The objection is pedantic: the Gentiles most likely to be open to the gospel were those Gentiles who had already been attracted to

Judaism and attended the local synagogue as sympathizers or 'God-fearers' (see on 10.2). Paul's own recollection of how often he suffered under Jewish jurisdiction (II Cor. 11.24) confirms that his allegiance to the synagogue continued for a long time. In contrast, the fact that Luke records no opposition from the Cypriot Jews (in any of the synagogues) indicates that Jewish opposition to the gospel was not a Lukan fixation.

John, presumably the John Mark of 12.25, is described as the assistant or servant of Barnabas and Saul, a clearly secondary role. What it involved, however, is unclear.

13.6 In Paphos, at the western end of the island, they encountered one of the more interesting figures to appear in the Acts narratives – Bar-Jesus as the classic example of the wrong kind of Jewish integration into the wider religious world (a Jew who was both a magician and a false prophet).

(1) He is the only one actually described as a *magos*, 'magician', in Acts, even though the confrontation with magic is one of the main secondary themes in Acts (particularly 8.9–24 and 19.11–20). It appears from 13.7 that he was retained by the proconsul, presumably as a court astrologer. Here we should recall again that magic had a positive evaluation in the ancient world (see on 8.9); that Emperor Tiberius, for example, had retained an astrologer, Thrasyllus, among his close advisers would have been well known.

(2) He is also described as 'a Jewish false prophet': the confrontation is not only between miraculous powers (as in the case of Simon in ch. 8), but also between two prophets and the powers of inspiration presupposed (13.1–4). That there were such wandering prophets is attested elsewhere (cf. 11.27; 21.10; *Didache* 12–13; Josephus, *Antiquities* 20.169–71; Lucian, *Alexander the False Prophet*). At this point the tradition plugs particularly into the substantial history of false prophecy within Israel and the clearly perceived dangers it posed (classically illustrated in the episodes of I Kings 22 and Jer. 28; contrast Num. 23–24!); though we should also note that Bar-Jesus is not depicted as a representative Jew or as representative of Judaism. As so frequently in Old Testament and New Testament, the recognition of the reality of prophecy is qualified by the recognition of the dangers of false prophecy, and the need underlined to test and prove any claim to prophetic powers. Here the proof is unfolded in what follows: Bar-Jesus' opposition to the gospel (13.8), contrasted with Saul's Spirit-filled and devastating denunciation (13.9–11).

(3) Curious is the third feature, the name Bar-Jesus, 'son of Jesus'. In this episode the disciple of and believer in Jesus confronts and defeats the 'son of Jesus'. Endless bewilderment has been caused by Luke's note in 13.8 that the other name by which he was known, Elymas, was a translation of Bar-Jesus, since the two have nothing to do with each other. Perhaps 'Elymas' was a kind of nickname, but if so its point is too obscure for us.

13.7–8   In contrast stands Sergius Paulus, one of Luke's good Romans (cf. 10.1–2; 18.14–16; 27.43). Luke designates him correctly as proconsul, Cyprus being a senatorial province. The contrast with Bar-Jesus is deliberate and threefold: the embodiment of Roman authority, 'an intelligent man', open to and eager to hear the word of God, against the duplicity of the Jewish magician and false prophet, resisting the missionaries of the word and trying to turn the proconsul away from the faith they proclaimed.

13.9   The mention of Paul's second name, or transition from the Jewish 'Saul' to the Graeco-Roman 'Paul', comes in curiously at this point. It is unlikely that it reflects the course of the episode – Paul taking the name of his illustrious convert, as though accepting the status of Sergius Paulus' son or slave (the change is recorded before the proconsul's conversion!). But it could reflect a transition to a mission directed more overtly and immediately to Greeks and Romans, where the Graeco-Roman identity might facilitate relationships. And it does seem to reflect the emergence of Saul/Paul into the position of leadership in relation to Barnabas, reversing the earlier relationship.

The description of Paul acting under immediate inspiration of the Spirit provides a parallel with Peter (4.8) and explains the boldness with which Paul confronted Bar-Jesus and its effect.

13.10   The denunciation is comprehensive: 'full of all deceit and fraud' (the character of his magic and false prophecy), that is, a charlatan; 'son of the devil' (the real source of his false inspiration); 'enemy of all righteousness' (the proof of his chicanery); his present attempt to 'turn away' the proconsul from the faith is simply a further example of his practice in 'making crooked' the straight paths of the Lord, in contrast to the role attributed to the Baptist at the beginning of the Gospel (Luke 3.5 – same verb). Its biblical character is also clear (Prov. 10.9 and Hos. 14.10; Jer. 5.27; Sir. 1.30; 19.26).

13.11   Still in the inspiration of the Spirit, Paul passes judgment on Elymas. The language used ('the hand of the Lord', that is, God) deliberately recalls the language used in the ancient accounts of Moses' and Aaron's victory over Pharaoh and his magicians (Ex. 7.4, 5, 17; 9.3), and the judgment is as clear ('you shall be blind'; cf. Deut. 28.28–29), though somewhat tempered ('not seeing the sun for a time'; cf. 9.9!). Luke will certainly have been mindful that his hero had experienced the same judgment (9.8): the parallel both sharpens the contrast and leaves open some hope for Bar-Jesus (cf. 8.24). That such a denunciation could have its effect in a context of magic and spiritual power need not be doubted (see also Introduction to 5.1–11), though Luke, the good storyteller, does not miss the opportunity of heightening the drama.

13.12   The result is the conversion of Sergius Paulus; his household is not mentioned (in contrast to 10.2, 24; 11.14; etc.). Luke attributes the success to the impressiveness of the miracle of judgment, but describes the proconsul's astonishment as provoked by 'the teaching of the Lord'. Is this perhaps because he has described Sergius Paulus as an intelligent man, one who would not receive the missionaries' teaching lightly, or because he saw teaching and miracle as part of a single whole?

Paul's first sermon
13.13–43

13.13–16 and 42–43 provide the frame for one of the more substantial speeches in Acts, one which matches Peter's first speech (2.14–36, 38–39) both in length and character. The parallel is no doubt deliberate: Paul preaches the same message as Peter. The parallel is quite detailed: (1) first, the opening paragraph unique to each and appropriate to their respective contexts (13.16–25; 2.14–21); (2) then the core kerygma focussed on Jesus' death, instigated by his own people, and met by God's vindicatory resurrection ('but God raised him'), with his immediate disciples as witnesses (13.26–31; 2.22–24, 32); (3) next the fulfilment of prophecy, Ps. 2.7 serving in the place of Ps. 110.1, but Ps. 16.10 cited by both and invoking the same argument (13.32–37; 2.25–31, 33–36); (4) and finally the concluding appeal for belief and offer of forgiveness (13.38–41; 2.38–39).

Even more than in ch. 2, the emphasis is on continuity with Israel's past revelation: from the exodus, through the first prophet (Samuel) and first king (Saul), and particularly through David, to David's greater successor (13.17–23); Jesus as the fulfilment of promise through John the Baptist and earlier through David (13.23–27, 32–37); the message and the fulfilment are for all Israel (13:23–24). More striking, however, is the way the speech is directed not only to Israel, the direct heirs of Abraham, but also to those who feared God (13.16, 26), God-fearers = sympathetic Gentiles (see on 10.2), (and?) 'devout proselytes' (13.43). What is striking is that they are included equally in this continuity – 'our fathers' (13.17), 'what God promised to the fathers he has fulfilled to us their children' (13.33), 'brothers' (13.26, 38), 'to us', 'us their children' (13.26, 33). The speech itself expresses an openness which is only hinted at in Peter's earlier speeches (2.39; 3.25; but also 10.34–35).

Here, as usual, Luke's intention was not to present the sermon Paul actually delivered on the occasion, but to provide in cameo form (a perfectly rounded miniature which would take a little over three minutes to deliver) an indication of what Paul would have said on the occasion. The double emphases just noted (continuity with Israel and openness to Gentiles) are certainly Pauline in character. On the other hand, the concluding peroration is much less like Paul: in his letters Paul hardly speaks of 'forgiveness', and 13.39 reads oddly as a report of Paul's view of the law. Yet the tradition, as in ch. 2, is old, and includes what sounds like an early christological use of Ps. 2.7, where God's begetting of Jesus as his son is linked to the resurrection (13.32–33). So Luke exercises some freedom on the matter, as we might expect, either in using preformed material, Pauline but not Paul's as such, or in the degree of casualness for the terms in which he represents Paul speaking. All this would be quite acceptable for the times.

13.13–14 Why John Mark left Paul and Barnabas is not stated. Possibly because the enterprise was becoming more ambitious than he had bargained for. Possibly he fell out with Paul, somewhat resentful at the way Paul was taking over the leading role from the more mild-mannered Barnabas. At any rate, in consequence Paul regarded him as a quitter or deserter (15.38). Luke also gives no indication of why the company went to Perga in the first place (we know of no Jewish colony there), and, more surprising, pressed on into the highland interior, not, it would seem, following any well-established road and involving a demanding one hundred or so mile trek. The best guess we can hazard is that Paul had some serious ailment, affecting particularly his eyes (Gal. 4.13–15), which made it necessary for him to abandon the heat of the coastal plain for the cooler air of the high country.

13.14–16 We know so little about how the synagogue gatherings functioned at this time (but see Philo, *Special Laws* 2.62), so that a passage like this (as Luke 4.16ff.) is particularly valuable. Here we learn of readings from both law and prophets and multiple leadership (the Jewish comunity in Pisidian Antioch was probably substantial) who invite visitors (presumably of somewhat distinguished appearance) to offer 'a word of exhortation' (cf. Rom. 12.8; Heb. 13.22). It is Paul who responds, presumably with Barnabas' acquiescence. Luke notes what he may have known or understood to have been a characteristic mannerism of Paul – 'motioning with his hand' (also 21.40; but also 19.33).

13.16–25 Somewhat as with the speech of Stephen in ch. 7, we are given at first what appears to be a recital of Israel's history. But as with Stephen's speech, so here there are particular notes of emphasis which give the recital its point. We have already noted that the address includes 'you that fear God' (13.16). The initial description (13.17–19) is studded with scriptural language, particularly from Deuteronomy, recalling Israel's election as a people and deliverance from Egypt (Deut. 1.31; 4.34, 37; 5.15; 9.26, 29; 10.15). Distinctive, however, is the thought of Israel made great during their time in Egypt, whereas Deuteronomy recalled them more to their experience of slavery. This, together with the reference to the seven Canaanite nations destroyed before Israel (Deut. 7.1), makes for a double note of exaltation which may well reflect the need felt within diaspora Jewish communities to remind the larger majorities among whom they had settled that their nation had a high pedigree and an impressive history.

The second phase is designed to reach David as fast as possible (13.20–22). It is a pleasant speculation that king Saul is mentioned (for the only time in the New Testament) because it was his namesake speaking, also of the tribe of Benjamin (Phil. 3.5) and so probably named after his eminent, though tragic forbear. God set Saul aside and 'raised up' (same verb as in 13.30, 37) David (a word play similar to that in 3.26). In contrast to Saul, David found favour

with God (echoing Ps. 89.20, I Sam. 13.14 and Isa. 44.28). This enables
the direct leap to Jesus (13.23), in terms already used earlier – of
David's seed (2.30), a Saviour (5.31), in fulfilment of promise (e.g.
3.22–25). There is an allusion to II Sam. 7.12–14 (see on 2.29–32 and
7.46–47).

The flow of thought is ready for an immediate shift to verses
32–33, but at this point a sequence of more regular elements of
earliest preaching is inserted. (1) The Baptist as the beginning of the
good news (13.24–25; cf. 1.5, 22; 10.37). Intriguingly the words
attributed to the Baptist are a variation of the tradition used in Luke
3.16, but also mixed with a tradition found only in John 1.20–21.

13.26–31   (2) 13.26 echoes Ps. 107.20, as had 10.36, but using again
Luke's key term 'salvation' (as in 4.12). (3) The rejection of Jesus by
the Jewish leaders, acting in ignorance, but fulfilling the prophets in
asking Pilate to have him executed (13.27–29; see on 2.23). As in 5.30
and 10.39, the cross is again 'the tree'. (4) 'But God raised him from
the dead' (13.30; see on 2.24). (5) Appearances to the first disciples to
serve as witnesses to the people (13.31; see on 1.8). In this last
instance it is notable that Paul is presented as citing the witness of
the other disciples, not the resurrection appearance to himself on the
road to Damascus – in some contrast to his own practice in his letters
(I Cor. 9.1; 15.8; Gal. 1.12, 16), but reflecting the fact that in Acts Paul
does not qualify as one of the primary witnesses (1.21–22); see again
on 1.21–22 and 14.4.

13.32–37   The main proof from prophecy section (Jesus' resurrection as fulfilment of God's promise to the fathers) is constructed
round three quotations, two Psalms, naturally attributed to David,
and a reference to David in Isaiah. (1) Ps. 2.7 – 'You are my son;
today I have begotten you' (13.33). The same passage is cited with
reference to the resurrection in Heb. 1.5 and 5.5, and we find a
similar emphasis in Rom. 1.4, a passage usually assumed to be a
quotation of an early confessional formula. The emphasis is sometimes described as 'adoptionist' (God adopted Jesus as his Son when
he raised him). But the term is anachronistic (it is appropriate only
where the affirmation is also a denial that Jesus was already God's
Son). The language reflects simply the enthusiastic re-evaluation of
Jesus' status as an immediate consequence of the stunning event of
his resurrection (see also on 2.36). It does not imply that theological
reflection had gone any further than that. So the language is very

early. Later on Ps. 2.7 is echoed in the accounts of Jesus' reception of the Spirit at Jordan (Luke 3.22). And still later it becomes an article of the creed that the Son's sonship was from all eternity.

(2) In this speech Isa. 55.3 is drawn in to supplement the second Psalm citation (3) in 13.34, but in terms already presupposing Ps. 16.10. The link is made possible by the LXX translation (Paul would have preached in Greek) which, unlike the Hebrew, speaks of giving 'David's holy things', while Ps. 16.10 promises not to 'give your holy one to see destruction'. The logic, however, seems rather strained: Isa. 55.3 shows that David's words were for the benefit of others ('I will give you')?

(3) The citation of Ps. 16.10 and deduction drawn from it in 13.35–37 is simply a variation on the argument already used by Peter in 2.27–31. It is not clear what the reference to Isa. 55.3 added to the line of argument.

13.38–39 The conclusion is more typical of the Acts sermons (2.38; 5.31; 10.43) than of Paul's own writing: 'forgiveness' as a concept appears only in the later Paulines, Col. 1.14 and Eph. 1.7, though we should note also the quotation he uses in Rom. 4.7. Forgiveness is promised 'through this person' – a variant on 'in/through his name' (2.38; 10.43). Even more intriguing is the awkwardly formulated, 'from everything of which you were not able to be set free by the law of Moses, by this man every one who believes is set free' (literal translation). The sentence certainly picks up characteristic Pauline language – 'law of Moses', 'justify' (the more usual meaning of the verb here translated 'set free'), 'every one who believes'. But in his letters Paul never says anything quite like this; the closest would be Rom. 6.7 (using the verb in the same unusual way; cf. Sir. 26.29) and 8.2–3 (saying something the same in different language). Paul would more typically have spoken of deliverance from the power of sin (the law providing only a means of covering sin and its effects through the laws of sacrifice), or indeed of freedom from the law itself. It is difficult to avoid the impression that a Pauline sentiment has been only half grasped and used here, and in consequence it is less than clear what the 'everything' is from which the law does not provide freedom (see also on 15.10).

13.40–41 The sermon could have finished at that point, but, unusually, a note of warning against disregard for the message is appended in a quotation from Hab. 1.5. This quotation of a passage with a quite different context, and not presented as a foretelling prophecy, is more typical of Paul (cf. the scriptures used in Rom. 9–11). The logic is typological: that a word of warning in an earlier context of God's prophetic concern for his people can apply to a similar situation later on. Habakkuk proved itself amenable to this sort of updating: both the Qumran community and the first Christians saw Habakkuk as foreshadowing the crises and opportunities of their own times (Qumran Habakkuk commentary – 1QpHab; use of Hab. 2.4 in Rom. 1.17, Gal. 3.11 and Heb. 10.38).

13.42–43   Given that the more typical Jewish response to Paul's preaching elsewhere in Acts is hostile (9.22–23, 29; 13.45, 50; 14.19; 17.5, 13; 18.6 etc.) the response here is strikingly positive. Since Luke so often speaks of 'the Jews' as uniformly hostile to Paul, we should also note that according to Luke 'many of the Jews followed Paul and Barnabas', were as obviously attracted to their message as the many 'devout proselytes' (less closely attached God-fearing Gentiles are not mentioned), and that Paul and Barnabas 'sought to persuade them to remain in the grace of God'. The last clause implies either they had believed Paul's message (but why were they then not baptized?) or that Paul was content with their openness to the message, as itself already a sign of their being in the grace of God (cf. 18.19–21; 28.30–31).

The first rejection by the Jews
13.44–52

Luke now unfolds in archetypal terms the result of Paul's preaching the gospel to Jews and Gentiles: 'the Jews' reject it, Paul turns to the Gentiles in consequence, and the Gentiles receive it (13.45–48). The point, however, is not that Paul then turns his back on his fellow Jews and goes exclusively to the Gentiles. That is a too simplistic reading of Luke's narrative. On the contrary, Paul continues the same practice thereafter (first preaching in the synagogue in a new town or city; see on 13.5). The point is rather that the scenario repeats (18.6; 28.25–28). This is the character of the message and the lot of the preacher: the message is first and foremost for the people of Israel, and it must always be offered first to the Jews, even if only some of them accept it and the rest reject it. On this point Luke has captured a genuinely Pauline concern: 'to the Jew first and also to the Greek' (Rom. 1.16; 9.24; 10.12). The alternative, and unjustified conclusion, that God has abandoned his people because of their unbelief, is the first step towards Christian antisemitism (see further Introduction to 28.23–31).

A subordinate theme is that it is the hostility and persecution of 'the Jews' which forces the Pauline mission to keep moving into new territory (13.50–51; cf. 8.4; 11.19; 14.19–20; 17.10, 13–14) – God overruling human animosity to achieve his richer purpose (see on 2.23).

13.44–45 How much of the account is the result of Luke using a stereotype portrayal of Jewish rejection is unclear. What should not be ignored however, is the implication that the Jewish community in Antioch was substantial and influential. What had happened in the meeting place of the Jews quickly got about the whole city and attracted crowds ('almost the whole city' is a pardonable storyteller's exaggeration) presumably to the same meeting place. We also learn subsequently (13.50) that the godfearing women (adherents to the synagogue) were of high standing in the community, and that the local Jews were able to incite also the leading citizens. All this hardly suggests a small minority group whose traditions and practices were despised or ignored by the local populace. On the contrary, it fits with what we know of many Jewish ethnic minority groups within the cities of Asia Minor: that they were substantial in number and influential within local politics.

Against this background Luke's narrative makes more sense: it was not so much Paul's message which caused the offence to the bulk of Antioch's Jews as its surprising appeal to Antioch's wider citizenry. The fear would be of an untried and untested new sect upsetting and undermining the good standing and good relations which the Jewish community had established for itself within the city (minorities were always anxious about their legal and social standing since local and international politics were so unpredictable). Probably a more accurate rendering of Luke's phrase 'the Jews' would therefore be 'the Jewish community'.

We may also deduce that there would be a theological dimension in the local Jewish hostility. For Jewish self-understanding it was axiomatic that they were the people specially chosen by God (the speech had echoed such axioms – 13.17). But that also meant a degree of distinctiveness and separateness from other nations. The speech of Paul, however, indicates that proselytes and Godfearers could also regard themselves as heirs of the promises to Israel (see Introduction to 13.13–43). Such a note could well have provoked that 'zeal' to maintain Israel's set-apartness, which had motivated Paul himself in his career as a persecutor (22.3; see on 21.20), and to contradict Paul's arguments on the point with personal abuse directed against him. Luke's portrayal, in other words, is not at all farfetched.

13.46–47   The denunciation appears in the context of a bitter dispute over Israel's identity and over the relation of Gentiles to and within that identity. It is a defining moment in the emergence of Christian self-consciousness. For Luke, it was, and continued to be necessary for the word of God to be preached first to Israel. But denial and rejection of that word (that God's gracious purpose embraces equally all who believe) was a rejection and denial of the same grace that had first chosen Israel. Moreover, Israel itself had been given the task of being and bringing light and salvation to the Gentiles (Isa. 49.6). So all Paul and Barnabas were doing was fulfilling Israel's mission – 'to the end of the earth' (it is the same phrase in 1.8 and 13.47). In rejecting Paul and Barnabas, the Jewish community were also rejecting their own God-given commission as the servant of Yahweh. The fundamental theological issue is thus posed by Luke, and remains at the heart of Jewish and Christian mutual relations: whether Christianity in taking the word of God focussed in Jesus to the Gentiles was actually remaining more true to Israel's identity and mission than the Jewish community which so largely rejected that word (see also on 28.28).

13.48   In contrast 'the Gentiles' responded positively. Luke of course uses the terms to indicate a broad contrast between the two ethnically distinguishable groups. No more did all 'the Gentiles' believe than did all 'the Jews' reject. It is crowd psychology which is in view here. Luke himself makes a point of noting that the Gentiles who actually took the step of faith were (much) fewer in number – persuaded more by God than the sentiments of a volatile crowd. More to the point, he takes care to describe them as 'destined for eternal life', that is, for the eternal life which the Jewish community appeared to be rejecting (13.46). This is not simply a piece of arbitrary predestinarianism: it has been Luke's concern from the beginning to underline that everything had taken place in accord with the plan of God (see on 2.23 and 4.12); and here it is equally important to note that the Gentiles who believed were chosen by God every bit as much as Israel had been in the first place (13.17).

13.49   is one of Luke's summaries of gospel success (2.47; 4.4, 32–37; 5.14; 6.7; 9.31, 35; 11.21, 24; 12.24; 16.5; 19.20), but here presumably it covers a period which stretched well beyond the next episode (why Luke did not leave it until 13.52 is unclear). This could be when 'the churches of Galatia' (Gal. 1.2) were first established, if they included more than Iconium and Lystra. It implies a missionary enterprise stimulated by Paul's initiative but not solely dependent on his own immediate mission team.

13.50–51   From the time of Socrates onwards, to go no further back in time, teachers and preachers would have provoked a variety of reactions in the cities where they spoke; and when fundamental beliefs of influential members of the community, or their influence within the city was put in question by such teaching and preaching, the reaction could be violent. Who knows what vested interests might have been threatened by the kind of unrest Paul and Barnabas seemed likely to provoke? See further above (Introduction to the section and on 13.44–45). The action of the departing missionaries recalls the words of Matt. 10.14/Luke 10.11, a disowning of part in and responsibility for their fellow Jews who had rejected them.

13.52   The leading troublemakers having been removed, 'the disciples' were apparently left in peace. The tense used indicates a continuing experience of being 'filled with joy and the Holy Spirit' – the first time, oddly enough, that Luke has used the term in regard to Gentiles. The implication of the preceding verses is that, despite the initial responsiveness (13.43), the Jewish community, including their influential sympathizers, closed ranks against Paul's message, and that the resulting Christian group in Antioch (14.21–22) was composed solely of Gentiles (cf. Gal. 4.8).

The Mission from Antioch (2)
14.1–28

The pattern set in Pisidian Antioch is repeated in the south Galatian towns of Iconium and Lystra: initially the gospel message meets with enthusiastic response; but then hostility, particularly Jewish in inspiration, forces the missionaries to move on.

The absence of detail (vague time notes, and no names recorded of hosts or converts who Luke could have consulted for the beginnings of the churches in these places) again raises questions as to how good Luke's sources were for this phase of Paul's mission, and whether he has not here extrapolated a pattern which tradition told him had recurred elsewhere (the language is almost wholly Luke's). The questions are sharpened by two further factors. First, the letter to the Galatians (more likely than not to have been written to churches in this area) was provoked by other Jewish Christian missionaries from outside rather than by local opposition from Jewish synagogues (though cf. Gal. 4.29; 6.12). Secondly, the report that Paul and Barnabas appointed elders in these churches (14.23) is not borne out by anything we learn of the ordering of the Pauline churches in his early and principal letters.

On the other hand, the pattern is not simply repeated in a wooden way; for example, nothing is said of any opposition at the final port of call (Derbe). The repeated reference to Paul and Barnabas as 'apostles' (14.4, 14), where the sense must be 'missionaries sent out from Antioch', reflects an Antioch perspective behind the account more than Luke's own. And Timothy, who reportedly came from these churches (16.1–2), could have been a source of basic information. So we have once again the not unfamiliar mix of good tradition, storyteller's art and theological perspective.

The principal theological feature appears in the story which forms the heart of the chapter (14.8–18) – Paul's first encounter with pagan ideas about God. The dangers of confusing divine and human, God with human creation, have been a strong concern in Luke's history (particularly 8.10 and sequel; and 12.20–23). And in Cyprus Paul had already confronted the worst kind of religious syncretism (a Jewish false-prophet and magician). In Lystra, however, we read of a head-on clash with the simple worshippers of the traditional gods and with the belief that these gods could appear as men on earth. Luke takes the opportunity to show that the word preached to Gentiles was also a word about God: Jewish monotheism is a presupposition of the Christian gospel; God as not only the initiator and mover behind the mission, but also the content of its gospel. Rightly to receive the message about Jesus depends on a right understanding of God and of God's relation to creation and to humankind.

The word received and rejected in Iconium
14.1–7

The pattern of preaching in synagogue, met by favourable response from both Jews and Greeks, followed by Jewish opposition stirring up Gentile opposition is repeated. It is important to note that Jews and non-Jews are recorded as both accepting the message and as rejecting it. The fact that Luke does not speak uniformly of 'the Jews' but varies the reference (14.1 – 'a great crowd of Jews and Greeks'; 14.2– 'the unbelieving Jews'; 14.5 – 'both Gentiles and Jews') again warns against any inference that Luke was intent on denigrating the Jewish community as a whole.

14.1 For the synagogue as providing Paul's most natural platform see 9.20 and on 13.5. Luke presupposes that many Greeks, proselytes and God-fearers, attended the local synagogue – a perhaps exaggerated claim, but borne out by evidence elsewhere (see on 10.2). The tense of the verb, 'believed', would normally indicate conversion, and the converts are presumably referred to as 'brothers' in 14.2, though clear indication that a church was established is left until 14.22–23.

14.2 Literally 'the disobedient Jews', that is, the Jews who refused to believe; perhaps the Greek would allow the sense 'unpersuaded' Jews, but the note of culpable refusal accords with the following note of malice. Since few passions run so deep as religious passions, one could well envisage the opposition provoked by what must have appeared to many Jews as an aberrant form of their religion. Gentiles attracted to the synagogue would likely be influenced by the reaction of local Jewish leaders. Luke's portrayal has little lack in plausibility though his narrative is uncomfortably compressed.

14.3   The transition is awkward. Presumably we are to take it that the opposition did not gell immediately. But Luke's description of Paul's and Barnabas' continued ministry is more stereotyped: bold preaching (4.13, 29, 31; 9.27–28; 13.46); the Lord bearing witness to the word of his grace (13.22; 15.8; 11.23; 20.32); signs and wonders (see on 2.22).

14.4   Nothing is said of a build up of tension (contrast e.g. 6.8–14), and, despite 14.1, the implication is that the Jewish community as a whole, or in its representative leadership, was opposed to Paul and Barnabas. It is not impossible that such events in a town the size of Iconium could set the populace as a whole by the ears, though the hand of the storyteller is much in evidence.

The reference to Paul and Barnabas as 'the apostles' (also in 14.14) hardly makes sense within Acts as a whole, given the qualifications for apostleship laid down in 1.22 (see on 1.21–22), and Luke's use of the term elsewhere invariably to refer to the twelve in Jerusalem (within whose number Barnabas had not previously been included). The only obvious solution is that Luke's account here (and 14.14) reflects the story as told from an Antiochene perspective, Paul and Barnabas having been commissioned and sent forth as missionaries (= 'apostles') of that church (13.3; cf. II Cor. 8.23 and Phil. 2.25).

14.5   That a section of the populace could be provoked to strong action on an issue of religious concern is certainly possible, as we know all too well today. To be noted is the fact that Luke presents the action as a united front: the Jewish community was sufficiently well integrated into the city for their cause to become a common cause; stoning is a typically Jewish punishment (see on 7.58), but would also be a natural impulse for a crowd near to riot. The same tradition obviously lies behind II Tim. 3.11.

14.6–7   The town of Lystra was not far distant, though the further trip to Derbe would have been more demanding, and from there they could have returned to Syrian Antioch, via Tarsus, even though it would have meant trekking across the Taurus mountains (cf.

15.41–16.1). Quite what Luke envisaged by adding 'and to the surrounding countryside' is a puzzle, since he always depicts Paul's mission as centred in cities and the area was not well settled; the note was possibly part of the tradition he received, denoting the outskirts or vicinity of the cities mentioned.

The encounter with traditional religion in Lystra
14.8–18

Just as the healing of a cripple by Peter and John provided the occasion for a definitive encounter between the representatives of the new movement within its Jewish context and the Jewish authorities (chs 3–4), so here the healing of a cripple by Paul and Barnabas provides the occasion for a definitive encounter between the missionaries to the Gentiles and the representatives of the old gods of classical Greece. Luke's skill as a storyteller is clearly in evidence, in the vividness of the visual detail in the scene he evokes for the reader. The irony is striking: Jewish missionaries, rejected by their own community in Iconium, are now hailed as the gods of old Greece. But most important of all is that the episode gave Luke the opportunity to stress that the message of Paul and Barnabas is a message about the one God, Creator of all. He makes no attempt to portray Paul as going on to preach about Jesus: in this first encounter with Gentile paganism the first priority is the Jewish Christian proclamation of God.

As to Luke's sources, all we can say is that, despite a sophisticated modern Western scepticism to the contrary, there is nothing basically implausible in the rather farcical sequence of events and swings of mood recorded. Paul himself recalled one episode in his mission where things went so badly wrong that he was stoned (II Cor. 11.25), Timothy is known in Christian tradition as a native of Lystra (Acts 16.1), and II Tim. 3.11 retains a tradition of persecution at Lystra following a similar hostile response at Antioch and Iconium.

14.8–10   Luke makes no attempt to portray Paul and Barnabas as going to the synagogue: 16.1 may imply that there was some sort of Jewish community there; but 14.19 suggests otherwise. Instead Luke goes straight into one of his best stories, allowing the fact of Paul's preaching, presumably in the central market area, to come out by allusion (14.9). The parallel with the equivalent episode in Peter's ministry is enhanced by reference to the man being 'lame from his mother's womb', unable to walk, by talk of the 'intense look' of Paul, and by the description of the man 'leaping up and walking' (3.2, 4, 8); also by reference to the man's 'faith to be saved (= healed)' (3.16). By way of some contrast, Luke notes that the Lystran cripple listened to Paul speaking (cf. 3.5) and that Paul achieved the cure by voice only (speaking across a listening crowd?).

14.11–13   There is probably an allusion to the famous tale of Zeus and Hermes entertained unwittingly by the old couple Philemon and Baucis, which may have been linked with this region (Ovid, *Metamorphoses* 8.620–724). The implication is of an upcountry townspeople (they spoke in local dialect) whose beliefs in the traditional gods of Olympus were simple and heartfelt (the response is of ready welcome and reverence). The key sentence, which provides the principal reason for telling the story and which triggers off Luke's theological response, is 'The gods become like human beings have come down to us'. The episode confirms that Paul was the chief speaker (Hermes was popularly thought of as the messenger of the gods); but there may also be an implication that Barnabas had a more distinguished or venerable appearance (Zeus as the high god). The Greek suggests that the temple was called the temple of 'Zeus outside the city', like the abbey of 'St Paul outside the walls' in Rome.

14.14   Barnabas and Paul are again called 'the apostles' (the most likely text; see on 14.4); does the naming of Barnabas first also imply the perspective of an Antioch church for whom Barnabas was still the leader of the missionary team (cf. 15.12, 25)? The tearing of clothes is a characteristic Jewish expression of grief (e.g. Gen. 37.29, 34; Josh. 7.6; II Sam. 1.11; Judith 14.16) and of indignation at abuse of God (cf. Matt. 26.65). How effective was their communication (in Greek) with a people who were accustomed to speak in the local dialect (14.11)?

14.15–17   The storyteller was conscious of the constraints imposed by the scene he has decribed. So no lengthy speech follows, and the point is made at once. The good news is not of human beings with godlike abilities (cf. 10.26), but of the living God, Creator of everything. The thoroughly Jewish character of the message is clear: they should turn from such worthless vanity, typically expressed in

Gentile idolatry (cf. Jer. 2.5; Wisd. 13); the only god worthy of worship is 'the living God who made heaven and earth and the sea and everything that is in them' (citing a classic expression of Jewish monotheism – Ex. 20.11, Neh. 9.6 and Ps. 146.6). That the God of Israel was also God of all the nations (14.16; Deut. 32.8; Ps. 145.9; Wisd. 11.22–24; *I Enoch* 84.2) is a reminder that Jewish monotheism gives its fundamental creed a universal character. The description of God's providential care (14.17) also echoes typically (though not exclusively) Jewish reflection on God's goodness in the fruitfulness of creation (Lev. 26.4; Ps. 147.9; Jer. 5.24).

More striking is that this axiom of Jewish faith is now presented as part of the good news (14.15). There had been no shortage of Jewish apologists for their unique monotheism, and diatribes against Gentile idolatry were standard fare within Jewish diaspora communities (Wisd. 11ff.; Epistle of Jeremiah; *Sibylline Oracles* 3). But Judaism was not an evangelistic religion, and the call to repudiate such (false) conceptions of God was not typically part of Israel's apologia. It was precisely the evangelistic compulsion within earliest Christianity which made it necessary to turn its presupposition of Jewish monotheism into an active part of its proclamation. The gospel is first about God, and about God and creation; the message about Jesus follows from that. The argument is a variation on Paul's indictment in Rom. 1.20–23, and the need for Gentiles to make the same initial turn from a false understanding of God to the living God is reflected in I Thess. 1.9.

14.18 Luke has made no attempt to round off the speech, not even with its implied call to repentance and conversion spelled out. Nor does he say whether this resort to preaching the gospel by means of an appeal to what is usually called natural theology (the evidence of God in nature) was successful (cf. 17.22–34). He preserves the reality of the scene and the focus on the message about God.

The return to Antioch
14.19–28

Luke's main objectives in narrating the mission from Antioch are now more or less complete, concentrated as they were on the confrontation with syncretistic magic, Jewish unbelief and the old

191

religions, expressed particularly in the two speeches attributed to Paul, and setting the pattern of mixed response and rejection from both Jews and Gentiles. The return journey is narrated in the briefest of terms, Luke pausing only to fill in a few details and to confirm the character and success of the mission. The fact that Luke passes over thus so briefly long days of arduous travel simply reminds us that Luke as a good storyteller knew how to retain his audience's attention.

14.19–20   Iconium was not far from Lystra (some six hours by foot), but Pisidian Antioch was more than a hundred miles distant, though there was evidently regular communication between them. That some Jews (not 'the Jews') should be so antagonistic to a message which seemed to call in question the uniqueness of Israel's election that they travelled such distances to oppose Paul would be surprising but not incredible (we may recall the vehemence of Paul's own previous hostility to the new movement). No local Jews are mentioned, and the pursuing pack succeeded only in catching up with Paul (where was Barnabas?). This is presumably the occasion to which Paul himself refers in II Cor. 11.25, so Luke knew this tradition (as, again, also II Tim. 3.11). The severity of a typical stoning is reflected in the assumption that the prostrate body was dead. In contrast, Luke's report that Paul was able immediately to return to the city (where had 'the disciples' come from?) and on the very next day to undertake the demanding journey to Derbe (some sixty miles away) inevitably causes some eyebrow raising. Luke has evidently been cutting some corners and for some reason (despite 14.22!) has chosen not to make much at all of the severity of Paul's sufferings (but see Introduction to chs 21–28).

14.21–22   The success in Derbe (again no synagogue is mentioned) is described uniquely in Luke-Acts with the verb 'make disciples' (a word probably used in the tradition available to Luke). Instead of pressing on eastwards to more familiar territory, Paul and Barnabas then turn round to retrace their steps. Paul's letters confirm that he was a church founder who was equally anxious to ensure the upbuilding and maturity of his churches; so a follow-up visit would likely have been one of his priorities (cf. 15.36). That Paul and Barnabas were able to re-enter cities from which they had been ejected need mean only that the opposition had been a crowd phenomenon which subsided as quickly as it had boiled over.

The description of the missionaries' consolidation of their converts is given in terms regularly used by Luke and Paul: strengthening (15.32, 41; 16.5; 18.23; Rom. 1.11; I Thess. 3.2, 13) and encouraging/exhorting (15.32; 16.40; 20.1–2; Rom. 12.1; 15.30; etc.). Less characteristic of Luke and more typical of Paul is the concern that his converts should 'remain in the faith', or better, 'remain in their faith' (cf. Acts 11.23; 13.43; I Cor. 15.1–2; Gal. 1.6), and that suffering was an unavoidable gateway into the inheritance of God's kingdom (cf. Rom. 8.17; II Thess. 1.5). In both cases the latter insight can be the basis either of a kind of Christian fatalism or of a positive theology of suffering. For the whole verse cf. particularly I Thess. 3.2–4. For Luke's references to 'the kingdom of God' see on 1.3; and for 'entering' the kingdom see Luke 18.24–25 and 23.42.

14.23   The reference to elders being appointed creates a historical anomaly. There is no indication from 13.1–3 that elders were a feature of the sending church (Antioch). And in none of the undisputed Pauline letters are elders mentioned, despite the fact that in several cases there were situations or crises in which elders, had there been any, would have been appealed to or called to account. In contrast, elders first appear in the Pauline corpus in the Pastoral Epistles (I Tim. 5 and Titus 1.5), generally regarded as written after Paul's death by someone from Paul's circle, and with the same thought of their being appointed by Paul or at his behest. It looks, then, as though Luke, both here and in 20.17, has either assumed the presence from the first of a practice and church structure which had become more common in his own day (the procedures of 13.3 were more 'charismatic'), or he has made more formal the sort of commendation of mature individuals such as we find in I Thess. 5.12–13 and I Cor. 16.15–18. Either way it tells us something of the character and objectives of Luke as a historian – a readiness to read the traditions he had from the founding period in a way which brought out the harmony of the early churches and the settled pattern of their organization from the first (cf. 11.30; James 5.14).

14.24–26   The return journey mentions preaching in Perga (of which nothing had been said in 13.13–14) and omits the Cyprus stage of the missionary journey. The reminder that Syrian Antioch was the place where 'they had been commended to the grace of God for the work which they had now fulfilled' (alluding back to 13.3) nicely rounds off the mission from Antioch and reminds readers that Paul and

Barnabas had carried it out as missionaries of the church there (14.4, 14) and that the story of their exploits had been told from an Antiochene perspective.

14.27   The Antioch church was still of a size able to be gathered in a single place (large house). The report emphasizes that it was all God's doing, and that it was God who had opened a door of faith to the Gentiles: the image is a favourite one of Paul's (I Cor. 16.9; II Cor. 2.12; Col. 4.3); and the emphasis is one we would expect from Paul (faith as the Gentiles' means of entry into Israel's heritage), but one (faith) which Luke has repeated throughout the preceding two chapters (13.8, 12, 39, 41, 48; 14.1, 9, 22, 23) in preparation for the climax of the Jerusalem council (15.7–11). The mention of Jewish converts (and of Jewish opposition) was less to the point: the principal significance was the fact that Gentiles had responded in significant numbers and that churches composed substantially, in some cases wholly of Gentiles had been established. A new phase in the development of the new movement and in the transformation of its identity had clearly opened up, with consequences which Luke proceeds to describe.

14.28   The final sentence (14.28) portrays Paul and Barnabas resuming their role as active members of the Antioch church.

The Council at Jerusalem
15.1–41

Chapter 15 is a watershed in Luke's whole narrative. It comes close to the beginning of the second half of Luke's account, and the coherence of the two halves depends in effect on the success of the Jerusalem council's deliberations. In historical terms what was at stake was nothing less than the very existence of the new movement itself, both its identity and its unity – in particular, whether what had begun in Jerusalem was going to remain in vital continuity with Jerusalem and all that Jerusalem represented, and whether the new outreach into the Gentile world now taken up as a life's work by Paul was going to become something else.

Luke had already prepared the ground to deal with this potential crisis: in cloaking the seriousness of the tensions within the Jerusalem church, initially between Hebrews and Hellenists, and consequent upon the death of Stephen and the resulting persecution; in ensuring that the acceptability by the Jerusalem leadership of the converted Saul and of the developments in Antioch was clearly documented; and in highlighting Peter's acceptance of Cornelius as the crucial precedent for Gentile mission. But even so, the counter-tendency to present the Jewish communities encountered by Paul's mission as almost uniformly hostile to his open invitation to Gentiles (chs 13–14, 17–19) was bound to stretch and strain that continuity through Jerusalem with the movement's Jewish heritage to breaking point. It was therefore imperative, before Paul's mission became more extensive and less under Antioch's (and Jerusalem's) over-sight, to address the problems caused by the success of Paul's mission for what was still essentially a Jewish sect, and to show how harmony between Jew and Gentile within the new movement could be maintained without sacrificing the continuity with and through Jerusalem.

The goal is achieved in a skilful way. (1) The initiative of God is brought out repeatedly (15.4, 7–10, 12, 14, 16–18, 28). (2) Those provoking the issue (whether Gentile believers should not be circumcised) are marginalized (15.1 – 'certain from Judaea'; 15.5 – 'some believers from the sect of the Pharisees'). (3) The full panoply of the leadership is engaged and agreed – 'the apostles and the elders', Peter, James, and Barnabas and Paul; the unity of the agreement is stressed (15.22, 28). But within that united front, (4) the precedent of Peter's acceptance of Cornelius provides the decisive argument (15.7–11), (5) the contribution of Barnabas and Paul (in Antiochene order of precedence) is touched on only briefly (15.12), and (6) James is portrayed as giving a chairman's summing-up and making the determinative recommendation (15.13–21) – all of which lean over to stress that the continuity of Christianity with the ministry of Jesus and its Jewish character is secure and determined by those most representative of that continuity. (7) James' speech focusses on a scripture which combines a restoration (of Israel) theology with openness to the other nations (15.16–18). (8) And the ruling recommended by James and agreed by the conference assumes that the common ground for Jew and Gentile within the new movement are the traditional Jewish concerns over Gentile idolatry, sexual license and meat from animals improperly slaughtered (15.20, 29). (9) Finally, Barnabas and Paul are presented as explicitly endorsed by the apostles and elders and as the emissaries of the agreement to the churches of the Antiochene mission (15.23, 25, 30; 16.4).

That there was such a conference and that the issue was whether Gentile believers should be circumcised is hardly to be questioned. In Gal. 2.1–10 Paul describes a consultation in Jerusalem on that very issue, involving Barnabas, with the protagonists of circumcision even more marginalized (Gal. 2.4), and achieving a formal agreement that circumcision was not required, endorsed by the Jerusalem leadership, James, Peter and John (Gal. 2.7–9). That there were two such consultations/conferences (the one a virtual repeat of the other) is unlikely, despite minority support by Bruce and others. The differences between the two accounts are readily explainable when the different perspectives of the two who provide the different accounts are taken into consideration. Thus, it is hardly surprising that Paul, in addressing the Galatians, focusses on his own part in the agreement; whereas Luke, with a wider audience in view, focusses on the role of Peter and James. That the latter's opinions were absolutely vital can hardly be doubted, and Paul's own language unwillingly acknowledges his dependence on them at this point (Gal. 2.6, 9).

The most serious divergence between the different versions is the presence of 'the apostolic decree' in Acts 15.28–29, taking up the recommendation of James in 15.20. Paul, for his part, makes it clear that 'the pillar apostles' 'added nothing' (Gal. 2.6), leaving little or no room for a formal agreement like 'the apostolic decree', and he never alludes to such a decree in I Cor. 8–10. The solution, however, may be straightforward. On his own side Paul naturally wanted to stress the one clear point of agreement (on circumcision, though including the codicil of Gal. 2.10). James and others in Jerusalem, however, probably took certain corollaries for granted, including traditional ground rules for association between Jews and Gentiles; such in part at least is the unavoidable implication of Gal. 2.12–13. Luke for his part probably felt free to indulge in a further case of concertina-ing, putting into close proximity what had actually developed over a longer period. That is to say, whatever had been assumed in the Jerusalem agreement and whatever had been formally agreed, the practice of association which steadily became more established within mixed churches of Jews and Gentiles thereafter had assumed the sort of religious, moral and social meeting ground which 'the apostolic decree' allowed for. Luke's squeezing of history, as in his account of Saul's involvement in the earliest persecution (8.1–3) and in his record of Paul and Barnabas appointing elders in the Galatian churches in 14.23 (see Introduction to 8.1–3), therefore, may simply have consisted in the retrojection to the Jerusalem conference of the formal agreement regarding a practice which from early days of the Gentile mission had in the event provided the informal terms of association between Jewish and Gentile believers.

Likewise, although there is nothing in the Pauline letters to support Luke's portrayal of Paul as an ambassador for 'the apostolic decree', it is a fact that Paul in his exhortations to Gentile believers was equally as inflexible in his opposition to idolatry and sexual licence (e.g. I Cor. 6.9; 10.7, 14; see on 15.20(2)), and equally as ready to encourage Gentiles to respect the food scruples of Jewish believers (Rom. 14.1–15.6; I Cor. 8–10). If we should be sensitive to Luke's readiness to concertina his historical record, we should be equally sensitive to the fact that Galatians was written when Paul was in incandescent mood and that his ethical counsel in other letters was (could be) a good deal more moderate.

Despite these divergences, the outcome in both versions indicates a genuine commitment on both sides to hold together, including some readiness to compromise on favoured positions for the sake of unity by both James and Paul in particular. In both versions the agreement was of epochal significance for the future of Christianity and in crystallizing its character as a Jewish movement opening out to accept Gentiles as such as full members.

The issue of circumcision raised once again
15.1–5

We have already observed how central circumcision was to Jewish identity (10.45; 11.2–3). This is entirely understandable, given its absolutely fundamental character in Israel's self-understanding as laid down in Gen. 17.9–14: the covenant made with Abraham (on which Israel's identity was premised) was a 'covenant of circumcision' (Acts 7.8; Gen. 17.11), an everlasting covenant in their flesh (17.13); no circumcision, no covenant, no promise, no nation (17.10, 12–14).

Two centuries before Paul the importance of circumcision as Israel's essential identity marker had been massively reinforced by the Maccabean crisis: for the crisis had been occasioned by the attempt of Israel's Syrian overlords to destroy Israel's distinctiveness, precisely by forbidding circumcision (I Macc. 1.48, 60–61); and the Maccabean defence of Judaism consequently had included among its first priorities the reassertion of circumcision as indispensable for all Jews (I Macc. 2.46). Thus, for the great bulk of Jews, the link between 'Jew', 'Judaism' and circumcision was axiomatic; an uncircumcised Jew was virtually a contradiction in terms. And since circumcision was thus so inextricably bound up with the covenant promise to Abraham and his descendants, no one, no Gentile could surely think to have a share in that inheritance without first being circumcised.

Such must have been the logic employed by the 'certain from Judaea'. And since nothing in the Jesus tradition encouraged the thought that the Gen. 17.9–14 requirement had been relaxed, it is hard to deny the strength of their case. It is true that a precedent had been established earlier in the case of Cornelius, but it is Luke's account which puts that precedent in the spotlight (10.1–11.18), and its strength had yet to be tested (15.7–11). Whether the acceptance of such a God-fearing Gentile as Cornelius counted as an anomaly or as the beginning of a new pattern had not yet been demonstrated. Even after the still clearer precedent of Titus had been established in Gal. 2.1–10, the requirement for the circumcision of Gentile believers could still be put by the other missionaries in Galatia (Gal. 5.2–12). So there is no difficulty in envisaging Christian Jews who still regarded circumcision as axiomatic for Gentiles who wished to share in Israel's blessings.

What we have here, then, is a, possibly even the, classic confrontation between old revelation, confirmed by centuries of history, and a new insight, given not through Jesus himself but in the course of an expanding, developing mission. It would have to take clear indication of divine approval and tremendous confidence in the agreed judgment of the leadership for such an epochal step and breach with unbroken tradition to be taken. With the Christian mission continuing to develop today, the church cannot avoid being confronted with similar hard questions in the resolution of which not all will be satisfied.

15.1   The 'certain men' are not identified, except as coming from Judaea. They are presumably the same as or associated with the believing Pharisees mentioned in 15.5. Paul calls them or those like them 'false brothers' (2.4), though their acceptance as part of a Christian debate indicates that they were baptized believers (Paul could be very dismissive of Christians whose policies he resented – II Cor. 11.13; Gal. 1.7–8). Acts 21.20 ('zealots for the law') indicates that they were or became a very strong, indeed dominant faction within the Jerusalem church. 'The custom(s) of Moses' was a common Jewish way of referring to the Torah as it had been practised over the centuries (6.14; 21.21; 26.3; 28.17).

15.2–4   Paul and Barnabas went up to Jerusalem as delegates and with the full support (15.3) of the Antioch church. This representative role is implicit also in Gal. 2.1–10, but kept in the background in Paul's account. If the churches in Phoenicia and Samaria were founded by the scattered Hellenists (8.4–5; 11.19) it is understandable that they would be more open to a diaspora mission and persuadable by the evident success among Gentiles. Luke certainly makes a point of the positiveness of their reception en route as also by the Jerusalem 'church and the apostles and the elders'. The appeal to what had happened as the initiative of God echoes the justification of Peter's action in Caesarea (11.17–18) and underscores a familiar Lukan theme.

15.5   If mention of Pharisees as members of the new sect comes as a surprise, that probably is because of the generally negative impression of Pharisees in Christian tradition (strengthened, of course, by Matt. 23). Luke had recognized that Pharisees were more diverse (see Introduction to 5.33–42). At the same time, the fact that Pharisees were attracted to the new movement, while still characteristically Pharisaic in their emphasis on doing the law, presumably indicates how conservative as regards the law the Jerusalem church was, an attitude to which Luke himself was by no means hostile (cf. 7.38, 53; 18.18; 21.26; and not least 23.6). That circumcision was simply part of a whole package (the Jewish law, the Jewish way of life) is the assumption behind texts elsewhere such as Gal. 5.3 and James 2.10.

Peter cites the decisive precedent
15.6–11

This is the moment for which the lengthy account of Cornelius' conversion and its repetition (10.1–11.18) had been preparing. Crucial to the whole strategy (whether God's or Luke's) was the fact that Peter had been forced by clear directive and approval from God to accept a Gentile, as a full member of the new movement (indicated in baptism), without requiring him first to be circumcised. That was the crucial precedent and in his last appearance in Acts Peter makes full use of it. It was this event and Peter's intervention here (both the event itself and Luke's account of it), more than anything said to him by Jesus (cf. Matt. 16.17–19), which made Peter the bridge-man who spanned and held together the Gentile mission of Paul and the conservatism of the Jerusalem church under the leadership of James.

15.6   The description ('the apostles and the elders . . .') presupposes that the Jerusalem church leadership had become thus formalized. Following this episode 'the apostles' disappear from view. With this crucial agreement achieved, their role in securing the new movement's link to the past was more or less complete.

15.7–9   This is the third (much briefer) rehearsal of the Cornelius episode. That it was God's initiative (in the early days of the movement) is the starting point. That Cornelius and his friends had indeed believed the word of the gospel was not in dispute; but their response of faith is stressed (15.7, 9). The decisive factor, however, was that God had given the Holy Spirit to them 'just as he did to us' (15.8; as in 10.47 and 11.15–17). The gift of the Spirit was God's testimony to them of their acceptability to him as Gentiles; God 'knows the heart' (cf. 1.24) and deals with his human creatures on that basis, not on the basis of ethnic descent or ritual markers (cf. I Sam. 16.7). His priority, therefore, was to cleanse the heart, not to secure observance of laws of clean and unclean (cf. 10.10–15), and this was effectively achieved through the individual responsive openness and commitment of trustful faith.

As in 10.34–35, 43–47 there is something of a tension between Cornelius' acceptability to God and his actual acceptance by God. The question of the acceptability of Gentiles as Gentiles is resolved by the fact of Cornelius' manifest acceptance by God. That was manifest by the gift of the Spirit. The cleansing of the heart is not assumed to have been an intermediate or distinct stage, which would simply confuse the basic point being made: it is the abolition or denial of any distinction/discrimination between Jew and Gentile which is the point of emphasis (15.8–9; cf. 11.12). Any difference in function between 15.8 and 15.9 would have the gift of the Spirit attesting Cornelius' acceptability, and only then the cleansing of the heart effecting his actual acceptance. But Luke could hardly intend such a meaning. His point is rather that he who knows the heart (counted the Gentile *per se* as acceptable) cleansed his heart (accepted him) by giving him the Spirit. As elsewhere in Acts, the Spirit is the central feature in the process of conversion-initiation (see Introduction §5(3)).

15.10–11   15.10 introduces an unexpected note: that the law requiring circumcision (and a whole way of life) was a yoke which their fathers and they themselves had been unable to bear (cf. Luke 11.46). This hardly accords with the generally positive attitude to the law in the Judaism of the day or with what we have read of a Jerusalem community attractive to Pharisees (15.5)! Is this Luke's nod to a Pauline tradition (cf. 13.39) which had found various features of the law as a slavery from which their Christian faith had brought deliverance (Gal. 4.1–7; 5.1–6)? At all events, 15.11 puts the emphasis back on the central point: that the grace of the Lord Jesus is both the necessary and the sufficient means of salvation for Jew and Gentile ('we in just the same way as they'). The denial of any significance for ethnic or ritual factors enables unconditional recognition of everyone's dependence equally on divine grace. Failure to acknowledge this is to 'test'/resist God (5.9).

The determinative ruling of James
15.12–21

James now emerges as the leading figure on the Jerusalem stage (cf. Gal. 2.9; see on 12.17). His speech falls into two parts. It begins from the precedent provided by Peter and uses scripture to build it into a basic principle (15.13–18). Far from being an anomaly, the Cornelius episode, confirmed by the reports of Barnabas and Paul, indicated a new stage in God's dealings, in which the restoration of Israel would incorporate Gentiles as such as also his people. The corollary (15.19–21) was that for Gentiles to be his people did not require them to become or to live like Jews. All that was required was that Gentile believers should adopt sufficient basic laws as to enable Gentile and Jewish believers to associate together in worship and in table fellowship.

In terms of Luke's overall strategy in portraying a coherent and unified Christian movement, this is probably the key statement. It gives absolutely no backing to the view that Luke saw Christianity as a completely new entity, thoroughly Gentile in composition and completely superceding and divorced from Judaism and Jews in general. On the contrary, its basic assumption, in what is clearly intended as the most eirenic statement on which Jewish and Gentile believer can unite, is that Jewish restoration and Gentile visitation/calling go hand in hand (cf. 1.6–8; 2.39; 3.25–26). At the same time, it is somewhat surprising that the centrality of Christ is not indicated (unless implicit in the reference to 'seeking the Lord' in 15.17, though 'the Lord' of 15.18 is clearly God), nor of faith in him. Rather it is God's initiative which is central (15.14, 16–18) and the importance of Gentiles turning to God which matters most of all (15.19).

So far as its historical value is concerned, the speech has certainly been written up by Luke (as use of the Greek version in 15.17 and proposal of 'the apostolic decree' in 15.20 most obviously indicate). Yet Paul's account also implies clearly a considerable degree of accommodation and a higher degree of good will on the part of

James on the key issue (Gal. 2.7–9) than either subsequent account would have led us to expect (Gal. 2.12; Acts 21.17–22). There is more behind the text here than simply Luke's grand plan.

15.12 Barnabas is accorded first place before Paul, again (as in 15.25), reflecting a more Antioch/Jerusalem perspective. Their report is given the briefest of mentions. There are suggestions of a sceptical audience (why does Luke say 'they kept silence'?), that Paul may have taken more of a back seat (already a more controversial figure on this topic?), and that Luke has made a point of putting their report in terms of the 'signs and wonders' which in his account had marked the earliest community itself (2.43; 4.30; 5.12; see on 2.22). By way of contrast, in Paul's account (Gal. 2.7–9) it was the report of the grace clearly and effectively manifested through Barnabas and himself in their preaching of the gospel to the uncircumcised which proved decisive in the consultation.

15.13–14 James begins by citing only Peter (referred to here by the old form 'Simeon', as in II Peter 1.1), and, interestingly, not Barnabas or Paul. The point of emphasis is recognized: that God had taken an initiative which they could not gainsay. The language is deliberately scriptural in tone: God visited to fulfil his promise and saving purpose (Gen. 21.1; 50.24–25; Ex. 3.16; 4.31; Judith 8.33; Luke 1.68; 7.16); to take from the nations a people for his name, that is, for himself (cf. Deut. 14.2; 26.18–19; 32.9; Ps. 135.4). By using the emotive idea of 'God's people' the speech implies that the calling of Gentiles is of a piece with Israel's own calling and an extension of it (cf. Paul's use of Hos. 2.23 and 1.10 in Rom. 9.24–26).

15.15–18 The scriptural proof or confirmation is essentially Amos 9.11–12, with the opening phrase possibly drawn from Jer. 12.15 and the closing phrase from Isa. 45.21. The incorporation of these secondary allusions would be understandable, since the Jeremiah passage envisages a restoration of Israel's hostile neighbours and integration with God's people (Jer. 12.14–16), and the Isaiah passage is part of the famous denunciation of false gods. Amos 9.11 is also cited by the Qumran community in reference to itself (CD 7.11; 4QFlorilegium 1.12). So the text featured in Jewish speculation of that period about the restoration of Israel, of the Davidic kingdom (rebuilding the ruins of David), and it would not be surprising that a new sect concerned about its own identity in relation to Israel should draw upon it.

The difference here is that the quotation follows the Greek version of Amos and that the crucial line (verse 17a) is quite different in the Hebrew (did James address the conference in Greek?). According to this version Amos envisages a restoration of Israel with a view to the rest of humankind seeking out the Lord, that is, the Gentiles over whom God's name had been called (REB – 'all the Gentiles whom I have claimed for my own'). What is clearly intended is an understanding of a people of God in which Jew and Gentile are one, a restored Israel into which Gentiles called by God in their own right, and not as petitioning proselytes, are integrated (not assimilated). The implied exegesis is bold but gives Luke (and James) a sound scriptural basis for his vision of the new movement and its integrated Jewish-Gentile identity.

15.19   The critical factor in the acceptability of Gentiles to the believing Jews should be the fact of their conversion to God and thus acceptance by God. The key term is again 'turn to God' (as in 14.15; 26.20; cf. 3.19; 9.35; 11.21; 26.18; 28.27). James seems to imply that even for a non-Christian Jew, a genuine turning to God by a Gentile should be sufficient ground for the former to drop most of the ritual barriers to association with the latter (to stop bothering/harassing Gentile converts on the point). In this case, presumably, the genuineness of such a conversion would be sufficiently attested by belief in Christ, the gift of the Spirit, and baptism in Jesus' name (the precedent is Cornelius), whereas the traditional marker of such conversion had been circumcision.

15.20   The minimum terms for mutual recognition and association between Jews and Gentiles in the churches are spelled out. The problem was not a new one. Jews in the land of Israel had always been confronted with the problem of 'the resident alien' and had included them in the basic legislation envisaged here (Lev. 17.8–9, 10–14; 18.26). Subsequently the Noahide laws (including the prohibition of idolatry, adultery and incest, bloodshed, and eating the flesh of a limb cut from a living animal) became the basis for association, and such rules of association were probably already operative (Gen. 9.4–6 had already warned against both eating flesh in which the blood still adheres, and murder). We have also already noted the prominence of Gentile God-fearers within the ambit of the diaspora synagogues (see on 10.2), which presumably involved some social intercourse. So this represents an attempt to formulate for the

Christian communities, on the basis of much longer experience, what could probably be regarded as best practice at that time. It is of course assumed that circumcision should not be regarded as a precondition for association between Jewish and (uncircumcised) Gentile believers; but next to circumcision maintenance of table purity was close to the heart of Jewish identity (cf. I Macc. 1.60–63; IV Macc. 4.26).

What the actual terms of 'the apostolic decree' were is a matter of some confusion in the textual tradition, though that very confusion is a reminder that the terms of association continued to be debated and revised during the period when 'the apostolic decree' played a vital role as the basis of mixed churches. The earliest form probably included four elements, covering three areas of concern on the Jewish side.

(1) Gentiles should avoid 'things polluted by (contact with) idols'. The noun ('things polluted') occurs only here in the Bible but presumably is equivalent to 'what has been sacrificed to idols' in the corresponding letter (15.29; 21.25). The reference, then, is to the fact that in most cities the meat available for purchase in the meat market would be supplied primarily from the local temples and from the sacrifices offered there (as in the Jerusalem temple only part of the animal's carcase would be used in the ceremonies). In most pagan households also, before wine was drunk a libation to some god or goddess would be poured out. In both cases the problem for devout Jews was that the meat/wine had been consecrated to an idol, and to partake of it would be to tarnish (render unclean) their own dedication to the one God (Ex. 34.15–16). The fear of having anything to do with idolatry was a major determinator of social behaviour for most Jews, because of the supreme importance of the first two commandments (Ex. 20.3–6); a whole tractate of the Mishnah was subsequently devoted to the issue (*Aboda Zara*). Strictly applied the rule would prohibit most social intercourse with Gentiles and prevent Jews from holding many posts and from participating in civic ceremonies. The care with which Paul deals with the issue in I Cor. 8–10 indicates its sensitivity in the early churches.

(2) Also to be avoided was *porneia* (also 15.29 and 21.25), best taken to indicate not just adultery or fornication but every kind of sexual licence, though in this context with special reference to sexual union within the prohibited degrees (Lev. 18.6–18). As Paul's own indictment of humanity (seen from a Jewish perspective) indicates (Rom. 1.22–27), a link between idolatry and sexual license was taken for

granted (e.g. Jer. 3.6–8; Ezek. 16.15–46; Wisd. 14.12; *Testament of Reuben* 4.6–8; Rev. 2.14, 20). Israel's own failure over the golden calf at Sinai was remembered as a dreadful warning (Ex. 32.6; I Cor. 10.7–8). Paul warns his own converts against *porneia* regularly (I Cor. 6.13, 18; II Cor. 12.21; Gal. 5.19; I Thess. 4.3). As these references indicate, the rationale behind the prohibition was not some narrow-minded prudery, but the realistic recognition that such lack of self control usually came to expression also in other self-indulgences and vices.

(3) The third term probably means 'strangled, choked to death', though it occurs only here (and 15.29 and 21.25) in biblical Greek, and only in these passages in this sense in secular Greek. It no doubt refers to the prohibitions in Jewish law against eating the flesh of animals from which the blood had not been properly drained (Gen. 9.4; Lev. 7.26–27; 17.10–14); strangulation killed without allowing the blood to drain from the beast. The importance of adequate provision for kosher meat was one of Israel's traditional identity markers (as still today), part of a complex of food laws which also covered clean and unclean and the dangers of idol meat (cf. IV Macc. 5.2). It was not a dietary fad but part of the Jewish way of life which identified it as Jewish. The Cornelius episode had called in question the need to retain the laws of clean and unclean (10.11–15), but Jewish sensitivities could be respected by observing the kosher laws.

(4) The fourth element, 'blood', could denote murder (cf. Gen. 9.6; Deut. 21.7–8), the shedding of blood rather than the consuming of blood, but probably goes with the previous item and highlights the reasoning behind the kosher laws. It was precisely because 'the life (of the animal) is (in) the blood' (Gen. 9.4; Lev. 17.11, 14) that the blood had to be drained away: human dominance over the animal realm permitted human consumption of some animal flesh, but not the absorption of their life.

15.21   The implication is that knowledge and observance of the law was well sustained in diaspora synagogues and not at all threatened by the compromise proposed. The hope would be for a mutual respect within the extended communities between Jews who insisted on stricter practice and those who consorted with Gentiles on the basis of the rules just proposed. Again it should be noted that the whole proposal is put from a Jewish perspective and is geared to maintaining relationships across the Jewish spectrum. The thought is not of Christian communities as such, the basis of whose fellowship was their common faith in Christ (again we note the absence of any overt reference to Jesus). The thought is rather of communities whose basis for fellowship is continued respect for the law.

Consensus achieved
15.22–29

The proposal of James ('from the chair') brings discussion to an end. All that remains is to discuss its implementation. The formulation of James' proposal in a letter sent to the churches of the Antioch mission reinforces his authority with regard to the Jerusalem church (cf. 21.18–25). More important, it secures in a lasting and definitive way the continuity with Jewish law which holds the new churches true to their Jewish origin and heritage. The maturity displayed in the whole proceedings is remarkable. The mention of Judas Barsabbas and Silas (15.22) must come from Luke's tradition (only Silas is really relevant to his ongoing story), and the reference to the churches of Antioch, Syria and Cilicia alone probably indicates that in the event the compromise emerged in relation to the churches of the immediate Antioch mission (perhaps even as early as the aftermath of the incident referred to in Gal. 2.11–14). The letter begins and ends with the traditional Greek greeting and conclusion, rather than the more distinctively Christian forms developed by Paul.

15.22   That a genuine consensus, without dissenting voice, was achieved is emphasized ('the whole church'); the believing Pharisees (15.5) either go along with the consensus or maintain a diplomatic silence. The appointment of delegates to return to Antioch reinforces the continuing links between Jerusalem and its most expansive daughter church. Is Judas Barsabbas the same man mentioned in 1.23? Silas was to become Barnabas' replacement in Paul's further missionary work (15.40). It is interesting that they are described as 'leading men among the brothers', but are neither apostles nor elders, though both are later described as 'prophets' (15.32). At any rate their mention is a sign that Luke's information here was provided by tradition.

15.23   The letter is sent by 'the apostles and elders', but presumably in the name of 'the brothers' at large. It is addressed to the Gentile believers only, since it was a plea to them to adopt the minimum degree of law observance reckoned necessary to enable conscientious Jews to consort with Gentiles. It is not insignificant that the recipients (the churches of 'Antioch, Syria and Cilicia') accord with Paul's own version of his missionary work prior to the Jerusalem consultation (Gal. 1.21). But in both cases the list presumably includes the work in Cyprus and southern Galatia as part of the mission from Antioch.

15.24–27   The disowning of the troublemakers is explicit (15.24; does Paul's use of the same term in Gal. 1.7 and 5.10 indicate some awareness of such a disowning?). The fact of consensus is emphasized (15.25; with one of Luke's favourite words). And the commendation of Barnabas and Paul (again named in their Antiochene order of precedence) is warm (15.25–26).

15.28   A little late in the letter comes the acknowledgment of the Spirit's guidance. Is it significant that in the course of this crucial event Luke has related no heavenly vision and no word spoken under inspiration, in contrast to his common practice elsewhere? Perhaps a church council is a different kind of operation! Or is it simply the realism of ongoing daily life that Christian communities have to make important decisions without depending on vision and prophecy and in trust that a genuine seeking for and openness to God's will can be expected to produce decisions which are indeed inspired by the Spirit? If so, we should recall two points of importance: that the discussion and decision seems to reflect a genuine willingness to come together on both sides (see Introductions to ch. 15 and 15.12–21); and that the decision is presented as a genuine consensus and not as a power play by one faction dictating its will to the rest.

The talk of 'no greater burden' reflects nothing in James' speech, but echoes Peter's Paul-like comment in verse 10. Its presence again may suggest a statement composed to represent in at least some degree a Gentile perception (many Jewish traditions burdensome – cf. Rom. 14.2–3, 6) as well as minimum Jewish essentials for fellowship beween Jewish and Gentile believers.

15.29   'The apostolic decree' is repeated, though with a different term for the first item (see on 15.20), and with the remaining items in reverse order, though there is similar evidence of disturbance in the manuscript tradition of the text (see on 15.20). The parting encouragement reinforces the impression of a thoroughly Jewish perspective – the verb 'keep' denoting the quality of covenant faithfulness (Gen. 17.9–10; Deut. 33.9).

The transition to the next phase
15.30–41

Luke's concern here is to bridge the gap between the end of the Jerusalem council, as he has recorded it, and the next phase of Paul's mission. This stresses Paul's role both as emissary for the apostolic decree (15.30–31, continued into 16.4) and as representative of the Antioch church (15.35). The fact that Paul subsequently chose Silas to be his companion also enables Luke to suggest that Paul's link to and continuity with the Jerusalem church remained strong (15.40).

This latter fact also enabled Luke to pass over with brevity the most awkward feature of the transition period – the breach between Paul and Barnabas. He does not hide the fact that there was a sharp dispute, but he relates it solely to the question of John Mark's resuming the role of their assistant (15.37–39). Yet, almost certainly it was within this period that the dispute at Antioch took place, which Paul's record (Gal. 2.11–14) shows to have been exceedingly distressful to Paul, and not least for his relationship with Barnabas (Gal. 2.13 – 'even Barnabas was carried away by their hypocrisy'). Paul had clearly felt that the question of Jewish and Gentile believers sharing table-fellowship together raised the same fundamental issues as had the question of Titus being circumcised (Gal. 2.1–10); but Peter, Barnabas and the rest of the believing Jews (even in Antioch) had disagreed. Since Paul gives no indication to the contrary, it is likely that he failed to persuade them otherwise – a failure which evidently still rankled as the tone of the letter to the Galatians itself shows. With such a failure to secure backing on an issue which he himself regarded as crucial, it is unlikely that Paul was able to continue serving as a representative and missionary of the Antioch church. The breach, in other words, was not only with Barnabas, and it was much deeper than disagreement over Mark's suitability. Over these more important dimensions to the breach between Paul and Barnabas Luke has chosen to draw a veil. He maintains the portrayal of Paul's solidarity with Jerusalem at some cost to the Pauline side of the story.

15.30–32   There is a blandness in Luke's account: the letter from the apostles and elders in Jerusalem resolved all problems and was received with universal rejoicing. The fact that Judas and Silas were also prophets is noted in passing, presumably to explain the effectiveness of their exhortations; was the title 'prophet' accorded to all who spoke with such effect? The language ('exhorted and strengthened the brothers') is again fairly stereotyped (see on 14.22).

15.33–35   The reported return of Silas to Jerusalem (15.33) created an obvious problem in the light of 15.40, which some scribes resolved by inserting verse 34. We should probably deduce that Luke was simply cutting one corner too many and failed to notice the anomaly his concertina-technique left in his narrative. The description of Paul and Barnabas continuing their ministry in Antioch, as both teaching and evangelizing (cf. 5.42), with many others (no more fully identified) also likewise suggests a casualness or haste in composition.

15.36   An indefinite time note allows Luke to hide the fact that he has passed over the serious Antioch incident (Gal. 2.11–14) in silence. That Paul should want to revisit the churches he had established is certainly consistent with what we know of Paul's pastoral concern from his own letters (see also 14.21).

15.37–39   The dispute (the Greek verb implies deeply felt irritation and anger) between one of the most conciliatory of men (Barnabas; see on 4.36–37) and one of the most dynamic and forceful of Christianity's early missionaries is inexpressibly sad, but reminds us of how impossible it is to separate human temperament from heart-felt commitment. The reference is back to 13.13; whatever the reason for Mark's return to Jerusalem, Paul thought it revealed a weakness in character which made Mark an unreliable associate. There are, however, subsequent hints that Paul and Barnabas were reconciled (I Cor. 9.6; Col. 4.10), and that when given a second chance by Paul, Mark did not fail him again (Col. 4.10; Philemon 24).

15.39–41   Barnabas and Mark followed Paul's earlier suggestion (15.36) and returned to Cyprus – despite the fact that Luke had given no real indication of success or church founding there. Paul chose Silas (because he was a prophet, or a link with Jerusalem?) and took responsibility for revisiting the other half of the previous Antioch mission (again described in terms simply of Syria and Cilicia – cf. 15.23). That they were commended to the grace of the Lord (God – 14.26? or Jesus – 15.11?) by the brothers in Antioch may owe more to Luke's assumption that relations were still strongly positive than to any record from Paul's side. Yet the fact that Silas/Silvanus was a close associate of Paul in the phase about to be launched (II Cor. 1.19; I Thess. 1.1; II Thess. 1.1) may mean that Paul himself made efforts to keep his lines of communication with Jerusalem as open as possible despite the catastrophic outcome at Antioch.

PART IV
The Aegean Mission
16–20

The next phase of Luke's record of Christian beginnings is usually referred to as 'the second and third missionary journeys of Paul'. This is based on a misperception and is a misnomer. What we actually have is the account of a sustained mission around the coasts of the Aegean sea. Luke presents it as a coherent and integrated unit. It has a clear beginning: the mission was entered upon with all the marks of divine prompting (16.6–9). And it has a clear end: that period of mission, as indeed Paul's whole period of unrestrained missionary work, is climaxed and concluded with a speech which has all the appearance of Paul's last will and testimony (20.18–35). In between, the initial circuit of the northern and western side of the Aegean (chs 16–17) is followed by a lengthy stay in Corinth, Paul's effective headquarters for eighteen months and more (ch. 18). Subsequently, Ephesus, on the other side of the Aegean, served similarly as Paul's headquarters for a further two years (ch. 19). The trip back to Antioch between these two halves is passed over in the briefest of terms (18.22–23) and was evidently not regarded by Luke as particularly significant.

This accords well in substance with what we know of and can deduce about Paul's missionary work from his own letters. We have already noted the likelihood that the incident at Antioch occasioned a breach not only with Barnabas, but also with the church of Antioch, and *a fortiori* with the leadership of the church in Jerusalem (see Introduction to 15.30–41). In which case it is probable that Paul more or less cut his links with Antioch: he could no longer serve as a missionary (apostle) of a church which had not backed him in the Antioch incident over the terms on which Jews and Gentiles should be able to associate within the mixed churches established by Paul (Gal. 2.11–21). The movement into the Aegean region, therefore, was

212

much more like the establishment of a separate or even independent mission than the extension of the mission from Antioch into a second missionary journey. Paul's fierce resentment at encroachments on his mission subsequently is clearly expressed in passages like Gal. 1.6–9, II Cor. 12.11–13 and Phil. 3.2, and the terms of independence on which he worked are clearly indicated in II Cor. 10.13–16.

Likewise it is clear that the Aegean mission was the heart of Paul's missionary work for Paul himself. Apart from Galatians and Romans, all the letters written by Paul or in his name were to churches founded in this period: Philippi, Thessalonica, Corinth, Ephesus, and also Colossae, only a hundred miles or so from the Aegean coast. More important in the long term, almost all his letters were written during this period from his Aegean bases. (Somewhat surprisingly from our perspective, Luke makes no mention of this activity which was to give Paul his lasting influence.) Paul himself also seems to recall the move into Macedonia as a new beginning (Phil. 4.15); and he certainly regarded the closure of this period as the end of what was to be the main phase of his work as an apostle (Rom. 15.18–21). So the Aegean mission was indeed the principal period of Paul's missionary work and the one which has made the most lasting impact on Christian development and thought.

In it Luke, as usual, advances his own other concerns. (1) The reader is regularly reminded that the mission was ever at divine initiative and with divine approval (16.6–10, 14; 18.9–10; 19.11–12). (2) The success in attracting to faith both Jews (16.1; 17.4, 11–12; 18.4, 8, 19–20, 24–28) and God-fearing Gentiles is fairly constant (16.14; 17.4, 12, 34; 18.4, 7), as also the hostility of the Jewish community (17.5, 13; 18.6, 12–17; 19.9; 20.3, 19). (3) The theme of the gospel's superiority over other spiritual forces is effectively developed (16.16–18; 19.11–20). (4) The encounter with Greek philosophy in Athens enables Luke to further the theme that the gospel's encounter with paganism includes the proclamation of God (17.22–31). (5) The apologetic theme is steadily maintained that the new movement and its missionaries pose no threat to the civic authorities and should be treated with respect (16.35–39; 18.12–17; 19.23–41). (6) Not least, we should note the way in which Luke the accomplished raconteur delights in such wonderful stories as the episodes in Philippi and in Ephesus (16.11–40; 19.23–41).

3: Paul's Aegean Mission

Beginnings in Philippi
16.1–40

In a brief prolegomenon Paul strengthens his team but loses his way (16.1–10). Divine guidance through a vision opens the door to the richest and most fully documented of Paul's missions. The outreach into Europe begins in Philippi, and begins with the first of Paul's converts that Luke can name personally – Lydia, a woman of significant social standing (16.11–15). The following account of an exorcism is also the first to be particularized in Acts (16.16–18). And the vividly-told story of the imprisonment and deliverance (by divine providence) of Paul and Silas provides the occasion for Paul to confront the local authorities and to secure the standing of the new house church (16.19–40). Such detail and the first appearance of the personal 'we' on the part of the narrator (16.10–17) suggests that Luke was personally involved in most of the events he records or at least was able to draw on first-hand eye-witness memories (see Introduction §1).

The recruitment of Timothy and the call to Macedonia
16.1–10

This section is primarily intended to demonstrate how it was that Paul first brought the gospel to Europe, or at least into the Aegean basin. That the Spirit warned off from as well as directed towards or confirmed is an unusual feature in Acts. But the account serves effectively to explain why Paul did not head in more obvious directions and how he was boxed into his unusual course. We may be confident for the same reason (the surprising character of Paul's route) that Luke's account reflects Paul's own version of the matter. Luke's objective is not advanced by the prior account of the recruitment of Timothy, so we can be equally confident that Luke drew this too from good tradition, possibly even Timothy's if not Paul's own recollection.

16.1   Timothy is introduced as already a 'disciple'. When he became one is not stated, and it is somewhat surprising that Luke did not pick him out in his account of the preaching and church founding in Lystra. But that could simply be the result of the rather allusive way Luke referred in that account both to Paul's preaching and to the establishment of a group of disciples there (14.9, 20–23). At all events, Timothy was to become the most important of Paul's team of associate workers (Acts 17.14–15; 18.5; 19.22; 20.4; Rom. 16.21; I Cor. 4.17; 16.10; II Cor. 1.1, 19; Phil. 1.1; 2.19; Col. 1.1; I Thess. 1.1; 3.2, 6; II Thess. 1.1; I Tim. 1.2, 18; 6.20; II Tim. 1.2; Philemon 1; Heb.13.23), and, according to I Tim. 1.2 and II Tim. 1.2, there was a special bond between the two.

Timothy's mother ('Eunice' by name, according to II Tim. 1.5) had married a Greek. Such intermarriage was strongly discouraged within most Jewish communities (recalling not least Neh. 9–10), but still took place often enough. The fact that Timothy had not been circumcised may also indicate that his mother had ceased to practise as a Jew. On the other hand, II Tim. 3.15 speaks of Timothy as having been taught the scriptures of his people from his childhood, so it may be that it was Timothy's Greek father who refused to allow him to be circumcised. As one regarded as an uncircumcised Jew, Timothy presumably did not attend the synagogue, but conceivably his parents were wealthy enough for his mother to have some Torah scrolls of her own. At any rate, Timothy's mother was sufficiently open to this Jewish gospel to have become a believer herself (was her husband now dead?).

16.2–3   The report that Paul himself circumcised Timothy is often regarded as quite inconsistent with Paul's opposition to circumcision elsewhere (15.2!; probably already in the view reported in Gal. 5.11!). But Luke explains the matter clearly enough. Since Jewish identity was regarded as coming through the mother, Timothy was a Jew (this is clearly what Luke understood to be the case). As a Jew, Timothy's lack of circumcision would have been an affront to most Jews. That Paul should regard the circumcised status as still quite acceptable for Jews is confirmed by Gal. 5.6, 6.15 and I Cor. 7.18, 9.20; it was the insistence that *Gentile* believers *had* to be circumcised to which he objected. Luke's account here, then, is further indication that Paul saw himself as having a continuing mission to his own people and that Luke himself did not see Paul as operating on the other side of an irretrievable breach with 'the Jews'.

16.4   This verse is of a piece with 14.23. In both cases Luke evidently assumed that Paul approved of and instituted practices in a formal way whose establishment as formally agreed practice probably took some time to come about (see on 14.23 and Introduction to ch. 15 [pp.195f.]). That he delivered the decree only to the churches founded as part of the mission from Antioch confirms its initially limited scope (see on 15.23).

16.5   One of Luke's summary statements (see on 13.49) which serves both to extend the storyline regarding these churches beyond the horizon of Luke's own account and to indicate some unspecified passage of time.

16.6–8   The most natural route for an extended mission westwards was through Apamea and Colossae to Ephesus. A more northerly route through Phrygia (and Galatia?) would indeed lead to Bithynia, a region with several well established and significant coastal cities (cf. I Peter 1.1). This is often taken to be the journey in which the churches of (northern) Galatia were established and to which Galatians were written (cf. also 18.23). But Luke gives no indication that this was a preaching mission (which he was quite capable of doing with brief summary statements). The impression is rather of a prevailing uncertainty among the mission team, looking for new centres of operation in the aftermath of the breach with Antioch. Those passed by included the important centres of Jewish settlement in Sardis, Smyrna and Pergamum.

The guidance is perceived as negative guidance – not as a prophetic word or vision, but presumably simply as an inner conviction on at least Paul's part. Such too could be heard as the voice of the Spirit (cf. 8.29; 10.19). This whole journey of several hundred miles was undertaken without any clear sense of positive direction. Such would appear to be often the way when the mind of the Spirit is sought – a moving on even if only to explore and abandon false trails.

The Spirit is called both 'the Holy Spirit' and 'the Spirit of Jesus'. Why the latter at this stage is again not clear. In his subsequent writing Paul recognized the Spirit of God by the 'Jesus character' of its manifestations (Rom. 8.15–16; I Cor. 12.3; 13). Here the 'manifestation' could be as simple as a common conviction or sense that it was not (yet) 'right' for the gospel of Jesus to be preached here or there.

16.9–10   The uncertainty is ended with a vision; as in chs 9 and 10, the vision is given more weight in determining fresh and unexpected courses of action. Notable is the fact that the vision is neither of Christ nor of an angel (cf. 18.9–10; 23.11; 27.23–24); would we today have described it more as a dream ('in the night')? Either way the psychology might be relevant: through the subconscious God is able to speak a message which the unconscious mind may have been blocking. At the same time we should note that a process of evaluation of the vision is implied in verse 10, a process in which the team as a whole was involved; as usual, what is put forward as divine guidance needs to be tested before it can be received as divine guidance. It is a pleasing speculation (with a long pedigree) that Luke himself was 'the man from Macedonia'. At all events the 'us' of the vision is matched by the 'us' of those who concluded that they were being called to take a major step forward in mission by crossing into Europe.

The founding of the church in Philippi
16.11–15

The previous uncertainty is not wholly resolved at once. Philippi was the obvious first destination, as the most important city of the region. But without an established Jewish community where should they start? Luke does not record that they went immediately into the market place and preached there. Rather they spent some days apparently simply familiarizing themselves with the place, and then went tentatively to a place where they thought prayer was made. The uncertainty is resolved by the conversion of Lydia and the baptism (the first attributed to Paul) of her household. This is the first church that we can clearly identify from Paul's letters whose founding is recorded. Luke's sources of information were probably much richer here than in any of the preceding cases.

16.11–12   What precisely Philippi's status was is unclear from the text (Thessalonica was the capital of Macedonia). But it was a Roman colony (that is, settled by Roman soldiers, and governed by Roman law), and located as it was on the principal Roman road from Byzantium to Rome (the Egnatian way) it was a major step on Paul's road to Rome itself. The symbolic significance of the step taken in response to the appeal of the man from Macedonia is enhanced – into Europe and more direct confrontation with Roman authority.

16.13   The implication is that Paul and his companions had been searching for a Jewish house synagogue in Philippi, without success. There were not even ten male Jews in Philippi for a synagogue to be constituted. The best information they could gain was that some Jewish women and sympathizers met on the sabbath (this is the clue) at an appropriate spot outside the city gates, beside the river, for the prayers usually said in the synagogue (the diaspora synagogue is regularly called 'the (house of) prayer' in Jewish Greek literature). What is then envisaged is more in the nature of conversation (sitting and speaking with) than of preaching.

16.14–15   Lydia was a woman with a substantial business in luxury goods (only the wealthy could afford clothes which had been treated with the expensive purple dyes; so e.g. Luke 16.19). She also had a house big enough to provide hospitality for the band of four, and household servants. That presumably meant she was an unmarried daughter or widow. She was another God-fearer, that is, probably a Gentile (see on 10.2), having possibly been already attracted to Judaism in her home town of Thyatira in Asia (we know of a Jewish community there). Luke makes a point of attributing her attentive openness (cf. Luke 24.32, 45) to the Lord; this notable success would have been an important vindication of their coming to such an unpromising location as Philippi. Lydia is the first of the women of high social standing who are remembered as associates of Paul in his work (including Phoebe – Rom. 16.1–2; Priscilla – see on 18.2–3, 27–28; Junia – Rom. 16.7; and Nympha – Col. 4.15). Her house would presumably have been one of the houses large enough for the church in Philippi to meet in, so that she probably functioned as a leader of the church in Philippi, at least in its early months (16.40; cf. Rom. 16.5; Col. 4.15). Her non-appearance in Philippians could have many reasons, of which only one was her absence on business. By then other women were prominent in the leadership of the Philippian church (Phil. 4.2–3).

Lydia's baptism correlates with her heart being opened to pay attention to Paul's words; in baptism her attentiveness became commitment. 'Faithful to the Lord' here will mean fully committed (as presumably also in 16.1), since 'faithfulness' (sustained commitment over time and in testing circumstances) would cover a longer period than had here elapsed. Lydia's is also the second of the household baptisms recorded by Luke (10.48; again note how the detail has become more explicit). 'Household' here need not include children since the term was as commonly used to include household slaves and retainers (see further on 16.32–34).

Success and tribulation in Philippi
   16.16–40

This is one of the most vivid stories in Luke's second volume. It serves Luke's various purposes: a further triumph over magic, a miraculous example of divine providence (but not attributed to divine intervention as such), with acquisition of further converts as a direct result, and the respect of Roman authorities wrested from them unwillingly but nevertheless formally accorded by them. But the space Luke gives to the episode is as much explained by the fact that it was a great story in itself. Although parallels of such miraculous deliverance from jail can be readily produced from the literature of the time it is hard to doubt that this story, with all its detail, was the story the Philippian church told about its own foundation. Paul himself recalls various miracles (including Luke's favourite 'signs and wonders') as part of his missionary success (Rom. 15.18–19; II Cor. 12.12; Gal. 3.5). A not insignificant detail is the fact that Luke has rightly recorded the popular designation (*strategoi*) for the two chief officials in the Roman colony (16.20, 22, 35–36, 38). We should also observe that Paul himself recalled being beaten with rods (II Cor. 11.25) and 'shameful treatment in Philippi' (I Thess. 2.2).

16.16   To be noted is the implication that Paul and the others continued to attend at the place of prayer (16.13). They did not immediately hive off into a small prayer group on their own in Lydia's house. They continued to regard themselves as part of the place of Jewish prayer as well as the place where they would find those most prepared for and open to their message.

16.16–17   The implication of the language used by Luke is that the girl spoke as in a trance: she was inspired, like the priestess at Delphi, by Apollo, who was symbolized by a snake (the python); like the Delphi priestess she 'gave oracles' (in a trance or in ecstasy). Her utterance is quite conceivable in the circumstances, since it required only a superficial knowledge of Jewish apologetics or of early Christian preaching. 'The Most High God' was an obvious title for Jews to use in speaking of God (it appears over one hundred times in the LXX for Yahweh), even though it would probably cause confusion given the many high gods in Graeco-Roman polytheism. And 'the way of salvation' echoes language evidently quite common in the early mission ('way' – see Introduction to chs 1–5(5) [p.2]; 'salvation' – see Introduction §5(5e) and note 16.30–31). One can well imagine, for example, a dim-witted slave girl, who had picked up phrases used of and by the missionaries, following them round and calling them out in the way Luke records; such a case would be attributed to possession in the common understanding of the time.

16.18   That Paul responded, after many days of this, with annoyance (the same word is used in 4.2) has an authentic ring. Luke does not dress up the episode as Paul acting out of compassion or out of a desire to confront evil head on. This is the first Christian exorcism as such recorded in detail. The comparison with Jesus' exorcisms is worthy of note. He exorcised in his own authority; they performed exorcisms in his name, invoking the authority represented by his name (see further on 19.13–16). Such was the normal pattern of exorcism and evidently such exorcisms had a significant success rate (cf. Matt. 12.27; Luke 9.49); for the power of Jesus' name see on 3.6 (and Introduction to ch. 3). The success here would be indicated by the fact that the girl fell silent and ceased to function as an oracle giver. A less satisfying note is that the girl immediately drops from the story, with nothing said as to whether Paul and the others tried to help her in any way.

16.19–24   The tale now unfolds with rapid strokes, the storyteller well into his stride, though no longer as a personal participant (the 'we' disappeared after 16.17). The owners of the slave girl (probably a small syndicate) saw that their hope of gain had 'gone out' with the spirit (same verb as in verse 18 – a nice Lukan pun). More concerned for profit than for their slave, they made a citizen's arrest and hauled Paul and Silas before the magistrates. As Roman citizens in a Roman

221

colony they would carry weight with the praetors or duumvirs responsible for administering the law; with slavery such an important economic factor in ancient society, responsibility for loss of slave value was a serious matter. Their charge, however, was not of robbery. Instead, Luke tells us, they adopted a tactic repeated countless times in the history of communities the world over: the appeal to prejudice against small ethnic minorities commonly known for their peculiar customs. Such prejudice among Roman intellectuals against the Jews for their customs of circumcision and dietary regulations is well attested for the period. In view of the tensions between Paul and 'the Jews' elsewhere in Luke's narrative, it is important to appreciate the fact that in Philippi it was precisely as a Jew that Paul suffered.

That popular resentment among the local mob could be counted on against 'strange superstitions' from the east would be consistent with all this (the Jewish community in Alexandria had suffered on several occasions from such popular hostility), as also the readiness of magistrates to concede to such pressure on the assumption that those charged were guilty of some serious crime and worthy of punishment. The punishment is not merely salutary but severe: they are stripped, beaten publicly (by the 'rodbearers' of verse 35) and put into the innermost cell with their feet in stocks. Why did Paul not claim his Roman citizenship (as in 22.25)? Possibly because a charge of depriving slave owners of the value of their property or of teaching foreign superstitions (in a Roman colony) would have involved a protracted trial with an uncertain outcome.

16.25–26 The climactic scene is vivid: Paul and Silas not at all downcast; their prayer and singing hymns to God (at midnight!) holding the other prisoners' attention (rather than inciting abuse); and the earthquake leaving all doors opened and all fetters unfastened. It sounds too good to be true (various parallels, cited e.g. by Johnson 300, indicate a recurring pattern in escape stories of the time), but presumably this is how the story quickly circulated within the Christian community if not further afield.

16.27–31 The drama is heightened by the jailor's actions. His assumption that he would be held responsible for the prisoners' escape is quite plausible, and in an honour/shame society that would be quite sufficient motive for suicide. On the other hand, the fact that Paul was able to prevent the other prisoners escaping again sounds rather novellistic (but we are not told how many prisoners there were). The jailor's question, 'What must I do to be saved?', echoes the words of the slave girl (16.17) and further suggests that the imagery of salvation (healing and wholeness) had been a feature of Paul's teaching in Philippi (the theme of 'salvation' occurs slightly more often in Philippians than in Paul's other letters – Phil. 1.19, 28; 2.12; 3.20). That 'belief in the Lord Jesus' is sufficient would certainly have been Paul's answer to the question (cf. 5.14; 9.42; 11.17).

16.32–34 The offer/promise of salvation to the jailor was to 'you and your household' (16.31). The word was spoken to 'all in his house' (16.32). He was baptized forthwith 'and all of his' (16.33 – usually translated 'and his entire family'). And he thereafter 'rejoiced with all his household' (16.34). This is the third household baptism in Acts (see 16.15) and it is equally unclear whether household slaves and other adults alone are in view or also children (as also 18.8). The baptisms apparently took place in the middle of the night, so presumably they were not baptized by immersion in the local river! – more likely at a well in the courtyard. Note also that their belief is now described as 'belief in God' (16.34).

16.35–39 Equally, if not more enjoyable for the retellers of this story in the Philippian church would be the sequel. The two magistrates either have qualms about their too peremptory judgment and try to shuffle the affair under the carpet, or are satisfied that a sufficient warning and example have been given; the departure of the main culprits from the city should effectively 'close the book'. The appropriate officers (literally those who carried the bundles of rods and axes symbolizing their masters' authority to inflict corporal or capital punishment, the lictors, equivalent to policemen) are despatched to send them on their way without further fuss. Paul, however, himself a Roman citizen (a fact not previously disclosed; see on 22.24–29), and therefore exempt from such arbitrary punishment, was able to humble the authorities: they had exceeded their authority (a charge against Roman citizens had to be investigated properly), and were themselves liable to serious retribution (cf. 22.29). The public apology thus secured was presumably, in Paul's mind, not simply a matter of rubbing his persecutors' face in the dirt, or of retrieving his own honour (cf. again I Thess. 2.2), but of establishing the status of the fragile new community, free from the spite of any other important citizens they happened to offend. Whether the tactic was successful may depend on the interpretation of Phil. 1.27–30. The fact that Paul and Silas nevertheless leave the city more or less at once implies that there was some face-saving on both sides.

16.40   The only port of call before their departure is Lydia, that is, presumably Lydia's house, where the brothers were gathered.

Crisis in Thessalonica and Confrontation in Athens
17.1–34

The period following the first church founding in Europe (Philippi) was an unsettled one. The missionary strategy is clear: (1) to concentrate on the principal cities (Thessalonica was the capital of the province); (2) to focus the missionary effort in and through the synagogue. The pattern which emerged in the mission from Antioch (13.44–14.20) is repeated – initial interest and positive response among Jews and Gentile sympathizers, followed by Jewish opposition, resulting in civic unrest and departure to another city (17.1–16). The pattern is one which Luke may have shaped or extended, but he assuredly did not invent it, since Paul himself recalls such trials and tribulations, including Jewish involvement, on what must have been several occasions (II Cor. 6.4–5; 11.23–27).

The climax of the chapter is the encounter with the Greek philosophies and their religious presuppositions in Athens, the historic and famed centre of Greek culture. In what becomes the last evangelistic sermon attributed by Luke to Paul, Paul again preaches God and appeals to the first principles of a natural theology against the false human misconceptions of God, with the distinctive Christian message drawn in only allusively at the end (17.22–31). The response is equally as disappointing as that of the Jewish communities: a few believe, but most hear the distinctive Christian claim with scorn (17.32–34). As Paul himself was to note, the typical Jew and Greek thought that the Christian gospel had little appeal and made little sense (I Cor. 1.22).

Success and opposition in Thessalonica and Beroea
17.1–15

A feature of Paul's evangelistic tactic is brought to the fore in this sequence – the appeal to and exposition of scripture as providing proof of the claims made regarding Jesus (17.2–3, 11). Although the tactic was in effect acted out in the speech in Pisidian Antioch (particularly 13.32–37), Luke said nothing of it during the rest of the mission from Antioch. But here it constitutes the whole of the message delivered by Paul in the synagogues of Thessalonica and Beroea. We may deduce that the various shifts in focus of emphasis reflect at least in part Luke's editorial decisions, to prevent the reports of successive preachings from becoming too repetitive. But the emphasis is one which both Luke (Luke 24.27, 44–47) and Paul (e.g. I Cor. 15.1–4) shared, so there is no call to play the one off against the other here.

According to Luke the Thessalonian mission covered little more than a three week period, but I Thess. 2.9 and Phil. 4.16 suggest a longer period – another example of Luke's concertina-ing of history? On the other hand, the report that Paul's preaching attracted mainly Gentiles, and that it provoked Jewish resentment at and opposition to preaching to Gentiles is confirmed by I Thess. 1.9 and 2.14–16. A further indication that Luke has been able to draw on good tradition is the mention of Jason (17.5–9) without introduction or further identification as one whose name was sufficiently well known; he may have provided the work of which Paul speaks in I Thess. 2.9, though characteristically Luke only alludes to such day to day details in passing later on (18.3 and 20.34). Here also it is noteworthy that Luke was well aware of the proper title for the authorities in Thessalonica ('politarchs').

17.1–3   The route follows the main highway, the Egnatian way, following the northern coastline of the Aegean (a distance of nearly one hundred miles). Luke here notes that attendance at the synagogue was part of Paul's custom. The structure of the sentence implies that the purpose was to use it as a base for his preaching (see on 13.5); but the thought is not excluded that, as with Jesus (Luke 4.16), it was his custom to attend the synagogue on the sabbath anyway, that is, as the appropriate place for a Jew to take part in communal devotions. The implication is that, as a distinguished visitor, Paul was invited to give a word of exhortation on the basis of the

scriptural readings (cf. 13.15), and that his first exposition proved
sufficiently interesting for the invitation to be renewed for successive
sabbaths (cf. and contrast 13.44–45). It was as natural (and proper)
for Paul to take the scriptures as his starting point in the synagogue
as it was later to take the poets as his starting point in Athens
(17.28–29). For the scriptures referred to see on 17.11. The central
claim should probably best be translated as, 'This is the Messiah,
Jesus whom I am proclaiming to you' (NRSV) (similarly 18.5, 28).

17.4   The verb usually translated 'joined' means literally 'were
allotted or assigned to (Paul and Silas)' – the implication being that
this was by divine action (cf. 2.47; 13.48). The 'some' who were persuaded must be Jews. It is taken for granted that participating in the
synagogue devotions were a substantial number of Godfearing
Greeks, including a fair number of women of high social status. This
certainly accords with the impression given in other sources that
many Gentiles did find the Jewish religious and ethical traditions
attractive, including the respect accorded to women within Judaism
(see on 10.2). Once again we should note that the Jewish community
in a major city was not a small despised group but of sufficient social
status to attract significant numbers of Gentile adherents. This is
what gives realism to the repeated pattern in Luke's account of
Paul's missionary work: that Paul won both Jews and Greeks to the
gospel. At the same time we should note the contrast between
'certain (Jews)', and 'a great crowd' of Godfearers and 'not a few'
women of high standing: only a few Jews were attracted, but many
Gentiles. The strength of Christianity's appeal to women was a
feature from the first. Paul himself vividly recalled the character and
effectiveness of his preaching in Thessalonica in I Thess. 1.5–2.13.

17.5   The bulk of the Jews take offence at this success – the term, 'the
Jews', again indicating the predominant feeling of the Jewish community in the city. The description of their 'jealousy' again may
include an allusion to Jewish 'zeal' (same word) to maintain Jewish
ethnic and religious distinctives in the face of assimilating or
syncretistic pressures of a major Greek city (see on 13.45 and 21.20).
The pleasure at Gentiles expressing interest in affiliation or even conversion to Judaism would be replaced by anger that a liberal Jewish
sect which sat light to the Jewish distinctives was proving more
attractive. Again the fact that 'the Jews' could arouse such popular
resentment among the city mob (the term indicates those who hung

about the market place) is an indicator that the Jewish community was part of the city's establishment, able to trade on populist resentment at new and strange teachings brought into the city (cf. again I Thess. 2.15–16). Luke displays some class consciousness in the different descriptions used in verses 4 and 5, as again in verses 11–13.

17.5–7   The story assumes and does not need to explain that the otherwise unknown Jason was acting as host to the visiting missionaries. It is not said whether he was Jew or Gentile (the Greek name in itself is not decisive on the point), but he was evidently a man of some substance, with a house large enough to provide such hospitality and where the brothers could meet. The implication is that those who had been persuaded and joined the missionaries had been baptized forthwith and formed one or more house churches; also that Paul and Silas were not present in Jason's house at the time of the disturbance. Luke the storyteller evidently felt no need to complete every pedantic detail (cf. 14.20, 22, and the silence in 16.19 regarding Timothy and the one implied by the 'we').

The accusations against Paul and Silas (in absentia) and Jason reflect the degree to which religion and politics of state were closely related in those days. They also express the sort of exaggerated populist rhetoric so readily drawn upon in all ages on such occasions of public confrontation. To 'turn the world (or empire) upside down' was to threaten the foundations of established order and custom (cf. 16.20); new ideas can always provide an excuse for populist conservative reaction, though if Paul's teaching in Thessalonica included a strong eschatological emphasis (cf. I Thess. 5.1–11; II Thess. 2.1) one can see how the accusation might arise. So too any proclamation of a new focus for religious commitment linked to talk of God's kingdom (cf. 14.22; 19.8; 20.25; I Thess. 2.12; II Thess. 1.5) could be readily presented in populist rhetoric as a seditious threat to Caesar's rule (cf. Luke 23.2), however farfetched the accusation might seem to a more objective onlooker.

17.8–9   The people at large as well as the authorities were bound to be disturbed by such accusations. The authorities take security (bail money) from Jason and the others, presumably to guarantee the departure of Paul and Silas, and then let them go. The response suggests that they recognized the realities of the situation and knew how to defuse a potentially dangerous situation involving an uncontrolled mob. Use of the mob was a well known demagogic tactic within the history of Greek democracy, so they would not be short of precedents.

17.10–12   The pattern is repeated. Paul and Silas slip away by night – but it would take more than one day's journey to reach Beroea (about sixty miles to the southwest). On arrival they head at once for the synagogue. Here, however, the response from the local Jews is presented as much more positive: they were more 'noble', 'fair-minded' (REB), received the word eagerly, and 'scrutinized/critically examined' the scriptures daily to see if the scriptures supported the interpretation put upon them by Paul and Silas. The implication is that the synagogue in Beroea functioned as a house of study, where the scrolls were kept, and where members of the Jewish community could attend daily (not just on the sabbath) for scripture study. The success is greater among the local Jews ('many', as opposed to the 'few' in Thessalonica), with a similar number of Gentile women of high status ('not a few' on both occasions) and Gentile men, also of high social standing. Again the resulting church consists of Jews and Gentiles. The reference to Sopater of Beroea in 20.4 (= Sosipater in Rom. 16.21?) indicates that the church became established, even though it is mentioned nowhere else.

17.13–15   As in the mission from Antioch (14.19), the troublemaking Jews who stirred up opposition in the previous mission posts saw Paul's message as a threat not only to their own community but to Jewish self-understanding. No doubt the fears were occasioned by a message which treated Gentiles as already equivalent to Jews in their acceptability and thus threatened Jewish identity as the people of God set apart from the other nations. Here again the attractiveness of the synagogue community to women and men of high social standing and the ability of the Jews from Thessalonica to stir up the local mob indicates that the Jewish community itself was not a target for local hostility to strangers.

The fact that Paul alone is sent off presumably indicates that he was the main exponent of the new message and so drew the fire of the opposition on to himself. That his companions escorted him to Athens (probably by sea) before returning to Beroea suggests either that they feared for his safety or that they wished to introduce him personally to friends or relations in Athens. The communication from Paul which his companions were to take back to Thessalonica foreshadows the extensive letter writing and network of communication Paul was soon to establish for his churches.

The gospel of God encounters Greek philosophy
17.16–34

It is important that the next section be taken as a unit and that the famous speech on the Areopagus is not studied in isolation from its context. For Luke describes the context out of which the speech arises with some care; the speech addresses the concerns raised in the paragraph which introduces it. So although the initial strategy is the usual one, to seek out Jews and Godfearers (17.17), it is the prevalent idolatry of the city which first catches his attention (17.16), and what then happens takes Paul into a new dimension of apologetic and evangelism. He encounters Epicurean and Stoic philosophers who find his talk of Jesus and Resurrection (two new deities?) confusing and give him the opportunity for a fuller exposition (17.18–20).

The speech which follows is one of the briefest of the more substantial speeches in Acts. At its heart is a twofold protest: against the multiplication of deities as the proper expression of religiosity; and against the assumption that God can somehow be contained within humanly made shrines or images. The first claim, then, is not presented in terms of the Christian story, but starts with a proper understanding of God, of the one God, Creator of all that is. The language used builds as much as possible on contacts with the wider philosophies of the time (particularly Stoicism) but is basically Jewish monotheism and creation theology presented in its universal implications. God, the Creator, is sovereign, maker of all things and of all nations. God's creation means that there is a God-given relatedness between God and humanity, which only finds appropriate expression in a non-idolatrous worship. Human attempts to manipulate God through the service offered him in shrine and cult, or to image God in representations of gold, silver or stone, are thus things of which to repent. In this way the expression of Athens' religiosity in the multiplication of idols is corrected, and the complete continuity of Christian preaching with already traditional Jewish apologetic and polemic within the wider Hellenistic world is reaffirmed. Implicit also is the fact that this strand of Jewish

230

theology provides a different basis for relations between Jew and Gentile than had developed within mainstream Judaism. Here it is humanity as a whole which is in view, at a more basic level than that of Jew versus Gentile, or indeed of Greek versus barbarian.

To this basic apologetic for Jewish anti-idolatry monotheism is added at the end, somewhat abruptly, reference to the 'man' appointed by God to judge the world and raised by God from the dead (17.31). This is the extent to which the Christian story is drawn upon. But the terms used to do so are worth noting. (1) Jesus is not identified and so the story of his continuity with Israel's history and prophecy is not a factor – in marked contrast to the speeches to Jews (chs 2 and 13 in particular). (2) Jesus is named only as a 'man whom he (God) has appointed', so that the basic monotheistic thrust of the overall speech is not compromised and the misunderstanding implicit in the philosophers' impression in 17.18 is corrected. (3) The attempted point of contact is through the idea of final judgment and resurrection; no mention is made of the cross. In short, the christology is subordinated to the theology; the developing christological distinctives of Christian faith are subordinated to the prior task of winning appropriate belief in God. At the same time, the focus on resurrection in both 17.18 and 31 confirms that in a Greek context as well as a Jewish (see on 2.24; also 4.1–2 and 23.6) the claim that God had raised Jesus from the dead stood at the centre of the Christian gospel.

As usual this speech will be Luke's attempt to portray the message which he thought was appropriate to Paul's mission to the Greek philosophers or what Paul would have said on the occasion. Again it is a cameo rather than a real exposition (a speech of some ninety seconds, and with such an abrupt reference to the resurrection of an unidentified man would hardly have done justice to the occasion). Luke hereby displays the diverse character of preaching necessary for the Christian mission, and his recognition (as also in 14.15–17) that the message about Jesus and his resurrection can only be rightly understood within the context of Jewish belief in the one God and Creator of all (a context which could, of course, be assumed in preaching to fellow Jews). Whether or not Luke presented this as some model for Christian apologetic to sophisticated Gentile audiences is less clear; but his account of the relatively modest success of the attempt (17.32–34) was probably realistic.

That Paul was quite capable of such an apologetic approach is confirmed by the differently angled Rom. 1.19–32 (and cf. again

I Thess. 1.9–10). The more restrained presentation of Christ (a man appointed as judge of the world and raised from the dead) also strikes a chord not only with a passage like II Cor. 5.10 but even with the more developed christology of passages like I Cor. 8.6 and Phil. 2.6–11, where Paul takes care to maintain the monotheistic framework intact even while speaking of Christ's role in terms of deity. Paul also preserves a memory of the mockery of Greek sophisticates at the gospel, as also of a limited success in winning men and women capable of sophisticated reflection on the cosmos (I Cor. 1.23, 26); Luke's source recalled two of their names.

17.16   The reaction of Paul to the many statues and representations of the gods in Athens (a feature noted by other ancient historians) is characteristically Jewish; the verb is strong – 'outraged' (REB), 'deeply distressed' (NRSV). Nothing aroused Jewish contempt for the other religions of the Mediterranean and Mesopotamian world so much as idolatry (see on 7.41, 48 and 17.29). On their side polytheists found such Jewish abhorrence puzzling and atheistic, even though the austere worship of the supreme God as invisible did attract some. On the whole, however, this was one of the points of mutual incomprehension between Jew and Gentile which helped protect Jewish distinctiveness. The tensions within later Christianity between a worship aided by icons and images and a worship focussed on the word reflect something of the same dichotomy in human perception of the divine.

17.17   Quite why Paul should debate with his fellow Jews and the usual God-fearers, presumably on the subject of idolatry, is not clear. Has Luke added the note because he assumed Paul always started with the synagogue? Or does he imply that Paul criticized his fellow Jews for not protesting more about the idolatry in Athens? In which case Paul would be criticizing his fellow Jews for not being Jewish enough; his Christian apologetic would be out-Jew-ing the Jews!

The debate in the market place implies a different tack in evangelistic strategy – as implied also in 14.9. Or was it simply that Paul could not contain his irritation at the number of images? Certainly the market place in Athens would be a natural location if one wanted to encounter other views and to engage in discussion. Paul's activities echo those of Socrates, and the 'open air' teaching of Cynic philosophers in particular is attested by other sources from the period.

17.18 In such an openness to dialogue, encounters with some of the most prominent philosophies of the day would be unavoidable, especially in Athens, where they held established and subsidized teaching positions. The portrayal of Paul ready to engage in argument with the leading thought of the day has rightly been inspirational for all eager to take their witness beyond the bounds of home and church and to engage in debate with contemporary ideologies. As the speech will demonstrate, the strategy includes a readiness to start where the audience is and to build on common ground as far as possible.

Epicureanism was a practical philosophy whose objective was to secure a happy life and to maximize the experience of pleasure. Among other things it taught that the soul died with the body (giving freedom from fear of death), and that the gods do not interfere with the natural world (giving freedom from fear of the supernatural). The relevance of a message such as Paul's to Epicureans and the likelihood that it would find little resonance with Epicureans is at once clear.

The more influential Stoicism taught that the aim of the philosopher should be to live in harmony with nature, guided by the reason which they identified with God and which manifests itself both in providence and in human reason. To live in harmony with this reason is the only good; everything else is a matter of indifference. Here again it should be obvious where the speech of Paul attempts to build on points of contact and commonality between Stoicism and Jewish monotheism (17.26–29).

The initial impression gained by the adherents of these older (as they would see them) philosophies was, however, dismissive and disparaging – particularly, no doubt, on the part of the Epicureans. The term used of Paul, 'babbler, chatterer', evokes the image of one who made his living by picking up scraps, a peddler of secondhand opinions. The charge of proclaiming 'foreign deities' echoes that brought against Socrates (particularly in Xenophon, *Memorabilia* 1.1.1 and Plato, *Apology* 24B). This was no doubt deliberate on Luke's part, since the trial and death of Socrates in 399 BC was one of the most famous episodes in Athens' history. The implication of Luke's description is that Paul was both misunderstood and a teacher of integrity, like Socrates himself.

In Luke's perspective, then, and despite the presence of a Jewish synagogue, the Athenians seem to have had little conception of a coherent and ancient theistic system like Judaism. In particular, they could make little sense of Paul's preaching about Jesus. According to Luke, they thought Paul was proclaiming two new 'foreign deities', namely, Jesus and Resurrection. From this we may deduce that Paul focussed his teaching on the central features of the Christian message (cf. again 4.2; 23.6), and that without a context (knowledge of Jewish history and religion) it proved meaningless to them. The point needs to be remembered wherever the gospel is proclaimed, that without an appropriate background of language and tradition the gospel is always likely to meet with incomprehension and misunderstanding. The speech attributed to Paul indicates that this was a lesson Luke wished to bring home to his readers and that Paul had learned it.

17.19–21 The Areopagus, or Hill of Ares (Ares being the Greek name for the God of war, Mars, so Mars Hill) was located to the northwest of the Acropolis. Here, however, it refers not so much to a place where speakers could hold forth (like Hyde Park Corner in London, or the Mound in Edinburgh) as to a council which met (or had met originally) on the hill. Among its functions was probably that of supervising education, not least in controlling the many lecturers who relished the honour of teaching in Athens. The picture Luke paints fits well within this context. His description of the Athenians and the foreigners who had taken residence there as interested in nothing other than 'talking or hearing about the latest novelty' (REB) is rather dismissive. But it catches well the sense of decadence and somewhat faded glory which had probably characterized the university town for many decades, despite its continuing high reputation as the city which more than any other evoked and preserved the greatness of Greek culture.

17.22–23 The opening of the speech makes a cultured compliment to the distinguished audience. The term used can often mean 'superstitious' (cf. 25.19), but the line between religiosity and superstition was recognized to be a fine one, so we should probably take it in a positive sense, as denoting a praiseworthy fear of or reverence for the deity. This religiosity was attested not simply by the abundance of altars to named gods and goddesses, but by their care to ensure that no manifestation of deity was left out. Such scrupulosity is well attested in other records, though in the plural form ('unknown gods'). It is this openness of Athenian religion which gives Paul the point of contact: he proclaims no new god, but one they had themselves recognized, albeit inadequately. At the same time, however, the objective will be to proclaim this unknown God as the only God. A too liberal religiosity had lost all focus and coherence, to which the religious sense of Jewish monotheism was the answer.

17.24–25 The starting point and axiom of Jewish (and Christian) religion is that there is one God ('the God'), who has created all things ('the world and everything in it'), and who is the sole sovereign ('Lord of heaven and earth'). The claim is wholly consistent and continuous with fundamental Jewish self-understanding and apologetic as enshrined also in the Jewish scriptures (Ex. 20.11; Ps. 145.6; Isa. 42.5; Wisd. 9.1, 9; similarly Matt. 11.25 and Acts 4.24).

It follows, with the same traditional logic, that this God is not dependent on anything made or provided by human beings. The relation is completely the reverse: humanity is wholly dependent on God for everything, from life and breath itself to everything else (Isa. 42.5; 57.15–16; Wisd. 9.1–3; II Macc. 14.35; see also Acts 7.48). The implication is that humankind understands itself only when it understands its fundamental dependence on God, with the corollary that such an understanding calls for an appropriate worship (verse 27). The line of argument would be meaningful to both Epicurean (God needs nothing from humans) and Stoic (God as the source of all life).

17.26–27 The chief thrust of the argument, however, continues to draw directly on fundamental tenets of Jewish monotheism. Humankind is made from one common stock (Gen. 1.27–28; 10.32), an idea less familiar to Greek thought. God fixed the seasons (or epochs of history) and the boundaries of the nations (Gen. 1.14; Deut. 32.8; Ps. 74.17; Wisd. 7.18). His objective was that they should seek God (Deut. 4.29; Isa. 55.6), recognizing that only in relation to and dependence on this beneficent and overseeing God would they be able to recognize their status and function as individuals and peoples (similarly 14.17). The verbs used here ('if perhaps they might grope for him and find him') capture well the sense of uncertain reaching out in the dark of those moved and motivated by such considerations of natural theology (God at work in and manifest in an obscure way in the world). The world is full of people with such unformed and indistinct religious feelings and aspirations. The critique of a religion and theology drawn only from the testimony of nature should be noted. The hope in an apology like Paul's would be that the clearer illumination provided by such scriptures will help dispel the darkness and uncertainty with the light of revelation (cf. Wisd. 13.5–9).

17.27–28   The clinching consideration is that this Creator God has not created a hunger for God within humankind only to leave it unsatisfied. This same sovereign Lord is not far from each of his human creatures. Again the thought is drawn immediately from the (Jewish) scriptures (Ps. 145.18; Jer. 23.23). But precisely at this point two sayings from Greek poets can be cited as amounting to the same thing. The first has an unknown source – 'In him we live and move and are'; but the second is drawn from the Stoic poet, Aratus, *Phaenomena* 5. At this point the Jewish-Christian understanding of the relationship between God and humankind draws close to some traditional Greek religious sentiments and provides a bridge across which apologists could attempt to venture in the hope of drawing their audience over to their own side.

17.29   But the apologetic effort is not expended in simply looking for points of contact and possible cross-over. The challenge to what any Jew would regard as an inferior and inadequate conception of God must be made. The point of common perception ('we are God's offspring'), therefore, provides the basis for the thoroughly Jewish corollary that God should not be represented by images of gold, silver or stone, or any work of human imagination (cf. Deut. 4.28; Isa. 40.18–19; 44.9–20; Wisd. 13.10; see also on 7.41). Even if the response were made that such images are only aids to worship, the Jewish/Christian reply would be that the symbol too quickly comes to stand for that which is symbolized, too much invested with the aura of the divine as if in its own right; the icon becomes the idol, itself the focus of worship and the definition of the divine. Such a critique of popular Greek religion would not be new to sophisticated philosophers.

17.30   What has been an apology for the Jewish understanding of God becomes an evangelistic thrust. Such misunderstanding should now be seen as a form of ignorance (cf. 14.16) and should now be repented of. As the Jews of Jerusalem should repent over the misunderstanding which occasioned Jesus' death (3.17–19), so idolaters should repent of their idolatry in the face of this clearer understanding of God and of God's relation to humankind. That repentance was necessary for all nations was clearly envisaged in Luke 24.47.

236

17.31   Somewhat as in 10.42, the first preaching to a Gentile, the conclusion is reached in a rush. Repentance is necessary, since this same God who began all things will bring all things to a conclusion with a day of judgment. The concept of a day of judgment is thoroughly Jewish (cf. e.g. Isa. 2.12 and Amos 5.18) and was carried over into Christian theology as a basic datum (e.g. Rom. 2.5, 16; I Thess. 5.2; II Thess. 1.10). The further description ('he will judge the world in righteousness') is drawn directly from the Psalms (Pss. 9.8; 96.13; 98.9). It is thus, once again, thoroughly Jewish in its conception – 'righteousness' as a word expressive particularly of the mutual obligations taken upon the covenant partners in the covenant between God and Israel (cf. e.g. Pss. 31.1; 35.24; 45.8; Isa. 26.2; 45.21; see also on 10.35). Some of the language would make sufficient sense to a Greek audience – 'righteousness' as referring particularly to the prescribed duties towards the gods. But one wonders what impact such a brief allusion to the theme of final judgment could have had on such a sophisticated and sceptical audience. At this point the cameo character of Luke's presentation, simply alluding in a phrase to a whole theme requiring a much fuller exposition, diminishes the credibility of the picture he here paints.

Still more audacious and straining of credulity would have been the abrupt allusion to the 'man appointed (to serve as judge)' in the final judgment. Here again the thought would not be new to a Jewish audience (see on 10.42). But what a Greek audience would make of it is much less clear. The final straw would be talk of resurrection from the dead. The idea of a man ascended to heaven would be familiar in both Jewish and Greek thought, but resurrection from the dead was a peculiarly Jewish conception, implying, as it presumably would, a resurrection of the body. But Greek thought generally took for granted a basic dichotomy between spirit and matter (the latter including the body), so that deliverance was conceived as of the soul liberated from its material encumbrances.

Luke cannot have been unaware of the offensive character of such an abrupt and bald declaration. It is almost as though he wanted to set in the sharpest possible contrast the fundamental claim of Christianity and the mocking rejection of the Athenian sophisticates. In so doing it is possible that he was echoing Paul's own sharp contrast in a passage which could also reflect the influence of the Athens confrontation (I Cor. 1.17–25).

17.32–34   The conclusion is briefly told. The message with its call to repentance for idolatrous conceptions of God might have struck a chord with some; Jewish apologetic would no doubt already be familiar to any who were 'groping after God' (17.27). But such a hopelessly brief allusion to the distinctive Christian claims regarding judgment and resurrection would have been bound to meet with incomprehension and dismissal, and a lengthier exposition would have demanded too great a leap in basic assumptions and conceptuality for most. Those more comfortable with their own philosophies or inattentive to what Paul would have said would indeed have been dismissive (particularly the Epicureans). Assuming a more sustained presentation by Paul, others might well have wished to hear more.

The actual recruits who take the step of believing were few – 'some men'. Among them Luke's sources recalled Dionysius, a member of the Areopagus council, a man of high social status, and a woman named Damaris. Of neither do we hear any more in the New Testament. But it is not even clear whether a viable church was established. Paul is recalled as having left almost straight away (18.1), an unusual step for him where a new church was there to be nurtured. Athens does not feature in Acts after 18.1; nor does the only other New Testament reference (I Thess. 3.1) tell us anything. And elsewhere Stephanas of Corinth is given the honour of being called 'the first convert in Achaia' (I Cor. 16.15). All told, the experiment in meeting Greek philosophy in Athens head on does not appear to have had a lasting success and probably left its most lasting influence in Paul's formulations in Rom. 1 and I Cor. 1 (not to mention Acts 17).

A Firm Foundation in Corinth
18.1–28

The move to Corinth, the next obvious target location, allows Luke to develop his portrayal of Paul's mission with significant details. (1) He provides, for the first time, details of how Paul sustained himself financially (18.2–3). (2) The regular pattern, of initial preaching to Jews followed by opposition, is met by the second denunciation of Jewish intransigence and announcement that the gospel will thenceforth be taken to the Gentiles (18.4–6). (3) A clearer picture than ever before is provided of the transition from a synagogue-centred ministry to a house church (18.7–8). (4) Corinth is clearly singled out as a centre in which Paul's mission became established over a lengthy period (18.9–11). (5) The Roman authorities give a judgment favourable to the legal status of the church by ruling that it still belongs within the protected sphere of Judaism (18.12–17).

The rest of the chapter is rather bitty. The main objective was evidently to provide the transition to the next important centre of the Aegean mission – in Ephesus. This is done by relating Paul's brief visit to Ephesus on the way from Corinth (18.19–20), and the intervening visit of Apollos (18.24–26), who was to become a powerful counterpoise to Paul in the Aegean mission. Any challenge or even threat he may have posed to the Pauline mission (cf. I Cor. 1.12; 3.4–7; 4.6–7) is defused by the report of his fervency in Spirit and fuller instruction by those prominent members of the Pauline team, Priscilla and Aquila, introduced at the beginning of the chapter (18.2). In between, the details of Paul's vow (18.18), indicating his continuing loyalty to Jewish traditions, and his visit to the church (in Jerusalem) and Antioch (18.22) are inserted briefly to maintain the link between the Aegean mission and both Jewish tradition and the original sending churches.

Establishment in Corinth
18.1–17

This half chapter, together with the two letters to the Corinthians, give us the fullest and most detailed record of the establishment of a church and its early history available to us. For Luke it was important that this successful foundation was the result of a happy combination of providential events and divine assurance provided directly. Thus on the one hand, the foundation period was bracketed by two events involving the Roman authorities. The first was the beginning of one of the most fruitful partnerships in all Paul's career as a missionary, when the expulsion of Jews from Rome provided the occasion for Paul to meet up with Aquila and Priscilla (18.2–3). The second was the favourable ruling of the proconsul Gallio in Corinth itself, which ensured that the manipulation of public sentiment against the missionaries (as in 17.5–7 and 13) could not happen in Corinth (18.12–16). More important, on the other hand, was the vision of the Lord which gave Paul the initial confidence he needed to settle himself in Corinth for a lengthy ministry (18.9–11). That God could thus be seen to be behind and directing Paul's mission was of first importance for both Paul and Luke.

For the historian it is also important that so much of the detail can be corroborated and located within the wider history of the period. The expulsion of Jews from Rome can be dated to 49, and Gallio's period of office can be dated likewise with some precision to 51. The mention of the names, Priscilla and Aquila, Titus Justus and Crispus, and also Sosthenes, with detail of status and location, as usual give some assurance that Luke had good sources to draw on. And although the pattern of synagogue preaching and rejection is so characteristic of Luke, even here there are indications that resistance from local Jews accompanied the foundation of the church in Corinth (I Cor. 1.22–23) and that there was a Jewish dimension to the tensions within the Corinthian church itself (cf. I Cor. 1.12; 8–10; II Cor. 11).

18.1   Corinth was the next obvious city to seek to evangelize. It was the capital of Achaia, and its position as an important business and commercial centre, for both north-south and east-west trade (on the isthmus of Corinth), gave it a particularly strategic prominence. The opportunity to reach out to travellers and those engaged in itinerant business, both Jews and Greeks, would be unsurpassed.

18.2–3   The expulsion of Jews from Rome by Emperor Claudius (most probably in 49) is referred to in a famous passage by the Roman historian, Suetonius: Claudius 'expelled Jews from Rome because of their constant disturbances at the instigation of Chrestus' (*Claudius* 25.4). The almost universal assumption is that by 'Chrestus' Suetonius must mean 'Christus', and that he is referring to disturbances within the large Jewish community in Rome occasioned by early preaching about Messiah Jesus by Christian Jews. It is less likely that Claudius expelled the whole Jewish community (reckoned at more than 40,000). So Claudius' edict was probably directed against those regarded as the main participants and ringleaders in the troubles (though Luke assumes that *all* Jews were expelled from *Italy*). In which case we can assume that Aquila and Priscilla were already Christian before they met Paul, and that they had already demonstrated their leadership qualities in the intra-Jewish debates in Rome. This is borne out here by the fact that Luke includes no record of their being converted by Paul. Their arrival in Corinth was 'recent'; possibly the abruptness of their expulsion meant that they had to give all their attention to business affairs and had not been able to continue 'agitating' on behalf of Christ. Even so, their mutual commitment (as well as their mutual trade) would ensure that they and Paul 'hit it off' together (Paul's references below to the couple indicate a particularly warm bond between them).

Aquila and Priscilla probably ran a substantial business (in tent-making, or more generally, leather-working) and were well to do. They moved around freely; they are located in turn at Corinth (here), Ephesus (18.26) and Rome (Rom. 16.3). And their houses were large enough to host the local churches (I Cor. 16.19; Rom. 16.5). They could therefore take Paul on and provide him with a living wage. Luke says nothing more at this point, but I Cor. 9.15–18 and II Cor. 11.7–9 indicate that Paul saw it as a point of principle not to be dependent on his converts for his livelihood. 'Working with one's hands' was quite acceptable in rabbinic circles, but would generally be regarded as beneath the dignity of the well-to-do; in the formal sense Paul became a client of his employers. Consequently we have to assume that Paul spent each week working at his trade, and that he was not free to range around looking for people to argue with. On the other hand, a tentmaking stall in or close to the market (archaeology has revealed such small shops in Corinth) would give plenty of opportunity to engage with passers-by and customers. Paul probably witnessed to his faith at and by means of his work.

241

18.4   On the sabbath, however, he focussed his energies on the synagogue (we have archaeological evidence of such a synagogue). Despite the tiredness which such physical labour must have caused (cf. I Cor. 4.11–12; II Cor. 11.27) he did not take the day off, but continued to use the synagogue as the obvious place and platform for his preaching of the word (13.14; 14.1; 17.1–3, 10). Here too Luke takes it for granted that there were Greek proselytes and/or Godfearers who attended the Corinthian synagogue on the sabbath (see on 10.2).

18.5   But when Silas and Timothy arrived from Macedonia Paul began to devote himself (more fully) to preaching. Probably they brought funds from the Macedonian churches (cf. II Cor. 11.8–9; Phil. 4.15). But possibly also the larger team allowed a better balance between work and ministry. As in 17.3 the thrust of Paul's argument was that the Christ/Messiah (of Jewish hope and expectation) was none other than Jesus (so also 18.28). The involvement of Silas and Timothy in the early days of the Corinthian church is attested also by Paul (I Cor. 4.17; 16.10–11; II Cor. 1.19; I Thess. 1.1 – written from Corinth).

18.6   For the second time the opposition of the bulk of the Jewish community leads to a frustrated denunciation: they were rejecting a message to which Gentiles were responding positively and with joy; the obvious corollary was that the Christian message should be taken more directly to the Gentiles. The account uses language similar to that in 13.45, but the denunciation is stronger than in 13.46, and fiercer even than the final denunciation in 28.25–28. The other two denunciations provide a scriptural rationalization (13.47; 28.26–27). But here an allusion to Ezek. 33.3–5 is judged sufficient (cf. Acts 20.26–27). There is a clear implication of culpable guilt, now not so much for Jewish complicity in the death of Jesus (the usual earlier ground for calling for Jewish repentance; see on 2.23), but for failure to accept Jesus as the hoped for Messiah.

Whether this was simply an outburst of frustrated concern on Paul's part (cf. 13.51) or a Lukan motif (or both), it once again is not final. Paul continues his strategy of going first to the synagogue (18.19; 19.8) and in engaging first with his fellow Jews where possible (28.17, 23). There is no final breach between the Pauline churches and the synagogues of the Jews, but a sustained obligation to recognize the Jewish character of the gospel of Messiah Jesus and his own people's first claim upon it (see further on 28.23–31).

18.7–8 Despite the opposition of the bulk of the Jewish community, there were those among the listeners who were convinced and believed. Titius Justus, possibly referred to again in Col. 4.11, is named first. For, although a Godfearer (his name suggests that he was a Roman citizen), his house is mentioned, presumably because it provided the base for the new congregation to meet. The dynamics are those of a schism in the synagogue community (similarly 19.9 – a familiar tale often repeated then and thereafter in religious groupings), but the implication that the new church met next door to the parent body gives the report a peculiar piquancy.

More important was the conviction of Crispus, the chief man or president of the synagogue, regarding Messiah Jesus as Lord ('trusted the Lord' is sufficient indication that a life-determining decision was made). To win such a prominent Jew was a confirmation that other Jews as well as Paul saw the new teaching as wholly consistent with and a fuller/further expression of their ancestral religion. This is the fourth household to be recorded as committing themselves to the new sect (cf. 10.48; 16.15, 33), and again it is not clear whether a family is in view or simply the household slaves and retainers (see on 16.32–34). Paul remembered the occasion well having personally baptized Crispus (I Cor. 1.14).

The many other Corinthians who heard (Paul or about Crispus), believed and were baptized presumably refer primarily to the rest of the synagogue community (Jews and Godfearers) who joined the breakaway group, but could include those attracted to the gatherings in the house of Titius Justus. Luke evidently did not share either Paul's knowledge or his opinion that the household of Stephanas were his first converts in Achaia (I Cor. 16.15). He also missed the opportunity to report the conversion of another local notable, Gaius (I Cor. 1.14; Rom. 16.23).

18.9–10 'The Lord' here is presumably Christ (cf. 18.8). The vision came in the night (a dream?). Once again a vision was to play a decisive role in shaping a policy and determining a course of action (cf. 9.10; 10.3; 11.5; 16.9–10). On this occasion it is the assurance that the Lord would be with him to protect him and to add many to his newly founded church which is decisive in causing Paul to settle for a long period in Corinth. It was this token of heavenly approval which caused Paul to make Corinth the first headquarters of what was now a mission independent both of Antioch and of the local synagogue. The language used ('a great people') echoes 15.14 and may well indicate a scriptural template for the report (Josh. 1.9; Isa. 41.10; 43.5; Jer. 1.8, 19; also Matt. 28.20). But Paul does recall a considerable degree of trepidation in his early preaching in Corinth (I Cor. 2.3) and an abundance of visionary experiences over the years (II Cor. 12.7). He also thought of the believing Gentiles as one with God's people (Rom. 9.25–26; 15.10; II Cor. 6.16). So Luke's picture is entirely consistent with Paul's own recollections and subsequent reflections.

18.11   is in effect another of Luke's summaries (see on 13.49), but gives a more precise indication of the span of time than usual.

18.12–13   Although we know the dates of Gallio's proconsulship fairly accurately (an inscription dates it at 51), it is not clear at what stage during Paul's time in Corinth or during Gallio's time as proconsul the events now described took place. The pattern of Jewish opposition takes a significant turn here. It is 'the Jews' once again who take the lead – that is, obviously, the bulk of the Jewish community following the defection(?) of some of their leading members, or the leaders who succeeded Crispus. But on this occasion, instead of trying to manipulate either the city's elite (13.50; 14.5) or the mob (14.19; 17.5, 13), they take their case directly to the highest court in the region. The charge is also significantly different – not of fomenting civil and political unrest (17.6–7; cf. 16.20–21), but of 'persuading people to worship God contrary to the law'. The last phrase is probably ambiguous. On the one hand, it would be intended to trigger Roman suspicion of new sects and various rulings in the past which had been made to prevent such sects making inroads into the traditional and civic cults (with consequent disturbance of civic functions and good order). On the other, it would express the synagogue's real complaint: that Jews and Godfearers affiliated to the synagogue were being encouraged to worship without regard to the (Jewish) law (that is, its distinctively Jewish features).

18.14–15   The peremptory ruling which followed (there was no need even for Paul to respond), addressed to all the participants as 'Jews', was of supreme importance for the young Christian church. In the first place, it refuted the suggestion that the believers in

Messiah Jesus were in breach of any Roman law, whether in their worship or in their evangelism. In the second place, it affirmed that the disputes between the young church and the synagogue were internal to the Jewish community, issues to be determined within their own jurisdiction (cf. the Jewish jurisdiction implicit in II Cor. 11.24). The consequences of such a ruling and precedent from such a prominent Roman authority would have been immense. (1) On the legal and political front, the young churches would be freed at a stroke from the threat of criminal actions against them. They could shelter under the legal protection afforded to synagogues – a vitally important immunity in an empire constantly fearful of combinations and associations which might foster unrest against the state. (2) On the social and theological side it was equally important that the new groups of disciples should be recognized as part of diaspora Judaism. Nascent Christianity was not yet seen as something distinct from its parent religion; the young churches were still recognized to be both continuous and of a piece with the network of Jewish synagogues scattered round most of the Mediterranean world.

18.16–17   With this ruling the case was brusquely dismissed ('he drove them away from the rostrum'). Why 'all' should then seize and beat Sosthenes, the ruler of the synagogue, is hardly self-evident. If 'all' denote the Jewish plaintiffs, we presumably have to envisage that they had cause for complaint against Sosthenes: had he also joined the disciples of Messiah Jesus (cf. I Cor. 1.1), a second president of the synagogue (in succession?)? or was he more accommodating to the new sect ('the Jews' were not so united after all)? Alternatively, if the 'all' are the market layabouts, is this a case where the Jewish community was not so highly regarded within the city (cf. 19.34; but contrast 13.50; 14.2, 19; 17.5, 13), so that the adverse ruling gave opportunity to express antagonism against an ethnic minority group? Either way, Gallio left the Jewish community to its own affairs and to stew in their own juice. The ruling and its beneficial effects for the young church was left unchanged. The promise to Paul in particular of protection while in Corinth (18.10) did not fail.

Preparing the ground for the next phase
18.18–23

Almost as an echo of Gallio's ruling in Corinth – deliberate on Luke's part, no doubt, but possibly also on Paul's – the immediately following record is of the firm decision to return to the East, Paul's Nazirite vow, a positive response from the synagogue in Ephesus, and the visit to the churches in Jerusalem and Antioch (18.18–22). Gallio's judgment was correct. This is indeed an intra-Jewish movement. Its chief exponent demonstrates concern for continuity with and maintenance of Jewish traditions. And he is well received both by the synagogue in one of the chief centres of diaspora Judaism (Ephesus) and by the mother churches of the Christian mission whose bridge-building loyalty to Jewish distinctives had already been well documented (ch. 15).

18.18   Another of Luke's vague time references leaves room for various sub-missions in the region (the church at Cenchreae, the eastern seaport of Corinth, was to have the redoubtable Phoebe as its patron – Rom. 16.1–2). Also for the letter-writing which became a substantial feature of Paul's Aegean mission (Thessalonians and Galatians were probably written during the time in Corinth). Of this Luke says nothing. Nor is it clear whether the 'many days' are part of the eighteen months of 18.11 or in addition to it.

'Syria' (as in 20.3) could simply refer to the eastern Mediterranean seaboard (Palestine being treated as a subprovince of Syria at that time), and therefore would be inclusive of a visit to either Jerusalem or Antioch or both. But in Acts it would more naturally be taken to refer to Syria proper (15.23, 41; 21.3), and with the visit to Jerusalem passed over without the city itself being named (18.22), the implication is that Paul wished primarily to visit Antioch, the church which first formally commissioned him (13.3).

The vow was probably analogous to the Nazirite vow described in Num. 6.1–21. In which case the vow was not to cut his hair during a specified period, so that what is described in conjunction with it here would be Paul's final haircut before the vow took effect. Since such a vow could only be completed at the central sanctuary (offering up the previously unshorn hair – Num. 6.18) the implication of Acts 21.23–24 is probably that the vow was maintained until Paul's final visit to Jerusalem. The action tends to support the suggeston that Paul intended his visit to Syria to be one of reconciliation. He made a vow which demonstrated his willingness to follow the Torah in matters of personal spiritual discipline in order to demonstrate his 'good faith' to the Torah conservatives in Antioch (and Jerusalem) and to heal any continuing rift with them. The report as such is not confirmed by Paul in his letters (there was no occasion for him to do so), but it is wholly consistent with his own pastoral strategy laid down in I Cor. 9.20, and should not be dismissed as merely a Lukan fabrication.

18.19–21   Ephesus was the capital of Asia and a very important religious and commercial centre, with a large Jewish population. Paul's trip across the Aegean presumably coincided with a business trip of Priscilla and Aquila (see on 18.2); the naming of Priscilla before Aquila both here and in verse 26 presumably indicates that Priscilla was the more dominant personality. Although *en route* to the East, Paul follows his usual custom of meeting with his own people at the synagogue (17.2) and, inevitably, becoming involved in discussion regarding his good news. Here, notably, the pattern does not (yet) repeat: the message is received with interest; it is 'the Jews' with whom he had debated who ask him to stay longer. In Paul's mind, however, the visit probably had the nature of a reconnoitre: the mission being now so well established in Corinth it was time to consider setting up base in another major centre. So he takes ship on his way with a promise to return, God willing – a typical Pauline qualification (Rom. 1.10; 15.32; I Cor. 4.19; 16.7).

18.22–23   It was possible to sail direct to Caesarea, or at least without calling at the northern Syrian ports. So even if Paul had wanted to go only to Antioch, availability of passage or adverse winds may have left him no option other than to go to Caesarea. And once there, a trip to Jerusalem would have been unavoidable. Despite his awareness of Paul's unpopularity in Jerusalem (9.29; 21.21, 27–36), Luke passes over the visit in almost embarrassed silence – 'having gone up and greeted the church (Jerusalem itself is not mentioned), he went down to Antioch'. Mention of the visit to Antioch is almost as brief: beyond the fact that Paul 'spent some time there' nothing more is said. Luke was presumably content thus to reaffirm the impression that the threads linking Paul's mission to the mother churches of Syria remained unbroken. Nothing more need be said. The minimalist reports, however, intrigue historians, who tend either to dispute whether the visits took place or to build them up into something more significant. But Luke clearly thought them of little importance (a brief interlude in the Aegean mission). This may be simply because for Paul they were intended as visits of reconciliation for the earlier breach (see Introduction to 15.30–41); whereas for Luke, since he had passed over that breach in silence, there was nothing else of substance that he could report.

A decision to return to his main focus of mission in the Aegean by land would be understandable as it allowed further visits to the churches of the earlier mission from Antioch (13.14–14.23; 15.41–16.5), ensuring their solidarity with the developing Pauline mission. Paul had probably written to the Galatians by now and the visit would consolidate his position among them and allow him to set in hand what became one of his principal preoccupations in the latter phase of the Aegean mission – the collection for the poor among the saints in Jerusalem (Rom. 15.25; I Cor. 16.1; II Cor. 8–9). This may have been sparked by such a visit to Jerusalem, which had made Paul aware of the poverty of the church there. And the churches of Galatia are mentioned as among the first to be given instructions about it (I Cor. 16.1). Of all this and the long days of travel covered in these verses Luke says nothing, content to summarize the purpose of the land journey by one of his standard phrases (14.22; 15.32, 41). For the reasons noted above (Introduction to chs 16–20 [pp.212f.]) this should not be described as the beginning of a 'third missionary journey'.

Integrating Apollos
18.24–28

The interlude in Paul's Aegean mission allows Luke to insert the story of Apollos, whose function is twofold. First, Apollos, together with the 'disciples' in the following episode (19.1–7), could represent all the groups on the fringes of the new Christian movement. There would no doubt be many such who had heard (or heard about) the preaching of John the Baptist, or incomplete reports of Jesus' ministry, or a garbled account of the early Christian preaching, and who had made some commitment on its basis. In the early years of a movement like Christianity, defining characteristics and boundaries are always less distinct than hindsight cares to admit. It was precisely one of the major functions and achievements of Paul and

Luke to fill out the Christian identity, its characteristics and boundaries.

Secondly, Apollos in particular became a prominent figure within the Aegean mission, as Luke knew well (18.26–28). We know also from I Corinthians that he became a focus for some dissatisfaction and disaffection regarding Paul (I Cor. 1.12; 3.4–7; 4.6), a kind of George Whitefield to Paul's John Wesley, as we might say. In other words, in his case there was a real danger of an off-centre or out of focus kind of Christianity developing round Apollos, particularly as he had rhetorical skills which Paul evidently lacked (cf. Acts 18.24, 28; I Cor. 1–4; II Cor. 10.10). It was important, therefore for Luke to be able to tell the story of how Apollos, for all his fervency in Spirit and accurate knowledge about Jesus, still had to be and was instructed more accurately in the way of God (18.25–26). The Christianity established in the Aegean region was the Christianity of the Aegean mission, the Christianity of Paul and his team. That Paul did regard Apollos as a fellow worker subsequently is confirmed by I Cor. 16.12, with Priscilla and Aquila also close at hand (I Cor. 16.19). The account here was probably derived ultimately from Priscilla and Aquila or from Apollos himself.

18.24   With Barnabas, Apollos is one of the most intriguing figures in earliest Christian history; the several brief references to whom only serve to stir curiosity still further. Not least in the fascination he exerts is the fact that he is the one man who provides a clear link between earliest Christianity and Alexandria, the second greatest city in the Roman Empire, a major centre of learning and of Jewish settlement and the source of most of the diaspora Jewish literature which we still possess (including the Greek translation of the scriptures, the LXX, several of the writings preserved in the Apocrypha and the extensive expository writings of the Jewish philosopher Philo, Paul's older contemporary). The following description of Apollos gives some credibility to the suggestion that the beginnings of Christianity in Alexandria were not entirely 'orthodox' (to use the later term).

This background in turn makes all the more intriguing the description that Apollos was 'an eloquent or learned man, well-versed in or powerful in (his exposition of) the scriptures'. There is an open invitation here to imagine one who expounded the scriptures in the manner of the Wisdom of Solomon or of a Philo or other Jewish apologists. Since these writings provide examples of how diaspora Judaism confronted wider Hellenistic religion and philosophy, both exemplary for and alternative to Christian apologetic, we can well understand how it is that Apollos appears in the New Testament as a somewhat ambivalent figure, and how some could attribute the authorship of Hebrews to him.

18.25–26   The impression that Apollos was a figure somewhat on the edge of mainline developments is confirmed by the description here. He had been 'instructed (catechized) in the way of the Lord'; he was 'aglow with the Spirit'; 'he spoke and taught accurately the traditions about Jesus' (cf. 28.31). But he had been baptized only with 'the baptism of John'; his instruction in 'the way of the Lord' indicates further influence from Baptist traditions (cf. Luke 3.4); and his knowledge of the way was not wholly accurate. The implication is that his knowledge of Jesus came from reports of Jesus' ministry prior to his death and resurrection (the 'Galilean gospel'), perhaps even from the period of overlap with the ministry of John the Baptist (John 3.26): he had responded to the challenge made by Jesus himself, and had responded in the way the first disciples had done – by undergoing the baptism which the Baptist had instituted. Whatever the uncertainty, Luke's description confirms that for him John's baptism marked the beginning, but only the beginning of the gospel (cf. 1.22; 10.37; 13.24–25).

There must have been many such as Apollos – men and women who had heard and responded to early or incomplete or distorted accounts of Jesus and the gospel. The question would then be: whether they should be regarded as already full disciples, or how should their deficiency be rectified? In this and the next episode Luke gives his answer. In the case of Apollos it was important that his teaching of Jesus tradition was accurate, that he had received the baptism associated with John the Baptist, and that he spoke boldly in the synagogue (cf. 9.27–28; 13.46; 14.3; 19.8). But the decisive consideration was probably that he was 'aglow with the Spirit' (cf. Rom. 12.11). In consequence, all that he needed was some further instruction. Unlike the 'disciples' in the following episode he apparently did not need to be baptized in the name of Jesus: John's baptism complemented by the gift of the Spirit was sufficient – as in the case of the first disciples themselves (1.5). In contrast, it was precisely because they had no inkling of the Spirit that the twelve dealt with next by Paul had to go through the whole initiation procedure (19.2–6). In both cases it was the presence or absence of the Spirit which was decisive; the assessment of Priscilla and Aquila on the issue was as Paul's. For Luke here again it is the coming of the Spirit which is the central and most crucial factor in conversion-initiation and in Christian identity.

18.27–28 To be noted is the implication that there was already a church established in Ephesus ('the brothers') – quite possibly by Priscilla and Aquila themselves, following up Paul's sole visit to the synagogue (18.19). Also to be noted is the fact that Priscilla and Aquila continued to attend the synagogue, where they first heard Apollos (verse 26). Most likely the 'brothers' at this stage were simply a group within the synagogue, who probably met during the week in the home of Priscilla and Aquila (Priscilla as the main leader). But they were sufficiently conscious of their identity as disciples of Jesus to communicate with the more established church in Corinth, where a breach with the synagogue had already occurred. Such letters of commendation evidently became a common practice as believers travelled from place to place (cf. Rom. 16.1; Col. 4.7–17; cf. II Cor. 3.1) and a major means of cementing the scattered churches into a single identity.

Apollos' connection with the Corinthian church is strongly confirmed by Paul in I Cor. 1–4, where his ministry in succession to Paul and the power and effectiveness of his speaking are also clearly implied. The way he helped the believers there, Luke tells us, was by vigorously refuting the Jews in Corinth on the central issue that the Messiah was Jesus (as in 17.3 and 18.5). Here we may note again that, although the Corinthian church had already established itself separately from the synagogue, there was still substantial discussion about Jesus and the messianic prophecies between them, though it took place 'in the open, publicly'. Gallio had been right: this was still a Jewish sect and an intra-Jewish argument.

A New Centre in Ephesus
19.1–41

The second main phase of the Aegean mission was centred in Ephesus. Luke begins his account by telling a story complementary to that of Apollos (18.24–28). As Priscilla and Aquila brought the imperfect instruction of Apollos into the fulness of the Pauline gospel, so Paul himself brings the imperfect discipleship of the group of twelve into the fulness of the Spirit (19.1–7). The pattern of synagogue preaching, opposition from within the synagogue, a schism within the synagogue, and a steady growth of mission still attracting Jews as well as Greeks, is repeated in brief outline (19.8–10). More important for Luke was the further and final contrast with syncretistic religious practices and magic, where the word of God achieved a signal triumph (19.11–20). Still more striking for Luke, in terms of the space devoted to it, was the major confrontation between the representatives of the most important religious cult in Ephesus, one of truly international significance, and the representatives of the new way. What mattered not least for Luke was both the public identification of the new way with 'the Jews' and the fact that the local authorities had shown their clear disapproval of such mob resentment to Christian success (19.23–41).

That the account serves Luke's continuing interests is clear: the Spirit as the key factor in determining Christian identity (19.2–6); the name of the Lord Jesus as the other crucial identity marker (19.5, 13, 17); the split within the synagogue caused by a message still manifestly Jewish in character and still directed to both Jews and Greeks (19.8–10, 17, 26, 33–34); the contrast with misconceptions and corruptions of the message of Jesus and the public triumph of Christianity over magic and one of the greatest religious cults of the day (19.13–17, 23–27); the reaffirmation that Gentile perception and portrayal of God is false (19.26); and the protection given to the new sect by important provincial and civic authorities against the hostility of the mob (19.31, 35–41).

None of this is to imply that Luke's hand was the sole originator of these accounts. There is a suspicious vagueness about the opening episode, to be sure; but the concern and emphasis expressed in the story is wholly Pauline and even echoes his own language (cf. 19.2 with Gal. 3.2). With this correction of incomplete discipleship Luke is willing to leave ambiguous the question of whether Paul was the real founder of the church in Ephesus (cf. 18.27). The traditional language ('the kingdom of God'; 'the way', a term particularly used in Ephesus – 18.25–26; 19.9, 23), the detail of location (hall of Tyrannus) and the time notes (three months, two years) give some confidence even regarding the brief record in 19.8–10. Likewise the note of particular names and titles in the other episodes (Sceva, Demetrius, Asiarchs, Alexander) and the involvement of Paul's associates (Timothy and Erastus, Gaius and Aristarchus) suggest a first hand knowledge behind the story in each case. Perhaps most striking of all, Luke devotes substantial space to two further episodes in which Paul, though named, is not actually at the centre of the story (making four such episodes in two chapters – 18.12–17, 24–28; 19.13–19, 23–41), a strange procedure from one for whom Paul was the principal figure and great hero – presumably because the stories came to him in this form. As in most cases, the words are the words of the storyteller (Luke), but the stories he drew from earlier sources and eyewitnesses.

In larger historical terms, the significance of Paul's time in Ephesus can hardly be exaggerated (20.31 indicates that he spent longer there, three years, than anywhere else). Ephesus was ideally suited as a centre for an expansive ministry. As the capital of the province there was frequent travel to and from it. We can well imagine mission teams being sent out from it, southwards to Magnesia and Miletus, north to Smyrna and Pergamum, and up the river valleys to the cities of the Lycus valley (Laodicea, Hierapolis and Colossae), to Sardis, Philadelphia and to Thyatira. This is not merely a matter of imagination, since we can see from Col. 1.5–8 and 4.12–13 that this is how the Lycus valley mission came about; and letters were being written to churches in most of the other cities mentioned above over the next two generations (Rev. 2–3 and Ignatius). Even if the actual origins of the church at Ephesus are uncertain, then, it was probably Paul's choice of it as centre of the eastern Aegean mission which largely accounts for the prominence it came to enjoy within early Christian history. From there Paul wrote some of his various Corinthian epistles (and visited Corinth at least once – II Cor. 2.1). Many think that it was from prison in Ephesus (cf.

II Cor. 11.23) that Paul wrote Philippians, Colossians and Philemon (trying to correlate the crisis alluded to in I Cor. 15.32 and II Cor. 1.8–9 with the events recorded here). The letter to the Ephesians speaks for itself, and I and II Timothy are also associated with Ephesus. There is also a tradition linking the apostle John in his later years to Ephesus. No wonder, then, that Luke gives so much attention to Paul's time in Ephesus. He would have had no difficulty in gathering the material he has used.

Disciples without the Spirit!
19.1–7

What the relation of this episode is to the last (Apollos) is not clear. It is natural to assume that the twelve or so disciples whom Paul met and who knew only the baptism of John were somehow associated with Apollos, possibly converts won by him. On the other hand, nothing is said by Luke to support this association. Their state of preparedness is markedly different: Apollos already 'taught accurately the traditions about Jesus', and was 'aglow with the Spirit'; whereas the twelve had never even heard of the Holy Spirit. And the treatment of each is also different: Apollos needed simply to be given 'more accurate' instruction, and nothing is said of him required to be or being baptized in the name of Jesus; whereas the twelve had to be put through the complete initiation procedure.

The difference seems to lie in the fact that Apollos already had the Spirit, and so did not need to be baptized in Jesus' name; whereas the others, not having the Spirit, were treated as new converts. This, at least, seems to be Luke's point. He highlights it by having Paul ask the crucial question: 'Did you receive the Holy Spirit when you believed?' (19.2). The question of baptism is secondary to that (19.3). In terms of Christian identity, it is the gift and reception of the Spirit which is determinative and decisive – as with the archetypal precedent, Cornelius (10.44–48; 11.15–18; 15.7–9). As with the Samaritans, even belief and baptism (in their case in the name of Jesus!) was inadequate fully to constitute Christian identity (8.14–17). So here, discipleship without the Spirit is self-evidently a contradiction in terms. Luke was presumably content to leave the rest of the details of the story vague (including its links both to the Apollos episode and to the account of Paul's mission in Ephesus) in order to focus attention on the point of primary importance for him. In this way other dubious claimants to the title 'disciple' or definitions of discipleship are corrected and integrated into the mainstream flowing from Jerusalem through Antioch and Paul.

19.1   Paul follows the route which was denied him on his previous trek through the Anatolian highlands (16.6), descending to Ephesus either via the Lycus valley (so including Colossae, though only in transit – cf. Col. 2.1), or through the next more northerly valley at whose mouth Ephesus lay.

The description of the 'certain disciples' and the circumstances in which Paul met them is vague. Luke presumably wanted them to stand for all who claimed to be disciples but were not part of the local church ('the brothers' of 18.27). As noted in reference to 18.24–28, there were bound to be many such – that is, many who claimed to be in a learning/following relation to whatever message regarding Jesus they had heard; Luke would probably know such groups at his time of writing. Luke's point, then, is to clarify what really counts as discipleship, to emphasize that bearing the title 'disciple' is not enough in itself.

19.2   The sequence of questions is important. The first and decisive question is whether they had received the Spirit – not whether they had been baptized with the correct formula, or had apostolic hands laid on them. The question is authentically Pauline; Paul shared the same concern and conviction: it is reception of the Spirit which constitutes a person as a member of Christ (Rom. 8.9; I Cor. 12.13; Gal. 3.2–3). Some in the classic Pentecostal tradition would argue that the question should be translated, 'Did you receive the Holy Spirit after you believed?' But the superior translation is, 'Did you receive the Holy Spirit when you believed?' As the above passages show, Paul could not conceive of a Christian without the Spirit; on the contrary, the gift of the Spirit was synonymous with belonging to Christ. And in his sequence of stories on the theme (8.14–17; 10.15–18; and here) Luke seems to be making the same point through the various accounts which came to him.

19.3   Their complete ignorance of the Spirit puts a question mark against the status of their discipleship. Whereas Apollos had accurate knowledge of Jesus (18.25), these disciples had at best a confused understanding of even the Baptist's message (cf. Luke

3.16). The second question (despite its puzzling form – 'Into what . . .?') therefore evidently seeks to uncover the grounds of their claim to discipleship. It assumes two things. First, that discipleship presupposes baptism. Secondly, that baptism in the name of Jesus would normally be part of a conversion-initiation event whose climax was the gift of the Spirit (2.38; 19.5–6). Since they had been baptized (they were disciples), but had not even heard of the Spirit, what sort of baptism (what sort of discipleship) was it?

19.4   The Baptist's baptism was essentially preparatory: the point had already been made twice in Acts (1.5; 11.16). John himself had made that clear by telling people (that is, particularly those baptized by him) to believe in the one coming after him, now identified as Jesus. Implicit here is the association: those who believe in Jesus will receive the Spirit (Luke 3.16; Acts 11.17). The lack of the Spirit therefore indicated an incomplete initiation process, a faith not yet directed to Jesus, the bestower of the Spirit (Luke 3.16; Acts 2.33). Once again, as in 1.22, 10.37 and 13.24, the Baptist stands at the beginning of the gospel, his significance neither independent of Jesus nor lost sight of behind Jesus.

19.5–7   Their belief, baptism and experience having proved so deficient, they are treated as in effect first time converts. Their previous repentance is completed (so it is implied – 19.4) by their belief in Jesus, they are baptized in his name, and the Holy Spirit comes upon them when Paul lays his hands on them. The theology is thus that of 2.38, but the process combines that of 8.17 and the experience of 2.1–4 and 10.46 (here is another point at which Paul mimics Peter). The implication seems to be: that laying on of hands is a beneficial aid, particularly when the normal, simpler procedure (repentance/belief and baptism) has not 'worked' for some reason; and that the coming of the Spirit may be manifested in inspired speech, the Spirit's presence being indicated both by loosened inhibitions and by the inspired speech itself (cf. 10.46). Paul evidently had witnessed such manifestations in his converts (cf. I Cor. 1.4–5; Gal. 3.5; 4.6). But neither Luke nor Paul imply that such manifestations are inevitable or uniform or necessarily of a particular kind.

Ephesus established as a centre
19.8–10

Typical of Luke is the brevity of what was probably the most crucial and successful period of mission in Paul's whole career. He was evidently content to sketch it in briefest outline – focussing on the schism within the synagogue and the emergence of an independent church more engaged with the wider community. With the instinct of a good storyteller he knows that the account of earliest Ephesian Christianity will be better served by means of the vivid episodes to follow.

19.8–9 The pattern of preaching within and opposition from the synagogue repeats with some modification. The potentially sympathetic response already foreshadowed in 18.20 is confirmed; for three months Paul is able to preach the word boldly. No mention is made of Godfearing Gentiles. Unlike earlier synagogue proclamations (13.50; 14.2; 17.5, 13), there was an openness to the message which characterized the bulk of the congregation. Does Luke's characterization of Paul's theme as 'the kingdom of God' signal a more carefully angled preaching which looked for more common ground (cf. 1.3, 6; 8.12; 28.23, 31)?

Only after three months did opposition arise, and only among 'some' (not 'the Jews'); indeed the 'some' are clearly a minority in the face of the community as a whole. To be noted, then, is the way in which the Jewish opposition in the diaspora synagogues seems to become less severe both in Corinth (18.4) and here, so that the final openness of the Jews in Rome (28.17–24, 30–31) comes as less of a surprise. Certainly if Luke had wanted to portray a breakdown between the Pauline gospel and 'the Jews' as complete and irrevocable he completely missed the opportunity to press home the point in relation to one of the major Mediterranean centres of the Jewish diaspora (though note also 21.27–29).

Nevertheless a split does occur. Quite why this needed to happen is unclear, but presumably the confrontation of two factions within the synagogue – the disciples, and the group (presumably of traditionalists) stirring up opposition to Paul – made for an intolerable atmosphere in the sabbath gatherings. The departure of one of the factions (most obviously the newer group), to form a new synagogue, was a sensible solution. The picture has a familiar ring to anyone acquainted with factionalism within a church. Here we

257

should note that Luke describes a separation and not an expulsion, and that he records no recriminations on either side. Evidently it would be inaccurate to speak of a confrontation between synagogue (as such) and church in Ephesus.

The implication of verse 9 is that Paul was looking primarily for a platform for his proclamation, though presumably 'the disciples' also met in homes for worship and fellowship. Paul must have gained wealthy backers by this time (the Asiarchs of verse 31?) since he was able to hire a lecture hall, though 20.34 indicates that he continued to work to support himself; the Western text adds that he debated daily 'from the fifth hour until the tenth' (11.00 am till 4.00 pm) – a plausible guess, allowing Paul the earlier morning for his tent-making. The transition of verse 9 also implies the move to a mission more immediately directed to the wider citizenship of Ephesus and indeed to the more leisured and intellectual strata of the society.

19.10   The wide-reaching effect ('all the residents of Asia heard the word of the Lord') is no doubt exaggerated. But it indicates how important a centre Ephesus was: many travelling to the capital from all over the province would no doubt take the opportunity to hear lectures like those of Paul. And in the Introduction to the section we noted the likelihood that Paul used Ephesus as a centre from which mission teams went up and down the coast or into the interior. Luke makes a point of indicating that the message continued to be heard by (and appeal to) Jews as well as Greeks (similarly 19.17).

A further triumph over syncretism and magic
19.11–20

Luke's continued delight in the miraculous (19.12–13) leads into a fascinating story (not involving Paul directly) which tells us much about the practice of exorcism in the ancient world (19.14–16). Which leads in turn into the account (again not particularly involving Paul) of the greatest of the triumphs recorded by Luke of 'the word of the Lord' over magic (19.17–20). The parallels with the accounts of Simon and Bar-Jesus in chs 8 and 13 are noteworthy. In each case Luke recounts a confrontation of the new Jewish sect with forms of corrupt or syncretistic Judaism (Samaria being part of Israel's traditional territory, Bar-Jesus being a Jewish magician, the exorcists being 'sons of a Jewish high priest') and the resultant victory of the disciples of Messiah Jesus. The implicit message is clear: true continuity with earlier Judaism and the true fulfilment of Jewish heritage is to be found in 'the word of the Lord', not in such syncretistic compromises with wider religious beliefs and practices in the Hellenistic world. Note also the contrast with 16.16–18: a successful exorcism by Paul demonstrates the power of the name of Jesus Christ in the right hands over black magic; whereas here the lack of success in an attempted exorcism demonstrates the perils of illegitimate use of Jesus' name but still provides the occasion for a further triumph of Christianity over magic.

19.11–12   The 'not just ordinary' miracles performed by Paul are equivalent to those attributed to Peter in 5.15. Both healings and exorcisms (notice that not all illness is attributed to evil spirits) were effected by handkerchiefs (sweat-rags) and scarves (aprons) which had had physical contact with Paul. Luke has played up such reports, of course, just as we today might want to play them down. Paul's own view of his miracles was somewhat ambivalent (Rom. 15.19; II Cor. 12.11–12). But given the same atmosphere of awe and fervent expectation as in 5.11–16 (here cf. verse 17), it would not be at all surprising that such cures did take place (see on 5.15). The belief that spiritual power can be conveyed through physical means is at the root of Christian teaching on the sacraments and on healing ministry as well as of the long tradition of relics within Christianity.

19.13–16   Jews had quite a reputation as exorcists. And, of course, we also know of other successful exorcists of the period (Luke 9.49; 11.19; Acts 8.7; 16.18). But the 'seven sons of a Jewish high priest named Sceva' sound something like a circus act, and that is probably how they should be regarded. Their title would certainly be contrived: whatever corruption there might have been in the high priestly families in Jerusalem, one can scarcely conceive of an outcome like this. On the other hand it is very possible to envisage a varied bunch of 'con-artists', or even of renegade Jews who tried to sell themselves as what we might call 'strolling exorcists'. We know of such characters from other literature of the time (e.g. Lucian's *Alexander the False Prophet*). The final phrase, 'out of that house', may suggest that they had been called in to deal with someone thought to be possessed by a demon.

Their technique would presumably be the standard one, as indeed we can see from other accounts. The key to successful exorcism was to be able to call upon a spiritual power stronger than that which was oppressing the sufferer (cf. 3.6, 16; 4.10, 12). The formula used here was the regular one: 'I adjure you by the name of . . .' (cf. its use, in reverse, in Mark 5.7; and the equivalent used by Paul in 16.18). The fact that the name of Jesus was used here indicates at once that Jesus was known to have been a highly successful exorcist in his time (cf. again Luke 9.49): to be able to call on Jesus was to call on that power which had proved itself in earlier exorcisms (cf. e.g. Luke 11.20); in later magical papyri the name of Jesus is one of those evoked in exorcistic formulae.

The rather amusing sequel serves as a serious cautionary tale. Paul was successful as an exorcist (it is implied) because he was a disciple of Jesus, who could therefore call upon the name of Jesus legitimately and with effect (16.18). The seven sons of Sceva in contrast were trying simply to manipulate formulae, depending on technique (and their impressive title). The lesson would be clear: spiritual power can be self-destructive in the wrong hands or where attempts are made to use it illegitimately. Only the one who follows in close discipleship upon Jesus and is led by his Spirit can act thus in his name (cf. 13.8–11 and again 16.16–18). At the same time we should recall that Luke did retain the tradition of Luke 9.49–50: it is Christ, not his disciples, who determines just who can act in his name.

19.17   The scene is entirely reminiscent of 5.5 and 11, and the exaltation of the name of the Lord Jesus in the sequence 19.5, 13, 17 is parallel to the sequence 2.38, 3.6 and 4.10. The name of Jesus continues to be an identifying mark of the new movement, but only as properly used (see Introduction to ch. 3 [p.38]). Again, as in 19.10, Luke makes a point of noting that the impact of the story was equally on Jews and Greeks.

19.18–19   The triumph over magic would be particularly sweet for Luke, for whom it has been a recurring theme (8.9–24; 13.6–12). Interestingly, Luke not only indicates that many of the believers had practised magic previously, but seems to imply that it was only some time after their commitment of faith that they confessed their practices (probably before the congregation, as subsequently laid down in *Didache* 4.14). This would not be surprising, given the melting-pot character of much religion of the time, and that magic had not such a negative connotation then as it has now (see on 8.9); the equivalent today could include over-reliance on prescribed drugs and sleeping pills. It is not clear whether those referred to in verse 19 were part of the 'many believers' of verse 18, but presumably there was at least some overlap. Ironically the same action (burning of books) could be the sign (then as now) both of the clearest break with an old way of life (when done of one's own volition) and of attempts at thought control (when done by others). The cost, fifty thousand pieces of silver, would amount to a substantial fortune.

19.20 The summary formula (as in 6.7 and 12.24) is used for the last time.

A first encounter with state religion
19.21–41

After inserting a brief note on Paul's plans Luke devotes the rest of the section (chapter) to a confrontation pregnant with significance for the future of Christianity within the Roman empire. For the cult of Artemis (Diana) in Ephesus was one of the greatest cults in the Mediterranean world (cf. 19.27). Artemis herself was one of, if not the most popular of the Hellenistic deities. As the cult centre for her worship and keeper (*neokoros*) of her image, Ephesus was itself a religious centre of immense importance. Artemis was the guardian of the city, and the city's political, civic, cultural and economic life must have depended to a considerable degree on the cult, the pilgrims it attracted and the trade it generated. The temple of Artemis in Ephesus was reckoned one of the seven wonders of the world, so magnificent was it.

These factors are important if the story told by Luke is to be fully appreciated. Against that background we can understand how the success of a new sect could have substantial economic consequences; sixty years later the younger Pliny records the devastation of the old cults by the success of Christianity in Bithynia (*Letters* 10.96). Likewise the ease with which a demagogic speaker could play on fears and local indignation to whip up a riot. Most important, from Luke's point of view, however, were two other features. (1) The fact that 'the Jews' were caught up in the riot and were regarded as on the same side as those threatening Artemis (19.33–34). The point already made in regard to 19.8–10 and 17 is thus reinforced: in Ephesus at least Christianity was seen to be of a piece with and able to shelter quite legitimately under the same legal banner as Judaism. (2) Even more important, men holding leading positions within the province (Asiarchs) are shown as among Paul's friends (19.31), and the town clerk quietens the riotous assembly by pointing out the lack of legal grounds for any complaint against the disciples of Jesus (19.35–41). Once again, as in 18.12–17, Christianity is shown to be still part of Jewish national religion and to constitute no threat to civic or Roman authority.

19.21–22   The two verses go oddly together: Paul resolves to depart, but then sends others ahead and stays put (cf. particularly I Cor. 16.5–9). But Paul was well known for his seeming vacillation on his travel plans (Rom. 1.10–13; II Cor. 1.15–18), as, presumably, circumstances, opportunities and demands upon him changed almost by the day (see also 20.3–4). His concern for his churches, and particularly to visit Corinth is well attested, as also his sending of Timothy as his emissary (I Cor. 4.14–21; 16.1–11; II Cor. 1.16; 2.12–13), and his determination to get to Rome following a visit to Jerusalem (Rom. 1.13; 15.24–25; II Cor. 1.16; 10.16). On Timothy see 16.1. The Erastus here was probably different from the man of the same name mentioned in Rom. 16.23, 'the city treasurer' of Corinth, but he is mentioned again in II Tim. 4.20. Even with points of unclarity remaining (why no mention of Titus?), the details of these two verses, therefore, are probably more easily correlated with the information which emerges from Paul's letters than any others in Acts.

The fact that Paul's planning was made 'in the Spirit' is the first of the notes to this effect in chs 19–21 which emphasize how much Paul's controversial trip to Jerusalem was undertaken with sensitivity to the mind of the Spirit (19.21; 20.22–23; 21.4, 11). The 'must' also indicates a sense of divine compulsion behind Paul's movements which no doubt Paul and Luke shared (see on 4.12; and note the repetition of the theme in 23.11 and 27.24).

19.23–27   The vividly told story requires little elaboration. Demetrius is a figure familiar to any visitor to religious shrines over the centuries. Also the particular mixture of religious and economic considerations; those who find the mixture a sign of inferior religious concerns have never borne responsibility for a listed religious building! Demetrius was able to summon other members of his trade guild. Luke, of course, would not have had a copy of Demetrius' speech to hand, but the sentiments and arguments were not hard to imagine. Rather cleverly he has Demetrius not only attest to the success of the new religion (19.26), but also to express the primary Jewish and Christian protest against the other religions of the time – the fundamental conviction that gods made with hands are not gods at all (cf. 7.41; 17.24, 29).

19.28–31   Demetrius disappears from the scene, but the clear implication is that the crowd became totally out of control. Archaeology has revealed the site of the theatre referred to – capable of seating some 24,000. Gaius we meet again in 20.4 – a different Gaius from the one mentioned in I Cor. 1.14 and Rom. 16.23. Aristarchus is also mentioned in 20.4, and again in 27.2, Col. 4.10 and Philemon 24 – one of Paul's main associate workers.

The Asiarchs were holders of high office in the league of Greek cities in the Roman province; three or four may have held office at any one time, but ex-office holders probably retained the title. Since the function of the league was to promote the imperial cult, Paul's friendship with some of the Asiarchs sounds odd. But the title probably was largely honorific and the office almost certainly awarded only to men of wealth and high social status. At any rate their support for Paul would at least imply that the new Jewish sect was not seen as any threat to the imperial cult or to Rome's authority.

According to Luke, Paul was dissuaded from going into the crowd. This makes it very difficult to correlate Paul's own account of the crisis in Ephesus (I Cor. 15.32; II Cor. 1.8–9) with anything in Luke's account. It seems that once again (as with the Hellenists in 6.1–6 and 8.1–4, and the Antioch incident in 15.36–41) Luke has chosen to draw a veil over a very unpleasant incident (this or some other), which in the event proved almost fatal to Paul.

19.32–34   The confusion of the irregular assembly/*ekklesia* (Luke notes dismissively that most had no idea why they were there) is compounded by the attempt of Alexander to 'make a defence'. Luke says both that 'the Jews' put him forward, and that some of the crowd wanted him to speak (though the precise meaning of the verb is unclear), but also that it was his being a Jew which triggered off the manic response of the crowd. The implication, therefore, is that he was a representative Jew, in good standing outside the Jewish community, and regarded as able to speak (presumably) on its behalf; but also that the crowd saw their grievance as directed against a Jewish teaching. And indeed, since Demetrius' speech had characterized Paul's message as directed against idolatry (19.26), it is difficult to see 'the Jews' distancing themselves from it. In other words, in a subtle way (too subtle for many commentators!), Luke has included the message of Paul within the defence proposed by Alexander. 'The Jews' of Ephesus are still not shown as hostile to Paul. In this way, not overtly but clearly enough, Luke is able to bring out once again that 'the way' preached by Paul was fully continuous and consistent with the religion of 'the Jews', properly understood now (as he would say) in the light of Jesus.

19.35–41   The 'town clerk' was probably the secretary or chief executive officer of the civic assembly, responsible for drafting and publishing its decrees. That he should be fearful for the city's standing of the consequences of an irregular assembly getting out of hand (they could easily serve as a cloak for seditious activities), and was one of very few men who could have commanded sufficient respect from the crowd is wholly to be expected.

That meteorites became sacred objects ('fallen from the sky') is also understandable, though the term by this time might have been extended to denote the heavenly origin of the image of the multibreasted Artemis. Either way the allusion could serve as an implied riposte to the Pauline/Jewish dismissal of idols as 'made with hands' (19.26).

The judgment that Gaius and Aristarchus (and Alexander?) were neither sacrilegious (cf. Rom. 2.22) nor blasphemers of Artemis was as important to note 'for the record' as Gallio's earlier judgment that the dispute in Corinth was an internal Jewish affair. The one meant that the way of Jesus still ran within the confines of the Jewish ethnic religion recognized by Roman authority; the other, that 'the way', like its parent Judaism, could not as such be considered a threat to traditional Greek religion. Commercial failure was not a ground for religious prejudice or complaint.

The Close of the Aegean Mission
20.1–38

This final phase of Paul's unrestricted missionary work has the character of a journey to Jerusalem. The parallel with Jesus' journey to Jerusalem, which in Luke's Gospel takes up more than half of Jesus' pre-Jerusalem ministry (Luke 9.51–19.45), can hardly have failed to occur to Luke, although he does not draw it out as much as we might have expected. In both cases, however, Jerusalem stands at the centre of destiny, where God's purpose for his people is acted out through his servants at the cost of rejection and great suffering to both. And in both cases the sense of divine compulsion and pro- phetic antipication of suffering is clearly marked out (cf. particu- larly Luke 13.33 with Acts 20.22–23).

The journey itself, therefore, is a farewell journey, taking in the whole sweep of the Aegean mission, though allowing a three month stopover in Corinth (it is implied), the earlier centre of the Aegean mission (20.3). As such it is a mixture of triumph (20.2), a specially cherished memory (20.7–12), and an increasing sense of foreboding, climaxing in the sorrowful farewells in 20.36–38. Within this sequence the speech to the elders of the church at Ephesus is given particular prominence (20.17–35), not simply as Paul's only speech to fellow believers, but primarily as forming in effect Paul's last will and testimony. It is this speech, together with the clear indication of 20.38, which indicates to the reader that this was the close, not only of the Aegean mission itself, but also of Paul's career as an indepen- dent missionary. This was not Luke's view alone, since Paul, writing during his last visit to Corinth, expresses the same sense of a major period of mission now at an end (Rom. 15.19, 23).

Why Luke chose to ignore the principal reason why Paul himself made the trip to Jerusalem is not clear. For Paul the primary object was to deliver the collection made by the churches of his foundation on behalf of the poor Christians in Jerusalem (Rom. 15.25–28). Luke includes a reference (20.4) to the bearers of the collection appointed by the churches (I Cor. 16.3; II Cor. 8.19, 23) without saying why they accompanied Paul. The Lukan Paul expresses the same trepidation about the outcome of the visit as does Paul himself (20.22; Rom. 15.31). And Luke later includes an allusion to the collection in a speech of Paul's (24.17). The most obvious reason for his otherwise complete silence on what was of such importance for Paul himself is that the collection was not welcomed and possibly not even received by the Jerusalem church – so deep was the antipathy which had grown up in Jerusalem and in the Jerusalem church itself towards Paul in the meantime (21.20–21, 27–28). In which case, this was another case of internal dissension within the churches over which Luke has chosen to draw a veil (as in 6.1–6, 8.1–4 and 15.36–41).

The speech also reflects Luke's concerns as much as or more than Paul's (see Introduction to 20.17–38). But otherwise we can be confident that Luke had good sources for his account. That a sweep through Macedonia to Achaia was Paul's preferred route for his return to Corinth, that he would want to spend some time in Corinth, and that he would wish to sail direct from Corinth to Judaea is indicated in I Cor. 16.5–7 and II Cor. 1.15–16. The names (20.4; Eutychus), the timing (20.6, 7) and the details of the route (20.13–16) all attest an accuracy of knowledge rather than the contrivances of imagination. Not least of significance is that at 20.5 the 'we' of personal involvement in the events narrated is resumed and continues until 21.18.

The farewell journey
20.1–16

The journey is narrated with an unusual amount of detail so far as the itinerary is concerned. It is as though Luke wanted to draw a clear line round the edge of the Aegean sea, including the locations where Paul had successfully ministered. In contrast, only one episode is picked out – a particularly choice one which would have been cherished by all those present. The combination of 'first day of the week' (Luke 24.1), 'upper room' (Luke 22.12; Acts 1.13) and 'breaking bread' (Luke 24.30–35) would be particularly resonant for Luke himself. In this way Luke rounds off the Aegean mission, leaving Paul only to make his exit speech before the curtain falls on the touching scene of the chapter's final paragraph.

20.1–2 The implication is that Paul left Ephesus because of the disturbances there and continuing threat to his liberty or life (cf. 16.40; 17.10) – the first such enforced departure for about four years on Luke's timescale. How the trip to Macedonia fits with Paul's own reference to a similar trip (II Cor. 2.12–13; 7.5–7) is unclear, but they are probably the same one (that part of II Corinthians having been written from Macedonia after the meeting with Titus). At any rate, here too Luke has chosen to make no record of the tensions between Paul and the church in Corinth reflected not least in these passages. Luke describes the trip solely as one of successful pastoral ministry (cf. 14.21–22; 16.4–5; 18.23).

20.3 The three months, presumably spent at Corinth, almost certainly gave Paul the time he needed to write Romans. It is in Corinth or Greece (not at all in Ephesus) that 'the Jews' re-emerge as a united opposition (cf. 18.12, 28 with 18.19 and 19.10, 17, 33–34; though note also 21.27–29) – the inference being that those who hatched the plot represented the bulk of the Jewish community in Corinth in their continuing opposition to the way of Jesus. Alternatively, since Corinth is not actually mentioned, and the plot is mentioned in close connection with Paul's travel plans, 'the Jews' may represent those Jews with whom Paul had been planning to travel direct to Jerusalem on a pilgrim ship; that such pilgrims could be hostile to Paul is indicated in 21.27. For the plan itself we have the corroborating testimony of Rom. 15.25. Last minute changes like this in Paul's travel plans caused much confusion and criticism (see on 19.21–22).

20.4 These named were almost certainly the representatives of the churches appointed by them to accompany the collection to Jerusalem (II Cor. 8.23), partly for safety reasons, no doubt, but also to express in personal terms the sense of fellowship and spiritual debt owed by the diaspora churches to the mother church in Jerusalem (Rom. 15.27). They came from the principal theatres of Paul's mission: southern Galatia – Gaius and Timothy (cf. 16.1–2 and 19.29); Macedonia – Aristarchus (see on 19.29), Sopater (= Sosipater? – Rom. 16.21) and Secundus (not mentioned elsewhere); Asia – Tychicus (Eph. 6.21; Col. 4.7; II Tim. 4.12; Titus 3.12) and Trophimus from Ephesus itself (21.29; II Tim. 4.20). Why no one is named from Achaia or Corinth in particular is not clear; possibly the abruptness of the departure came before the local arrangements were made or the delegate of the church appointed.

20.5–6   The separate travel could have been intended to confuse any hostile intent, or to allow Paul one last visit to the churches of Macedonia. To be noted is the fact that Paul remained at Philippi for Passover – celebrated as a traditional feast, though now with additional Christian significance (Luke 22.1, 7–20). The surprisingly long time taken for the journey from Philippi to Troas (contrast 16.11) could be explained by adverse winds. Luke shows no embarrassment at presupposing the existence of a church at Troas whose founding he has not narrated (but cf. II Cor. 2.12).

20.7a   This is the first clear indication that Christians had begun to meet on the Sunday (cf. I Cor. 16.2; Rev. 1.10). The implication of 20.6–7 is that Paul delayed so long in Troas (despite the urgency indicated in 20.16) because he wanted to share in the Sunday gathering. The purpose of the gathering was 'to break bread'. Elsewhere in Acts this phrase denotes a shared meal (see on 2.42 and 27.35–36), but the enacted memory of the last supper may well have been part of it (the Sunday in question being so close to Passover – 20.6), the whole meal being regarded as the Lord's Supper, about which Paul had written quite recently to the Corinthians (I Cor. 11.20–26; cf. subsequently *Didache* 14.1).

20.7b–10   The tragi-comic episode which follows is vividly recalled: Paul going on talking hour after hour; the lights; Eutychus sitting in the inset of a high window, dozing off and falling down; the immediate shock at his stillness (the narrative assumes he was dead); Paul ever the one to take the lead. The account of the healing action may reflect the influence of I Kings 17.21 and II Kings 4.34–35, but that influence could as well have been on Paul himself (as he pondered what to do) as on Luke. It will not be accidental that a miracle of raising from the dead is thus attributed to Paul as it had been to Peter in 9.40–41.

20.11–12   A further breaking of bread is presumably implied: they would hardly have delayed the purpose for which they gathered till after midnight; and taking place in the middle of the night and still part of the same gathering, it must assuredly denote the opportunity to assuage hunger. In fact, it would have been (and is) typical of Jewish hospitality on such an occasion that a lengthy period of fellowship took place round the meal table and was interspersed with opportunities to partake of fresh supplies of food and drink (to think in terms of a modern sermon and eucharist would be anachronistic). Luke chose to continue to focus on Paul's sustained discourse or conversation, and only then to complete the story of Eutychus; but it would be pedantic to assume that Eutychus was ignored in the meantime.

20.13–16 The account is given by one who was a participant and could remember such details (see map 3 on p. 214 for the places mentioned). That Paul should bypass Ephesus, despite the fact that it had been the most successful of his mission centres, is plausible, particularly if the crisis at Ephesus had been more serious than Luke has let on (see on 19.28–31). But the reason Luke gives would have been sufficient explanation, even if Luke does not elucidate it. For there could have been no more appropriate time than the feast of Pentecost to offer the firstfruits of the Gentile mission in Jerusalem (the collection) and to acknowledge to Jerusalem the debt which Gentile experience of the Spirit owed (Rom. 15.16, 27). See also 27.9.

The testament of Paul
20.17–38

Within Jewish circles the genre of testament was already well established (modelled principally on Gen. 49; but note also Josh. 23). Characteristic of the genre was the presentation of some revered figure from the past, prior to his death, giving farewell instruction to his immediate circle, drawing appropriate lessons from his own life, and warning of evil times ahead. Such *Testaments* attributed to some or all of the twelve patriarchs were already in circulation and probably also one attributed to Job. Luke does not make use of the genre as such, but the motivation seems to be similar (note particularly 20.24–25): Paul, who is about to be separated for good from all of his churches, takes the opportunity to review the character of his main missionary work, to forewarn of future dangers and to draw appropriate lessons for his churches.

The emphases are the ones which Luke assumed that Paul would have wanted to give. But the fact that he depicts Paul's audience as 'the elders' from Ephesus (20.17), who are also addressed as 'overseers' in 20.28, despite the fact that Paul nowhere refers to 'elders' in any of his letters from this whole period, suggests that Luke more than half consciously wrote with an eye to the churches of his own day (see further on 14.23; though note also Phil. 1.1). Most intriguing of all, verses 29–30 express a mood of foreboding which we more naturally associate with documents written towards the end of the century, and their language, as also 20.24 and 28, have given some credibility to the quite popular suggestion that Luke was also the actual author of the Pastoral Epistles.

Luke certainly takes the opportunity to underscore several of his principal themes which run through Acts: 'the counsel of God' (20.27) as the ultimate determiner of the most decisive events (see on 2.23 and 4.27–28); the Spirit of God as the inspiring and ordering power behind the church and its mission (20.22–23, 28; see Introduction §5(3)); Paul as one who received his ministry from the Lord Jesus (20.24; cf. 9.15–16; 18.9–10; 22.17–21; 26.16–18) to serve as the great model of the committed missionary and teacher (20.19–21, 24–27, 31, 34–5); the repeated theme of witness-bearing (20.21, 23, 24; see on 1.8); the gospel as about the grace of God and the kingdom of God (see on 1.3) and calling for repentance towards God as well as for faith in the Lord Jesus Christ (20.21, 24–25, 32; see Introduction §5(5e)); the tension between a message directed to Jews and Greeks (cf. 19.10, 17) but also threatened by 'the plots of the Jews' (20.19, 21; see Introduction §5(4)); and not least the subtle reinforcement of the message that Christianity (consisting of Jews and Greeks) fully shares Israel's identity (20.28 and 32).

At the same time there is a sequence of features which suggests that here too Luke has not simply created the speech from his own theological priorities, but that his own theological emphases may have been as much shaped by the reports and traditions available to him. Thus we note Paul's sense of being under criticism from within his churches (20.18, 26–27, 33), a surprising feature for the reader of Acts, but familiar from Paul's letters themselves. So too the emphasis on Paul's suffering (20.19, 23) is something on which Acts has not particularly dwelt. The mention of 'house to house' ministry (20.20) reminds us that Paul's chief work will often have been carried through in house churches, whereas Luke concentrated more on the initial ministry in the synagogues (see on 13.5). The reference to the church as 'obtained through the blood of his own' (20.28) is a theological reflection on the cross unique in Acts. Paul's emotional commitment to his churches (20.19, 31) and concern for 'the weak' (20.35) is reflected much more clearly in Paul's letters than elsewhere in Acts hitherto. The language of 20.32 is particularly Pauline in character (to some extent also that of verse 33). And prior to 20.34 Luke has said virtually nothing about Paul maintaining himself by his own labour, a point of principle for Paul himself. That Luke was justified in portraying this as Paul's last will and testimony, then, is a view which can be maintained with some confidence.

20.17 Somewhat oddly, Luke has made a point of mentioning elders in connection only with the churches of Galatia and Ephesus (see on 14.23). Miletus was some thirty miles to the south of Ephesus, so it would be questionable how much time Paul saved by bypassing Ephesus.

20.18 Paul's testament begins on a note of self-defence concerning his own life. That Paul did feel himself to be under criticism for various aspects of his ministry is well attested in his letters – over his travel plans (see on 19.21–22), on his preaching (I Cor. 1.17–2.4; II Cor. 10.10; 11.6), on his refusal to accept financial help (I Cor. 9; II Cor. 11.7–11), and so on. Already in his earliest letter he felt it necessary to appeal to his converts' knowledge of his conduct (I Thess. 1.5).

20.19–20 'Serving the Lord' is Paul's language (Rom. 1.1; 12.11; Gal. 1.10; Phil. 1.1) not Luke's, as also the terms 'humility' (e.g. Rom. 12.16; Phil. 2.3) and 'what is profitable/beneficial' (I Cor. 6.12; 10.23; 12.7; II Cor. 8.10; 12.1). Paul also recalls his tears (II Cor. 2.4), as well as danger from his own people and hindrances put in his way by 'the Jews' (II Cor. 11.26; I Thess. 2.14–16). Both 'in public and from house to house' implies that his teaching was always consistent: he did not say one thing in private and another in public; there was no esoteric teaching for a privileged inner circle.

20.21 forms a nicely rounded summary of Paul's preaching in Acts – repentance towards God and faith towards Jesus as 'our Lord' (e.g. 13.38; 16.31; 17.30; 19.4; 26.18). In Paul's letters themselves, note the equivalent balance of I Thess. 1.9–10, though 'repentance' is hardly a characteristic Pauline term (only Rom. 2.4 and II Cor. 7.9–10). It was important for Luke that God as much as Jesus was the content of the proclamation to the Greeks (particularly 14.15–17 and 17.22–31). Similarly, it is important to note that in Paul's last testament Luke retains the even-handed emphasis on a gospel for Jews as well as Greeks (9.15; 13.44–48; 17.4, 11–12, 17; 18.4–7; 19.8–10, 17; cf. Rom. 1.16; 10.12; I Cor. 1.24).

20.22–23   sustain the note first sounded in 19.21 that Paul's final visit to Jerusalem was at the Spirit's prompting and in full awareness of its dangers (21.4, 11). The mission which began with such clear signs of the Spirit's direction (13.2, 4; 16.6–7) ends on a similar note of conviction. The full scope of the commission given in 9.15–16 has still to be carried through. Paul speaks of his 'chains' and 'afflictions' on several occasions in his letters (cf. particularly Phil. 1.17).

20.24–25   Paul is conscious that it is his whole life's work which is being thus weighed. The sense of the weightiness of the commission is somewhat as in II Cor. 5.18–20, but the language is the same as that in II Tim. 4.7 ('I have completed my course'). Striking a note which reinforces the character of the speech as a final testimony, Paul himself assumes that prison or death will prevent any future face to face contact. That he preached the kingdom confirms that his preaching was in line with that of Jesus and the earlier preachers (see on 1.3).

20.26–27   The note of final statement of accounts is heightened still further. The mood is almost that of a solemn death-bed testimony: 'I have injured no one; I have declared the whole counsel of God'. The overtone and allusion is precisely the same as in 18.6: Paul has fulfilled the role of the watchman, who has discharged his responsibility towards his people with faithfulness and who cannot therefore be held responsible for any calamity which befalls them as a result of ignoring his message (Ezek. 33.3–5).

20.28   is one of the most difficult verses in Acts, not to mention the whole New Testament. The perspective once again is closer to that of the later Epistles than to anything in the undisputed Pauline letters: 'take heed to yourselves' (I Tim. 4.16); 'overseers' (I Tim. 3.1–7; Titus. 1.7); Spirit appointed leaders (cf. I Tim. 4.14; II Tim. 1.6); also elders (20.17) shepherding the flock (I Peter 5.2–3).

The chief difficulty arises in the final clause – '. . . the church of God, which he obtained through the blood of his own'; or should we better translate 'through his own blood' (cf. NIV)? The text caused such puzzlement (God's own blood?) that some of the scribes responsible for making copies of Luke's book evidently attempted to improve or clarify it – particularly by reading 'the church of *the Lord*, which he obtained through his own blood' (cf. Heb. 9.12). REB prefers this as the correct reading, but a good rule in textual criticism is that the more difficult text is most likely to be original. NRSV and NJB, in contrast, reads 'the blood of his own Son', assuming a reference in the phrase like that explicitly given in Rom. 8.32.

Reference to the blood of Christ (on the cross) is a regular feature in Paul's letters (Rom. 3.25; 5.9; I Cor. 10.16; 11.25, 27; Col. 1.20), but never as a reference to God's blood. Rather than assume a simplistic, or, alternatively, a highly sophisticated statement of God's action in Christ (cf. II Cor. 5.19), we should probably see here a not very clearly expressed reference to the death of Jesus. Even so, the christo-logy is beyond anything else we have read in Acts (Jesus as 'God's own'). Not only so, but nowhere else in Acts does Luke attribute a saving significance to the cross, whether as an act of martyrdom or as a sacrifice. Conceivably Luke himself was not entirely clear on the significance of the cross: all the other references to it in Acts express a suffering-vindication motif (see on 2.24). But possibly it is simply a jumbled reference to the more familiar and clearly formulated teaching of Paul.

In terms of the constantly underlying question of Christian identity there are several important features in this verse. (1) 'The flock' is a well-established Old Testament image of God's people (Ps. 78.52, 71; Isa. 40.11; Jer. 23.2; Ezek. 34; Micah 5.4). (2) This evocation of 'Israel imagery' for the churches founded by Paul is enhanced by use of the term 'acquire', used of God's choice of Israel in the Greek translations of Isa. 43.21 and Mal. 3.17. (3) 'The church of God' is the regular Old Testament usage ('assembly' of God), indicating that each gathering of believers, followers of the Way, Gentile as well as Jew, was of a piece with and in direct continuity with the congrega-tion of Israel.

20.29–30 The premonition that false teaching will arise in the future, from influences both without and within, again has the ring of later letters in the New Testament (I Tim. 4.1–3; II Tim. 4.3–4; II Peter 2.1–3; 3.3–4; similarly *Didache* 16.3 and other second-century Christian writings); whereas there is nothing quite like it in any of the undisputed Pauline letters (cf. also the warnings in Matt. 7.15, 10.16 and John 10.12, and the situation envisaged in I John 2.19). The mood is that of the end of an epoch, *fin de siècle*. Verse 29 became the basis of the subsequent view that heresy was always from outside the church, subsequent and secondary to orthodoxy.

20.31 'Keep awake' continues the same mood of eschatological foreboding (cf. Mark 13.35, 37; I Thess. 5.6; I Peter 5.8; Rev. 3.2–3; 16.15). The tone of final testimony, almost self-defence, is maintained, but the talk of his night and day concern and admonishing is Paul's (particularly I Thess. 2.9–11 and 3.10), and the emotional intensity is little different from that attested in II Cor. 2.4; Paul, we can be sure, was an intensely emotional man who cared deeply about the welfare of the churches he had founded.

20.32   The talk of commending to God has a Lukan ring (Luke 23.46; Acts 14.23; cf. I Peter 4.19), as also 'the word of grace (Luke 4.22; Acts 14.3), but the sentiments are Pauline. In contrast, the language of God's ability/power (Rom. 16.25; II Cor. 9.8), of upbuilding (I Cor. 8.1, 10; 10.23; 14.1, 17; I Thess. 5.11; though also Acts 9.31), and of inheritance (Rom. 4.13–14; 8.17; I Cor. 6.9–10; Gal. 3.18) among the sanctified (Rom. 15.16; I Cor. 1.2; though also Acts 26.18), is much more distinctively Pauline within the New Testament (for the full phrase – 'inheritance among the sanctified' – cf. particularly Eph. 1.18 and Col. 1.12). It is difficult to avoid the conclusion that, whether through tradition or through personal awareness of Paul's thought, Luke's attempt to represent Paul's mind at this point has been very successful.

The last phrase in particular is more significant for our grasp of Luke's perception and defining of Christian identity. For it strongly reinforces the idea that the new movement described by Luke was one not separated from Israel but integrated into its heritage. Talk of sharing the inheritance of the saints is unmistakably Jewish in character. For anyone familiar with the Jewish scriptures it would immediately evoke the characteristic thought of the promised land and of Israel as God's inheritance (e.g. Num. 18.20; Deut. 32.9; Jer. 10.16; 51.19; Sir. 44.23) and of the people of Israel as 'the holy ones/saints' (e.g. Deut. 33.3; Pss. 16.3; 34.9; Dan. 7.18; 8.24; Tobit 8.15; Wisd. 18.9). Here then were mainly (entirely?) Gentile church leaders being addressed as those who are to share fully in that promise to Abraham which most clearly set Israel apart from the other nations. Here, in other words, is Luke's way of indicating that both the vision of James (15.15–17) and the commission of Paul (26.18) were fulfilled in Paul's mission.

20.33   The denial here echoes Paul's sense of responsibility towards his churches (in money matters) more closely than that in 20.26 (cf. I Cor. 9.12, 15; II Cor. 7.2; 11.7–11), though the tone is again that of a final statement of accounts (the model perhaps provided by I Sam. 12.3–5). Oddly enough, Paul follows the pattern of mission laid down in Matt. 10.8 more closely than that of the parallel Luke 10.7. Coveting, acquisitive desire is a theme which appears nowhere else in Acts, but is a common Pauline concern (e.g. Rom. 7.7–8; I Cor. 10.6; Gal. 5.16, 24).

20.34–35   That Paul provided for his own needs by working with his own hands was a point of principle and pride for Paul (I Cor. 4.12; 9.15–18; I Thess. 2.9). The verse here adds the information that his labour provided for the needs also of those with him. But concern that the more able should assist the weaker was certainly another Pauline concern (Rom. 15.1–2; Gal. 6.2), and he was quite ready to put himself forward as an example of Christian conduct (I Cor. 4.16; 11.1; Gal. 4.12; I Thess. 2.9–12; 4.11; II Thess. 3.6–10).

The explicit quotation of a saying of Jesus is unusual in Paul (only in I Cor. 7.10, 9.14 and 11.23–26). But he seems to echo and allude to other teaching of Jesus at various points in his ethical exhortation (cf. particularly Rom. 12.14, 17; 13.7; 14.13–14; I Cor. 13.2; I Thess. 5.2, 13, 15). So we can well imagine that the first Christian churches had a common store of Jesus tradition, which was passed on to them when they were founded, which was preserved and rehearsed by the communities' teachers, and to which preachers could allude with confidence that their congregations would recognize the allusion. What is striking here is that the saying attributed to Jesus appears nowhere in the Gospels (though cf. Luke 6.35–36, 38). This simply reminds us that not everything taught by Jesus has been preserved, and that there are a number of such sayings preserved outside the canonical Gospels which may well go back to Jesus himself (e.g. Luke 6.5 Codex D; *Gospel of Thomas* 82).

20.36–38   The speech ends rather abruptly; but a word of the Lord was as good a note for the Aegean mission to end on as could be imagined. Anxious, as it were, not to diminish that as the final note of this central section of his book, Luke gives no further detail, even of their final prayer together. The weeping reinforces the impression that a final testament has been delivered (cf. Gen. 50.1–4). In this way Luke hastens to round off the penultimate movement of his great symphony with this last touching, melancholic sequence, where the emotional bonding between Paul and his converts is underscored, and where the last notes of the coda have an emphatic finality – they would see his face no more. After that, their escorting him to the ship almost evokes the image of a funeral procession (the verb was so used in the idiom of the time).

PART V

The Final Acts: from Jerusalem to Rome
21–28

If Paul's determination to go to Jerusalem in 19.21, 20.3 and 16 echoes that of Jesus in Luke's Gospel (Luke 9.51, 53; 13.33; 18.31), then the final section of Acts echoes the passion narrative in the Gospel still more strongly. Indeed, Acts 21–28 could be called the Acts passion narrative, the passion of Paul, with its own passion prediction on the road to Jerusalem (21.11; cf. 28.17), just like the passion predictions on the road to Jerusalem in Luke 9.44 and 18.31–33, and the repeated pronouncements of Paul's innocence (23.9; 25.25; 26.32; 28.21) echoing Pilate's threefold pronouncement of Jesus' innocence (Luke 23.4, 14, 22). This must be why Luke gives such a disproportionate amount of his second volume to Paul's final days in Jerusalem and in Roman custody, in the course of which the trials and tribulations of Paul reach their climax. The slowing down of pace, like that in the Gospel passion narrative, here allowing even for two further lengthy narrations of Paul's conversion and commissioning (22.1–21 and 26.2–23), gives the whole a greater gravitas.

Was this in fact why Luke made so little of Paul's earlier sufferings, largely ignoring the events catalogued by Paul himself in II Cor. 11.23–27, so that even the stoning recorded in 14.19 seems hardly to have touched him – that is, in order that like the Gospel, Acts too should have the character of a passion narrative with a lengthy introduction? If so, it underlines the importance which Luke attributed to the work of Paul for the beginnings and definition of Christianity: as the defence and vindication of Jesus was the definitive climax of his first volume, so the defence and vindication of Paul is the definitive climax of his second volume. Furthermore, the impression that Paul was a kind of tug-of-war rope being pulled in opposite directions by Jews and Romans (chs 21–26) vividly illustrates the character of the Christianity Paul represents (see particularly Introductions to chs 22 and 23 [pp.291,300]).

That Luke really did intend this as the final act in his drama of Christian beginnings (and not as the precursor to a third volume) is indicated clearly enough in several ways. The first has been already referred to – the way Acts 21–28 parallel the Lukan passion narrative. For not only do the motif of the journey to Jerusalem and the passions of Jesus and of Paul match each other. But in addition we may note that Acts 28 makes an interesting parallel with Luke 24. For the opening paragraph (28.1–10) contains a clear vindication of Paul which effectively parallels the vindication which the resurrection afforded Jesus; we recall the repeated, 'but God', in the early chapters of Acts (see on 2.24). And the open-ended character of the end of Acts, where Paul is left welcoming all who came to him, and preaching and teaching 'openly and unhindered' (28.31) effectively parallels the open-ended character of Luke 24.44–53. In both cases the reader is reassured and invited to look beyond the horizon of the final chapter. The narrative may have reached its closure point, but the reader knows well enough that the story is not at an end.

Secondly, the final scene in Acts is clearly intended to complement the opening scene in Acts. The kingdom of God is still being proclaimed (1.5; 28.31); witness is being borne at the furthest point from Jerusalem (1.8); a new centre of mission has been established in the capital of the civilized world; the reader can be sure that the responsibility to bear witness to the end of the earth will be completed (1.8). The narrative begun in Acts 1 has reached its natural closure point. The expanding circles of mission from Jerusalem (chs 1–5) to Samaria and Judaea (chs 6–12), from Antioch into the peninsula formed by Asia Minor (chs 13–15), and from there into the Aegean (chs 16–20), reach their natural climax in the journey to Rome (chs 21–28). To say any more, whether about Paul's martyrdom or even further missionary work by him, would only leave a sense of anti-climax. Luke, the master storyteller knew when to stop.

Thirdly, one of the chief points to be made in the Pauline passion narrative is that Paul's commission (9.15–16; reiterated in 22.15, 17–21 and 26.16–18) has been now completed. He has carried Christ's name before 'the Gentiles and kings and the sons of Israel' (9.15). Hence the repeated sequence of trials and hearings: before the sons of Israel (22.1–22; 23.1–10); before the Gentile governors (24.1–25.12); and as the climax, before the Jewish king (25.13–26.32; see Introduction to ch. 26). And he suffers greatly in the process

(9.16; 21.30–35; 22.22–25; 24.27), not least in the ordeal of storm and shipwreck (ch. 27). To complete the story of Paul, the great missionary to both Jew and Gentile, nothing more needs to be said. In a way which effectively foreshadows modern storytelling techniques, Luke provides a kind of 'fade-out' in the final scene, leaving the reader with a lasting impression of Paul the missionary, sitting now at the heart of the civilized world and still busy preaching the gospel to all comers . . .

Arrest in Jerusalem
21.1–40

Paul's journey to Jerusalem has the same outcome as that of Jesus –
rejected by his people and left to the mercy of the Roman authorities.
The whole narrative builds up to this, with its succession of warnings and forebodings (21.4, 11–14), the ambivalence of James and the
elders (21.20–22) and climaxing in the riot in 21.27–31. Thus once
again, and more sharply than ever, the issue of Christian identity is
posed. Should he have gone to Jerusalem (21.4, 11–14) and attempted
to reassert his Jewish identity (21.23–26)? What is it that he preaches
(21.20–21)? Is his message a threat to the law and temple (21.28)?
How are Gentile believers to see themselves and be seen in relation
to Israel's traditional identity markers (21.28–29)? And not least,
Who is this Paul, and how should he be understood, above all in
relation to his own people (21.21, 24, 28, 37–39)?

The journey to Jerusalem
21.1–16

The narrative reinforces the impression of the Miletus speech and
the conclusion of ch. 20. The only details included, beyond that of the
bare itinerary, are the increasing forebodings of imminent disaster
(21.4, 11–12), the consequent anguish of both Paul and his friends
(21.12–14), and the final leave-taking (21.5–6). Were it not for the first
person plural of the narrator ('we'), the reader would be unaware
that Paul had any companions with him. The spotlight falls exclusively on Paul highlighting his figure in his role of tragic hero.

One of the most striking features of the section is the confusion
within the narrative as to what God's will for Paul actually was.
Somewhat surprisingly, Luke has no hesitation in ascribing the
prophecy telling Paul not to go to Jerusalem (21.4) to the Spirit, and

apparently no qualms in presenting Paul as one who disregarded a clear-cut command of the Spirit (21.13–14; contrast 16.6–7)! Whether Luke saw any tension or even contradiction with 19.21 we cannot tell, although it could be significant that he does not repeat the reassurance of 19.21 at 21.13. On the other hand, Luke surely cannot have thought or intended his readers to understand that Paul went on up to Jerusalem in defiance of the Spirit! The issue is not posed so sharply in 21.11, since Agabus simply delivers the prophecy (speaking as a prophet), the same prophecy that Paul had himself delivered in 20.22–23, and it is the disciples at Caesarea (including 'we') who draw the conclusion that Paul should not go to Jerusalem. What Philip and his prophet daughters (21.8–9) in particular had to say we are not told. What can at least be said is that Luke's account retains a highly realistic character: the Christians were entirely divided about what was the right thing for Paul to do; discerning the will of God is not easy, and counsel will often be divided on it; in the end each must take responsibility for his/her own actions.

21.1–3   The route followed is the direct one. A suitably sized craft allowed them to take the fastest course, sailing under Cyprus straight to Tyre.

21.4   Apparently Paul had no personal contacts among the disciples at Tyre (despite 15.3). It would be interesting to know how inquiry was made: did Paul inquire at the synagogue? or were the followers of the way of Jesus well enough known as such within the city that directions would soon be forthcoming? Given the strong traditions of hospitality in the ancient world, but particularly among Jews (e.g. Lev. 19.34; Deut. 10.19; Job. 31.32; Luke 9.3–4; 10.5–7, 38–42; Heb. 13.2), the picture is as we would expect (cf. 9.43; 16.15; 21.8, 16). The implication is that in the course of the seven days together they met for worship, during which an inspired utterance was given telling Paul not to go on to Jerusalem (cf. 13.2). Surprisingly nothing more is said about it: it was accepted as a word of the Spirit, but Luke remains silent about any discussion or questionings which we would expect such a prophecy to cause (see also 21.10–14).

21.5–6   The scene is as affecting as that in 20.36–38, with the same term used to indicate a supportive escort. The character of the scene is enhanced by mention of wives and children; it was a family occasion. The readiness to kneel and pray together in public would have been less remarkable then; the note accords with Luke's regular emphasis on prayer (see on 1.14).

21.7–8   In contrast to Tyre (21.4), the church at Ptolemais was known to the travellers, and Philip well known as the leader (founder?) of the church at Caesarea (see on 8.39–40). Philip is now identified as 'the evangelist, who was one of the seven'. The combination of titles is striking. 'The seven' links him back to the narrative of 6.1–6, where he first appears (6.5); but 'the evangelist' indicates his more prominent role as described in ch. 8 (the title appears elsewhere in the New Testament only in Eph. 4.11 and II Tim. 4.5). If the note ('one of the seven') is not simply Luke himself pointing back to 6.5–6, then it strengthens the implication of the Hellenist episodes in chs 6–8 that seven leading figures from the ranks of the Greek-speaking disciples were singled out at that time (hence 'the seven') and that Philip became better known for his work as an evangelist (independent of his role as one of the seven).

21.9   Since nothing is made by Luke of this note we may assume that he records it because he knew it to be the case. The form of the verb indicates that they prophesied regularly; they were prophets. In a day when the ministry of women still raises questions in the minds of some Christians, it should be remembered that what Paul regarded as the two most important ministries within the churches (I Cor. 12.28; Eph. 2.20) were filled by women – apostle (Rom. 16.7 – Junia), and prophet (here and I Cor. 11.5).

21.10–11   Agabus we have met before (11.28) – a wandering prophet, that is, one who moved from church to church (presumably at the impulse of the Spirit) to minister there for a period (see on 11.28 and 13.6). In this instance and in the tradition of the biblical prophets (e.g. Isa. 20.2; Jer. 13.1–7; 19.1–13; Ezek. 4.1–17), he enacts a piece of prophetic symbolism. As noted in the introduction to the section, however, he simply delivers his message as a prophecy ('Thus says the Holy Spirit') of what is going to happen to Paul, without seeking to dissuade him (cf. 20.23); should we infer that 21.4 was a deduction which should not have been made from a similar word? A pun is probably intended: Paul goes to Jerusalem 'bound' in the Spirit (20.22–23) to be bound as Agabus predicts. The parallel with the passion predictions in the Gospel is striking (Luke 9.22, 44; 18.31–33; 24.7). As in the references to Jesus' death earlier in Acts, responsibility is placed on 'the Jews at Jerusalem' (likewise inaccurately, as the sequel indicates), while recognizing that it was the Gentile authorities who held the power of life and death (see on 2.23).

21.12 Paul's companions and the locals (local disciples, presumably) draw the obvious conclusion. The formulation would exclude Agabus; did he not draw the same conclusion from his own prophecy? But this line of deduction may be too pedantic.

21.13 Paul's response is not that the Spirit compelled him (cf. 19.21); to put it so might have made for too sharp a contradiction with 21.4. But the same indomitable determination is implied. The speech at Miletus had given the same evaluation of his life's worth and of his preparedness to lay it down if his mission required it (20.23–24). But Paul himself, writing before he set off from Corinth had expressed a similar foreboding and resignedness to God's will (Rom. 15.30–32). Note again that the determining factor which identifies the act as one of conscious commitment rather than of foolhardiness is 'the name of the Lord Jesus' (cf. particularly 5.41 and see Introduction to ch. 3 [p.38]).

21.14 In the sigh of resignation there is a further echo of the passion narrative (Luke 22.42; cf. also Acts 18.21). The regular phrase in the New Testament epistles is 'the will of God' (Rom. 1.10; 12.2; 15.32; etc.), but here 'the Lord' is probably Christ (cf. Eph. 5.17).

21.15–16 It is quite a party which ascends the sixty miles or so to Jerusalem. They stayed with Mnason (presumably a substantial householder). The fact that like Barnabas he was an early disciple and a Cypriot, and so more likely to be identified with the Hellenists/Greek-speaking Jews (cf. 11.20), may well be significant. They lodged with one who was more likely to be sympathetic to the whole diaspora mission. Is there also an implication that the more obvious hosts (James and the elders) would be less sympathetic? At the same time, if Mnason was indeed more of a Hellenist, it is significant that he lived in Jerusalem and functioned (presumably) as part of the Jerusalem church. As usual in such situations, allegiances would not be black and white and congregations not uniform in opinion. An obvious speculation is that Mnason ('an early disciple') was one of the 'we' author's sources for early information about the early days of the Jerusalem church and the Hellenists.

The attempted compromise
21.17–26

This is one of the most intriguing and potentially most illuminating episodes in Acts – particularly in terms of understanding both internal Christian relations (today we would say ecumenical relations), that is, between Jerusalem and the Gentile mission, and Jewish/Christian relations. It marks in fact a climax in the development of the church which began in Jerusalem (we hear no more of the Jerusalem church/believers/disciples hereafter in Acts; contrast 23.16–22 and 24.23), and leaves something of a gaping hole or huge unanswered question about the character of Jerusalem Christianity and its future relation to the wider mission represented by Paul (see further Introductions to ch. 23 and 23.1–11 [pp.300f.]).

Here we need to recall that the reason why Paul himself came to Jerusalem was to deliver the collection, gathered from the diaspora churches for the poor among the Jerusalem believers, with all the overtones of respect and ecumenical fellowship which it implied (see Introduction to ch. 20). The failure of Luke to mention it at this point (particularly if he was aware of it – 24.17) arouses suspicion that it was after all not welcomed and may even have been rejected by the Jerusalem hosts (Rom. 15.31 shows that Paul himself had been fearful of such an outcome). Such a reaction would be understandable in the light of 21.20–21: it would hardly be possible for the Jerusalem leadership (however sympathetic personally) to receive a gift from someone regarded with such suspicion and hostility among the Jerusalem believers. But if that is so, it shows how fierce was the antagonism towards Paul within the Jerusalem church itself. It also reminds us that deep division of opinion and resulting resentments were quite as much a feature of the first Christian churches (as of any human organizations) as they have been in subsequent centuries.

In these circumstances the suggested compromise was a bold and imaginative one – expressing still (or again) that measure of good will on the part of James which lay behind his earlier eirenic attitude and agreement (15.13–21; so also Gal. 2.7–10, despite 2.12). Some have questioned whether it is conceivable that Paul would have agreed to the compromise: how could someone in direct line of influence from Stephen (cf. 6.14; 7.48–49) act as though the Temple was still a factor in the lives of Jesus' disciples? How could the Paul usually remembered for his opposition to the law have acted as though he had never died to the law (Gal. 2.19–21)? Such a view, however, allows itself to be ruled too much by the rhetoric of such statements and plays down I Cor. 9.19–21, where Paul sets out clearly his own policy of compromise, or better, principle of flexibility and adaptability. It also shows too little imagination for the realities of a crisis situation such as is here envisaged. In such circumstances anyone who was not totally intransigent would have been open to some degree of compromise; had Paul been so intransigent would he have gone to Jerusalem in the first place? In consequence, we can say that ch. 21 gives us a classic example of Christian willingness to find a middle way between divergent views without sacrifice of personal integrity (conceivably the intention was to receive the collection at Paul's hand after he had given proof of his good faith). We need also to remind ourselves that the compromise did not succeed!

21.17–19   The story picks up afresh. The Jerusalem brothers (including Mnason?) welcome them. It sounds as though a formal meeting with James and the elders had to be arranged – an ominous note (James would not receive him privately?). Peter is no longer around. It also sounds as though Paul gave a formal report to the gathering – a detailed account of God's dealings. That God was the initiator and actor in the mission and its developments was also Luke's particular emphasis (cf. particularly 11.18 and see further Introduction §5(1)).

21.20   The response of the Jerusalem leadership has a *pro forma* character, but echoes 11.18. The narrative passes immediately to the matter of primary concern. Their report in turn, of thousands of Jews who have believed, echoes the hyperbolic numbers of 2.41, 4.4, 5.14 and 6.7 (see on 2.41). But we need not doubt that the sect of the Nazarene had attracted and won substantial numbers of Jews, a point on which Jervell lays particular emphasis.

The crucial fact, however, is that their faith in Messiah Jesus had not altered their zeal for the law. When James/Luke describes them as 'all zealots for the law' we should not think of the political revolutionaries who set the Jewish revolt in motion in AD 66. The zeal here in view was understood as a reflection of divine zeal/jealousy (the same word – Ex. 20.4–5; 34.12–16; Deut. 4.23–24; 5.8–9; 6.14–15). That is to say, it was a determined commitment to maintain Israel's set-apartness to God, to avoid or prevent anything which smacked of idolatry or which would adulterate or compromise Israel's special relationship with God as his peculiar people. Such zealots were like Phinehas who killed his fellow-countryman and his foreign concubine rather than allow their fornication (Num. 25.6–13; Sir. 45.23–24), or like Mattathias who likewise took the sword to prevent the corruption of his ancestral religion (I Macc. 2.19–27). Paul himself had been such a zealot before his conversion (22.3; Gal. 1.13–14; Phil. 3.6). The same attitude among strongly conservative Jews is attested by both Philo and the Mishnah.

> Philo, *Special Laws* 2.253 – 'There are thousands who are zealots for the laws, strictest guardians of the ancestral customs, merciless to those who do anything to subvert them'.

> Mishnah, *Sanhedrin* 9.6 – 'If a man . . . made an Aramean woman his paramour, the zealots may fall upon him. If a priest served (at the altar) in a state of uncleanness his brethren the priests did not bring him to the court, but the young men among the priests took him outside the Temple court and split open his brain with clubs'.

The picture painted here, therefore, is entirely credible. What is striking, however, is that the new Christian sect in Jerusalem had attracted such zealous protectors of Jewish distinctives and traditional practices – more extreme, it would appear, than even the Pharisees referred to in 15.5. Quite what this tells us about the character of Jerusalem Christianity is not clear, but it was certainly ominous for any hope of good relations between the home church and the burgeoning mission in the Aegean and beyond.

21.21   It would be hardly surprising that such rumours regarding Paul were circulating and actively promoted in these circles. The charge, it should be noted, was not that Paul had accepted Gentiles as full members of the Nazarene sect; that issue had been settled in ch. 15, that is, in Jerusalem and following the lead of James himself. The charge was rather that Paul taught his fellow diaspora Jews 'apostasy from Moses' by encouraging them to give up practising those laws and traditions which marked out Jew most distinctively from Gentile (circumcision and food laws would be most clearly in view). It was just such a threat to Israel's set-apartness which would inflame Jewish zeal. Even if there was some knowledge of Paul's advice on how mixed churches should conduct themselves (Rom. 14.1–15.6; I Cor. 8–10), it would be easy for the impression to be put about that the end result was loss of Jewish identity. The reader knows from 16.1–3 how unjust the rumour was.

21.22–24 The advice of James and the elders is carefully calibrated. They do not themselves disown these rumours. Instead they suggest that Paul disprove the rumours by his own action, by showing that he himself still lived in observance of the law. Obviously this was not the time to engage in theological debate on the role of the law for believers; passions needed to be cooled first (if at all). We may presume that it was such considerations which secured Paul's agreement.

The vow in question was a Nazirite vow (Num. 6.1–21). The period of the vow having been completed, those involved could now shave their heads. A purification is not part of the vow in Num. 6 as such, but it was impossible to avoid being rendered impure in day to day life (as Num. 6.9 recognized), and the need for purification in order to participate in the cult was a standard feature of Israel's religion (see e.g. Josephus, *Jewish War* 5.227; referring to the purity regulations of Lev. 11–15 and Num. 19). If Paul's vow at Cenchraea had anything of the same character (18.18) Paul would have been able to discharge it at the same time. But Luke says nothing of this. Alternatively the hope may have been that Paul would be willing to shoulder the expenses of the Nazirites (as Agrippa seems to have done a few years earlier, according to Josephus, *Antiquities* 19.294).

21.25 James confirms that the conduct of Gentile believers is not an issue in all this. The recollection of the apostolic decree matches the detail of the letter in 15.29 (see also on 15.20). Some again read verse 25 as though James was informing Paul of something new to him. But Luke could hardly intend such a meaning (he has already shown Paul delivering the letter itself to his early foundations – 16.4). Nor does the text require us to read it that way. Rather the repetition increases the sense that a formal statement was being made.

21.26 The process described follows the rules for the discharge of a Nazirite vow (Num. 6.13–15; 6.21 seems to envisage the payment of a further offering). Even if Paul himself had not undertaken such a vow or the vow of 18.18 did not last so long (see on 18.18), the fact that he had returned from outside the holy land meant that he had to purify himself for seven days. Where did Paul get the money necessary to pay for the men's expenses? Surely not from the unmentioned collection!

The compromise fails
21.27–40

The narrative proceeds with vigour. As usual when Luke goes into detail the word picture is painted with vivid colours, displaying once again Luke's storytelling skills. The detailed knowledge of the physical relation of the Roman garrison to the Temple platform, of the cause of the riot (diaspora pilgrims from Asia, Trophimus from Ephesus), of the deployment of garrison troops and manner of arrest, and of the recent revolutionary action mounted by the Egyptian, all give confidence that Luke once again has been able to draw on good eyewitness tradition (the 'we' narrative continued as far as 21.18), however much as a storyteller he felt free to elaborate it.

21.27–29 It is unclear whether by 'Asia' here Luke means the province or Ephesus in particular (as probably in 19.22 and 20.16). Either way the Jewish pilgrims would have been in a position to recognize Trophimus (one of the delegates listed in 20.4) or that he was a Gentile. But if Ephesus is meant, it is the first real indication that Ephesian Jews were hostile to Paul (contrast 19.8–10 and 33–34).

The accusation in 21.28 strongly echoes that levelled against Stephen in 6.13 ('he speaks against this holy place and the law'); Paul sparked off opposition and hostility like that which brought about Stephen's martyrdom. The allusion will be deliberate on Luke's part. The additional factor here ('against the people') well echoes the zealot's determination to protect the boundaries separating Jew from Gentile at all costs (see on 21.20). Consistent with that is the specific charge that Paul had brought a Gentile (Trophimus) into the Temple. By that will be meant that Trophimus had gone beyond the low fence which marked off the court of the Gentiles (which Gentiles were able to frequent) and the inner courts of women and of Israel, leading into the heart of the Temple where the sacrifices were offered. Notices fixed prominently on this fence (two of them have been discovered) warned Gentiles that the penalty for breaching this barrier was death – more or less the only power of capital punishment which Judaea retained. The fence, therefore, was a visible sign and symbol of Israel's obligation to keep itself apart from the nations – the obligation which zealots were sworn to defend.

Of course, the Jews from Asia (who make the accusation) are not identified as disciples, but the implication is that their attitude was little different from that of the zealots among the Jerusalem disciples. Does this tell us anything about the non-appearance of the Jerusalem disciples in the rest of the narrative – similar to Luke's silence in 8.1–2? Could it be that the Jerusalem Christians left Paul (like Stephen) to stew in his own juice? Or is it simply Luke's storytelling style (concentrating on the main actors) which arouses such suspicions?

21.30–36 The account of the riot is neatly drawn and quite plausible. The crowd gather, stirred more by passion and prejudice than by clear information. The object of their hostility is seized and dragged away from the sacred spot (cf. the account in Mishnah, *Sanhedrin* 9.6 cited at 21.20 above). The Temple authorities take steps to ensure their property is protected; we should presumably assume that the gates in view were those to the inner courts, the Temple proper. The fortress Antonia abutted the north-west side of the Temple platform, with a stair giving access directly on to it, so that in times of unrest a detachment of the local garrison could be rapidly deployed, here led by the commander of the garrison troops himself. The cause of the trouble (Paul) was the obvious person to arrest – if only to calm the situation and to allow fuller inquiry. The information offered on the spot is inevitably confused; we can guess what one account was (21.28), but what was the other?! The cohort beats an orderly retreat, protecting their presumably injured prisoner from the mob's further violence and taking him back up the stairs. The crowd is incensed at the loss of its prey.

21.37 A moment of humour relieves the intensity of the drama. The tribune's confusion mirrors that of the crowd (21.34). But his question also reflects the confusion regarding Paul's identity and teaching evident throughout the narrative (21.21, 24, 28). Paul's answer (21.38) will therefore be all the more important.

21.38 The Egyptian in question we know about also from Josephus (*JewishWar* 2.261–3; also *Antiquities* 20.169–62). A few years earlier an 'Egyptian false prophet' had led a crowd (Josephus says about 30,000) by a circuitous route from the desert to the Mount of Olives with the promise that they would be able to seize the city. They had been quickly dispersed (with many deaths) by vigorous action from the procurator Felix (see on 24.1), but the Egyptian himself had escaped. Luke's information indicated a much smaller crowd (4,000) and characterized them as 'sicarii' ('dagger men'). This was the name given to those in the early days of the Jewish revolt (begun in 66) who used daggers (*sica*, *sikarion*) to assassinate their political opponents. It is doubtful if it was already in currency at the time of Paul, so that Luke's report may recall the episode in the light of later developments.

21.39   Paul's reply gives information nowhere else available to us. He was not only a native of Tarsus (which we might have deduced from 9.30 and 11.25), but he had also been a citizen of that notable metropolis. For a Jew to be a citizen of the city of another country would be unusual; for a start he would have had to meet a substantial property qualification. But if Paul was also a Roman citizen (16.37; see on 22.28) the lesser dignity could well have been his by birth also.

More to the point of Luke's account, Paul identifies himself as a Jew. He responds to the confusion regarding his identity and work (see on 21.37) by indicating simply his identity as a Jew. This self-designation further undermines the impression which some have taken from Luke's references to the hostility of 'the Jews' elsewhere (e.g. 13.50; 17.5; 20.3, 19), that Christian identity had become wholly divorced from Jewish identity. Here the leading proponent of Gentile Christianity identifies himself straightforwardly as (still) a Jew: Jewish and Christian identity still overlap and here merge in the person of Paul himself.

21.40   The scene is somewhat contrived: Paul, securely guarded on the steps rising above the Temple platform, is able to calm the howling mob, as the tribune and his cohort had failed to do. But Luke the storyteller relishes the drama of the scene he describes – Paul motioning with his hands, a great and expectant hush quietening the crowd, and Paul beginning to speak in his native Aramaic tongue (cf. II Cor. 11.22; Phil. 3.5).

Paul's First Defence in Jerusalem
22.1–30

The central feature of the chapter is clearly Paul's speech of defence (22.1–21). But it is also important to bear in mind the framework in which Luke has set it; for Luke regularly uses the framework of a speech to 'set up' the speech, not only in terms of the developing narrative, but also in terms of the theological points he wants to be heard by means of the speech. In this case the framework is slightly obscured by the chapter division. But when we recognize that 21.37–40 functions as preface to the speech and 22.22–29 as its sequel, a striking feature becomes immediately apparent. This is the fact that at each end of the speech Paul identifies himself and does so in a way only paralleled in 23.6. In the preface to the speech he identifies himself as a Jew from the diaspora (21.39); and in the sequel he identifies himself as a Roman citizen (22.25–28). This framework structure is matched by the structure of the speech itself. For it begins with a reaffirmation of the same identity claim ('I am a Jew' – 22.3; see also on 22.4–5) and climaxes in the commission to go 'far away to the Gentiles' (22.21). Hence also the internal dynamic between the various elements within the speech – the strong emphasis on Ananias' Jewish identity (22.12), the Jewish character of Paul's commission to bear witness for the Righteous One 'to every person' (22.14–15), with its strong echo of Isaiah's commission (22.17–20), and not least Paul's own continuing identification with the Temple (22.17).

None of this will be accidental. Luke is making a clear point by means of this section: Paul, and the movement he represents, shared a double character and a double loyalty. He (and it) are both Jewish, standing well within the traditions of his people, but also with rights and obligations within and to the wider world. It was this twofold identity which caused all the problems now unfolding: fellow Jews who would not recognize the wider obligation as articulated by Paul; Roman authorities uncertain as to the continuing Jewish identity of Paul and what he represented. This is a theme Luke plays upon constantly in this and the following chapters, as Paul becomes a kind of shuttlecock batted back and forth between the two spheres – the physical to-ing and fro-ing of the main character in itself expressing the tensions which the twofold identity and double loyalty set up. The ever clearer definition of Christianity's identity is the subplot being played out in these chapters.

Paul's conversion rehearsed for a second time
22.1–21

For the second time Luke recounts Paul's conversion – this time from Paul's own lips (as also the third in ch. 26). As before (see Introduction to ch. 9), the constant focal point of the speech remains the encounter between Jesus and Paul (22.7–10; cf. 9.4–6 and 26.14–16), and the climax is the commissioning of Saul/Paul to take the gospel to the Gentiles (22.15, 21; cf. 9.15–16 and 26.16–18, 23). But here there are two principal shifts in emphasis. The first is the emphasis on Paul's Jewish identity, training and zeal, one who even after his conversion went naturally to the Temple to pray (22.3, 17), and on Ananias as 'a devout observer of the law' (22.12). The other is the way the speech passes over the element of commissioning in the Damascus road encounter itself (contrast 26.16–18) or even in relation to the meeting with Ananias (22.15; contrast 9.15–16), and leaves it till the subsequent vision of Paul in the Temple (22.17–21). Luke makes the commission to go to the Gentiles literally the climax of the speech.

In both cases the reason is obvious. The speech emphasizes the Jewishness of the two main characters because it obviously has the Jewish audience of the speech in view. And leaving the explicit commissioning to take the gospel to the Gentiles until the end makes it clear what it is the Jewish crowd object to: that this Jewish sect is eroding the set-apartness of Israel from the other nations, undermining the Jewish distinctives and in effect questioning Israel's special prerogatives as God's chosen people.

Did Paul deliver this speech in these circumstances? The dramatic context sketched out by Luke is not at all so far-fetched as many assume. In a day when public oratory was the principal means of disseminating information and canvassing public support for policy, the tradition of crowds giving a hearing to speeches would be well established. As usual, Luke would feel no obligation either to provide a transcript of what Paul actually said, or to refrain from recording any speech. In accordance with the conventions of historical writing of the day, it was enough for Luke and his readers that he could represent what Paul could or would have said on the occasion in question. The variation in the three accounts of Paul's conversion, reproduced by one and the same author, is a reminder both of the liberty an author felt in retelling the same story and that this was quite acceptable historiographical technique for the time (see further Introduction §4(3)).

22.1–2 The speech is introduced as a speech for the defence (*apologia*; cf. 24.10; 25.8, 16; 26.1–2, 24; I Cor. 9.3; II Tim. 4.16). Luke implies (cf. 21.40 with 22.2) that the 'great silence' of 21.40 was not so complete as he seemed at first to imply. Now, on hearing Paul speak in Aramaic, the hush deepens and becomes the more expectant. Of course Luke is squeezing every bit of drama he can from the account, but any public speaker knows the difference between a quiet and an expectant audience; Bruce suggests the parallel of someone regarded as a traitor (by e.g. Irish nationalists) being able to address a hostile crowd in the vernacular.

22.3–4 The information of 21.39 is repeated for emphasis and effect: Paul was a Jew. But now he lays out the full sweep of his *bona fides*, using the traditional three stages of birth, nurture and education (as in 7.20–22). He was a Jew of the diaspora (it was diaspora Jews who had started the trouble – 21.27). But he had been brought up in the city, and taught by one of the greatest rabbis of the time (Gamaliel – see on 5.34); despite scholarly questioning of this information (based on Gal. 1.22), it is hardly possible to conceive of someone training to be a Pharisee (23.6; 26.5; Phil. 3.5) anywhere other than in Jerusalem. More to the point, he had been trained in the strict understanding and practice of the ancestral law which was a mark of the Pharisees: the term he uses here (*akribeia*) was used by Josephus to describe the Pharisees and denoted their concern for exactness in interpretation of the law and scrupulosity in observing the law (so also its adverbial version in 26.5). And he had been 'zealous for God' (similarly Gal. 1.14; cf. Rom. 10.2). A Jewish audience would not fail to pick up the implication here in the junction of verses 3 and 4, for in Jewish history one 'zealous for God' was one who maintained and defended Israel's set-apartness with the sword (see on 21.20). It was out of this zeal that he had persecuted the church (Phil. 3.6), those who followed the way (9.1–2). In other words, Paul could speak as one who was a Jew through and through. He knew and understood from personal experience the fears and beliefs which had sparked off the riot in the first place (21.28).

22.4–5 repeats the information of 9.1–2 with some variations. One indicates that some of the persecution resulted in the death of followers of the Way (similarly 26.10); that is surprising since the power of the death penalty was strictly controlled by the Roman authorities; but perhaps the case of Stephen is in view (see further on 26.10). Another notes that his commission to Damascus was approved by the whole council of elders (the same term is used in Luke 22.66); he had acted as representative of the people as a whole. And a third refers to the Jewish community in Damascus as 'the brothers'. Paul continues to emphasize his Jewish identity.

22.6–8 is more or less a putting of 9.3–5 into first person terms. The only additional information is that the encounter on the Damascus road happened 'about noon'. The information has stimulated speculation about the effects of the midday sun in the vision Paul saw ('a great light'). Jesus also identifies himself by means of the fuller formula: 'Jesus the Nazarene' (as in 2.22; 3.6; 4.10; 6.14; 26.9).

22.9 This is the most glaring inconsistency between the first two accounts of Paul's conversion: in 9.7 those with him 'heard the voice but saw no one'; here 'they saw the light but did not hear the voice of the one speaking with me'. The inconsistency can be resolved (they heard the voice but could not make out the words). But it is more worthy of note that the same author could dictate both versions without any sense that such inconsistency was of any significance.

22.10–11 In this version the instructions of the heavenly one come in response to Saul's question, and the response alludes to the larger commissioning indicated in 9.15–16, here using the term ('appointed') which was used in 13.48 and which emphasizes divine ordering of events (cf. 26.16–18). Otherwise the account is the same as in 9.6 and 8. Talk of the 'brightness or glory' of the light ties into Paul's own recollection of the event in II Cor. 4.4–6.

22.12   In 9.10 Ananias was referred to as 'a disciple'. Here Paul describes him as 'a devout man (cf. 2.5 and 8.2) as defined by the law, well spoken of by all the Jews living there'. The point is obvious: the man who received the zealous Pharisee into the sect he had been persecuting was a wholly observant, respected and representative Jew. The same man could be a representative of both Jewish traditional values and of the way, because the two were not at odds with each other; they were cut from the same cloth.

22.13   abbreviates 9.17–18.

22.14   gives the information implicit in the ch. 9 version: that Ananias reported the substance of his own visionary instruction (9.15–16) to Saul. Thus the good storyteller builds up the fuller picture by giving complementary information in his successive versions of the same story. Here, once again, the language used underlines the continuity of Paul's commissioning with Israel's heritage. (1) The one who appointed Paul was 'the God of our fathers' (echoing the title used in 3.13, 5.30 and 7.32), as in 7.32 probably an allusion to the commissioning vision of Moses in Ex. 3.15; Paul's commissioning was in continuity with that of Moses. (2) Paul was appointed not simply to do but to know God's will – the aspiration of every pious Jew (Ps. 40.8; Ps. 143.10; II Macc. 1.3; Rom. 2.18). The implication is, of course, that Paul's new direction in mission is in full accord with the will of Israel's God, part of his ordering of history (see on 4.12 and 27–28). (3) The one he saw was 'the righteous one' (as in 3.14 and 7.52). Paul's converting vision and commission was entirely God's doing.

22.15   gives the justification for Luke's and Paul's repeated testimony to his conversion-commission. To be noted is the fact that Paul is here also commissioned to be a 'witness' (as in 26.16; but so also was Stephen, witness = martyr – 22.20). These are the only occasions on which Luke uses this term which was tightly linked with the apostles (1.8, 22; 2.32; 3.15; 5.32; 10.39, 41; also 13.31), and the closest he comes to conceding Paul's own fierce insistence that he was an apostle every bit as much as the earlier witnesses of the risen one (I Cor. 9.1–2; 15.8–11; Gal. 1.1, 15–16; see Introduction to ch. 1 [p.4]).

22.16   is a further variation on the previous version (9.17–18). In the former there had been no explicit invitation to baptism, but only reference to Saul's being filled with the Holy Spirit. Here there is no reference to the Spirit, but an actual theology of baptism is clearly implied (the Greek could be translated 'Baptize yourself . . .', but the more obvious rendering is 'Get yourself baptized . . .'). (*a*) Baptism is explicitly linked with the washing away of sins (cf. 2.38) – whether as a parallel or an effective symbolism is not made clear. The same question arises in I Cor. 6.11 (same verb) and Eph. 5.26. In Acts 15.9 the thought is of the cleansing of the heart effected by faith, and in Heb. 9.14 the cleansing of the conscience by the blood of Christ. (*b*) Baptism is understood as the occasion wherein or means whereby the baptisand 'calls upon the name' of Christ in confession and commitment (cf. 2.21; 9.14, 21; 15.17). It thus served as the most visible formal marker to identify those who placed themselves under the name of Messiah Jesus – apart, that is, from the gift of the Spirit (10.44–48). As an identity defining ritual in contrast to circumcision it was caught up in the tensions of Christian identity. And though it features little in the Jewish/Christian identity crisis in the New Testament (hardly prominent, for example, in Galatians), it was the visible and public character of baptism which gave it the same role and importance within subsequent Christianity that circumcision enjoyed within Judaism at the time of Paul.

22.17–20   is entirely fresh information, which Luke has held back till this point, in much the same way that he held back the issue of clean and unclean until ch. 10 and the accusation that Jesus would destroy the Temple till 6.14. In each instance the dramatic effect is powerful – as Luke no doubt intended.

We learn (22.17) that Paul continued to attend the Temple even after his conversion (despite the views on the Temple associated with Stephen), and not just as a convenient compromise in 21.26. This is as much of a defence against the original charge (21.28) as the speech allows: it is no longer the Temple as such which is at issue, it is the free opening of a Jewish gospel to the Gentiles. Here also is a further example of a vision coming at a crucial moment of decision for Paul (cf. the visions of ch. 10, 16.9–10 and 18.9–10; also 23.11). As in 10.10 and 11.5, Luke has no hesitation in describing it as a vision seen 'in ecstasy'; it is a way of denying that the vision was contrived (Paul was not controlling things).

The vision has some echoes of that of Isaiah in Isa. 6.1–10. As with Isaiah, the vision takes place in the Temple (Isa. 6.1). Like Isaiah, Paul's first reaction is to confess his unfitness (Isa. 6.5; Acts 22.19–20).

And like Isaiah, Paul is 'sent' and 'goes' (22.21) at the behest of 'the Lord' (Isa. 6.8); the 'Lord' here is implicitly Christ though not actually named (22.19; cf. John 12.41). Most striking is the link provided to Luke's theme of Jewish rejection, already highlighted in 13.46–47 and 18.6, and foreshadowing the final word of 28.25–28, where the same passage is cited (Isa. 6.9–10). As with Isaiah, Paul is given the depressing information that his own people will not accept his testimony (22.18). But the implication is the same: even so, he, like Isaiah, must continue to speak his message to his people (to Jew as well as Gentile; cf. 3.25, 13.47 and 26.18), as Paul in fact did according to 28.17–24 and 30–31.

The account rehearsed is very much Luke's version of things (cf. 7.58, 8.3 and 9.1–2). Quite how it squares with Paul's own insistence that his commission to the Gentiles came with the revelation of Jesus Christ on the Damascus road (Gal. 1.15–16; cf. Acts 26.16–18) is not clear. But it is entirely possible that, following his three years in Arabia and Damascus (Gal. 1.17–18), Paul needed a further commissioning boost before embarking on his evangelistic work in Syria and Cilicia (Gal. 1.21–23) – one of the abundant revelations which Paul confesses to in II Cor. 12.6.

22.21   provides the reason why the commission of Saul was left until the end of this version. It is the climax of the speech and becomes the occasion for the crowd to react (more so than the implied identification of Jesus as 'Lord', it would appear). This double function underlines that the commission to the Gentiles was at the heart of Paul's self-understanding as a missionary, and that it was this open invitation to Gentiles which provoked the hostility of Paul's fellow Jews (since, presumably, it called in question their own traditional self-understanding as the chosen people of God).

The reaction of Jewish crowd and Roman centurion
22.22–30

This is the second contrast between Jewish crowd and Roman authority – the latter protecting Paul from the former (as in 21.27–35). In it Luke continues to play off the mutual incomprehension of both as to who Paul was and what he was about. The crowd have heard Paul identify himself wholeheartedly with his ancestral religion, but cannot accept his commission to go to the Gentiles. The centurion on the other hand has learned from his first mistake: Paul is a Jew (and not 'the Egyptian'). But now he makes a second: he assumes that as a Jew he is no different from most other Jews, and so can be subjected to the arbitrary punishments allowed under Roman law. And when informed that Paul is in fact a Roman citizen he can hardly believe it. Luke dwells on the confusion at some length, since it is representative of his whole endeavour: to show that Paul is a typical and properly representative Christian; that is, a Jew through and through, but also a Roman citizen. As he spans two worlds, so the faith he represents can command a hearing in both worlds.

22.22–23   The 'word' which incites the crowd is the last (22.21). Despite the ambiguity of talk of those 'far away' (see on 2.39) and the promise of blessing to the nations contained within their own foundation promises (see on 3.25), they are not ready to face up to the consequences for their own prerogatives and self-understanding which 'to the Gentiles' involves (cf. Luke 4.24–29).

22.24–29   The detachment guarding Paul proceed up the rest of the stairway into the fortress Antonia. The procedure set in motion by the centurion was a common one – to interrogate a prisoner by means of physical torture. And torture it would have been, since the Roman scourge was usually a flail with knotted cords, or possibly in a severe flagellation with pieces of metal or bone inserted into the leather straps. Quite possibly it was the prospect of such a severe beating (in contrast to the relatively much less severe beating in 16.23) which caused Paul on this occasion to identify himself as a Roman citizen. The point was that the law explicitly safeguarded Roman citizens from such arbitrary punishment (16.37). The reaction of the tribune and those who had illegally tied Paul (22.29) is a fair reflection of the seriousness of what they had done as a breach of Roman law.

The interplay between centurion, tribune and Paul is a fine piece of storytelling: the tension builds as Paul is stretched out and tied securely at a whipping post or on a bench in preparation for the fearful scourging; the bombshell dropped by Paul and the incredulity and fear of the centurion and the tribune are vividly evoked; and the turning of the tables in 22.28 is highly effective (we know that Roman citizenship was sold during the reign of Claudius). But it serves Luke's point still more by underlining the depth of Paul's second identity, this time as a Roman citizen – something necessary since the emphasis on Paul's Jewish identity had been so thoroughly reinforced in the preceding paragraphs. That Paul could have been a Roman citizen by birth is a thought which causes some eyebrows to arch in surprised doubt. But many Jews had been sold into slavery in Rome after Pompey's conquest of Palestine in the 60s BC, and it was customary for such slaves to be granted citizenship when they attained freedom (as most did). Quite possibly, then, one of Paul's immediate forbears had gained Roman citizenship in this way. Alternatively, his father had done some significant service to the Roman authorities in Cilicia and had been granted citizenship by way of reward. At all events, the point is that Paul the Jew had also been a Roman citizen from the day of his birth. Such a double identity was not a contradiction in terms.

22.30   The chapter division would come more naturally between verses 29 and 30, but we will follow the accepted division here for convenience. At least it facilitates the parallel between chs 22 and 23, with Paul's speech of defence making the immediate impact on the reader. As usual the simple reference to 'the Jews' allows the inference that Luke was setting the Jewish nation as a whole over against Christianity. But that hardly makes sense of his repeated emphasis in these two chapters on Paul's own Jewish identity. And on Roman lips, an indiscriminate reference to 'the Jews' would hardly be suprising. Luke also effectively indicates the power of Rome vis-à-vis the Jewish authorities. The tribune, identified as Claudius Lysias in 23.26, has the authority (no doubt in the name of the procurator) to summon the leading Jews in a sanhedrin/council, not to try Paul as though he fell within their jurisdiction, but for them to elucidate Paul's status and the facts behind the riot in the Temple court. The issue is still, What is the real identity of Paul and of the movement he represents?

Paul between Jewish Hostility and Roman Protection
23.1–35

For the third time in successive chapters Luke sets out a contrast between Jewish hostility and Roman protection. The two preceding examples were part of the same episode, where Paul was attacked by and defended himself against the Jerusalem mob; as in the diaspora (17.5–8 and 19.23–41) so also in Jerusalem. But at Roman insistence (22.30) the next stage was naturally to have Paul confront his peers in a hearing before a council of Jewish leaders, presided over by the High Priest. Here will be clarified, the tribune hopes (22.30; 23.28), the issue of whether Paul was acting on behalf of or against his people. The resulting interplay between representative individuals and groups continues through the chapter, providing a kaleidoscope of impressions and raising as many questions as it solves.

In the initial exchange Luke's portrayal neatly juxtaposes a High Priest who acts in defiance of the law and Paul who cites the law as his authority (23.3–5). Paul stands more fully within the traditions of his people than its chief representative! Thereafter Paul's tactic is to seize the wedge between Pharisees and the high-priestly party, already evident in the early days of the beginning of the way (5.33–39), and to drive it deeper. He speaks as a Pharisee, and is able to claim that the whole issue of the validity of the new movement boils down to the question of 'the hope and resurrection of the dead' (23.6). Here is one somewhat drastic way to defend and maintain a continuing Jewish identity, that is, by siding with one faction within Judaism over against another. Whether the tactic succeeds is unclear, since the tribune fears that Paul might be pulled in half by the whole assembly (23.10) and has to rescue Paul once more. A further vision strengthens Paul's hand in the course he has taken (23.11).

Somewhat surprisingly, following this careful delineation between Jewish parties in 23.6–9, Luke then attributes the further plot against Paul simply to 'the Jews' (23.12). It is at once evident that he does not have 'the Jews' as a whole in mind; the number amounts to something over forty. But since the Jews go on to involve 'the chief priests and elders' in the plot to murder Paul (23.14–15), they can be said to represent the Jewish people. In this way the contrast between Jewish hostility to Paul and Roman protection for Paul can be the more sharply drawn. More to the larger point, within Luke's over-arching scheme this is the climax of Jewish hostility to Paul; from this point onwards Jewish hostility and its effectiveness steadily diminish.

Within Luke's larger scheme, it is also striking that the only one who rallies to Paul's support from within his own community is one who belongs to his own immediate family circle, and who also speaks of 'the Jews' as those who have laid the plot against Paul (23.16–23). Surprisingly, we might think, there is no mention of the brothers or the disciples or the believers rallying round Paul or involved in representations on his behalf. The tensions within the Jewish community are reflected in the tensions within the sect of the Nazarene (cf. 6.1–8.2). The upshot, once again, is to highlight the protective role of the Roman tribune.

This leads into the next scene in which the Roman authority gives its provisional judgment on the character of what Paul stood for and of the charges brought against him. As with Gallio (18.14–15), the point of primary importance is that Paul seems to be guilty of no infringement of Roman law. The issue is a purely internal Jewish matter about the Jewish law (18.15). In this way Luke indicates that, despite the tensions exposed within Judaism regarding Paul (and by silent implication, also within the church of Jerusalem), so far as the principal representative of the Roman Empire is concerned, Paul and what he represents is still a Jewish affair, still to be understood and identified in Jewish terms.

Paul's confrontation with the Jewish authorities
23.1–11

In ironic contrast with the 'defence' made before the Jerusalem mob (22.1), this second encounter before the highest Jewish court or legal gathering cannot be dignified with that title. If Paul starts with that intention, the encounter degenerates immediately into an angry exchange of insults. Despite, or in line with his double entendre apology (23.5), Paul sees that no useful exchange is in prospect and no realistic defence can hope to succeed. Instead he plays the factional card and does succeed in winning support from his (erstwhile) fellow Pharisees, but at the cost of the whole council degenerating into violent argument.

The contrast with the initial defences of Peter in chs 4 and 5 is also striking. There the bold proclamation of Peter left the council as a whole non-plussed, with Gamaliel's advice (5.34–39) pointing out an eirenic and pragmatic way forward. Here the Pharisees again come to Paul's aid, but now as part of an open confrontation. This trial gives no prospect of reconciliation between the two ends of the spectrum here facing each other – the official guardians of Israel's cult and Torah, and Paul representing the Nazarene sect's outreach into the ranks of Gentile proselytes and God-fearers. The breach is deep, the hostility sharp. The question left hanging, however, is whether rapprochement is still possible between those whose position is nearer to the middle of the spectrum – the Pharisees, who also believe in the resurrection of the dead, and some of whose members were also believers (15.5), and the thousands of believers still zealots for the law (21.20), whose absence from the whole affair has an ominous ring. The question, in other words, is whether the breach is between Judaism and Christianity, or more accurately between different factions within the religion of the Jews, or even between Jewish-Christianity and Paul!

As ever, we cannot be sure that such a confrontation did take place in just these terms. Luke could well have had good first-hand reports to draw on here, and the events described, though surprising, are hardly implausible. Paul's identification of himself as a Pharisee accords with Phil 3.5, and he shared Luke's conviction that the resurrection of Jesus was absolutely central to Christian faith (e.g. Rom. 10.9; I Cor. 15.14, 17). Perhaps more to the point, whatever the finer points of detail, Luke's portrayal has certainly hit the nerve of Jewish factionalism of the period, and of earliest Christianity's role within that factionalism.

23.1   As usual (see on 4.5–6), 'the sanhedrin' would be more accurately described as a council of leading Jews convened to consider a particular issue put before them of potential national importance. Did Paul address the council in Aramaic (Luke does not say so) or Greek (with an eye to the tribune and his soldiers nearby – 22.30 and 23.10)? The question has some point here, since Paul starts by attesting his 'good conscience', a conception (conscience) lacking in Hebrew, and only recently acceptable as good Greek. The introduction is certainly Pauline (cf. Rom. 9.1; II Cor. 1.12; II Tim. 1.3), but less appropriate here (in front of the Jewish assembly) than in 24.16. Paul's good conscience presumably covered his period as persecutor (he had had no qualms about it at the time), as well as his missionary work together with those he had previously persecuted, though the seeming contradictoriness of the two life-styles would probably have provoked further indignation on the part of his hearers. The address to the assembly as 'brothers' maintains the spectrum of ambiguity (both fellow Jews and fellow believers, including Gentiles, are 'brothers'; see on 1.15 and 9.17), but the choice of language and/or terms was less brotherly than it might appear.

23.2 Ananias, son of Nedebaeus, was High Priest from about 47 to 58. He had been sent to Rome by the governor of Syria in 52 under suspicion of involvement in disturbances between Jews and Samaritans, but pleas on behalf of the Jews by Agrippa II had been effective in securing his acquittal (Josephus, *Jewish War* 2.232–46; *Antiquities* 20.118–36). The affair will have done him no harm in the eyes of his own people and he was then probably at the height of his power, remembered subsequently for his wealth and influence, both of which he retained even after he was replaced as High Priest.

Why he should take offence at Paul's opening sentence is not clear. Possibly the use of Greek (language and/or conceptions) was offensive in the circumstances, or even Paul's mention of God, or that he spoke without awaiting an invitation/direction to do so. Paul's claim to have a clear conscience in itself would hardly merit such a response. But hostility towards one whom the High Priest no doubt already regarded as a renegade Pharisee could help explain an unjustified and peremptory act. Note the parallel with John 18.22.

23.3 Paul's temper was on equally short rein (the contrast with Jesus' demeanour in Luke 23 is striking). His response seems to be a mixture of allusion to Deut. 28.22 (God's punitive 'strike' against Israel's disobedience) and Ezek. 13.10–15 (whitewash obscuring the weaknesses of a wall ready to collapse; cf. Matt. 23.27); the Qumran sectarians made the same sort of allusion to Ezek. 13.10 in their criticism of the Jewish leadership – 'those who build the wall and cover it with whitewash' (CD 8.12). If so, it was a devastating indictment of a powerful figure, who may already have used his wealth to support his political manoeuvering and who was murdered at the outbreak of the Jewish revolt a few years later (66). The point of greater substance was that the high priest was acting illegally in calling for the punishment of one who had not yet been tried or found guilty (cf. Lev. 19.15; John 7.51).

23.4–5 The exchange maintains the high drama of the scene. Was Paul being ironic? – one would not have expected a High Priest so to act. A possible answer is that Ananias had recently been replaced as High Priest, although still influential enough to be asked to chair this ad hoc council; but here we become caught up in the uncertainties of the precise date/year on which Paul returned to Jerusalem (on the most commonly calculated date, 57, Ananias would still be High Priest). Another suggestion is that Paul's eyesight being poor (see on 13.13–14) he could not see who was presiding over the assembly. At all events, the scripture cited by Paul (Ex. 22.28) certainly has something of a sarcastic ring, since whoever was president of the council would be 'a ruler of the people'. The irony is deepened since it is Paul who cites the law in accusing the High Priest of breaching it: Paul is more law-abiding than the High Priest!

23.6–8 The impression given in the sequel is that Paul gave up any real hope of a fair hearing and chose to throw the apple of discord into the midst. The apple in this case was the belief in the resurrection of the dead.

The Pharisees were leading exponents of the view that the laws and beliefs by which the Jewish people lived had to be explained and their implications spelled out in order that obedience in the changed circumstances of their own day could be as faithful as possible. As part of this, as we might say, hermeneutical philosophy, they had embraced the still fairly recent view (only a couple of centuries old) that beyond death the faithful (or all human beings) could expect resurrection (cf. Isa. 26.19; Dan. 12.2; II Macc. 7.9–14; Mishnah, *Sanhedrin* 10.1). The Sadducees, on the other hand, were conservative in their beliefs and practices (as so often with the ruling class in a society); if it was not in the Torah, then it should not or need not be embraced (Josephus, *Antiquities* 18.16). Excluded on this criteria was not only belief in the resurrection (cf. 4.2), but also in the burgeoning hierarchy of angels and spirits which was also a feature of the intertestamental period. This was the issue, we may recall, in Jesus' dispute with the Sadducees on the same subject (Luke 20.27–38), where Jesus in effect sided with the Pharisees by deducing the fact of the resurrection from the Torah itself (Ex. 3.6).

More to the point of Paul's and Luke's apologetic is the fact that Paul here is shown as claiming still to be a Pharisee (so also 26.5 and Phil. 3.5). By 'son of Pharisee' he may refer to his being a disciple of Gamaliel (22.3; cf. I Cor. 4.17; I Tim. 1.2; II Tim. 1.2), since it would be unusual, not to say impossible for his natural father to have followed the Pharisaic discipline far off in the diaspora (Tarsus). Still more important was the fact that Paul could focus the key issue, on which the relation of the new sect to the rest of Judaism turned, on 'the hope of the resurrection of the dead'. That this was one of the primary identity markers, if not the decisive identity marker of the new sect (the belief that in Jesus the resurrection of the dead had already happened), was already evident in Luke's presentation (see Introduction §5(2)). But here it also becomes the defining issue in determining whether Christianity should be recognized as still part of the spectrum of Jewish sect, practice and belief. The tactic reveals that the belief in Jesus' resurrection was essentially Pharisaic in character and that the sect centred on that belief was as much of a piece with developing Judaism as the sect of the Pharisees. In Luke's own day the point would be the basis of any possible rapprochement between Christians and Pharisees (by then the only surviving and dominant party within a Judaism recovering from the failure of the 66–70/73 revolt). This assertion of common ground of shared hope becomes a repeated feature of the final chapters (see also 24.15; 26.6–8; 28.20).

23.9–10   The tactic is successful at least in part. Some of the scribes (cf. 4.5; 6.12) who counted themselves as Pharisees, hearing Paul speak as one of them, take his side (using a military metaphor). They rub salt in the wound by allowing the possibility that Paul was the recipient of fresh revelation (from one of the angels or spirits whose existence the Sadducees denied) which confirmed the Pharisaic interpretation of the Torah on this point (something like this had indeed happened! – 22.6–10). But the result was a clash of factions, of minds and also, it would appear, of fist (the scene is easily visualized). The tribune has to intervene once again and Roman armour protects Paul from Jewish theological dispute turned violent.

23.11   The Lord (Jesus) stands by him, presumably in a vision or a dream (cf. 16.9) giving him the same sort of assurance as he received in Corinth (18.9–10) and subsequently on his voyage to Rome (27.23–24). Both Paul and the reader can thus be assured that the purpose of God is still overseeing events (see on 4.12). It is unclear when the desire/compulsion to go to Rome arose in Paul's mind (cf. 19.21).

The plot against Paul
23.12–22

The dramatic tension is not allowed to slacken one whit. Now 'the Jews', or at least a die-hard group of Jews plot to assassinate Paul, and involve the same alliance of hostile authorities ('high priests and elders') as opposed Peter and John initially (4.5, 8, 23) in complicity. Over against them stands one young man, Paul's nephew; everything depends on him. The full report of the plot in 23.16–21 has the same purpose and effect as the repetition of 10.1–11.18 – to add weight to the episode, here by highlighting the sharp contrast between 'the Jews' on the one side and Paul in his almost complete isolation within his own people on the other.

Here again we have no way of corroborating Luke's account. All we can say is that the detail and the circumstances are entirely plausible for the time. There is no reason to doubt that Luke had good sources to draw on.

23.12–15   Whether those in view could have been called 'sicarii', those who assassinated political opponents with knives (see on 21.38) is not clear; Luke does not use the term here. But the date of these events (57?) was now less than ten years from the Jewish revolt (begun in 66), which was itself the culmination of a growing period of unrest and brigandage or, alternatively expressed, of incidents involving freedom fighters (the same disagreement over how such activists should be regarded was evident then as it is in regard to similar political movements today). We can readily imagine, therefore, a group of Jews dedicated to the cause of Israel maintaining its national identity in clear distinction from Roman interference and the corruption of Greek influences. Such a group could both regard Paul as a traitor (21.21, 28) and be willing to take the most extreme measures to remove him. The episode has high historical plausibility.

The plot was a simple one. That all 'the chief priests and elders' were involved is unlikely; it would be enough to draw one or two of the more influential members into the plot by way of complicity. That the circumstances of the time encouraged or excused such corruption would be no surprise. Luke, however, tells the story in order to bring out the contrast between Paul (quite isolated) and the representatives of the Jewish nation ('the Jews', 'the chief priests and elders') as sharply as possible. The motivation is primarily dramatic, but the theology implied underlines the fact that Paul's and Luke's claim for continuity of identity between Israel and Christianity is lost if it is put solely in ethnic or national terms. Luke no doubt would intend his readers to indulge in some dark humour at the thought of the plotters having condemned themselves to death by the failure of their plot; the Greek says literally 'put themselves under an anathema', that is, committed themselves to destruction (Deut. 13.15; 20.17; Josh. 6.21; etc.), if they did not succeed in their enterprise. Hence, presumably, the repeated reference to the vow not to eat until Paul was dead (23.12, 14, 21), just in case the reader missed the point.

23.16–22 This is the first we hear of Paul having relatives in Jerusalem. But why not? With whom had he stayed when he first came to Jerusalem as a student? Luke's technique is only to introduce such characters as and when the storyline requires it. How the nephew learned of the plot Luke does not tell; the storyteller prefers to leave such details to the reader's imagination. The fact that the nephew had free access (as a relative) to Paul in custody renders all the more eloquent Luke's silence regarding any other visitors who supported him. The detail implies that he was still relatively youthful (23.19), but with enough boldness to advise the tribune (23.21) – the initial Greek term itself (23.17) would cover anyone from twenty to forty years of age. Significantly, it is to the Romans that he turns: there is no help to be looked for within Judaism or even the Jerusalem church. Paul's isolation is complete; he depends wholly on Roman protection.

Paul under Roman protection
23.23–35

This episode is an essential link in the chain, explaining how it was that Paul was transferred to Caesarea, for a hearing before the higher tribunal presided over by the provincial governor, in due course to make his appeal to Caesar (25.11). We may be confident at least of the broad outline of events: no one doubts that Paul was sent to Rome under escort, still in Roman custody; and the tribune would no doubt have been happy to rid himself of this difficult and potentially dangerous case (hence the alacrity of his response to the nephew's news). How much of the detail of the transfer Luke could draw from personal knowledge we do not know (the 'we' report does not resume till 27.1), but troop movements would probably follow well-established and familiar procedures.

Nor do we need to assume that Luke or his source was privy to or saw a copy of the letter from the tribune to the governor, even though he knew the former's name (23.26). As with the speeches, Luke would feel free to compose a letter with terms and sentiments which he thought to be appropriate (Introduction §4(3)) and which reflected the generally favourable attitude towards Paul on the part of the Roman authorities during this whole period. At the same time Luke was able to advance his own concerns: the contrast between 'the Jews' and Paul the Roman citizen (23.27); but also the recognition that the dispute between them was not a matter of Roman law but an internal Jewish disagreement over interpretation of the Torah (23.29).

23.23–25   The detachment assigned to guard Paul is surprisingly large – about half the Jerusalem garrison. But the days were troubled (less than ten years before the outbreak of the revolt against Rome) and the hostility towards Paul was widespread. The main body escort Paul for only one day's journey (23.31–32), returning when the area of greatest danger had been left behind.

23.26–30   The letter is written in proper, formal style, giving the name of the sender, the intended recipient with his title as a superior official ('most excellent/Excellency'), and the appropriate greeting (on Felix see 24.1). Luke records the whole letter (though without any formal conclusion) in order to indicate that his version of events was also the offical Roman one – Paul a Roman citizen, accused by his fellow Jews, but on matters outside or not requiring Roman jurisdiction, and only retained in custody because of a threat to his life. That an inferior Roman official might well refer a potentially explosive issue to his superior, to avoid responsibility if things went wrong, is wholly understandable; the younger Pliny is known to us because as the Emperor's administrator or legate in Bithynia from AD 110 he kept writing to Emperor Trajan for advice on such tricky questions. It is also hardly surprising that the commander of the Jerusalem garrison, Claudius Lysias, comes over as one ready to bend the truth and to present himself in the most favourable light (rescuing Paul because he was a Roman citizen); the representation would hardly be unfair to the tribune. The new information provided is that Paul's case is herewith referred to the Procurator and that Paul's accusers have been ordered to present their case against Paul to him (28.30).

23.31–35   Luke goes into surprising detail on the troop movements, presumably an indication of a good source, although the distance covered in the first stage would have been considerable (forty miles). The governor holds a brief preliminary hearing, to clarify the issue of jurisdiction (23.34), and the scene ends on a note of anticipation and assurance of Paul's security. The 'praetorium' was the official residence of a provincial governor. Here it refers to the palace which Herod the Great had built for himself, and which now evidently served also as the Procurator's military headquarters and garrison.

On Trial before Governor Felix
24.1–27

Having twice portrayed Paul on trial before 'the sons of Israel' (chs 22 and 23), Luke over the course of the next three chapters portrays Paul testifying before 'the Gentiles and kings' (9.15). This is the first, and only trial proper, as is confirmed by the regularly recurring legal terminology (24.1, 2, 8, 10, 13, 14, 19, 20, 22). Luke was also evidently aware of the rhetorical style and flourishes which characterized such set pieces and introduces both the brief prosecution speech (24.2–4) and the speech for the defence (24.10–11) accordingly.

More to Luke's point, both accusation and defence allow Luke to advance his chief concern. The movement represented by Paul can indeed be called a 'sect' (24.5, 14), that is of the Jews (24.5; 28.21–22), like those of Sadducees and Pharisees (5.17; 15.5; 26.5). The accusation of temple profanation is wholly unfounded (24.12–13, 18–19). And the opportunity is taken to reaffirm Paul's resolutely strong Jewish credentials: he came to worship in Jerusalem (24.11); he worships 'the God of our fathers' (24.14); he believes everything set down in the law and the prophets (24.14); he shares the Pharisees' hope in the resurrection (24.15, 21); he has a clear conscience before God (24.16); he came to bring alms to his people (24.17); he purified himself in the temple (24.18). Luke (and Paul) continue to insist on the substantial overlap and direct continuity between Christianity and the ancestral faith of Israel. Paul was no renegade or apostate careless of Israel's founding principles and continuing priorities.

Felix's reaction and the freedom he permitted Paul in custody provide proof enough that the Procurator recognized there was no real case to answer (24.22–23). The further fact that Felix summoned Paul for conversation (not a legal term) on subsequent occasions (24.24–26) and kept him in custody only in hope of being offered a bribe and to do the Jews a favour (24.26–27) should leave the reader in no doubt as to Paul's unblemished credentials.

There is little that need be said on the regular question of the

310

historical value of Luke's account. There is no reason to doubt that there was a hearing before governor Felix in the administrative capital of the province, involving a deputation from the Jerusalem authorities and a hired spokesman (barrister) whose name was known. Nor that Felix felt free to leave a non-urgent case unresolved for the remainder of his procuratorship. The portrayal of Felix as giving private hearings to Paul is a nice story line, and not implausible. But the parallel with the encounter between Herod Antipas and John the Baptist is striking (both rulers stole other men's wives; and cf. particularly Mark 6.20), and Luke's omission of the Mark 6 tradition in his own Gospel may be a further example of his readiness to delay the impact of certain episodes until his second volume (see Introduction §3). On the other hand, Luke's deduction that Felix was looking for a bribe fits with other reports and may reflect their influence on Luke (see on 24.26).

As to the speeches, they are so conventional, they summarily rehearse previous episodes, and they serve to advance Luke's own agenda (Christianity as a legitimate Jewish sect; see particularly 24.14–15), that the hand of Lukan construction can hardly be denied (did the prosecution speech indeed last for only eleven lines?). The one feature which suggests that Luke may have been drawing on some recollection of the events is the allusion to Paul's purpose in coming to Jerusalem, to deliver the collection (see on 24.17).

24.1   The story continues without any real break, but as in the preceding chapter, the chapter division here helps the reader focus on the principal business of the chapter. The description indicates how much the control of affairs has slipped from Jewish hands. Ananias (see on 23.2) now comes down to Caesarea as a postulant rather than as president of the court, with only 'some elders' in attendance (contrast 4.5; 6.12; 23.14). The case now rests in the hands of a professional spokesman ('rhetor') – Tertullus. The Latin name need not imply that he was not himself a Jew, but Luke makes no attempt to bring out the point either way (cf. 24.9).

The governor was Felix. Unusually, he had been a slave who had been freed by Emperor Claudius; but he seems to have been a favourite of the Emperor, and Claudius was known for giving too much power to freedmen. He was procurator of Palestine from 52–59/60, a period of growing unrest (the Jewish revolt broke out in 66), for which his maladministration was blamed. His servile origins will not have helped when opinion turned against him at court;

Tacitus the Roman historian summed him up in one of the better one-liners of the period – 'he exercised the power of a king with the spirit of a slave' (*Histories* 5.9). See also on 24.22, 24 and 27.

24.2–4   The opening of Tertullus' speech illustrates the rhetorical style of the time, particularly the flattering introduction and address, 'Your Excellency' (24.2), the note of respectful gratitude for favours received (24.3), the promise to be brief and the request for a hearing 'with your (customary) graciousness' (24.4). If Josephus' account of Felix's disreputable record is to be trusted, this was flattery indeed.

24.5–8   The first two points of accusation use the image of pestilence and riot: 'this man is a source of disease, a plague carrier'; 'he foments discord/strife/rebellion'. Two more frightening prospects could not be put before the governor of a province. The intention would be to throw as much mud as possible at 'the sect of the Nazarenes'; the sect would naturally take its name from 'Jesus the Nazarene' (see Introduction to chs 1–5 (6) [p.2] and on 4.10), and 'Nazarenes' is still the name by which Christians are known in Hebrew and Arabic. The accusation is directed against Paul as such, but no attempt is made to exculpate the other Nazarenes from the implication that the dangers were posed by Paul in his role as ring-leader of the sect (the reader is expected to recall such episodes as 15.2, 17.5–8, 18.12–17, 19.23–41 and 21.27–36). The specific charge of desecrating the temple summarizes the initial accusation (see on 21.28); it is not so important for the storytelling that it needs to be spelled out more fully. Older translations include reference to the part played by Claudius Lysias (24.6c–8a) but the manuscript evidence shows clearly that these clauses were added later.

24.9 'The Jews' here presumably are the high priest and some elders mentioned in 24.1; they represent the official line of the Jewish leadership in Jerusalem. An echo of Luke 23.10 is probably intended.

24.10   Luke depicts Paul as familiar with the conventions of formal rhetoric and well able to perform accordingly. His expression of confidence in Felix's judgment need not have been entirely misplaced: Felix's marriage to Drusilla (24.24) would have given him an unusual degree of knowledge of Jewish affairs; and in other cases he seems to have been amenable to sensible argument (Josephus, *Antiquities* 20.178).

24.11–13 The initial response simply affirms a strongly positive intention in returning to Jerusalem, indeed as a pious pilgrim, and denial of any trouble-making in any context within Jerusalem; he had been in Jerusalem only twelve days (not counting the subsequent five days[?] – 24.1) – hardly time to foment a rebellion! The reply accords both with Paul's own stated policy of conduct within Jewish contexts (I Cor. 9.20) and with the low-key policy advocated by James and followed by Paul in 21.23–26. Verse 12 is interesting since it indicates that there were several synagogues, or gathering places (for different interest groups or nationalities) within the city (cf. 6.9).

24.14–15   is a particularly interesting sentence within Luke's overall apologia. It is presented as a 'confession': the term has the same judicial/religious ambiguity in Greek as in English. The confession is that the accused 'sect' (see Introduction to this section; on 'the Way' see Introduction to chs 1–5 (5) and (6) [p.2]) worships 'the ancestral God' (cf. 3.13) in accordance with the scriptures, and that they share the same hope of resurrection, of both just and unjust (cf. Dan. 12.2; John 5.28–29; Rev. 20.12–15; see on 23.6). Paul meets the exaggerations of the prosecution (24.5–6) with his own exaggeration: Ananias, as a Sadducee, did not believe in the resurrection; and only those among the elders who were Pharisees would have done so (23.8). But the exaggeration serves primarily, and not unfairly, to underline the chief point (for both Paul and Luke): that the Jesus sect was as consistently traditional in worship and as thoroughgoingly scriptural in belief as any other section of the Jewish people. Particularly notable is the theocentric focus of the confession: 'I worship our ancestral God . . . having hope in God.'

24.16   Following from this confession, Paul's affirmation of his clear conscience (see on 23.1) is that of the faithful Jew continuing to be such (21.39). The word 'clear' can mean either 'blameless' or 'giving no offence' (cf. I Cor. 10.32; Phil. 1.10). Since Paul could hardly assert the latter, the implication is that Paul's own conscience remained untroubled in the midst of the accusations levelled against him: he remained convinced that what he stood for was entirely in line with the fundamental principles and convictions of his own people.

24.17   This is the only allusion Luke allows to what Paul himself clearly regarded as the principal reason for his coming to Jerusalem – to deliver the collection (see Introduction to 21.17–26). The reference is obscure. Luke does not use any of the terms Paul himself had used in Rom. 15.25–28, I Cor. 16.1–3 or II Cor. 8–9 (though Rom. 15.16 speaks of 'the offering of the Gentiles'). Instead he speaks of 'alms and offerings'. These two actions were at the very heart of Jewish piety; in the Judaism of the period 'almsgiving' was more or less synonymous with 'righteousness' (see on 3.2–5); and in the context 'offerings' can hardly mean other than the means to offer sacrifices in the Temple. It may be, then, that Luke (or Paul) is here dressing up the more controversial collection (a free act of Gentile Christian generosity) as an act of traditional Jewish piety (but cf. Gal. 2.10). At all events, the effect is to reinforce the claim of 24.14–15: this movement/sect is still thoroughly Jewish in religious practice and ethos; and that (for those who knew the facts of the collection) included the pious concern of the Gentile churches for their Jerusalem brothers and sisters ('to my nation').

24.18–21   simply rehearses the previous accounts. Paul emphasizes that when the trouble first started the ceremony of purification had already run its course (seven days); he had been in the Temple as a good, observant Jew (21.26–27). And there had been no trouble during all that time. An effective legal point is scored: where are my accusers (21.27–29)? The present accusations are merely hearsay. The subsequent hearing before the council (ch. 23) reinforces the point: the council produced no finding of wrongdoing, only a dispute over the resurrection of the dead. The small variation from the wording of 23.6 is of no significance. But the crucial claim is effectively repeated: the new sect focusses entirely on the claim that God had raised Jesus from the dead, and this claim is entirely consistent with a conviction (the resurrection of the dead) strongly held even within the Jewish council itself.

24.22   The information that Felix had 'a more accurate knowledge of the things concerning the Way' (see Introduction to chs 1–5 (5) [p.2]) is somewhat surprising. It need not necessarily mean, however, that he was well informed on the beliefs and practices of the first Christians (though an effective procurator would have agents and spies everywhere). It could simply mean that he was well informed on the circumstances of the case, of the larger political and religious issues which lay behind this particular strike against Paul. Having a Jewish wife (24.24) would have given him an insight into national politics unusual among his predecessors. In which case, he did not really need a fuller report from Lysias (cf. 23.29), and the reason for the adjournment was simply an excuse (Luke certainly does not follow up the point in his account).

24.23   The terms of custody confirm that Felix saw no sound basis for the accusations brought against Paul: the latter was to have 'liberty', that is, literally, 'relaxation' (of the terms of custody); and his own circle (the first we have heard of Paul's support group for some time; see Introduction to 21.17–26) were to have unrestricted access to him to attend to his needs (that is, in bringing him food, change of clothing – and writing implements?).

24.24   Drusilla was the youngest daughter of Herod Agrippa I (see 12.20–23). According to Josephus, she was born in 37/38 and married Azizus, king of Syrian Emesa, in 53. She had previously been betrothed to Epiphanes, son of Antiochus, king of Commagene, but he 'had rejected the marriage since he was not willing to convert to the Jewish religion'. And the marriage to Azizus went ahead only after he had consented to be circumcised (*Antiquities* 20.139). She is said to have been very beautiful, and Felix was able to persuade her to leave Azizus and to marry him instead (*Antiquities* 20.141–4). The reports are thus conflicting: how much did the insistence on conversion and circumcision reflect Drusilla's own views (she was still less than twenty years old when she married Felix)? And was her abuse of traditional Jewish marriage law an abberation or characteristic (there was presumably no question of Felix being circumcised)? The fact that Luke bothers to mention her here suggests that he saw her presence as some kind of confirmation that the Jewish character of Paul's message was recognized by Felix.

24.24–25   The descriptions of the subject of their conversations are interesting. 'Faith in Christ Jesus' would be the agenda as perceived by both Paul and Luke (see e.g. 11.24; 15.9; 20.21; Rom. 1.17; 3.22; Gal. 2.16); Paul sought to convert the procurator (cf. 13.8). 'Righteousness, self-control and coming judgment', on the other hand, evoke something of the character of a philosophical debate. 'Righteousness', to be sure, is a thoroughly and almost distinctively Jewish term: in Jewish thought it denotes fulfilment of the obligations placed on the individual by membership of a people or a covenant (see on 10.35 and 17.31); but in Greek thought it would be comprehensible in the more abstract sense of 'justice'. The case is quite the opposite with the second item, 'self-control', for that occurs frequently in Greek thought and seldom in LXX and New Testament (e.g. Sir. 18.30; I Cor. 7.9; Gal. 5.23). In the former it is a key term as an ideal of philosophical ethics – self-control in regard to all human desires (including food, drink and sex). On the other hand, 'coming judgment' (not final judgment) would be familiar within both circles of thought (in Old Testament cf. e.g. Isa. 13.6–16; Joel 2.1–2; Zeph. 1.14–2.3). Either way, Luke portrays Paul as 'getting through' to Felix. Felix's response – to delay and put off the vital existential choice, between fleeting political power (he was deposed within two years), and a settled faith with its resulting self-discipline – makes him the unenviable paradigm of the temporizer.

24.26 According to Josephus, Felix bribed the most trusted friend of Jonathan the High Priest to arrange for Jonathan's murder by the *sicarii* (*Antiquities* 20.163). In any event it would be unusual for highly placed Roman officials not to accept gifts and favours which would help ensure their future prosperity; Josephus tells us that the only ones left in prison by Festus' successor, Albinus, were those unable to pay an appropriate bribe (*Jewish War* 2.273). So the attitude ascribed to Felix is quite in character. Is there an implication that Felix knew of the money (the collection; cf. 24.17) which Paul had brought up to Jerusalem with him, and that it was still technically in Paul's control (it had *not* been delivered to the Jerusalem church; see again Introduction to 21.17–26)? The picture of Felix summoning Paul frequently for private consultation evokes the impression of a man as much drawn by the character of Paul and his message as he was repelled by the consequences which would inevitably follow from acceptance of that message.

24.27 Felix was recalled in 59 or 60. Josephus reports that the leaders of the Jewish community in Caesarea pursued him to Rome with accusations of maladministration, but that Nero spared him at the entreaty of Felix's brother, the influential freedman, Pallas, who had been a favourite of Claudius (*Antiquities* 20.182). The fact that the complaint was brought only by the local Jewish leadership could conceivably mean that Felix's attempt to curry favour with 'the Jews' (the representative leadership in Jerusalem; cf. 25.9) by leaving Paul in custody, as reported here, had some success. But with such few facts to hand such correlation between Acts and Josephus is hazardous, especially as the portrayal here conforms to Luke's consistent attempt to portray the representative Jews of a place as uniformly hostile to Paul.

On Festus see 25.1.

The Build-up to the Hearing before Governor Festus and King Agrippa
25.1–27

In many ways this is the strangest chapter in the book. The business of Paul in Roman custody has already been drawn out for more than three chapters. And nothing would have been easier for Luke than to concertina the events narrated in this chapter into a brief sentence or two. Even if the appeal to Caesar is the dramatic high point of the chapter (25.11–12), a Luke, short of space on his roll or anxious to move the narrative on, could readily have included it at the end of the speech in ch. 26.

Why then this marking time and foot dragging delay, by the end of which we are no further forward than when we began the chapter? Sensitivity to the unfolding drama probably provides sufficient answer.

First, there is the dramatic effect of suspense being screwed up to steadily higher pitch. The previous hearing before Felix had ended by being adjourned. Now all hangs in suspense. How is Paul going to come out of this confrontation with the legal might of Rome? Previous encounters had ended most positively (13.12; 16.35–40; 18.12–17; 19.23–41). But Felix had passed over the opportunity to give a similarly positive affirmation of Paul and what he stood for (24.24–27). And the further delay poses the possibility of an alternative outcome in a tantalizing way. So Festus is shown as first standing firm before Jewish demands (25.4–5), but then as willing to accommodate them (25.9), opening up the possibility of dirty work at the crossroads (25.3). And even the appeal to Caesar, at once granted (25.11–12), is not allowed to settle the matter. Instead king Herod Agrippa II is introduced on the scene and the build-up to Paul's last great self-testimony (ch. 26) begins afresh, with the sort of marking time dialogue which imparts no new information but simply stretches out the suspense still more (25.13–27). This is Luke the storyteller and dramatist *par excellence* at work.

Secondly, within this sequence the manoeuvres of the principal parties help maintain the reader's interest. 'The Jews' continue to be implacably opposed to Paul, willing to stoop to treacherous means to dispose of him (25.2–3, 7). But their representative character is more clearly signalled (25.2, 7). And in the second half of the narrative they leave the stage, to take no further direct part in the proceedings, and to be replaced as representative of Jewish interests (26.2–3) by the much more pliable Agrippa (25.13–26.32). Festus himself is portrayed as being genuinely uncertain and unclear about the matter (25.20, 26), open to and needing firm guidance (so why does Luke not go ahead and provide it?). Only Paul is rock solid in his stance and in his repeated denial of any wrongdoing against his people (25.8, 10–11). But these replies are too brief. What the dramatic story-line cries out for is a final and complete refutation of the charges and the resolution of the suspense.

And so, like a well-staged play, with the grand processional entry of Agrippa and his consort, followed by the military staff, the chief notables and finally Paul himself (25.23; any film director worth his salt would recognize the potential of the scene), and then the prologue spoken by Festus (25.24–27), Luke at last brings us to the great climax of Paul's final defence and proclamation (ch. 26).

On the question of historicity, we again need entertain no doubt as to the main outlines of the tale. The portrayals of procurator Festus (25.1) and of king Agrippa (25.13) are in character with what we know of them from elsewhere. The variation in time notes ('three days', 'not more than eight or ten days', 'many days' – 25.1, 6, 14) suggests more than arbitrary choice. And even the pageantry of the final scene would fit well with the ancient love of display and as a setting for what comes close to a 'show trial'. But the detailed exchanges probably owe most to Luke's historical imagination and dramatic flair: he does not bother to specify the charges brought against Paul (25.7); Paul's response is equally vague (25.8, 10–11; apart from the reference to the Temple in 25.8); and presumably Luke had no record to draw on of the private conversation between Festus and Agrippa (25.14–22). On the other hand, given a degree of virulent hostility towards Paul on the part of at least some of the Jewish leadership in Jerusalem, the narrative has an overall plausibility which would fully satisfy Luke's canons of historiography. And somewhat surprisingly, Luke does little to advance his central claim that the movement which Paul led was Jewish through and through (contrast even 25.19 with 23.6 and 24.14–15); he must have thought the point sufficiently secure. Here it is the demands of the unfolding drama which override all else.

25.1 The year when Festus took over from Felix as procurator of Judaea is uncertain (probably 59 or 60); the year of 62 for his death (in office) is more certain. These dates provide valuable correlation for dating the latter years of Paul's life. According to Josephus, Festus was a much stronger and fairer Procurator than either his predecessor (Felix) or his successor (Albinus): he took firm action against bands of dissidents and handled a tricky situation regarding a wall constructed in the Temple area with sensitivity (*Antiquities* 20.185–95). The way he is portrayed in the following narrative conforms with this broad picture.

25.2 That Festus should make one of his first priorities a visit to Jerusalem is a reminder of the increasing tensions of the period (increasing brigandage, or guerrilla actions) and of the importance of commanding Jerusalem as Israel's capital and heart. That Paul should be high on the agenda of the chief priests and other leading Jews is equally understandable: the threat which Paul's mission to the Gentiles was seen to represent and embody, a threat to Jewish national identity and integrity, would have made his case stand out, whatever the other grievances of the time. The High Priest at that time was one Ishmael; but the narrative no longer depends on such details (cf. 23.1–5).

25.3 What were Luke's sources for postulating a further plot against Paul? Presumably these were not the same men as vowed to starve themselves in 23.13; two years had elapsed! Did Luke simply assume an equivalent strategy? In the increasingly tense and fervid atmosphere of the early 60s (the Jewish revolt began in 66) such a supposition would not necessarily be far-fetched.

25.4–5 Festus replies with the voice of authority: they must come to him and present their case at the place where he is in sole and complete control.

25.6–8 The absence of specific charges ('many and weighty complaints') and refutation suggests that Luke no longer wants to linger over details. At the same time, the delay of two years in proceedings might well have blunted or broadened some of the earlier charges. The reader, of course, would hardly need reminding (24.5–6, 17–21).

319

But Luke's concern was to set the scene with broad brush strokes and to evoke the atmosphere of continuing charge and denial. The important points for the reader to note would be the threatening attitude of the Jews (25.7 – they 'stood around him'; similarly 25.18), the absence of proof in support of the charges (25.7), and Paul's blanket denial of any offence – whether against the law, or the Temple or Caesar (25.8). The last (against Caesar) is a surprising new element in the charges, but it could reflect the similar tactics used against Jesus (particularly Luke 23.2), or an understandable attempt to bring home to the authorities the fundamentally subversive character of Paul's work as seen by the plaintiffs (cf. 16.21; 17.7).

25.9   Precisely the same phrase is used here as with Felix (24.27 – 'wishing to do the Jews a favour'). But the context is different: Felix, at the inglorious end of his career, seeking to buy off opposition from his former subjects which might prove fatal to him in Rome; Festus, at the beginning of his period in office, showing willing to come and go with his new subjects. In the shunting back and forth of Paul between Jewish and Roman authority, this was a point of real danger: were the case to revert in any measure to Jewish jurisdiction, that could be the end for Paul (quite apart from any extra-juridical plot – 25.3). That the trial would still be before Festus was some safeguard; but would it nevertheless be a fatal move in the wrong direction (cf. 25.11; and note the ambiguity of 25.20)?

25.10-12   Presumably some such thoughts would have been in Paul's mind: his chief hope of safety lay in his remaining in Roman custody and within the protection of Roman justice. The response is dignified, even noble: he had done his people, their representatives and what they stood for, no wrong (even Festus' brief acquaintance with the case would have made that clear to him); he was no wrong-doer and had done nothing deserving of death; there were no grounds for his being returned to Jewish jurisdiction (the real fear); 'I appeal to Caesar'. Nothing is said of it at this point, but Paul exercises the right of the Roman citizen – to be tried by the Emperor (in this case Emperor Nero, whose first five years, 54–59, were remembered as a period of good rule). Festus would know of Paul's citizenship as a matter of court record (23.27), and would have no reason to deny the citizen's right. Luke assumes that as one of Roman citizenship's most ancient and most basic rights it would be well known to his readers.

25.13   Agrippa II was son of Agrippa I (see 12.20–23). He had been only sixteen when his father died (AD 44). Emperor Claudius had decided he was too young to inherit and appointed a Roman gover- nor instead. In the intervening years, however, he had been given more and more of the north-eastern territories of Herod the Great's former kingdom. His reputation is disputed, but he seems to have functioned in Rome as a spokesman for Jewish causes; he is remembered as having engaged in legal discussion with the famous Rabbi Eliezer ben Hyrcanus; and it may have been at his insistence that the non-Jewish husbands of his sisters were first circumcised. So his interest in and knowledge of Jewish law and tradition was probably common knowledge: sufficient at least to justify Festus' seeking out his advice (25.14, 22, 26) and Paul's subsequent compli- ment (26.3). It was thus a very astute move on Festus' part to consult Agrippa: to have such an acknowledged authority on Jewish affairs advise and approve his judgment on Paul would provide excuse enough for Festus either for giving way to the pressures of the Jewish council or for acceding to them.

Bernice was Agrippa's sister. She had been twice widowed, and a third marriage had failed. She seems to have settled to the role of acting as consort or hostess to the unmarried Agrippa, inevitably giving rise to otherwise unfounded rumours of incest.

25.14–22   follows the familiar dramatic convention of letting the reader listen in to a conversation in which the events to date are passed in brief review. Little is added to the reader's knowledge and the variations in details are insignificant; but as already noted (Introduction to ch. 25 [pp.317f.]), the purpose of the paragraph seems to be rather to build up the suspense precisely by this failure to move the plot forward. In the course of it, however, the characteri- zation of Festus is strengthened: he comes across as a representative of Roman justice at its best (25.16–17), trying always to be fair and genuinely seeking the truth (25.20–21), in contrast to the ill-defined and malicious accusations of Paul's enemies (25.15,18).

The most interesting verse and the only one which really adds any- thing to Luke's narrative is 25.19. Far from any attempt having been made to substantiate the earlier charges of riot or sedition (24.5; 25.8–9) the whole case had proved to be entirely an internal Jewish dispute. Festus calls Israel's religion a 'superstition': that is, not necessarily a negative designation, but depicting Judaism as simply one national religion among many (see on 17.22). The important

321

word, however, is not 'superstition', but 'their own'. The echo of 18.14–15 and 23.29 in particular will be deliberate; the same word '(controversial) questions, issues' is used in 15.2, 18.15, 23.29, 26.3 and here. In this way the dramatic purpose is well served: if the affair is all a matter of internal dispute should Festus not conclude as Gallio had? – 'See to it yourselves' (18.15); lest the tension slacken, Festus omits the assurance that the trial in Jerusalem would be 'before me' (25.9, 20).

More important for the deeper theological claim of the book as a whole is the repeated affirmation (from the Roman perspective) that the new movement which Paul represented was an internal Jewish movement, which raised matters of controversy about but still within the religion of the Jews ('their own superstition'; 18.14–15; 23.29). Festus has even grasped that the controversial questions focus on the issue of Jesus' resurrection (cf. 4.2; 17.18, 32). The context makes it unnecessary to repeat that this not least is an internal issue (23.6; 24.15) and allows Luke to formulate the belief as one to whom the idea was strange – 'a certain Jesus, who was dead, but whom Paul asserted to be alive'.

25.23–27   The stage setting is dramatic: the entry of Agrippa and Bernice 'with great pageantry'; the procession of military and civic dignitaries; and, last of all, the entry of Paul – the real climax. Festus' preliminary speech again rehearses well known details, but, given the setting, some such prologue was necessary before Paul takes centre stage. The claim that 'the whole Jewish population' had petitioned him against Paul may be typical exaggeration such as we have seen earlier (cf. e.g. 2.5–6; 5.14, 16), but it helps reinforce the point that 'the Jews' in these chapters (21.11; 22.30; 23.20, 27; 24.9, 27; 25.9–10) are to be understood as those Jews most representative of their people. 'The Lord' here is the earliest literary evidence of the absolute form used for the Emperor, a usage which was to become steadily more frequent and more problematical for Christians.

It should be noted that the scene is not portrayed as a formal trial: no formal indictment is brought against Paul – on the contrary, he is declared innocent (25.25), for the second or third time (23.29; 25.18); and there is no speech for the prosecution (as in ch. 24). The format rather is that of a hearing (but in a magnificent setting; contrast 24.24–26), designed to give Paul's final complete self-testimony maximum effect. The final sentences in particular (25.26–27) give Paul the perfect opening: the slate is blank; let Paul write on it what he will.

The Hearing before Governor Festus and King Agrippa
26.1–32

This is the third account of Paul's conversion (after chs 9 and 22). As such, its significance is easily lost in a comparison of the variant details of the three accounts. That would be unfortunate. For ch. 26 forms the climax of the book of Acts in the same way that the crucifixion provides the climax of the Gospels. Luke will no doubt have intended to evoke that impression: the near conversion of Agrippa (26.28) parallels that of the thief on the cross (only in Luke 23.40–43); and the affirmation of Paul's innocence by both Festus and Agrippa (26.31–32) parallels the similar assessments of both Pilate and Herod regarding the case against Jesus (the latter again only in Luke 23.14–15). As we shall see, ch. 27 can then be seen to function as roughly equivalent to the burial of Jesus and despair of holy Saturday, and ch. 28 to the resurrection narratives.

Far from being a mere repetition of Paul's conversion, then, ch. 26 is the climax towards which the preceding narratives have been building. (1) This was evident from the character of ch. 25, as we have already seen (Introduction to ch. 25 [pp.317f.]): the lack of any real development in the narrative in that chapter simply screwed up the suspense and expectation, so that when Paul at last commands centre stage, the attentive reader/listener is ready for a climactic and conclusive declamation. (2) Ch. 26 is also the climax of the sequence which began far back in ch. 21. Paul has been in Roman custody since then – more than two years. In a variety of settings, he has confronted his own people, their leading representatives, and the Roman governor. Now he has opportunity to make a final and determinative defence (Luke will make no attempt to indicate that he was given a subsequent opportunity before Emperor Nero). This is no mere repetition of ch. 22 for the sake of emphasis, but the Lukan Paul's definitive answer to his Jewish critics – addressed explicitly to the king of the Jews (see also Introduction to chs 21–28). (3) Not only so, but we should also note that this speech, together with the account of Paul's conversion itself (ch. 9), brackets the main body of Paul's missionary work. Hence its character – very little directly addressed to the accusations laid against him, but reviewing the course and rationale of his whole life. Only so can the turns in his life which have occasioned the accusations be properly appreciated. This is Paul's 'apology' (the verb used in 26.1–2; cf. 22.1) – *Apologia pro vita sua*.

The key emphasis of the speech, therefore, is not simply to recall Paul's conversion. It is rather to nest the accusations against Paul within the context of his conversion, and his conversion within the context of his faithfulness as a Pharisee and the common hopes of his people. This is clear from the sections of the account where Luke departs significantly from the previous accounts – here particularly 26.6–8 and 18–23. Especially noticeable is the way the speech ties Paul's commissioning to the Gentiles so tightly into the total package: he received the commissioning from the risen Jesus himself on the Damascus road (contrast 9.15–16; 22.17–21); this commissioning is part of Israel's own commissioning (the echoes of Isa. 42.6, 17 and 49.6 in 26.18 and 23); and it is in fact integral to Israel's own messianic expectation (26.22–23).

This indeed is the climax of Luke's own defence of Paul, but also the climax of his own attempt to define the identity of the new movement about which he was writing, the climax, we may say of his own theology. Central to which is Luke's own conviction both that the Pauline mission was the driving force of Christianity and that the Pauline mission was in direct continuity with Israel's own self-understanding and claims (see Introduction §§2 and 5(4)). Paul and the Pauline mission were not at odds with or destructive of Israel's heritage; on the contrary, Paul was simply fulfilling Israel's own responsibility to be a light to the Gentiles. 'The Jews' in their role as representing the Jewish people were as mistaken in their opposition to Paul's mission as they were in their specific accusations against Paul. The final words of the speech – 'that as first of the resurrection of the dead, he was to proclaim light both to the people and to the nations' (26.23) – have a much more positive and conciliatory 'both-and' emphasis, which, finally, sets Paul firmly in the company of James (15.14–18).

The concluding paragraph (26.24–32) effectively maintains the dramatic quality of the scene while highlighting still further Luke's chosen emphases: the speech is cut short, outlining the final spoken words still more clearly as the speech's climax (26.23–24); the reaction of Festus seems uncalled for, except that it again brings out the exceptional character of the Christian claim – Christ risen from the dead, a light to both Jew and Gentile (26.23–25); and the reaction of Agrippa likewise indicates not so much the power of Paul's presentation but what should be the inherent appeal of this so Jewish message to this so Jewish king (26.26–28). The scene closes with Paul's poignant response (26.29) and fades out with the reaffirmation of Paul's innocence, with the final words ('had he not appealed to Caesar') providing the link forward to the penultimate chapter. In these two chapters in particular Luke shows that he would have made a first class screenplay scriptwriter.

As to the historical detail. Once again we need have no doubt that Paul was heard by Festus and that he was sent to Rome for his case to be settled. As already noted (Introduction to ch. 25 [pp.317f.]), Luke's account accords well with what we know of Festus and Agrippa from Josephus, though we may have to allow some dramatic licence for the final scene (26.24–29). The speech itself is constructed round the same two features as before – the encounter with Jesus (9.4–6; 22.7–10; 26.14–16) and the sending of Paul to the Gentiles (9.15–16; 22.15, 21; 26.16–18, 23). These were the constants of Paul's own recollection of the event (I Cor. 9.1–2; Gal. 1.15–16). The references to 'Jesus the Nazarene' (26.9; cf. 2.22; 6.14) and to 'the saints' (26.10; see on 9.13) also have a primitive ring. Otherwise, 26.2–23 is simply one variant of what must have been an often told tale, elaborated in part, and, of course, adapted to the circumstances (26.6–8, 21), but whether by Luke or by Paul himself would hardly make much difference. As observed before, if Luke could record three such variant accounts of the same event without qualm, he would hardly expect his readers to have qualms about the veracity of his portrayal of Paul on the ground of these variations (see also Introduction to ch. 9 [pp.117f.]).

26.1   It should be noted that Festus in effect hands over the proceedings to Agrippa: this is to be entirely an intra-Jewish affair; hence Paul's address is to 'King Agrippa' (26.2, 19). Paul's stretching out his hand (despite his chains – 26.29) may recollect a rhetorical device used by Paul (13.16) or form part of the dramatic stage directions which Luke included by instinct.

26.2–3   Paul observes the conventions of the day with his opening, gracious compliment (cf. 24.10). We have already noted that Agrippa may have been regarded, quite properly, as something of an expert in Jewish affairs (here 'customs and disputed issues'), especially by his Roman sponsors (see on 25.13), so the compliment could have been applicable as well as appropriate. Paul can speak of '(the) Jews' though both Paul and Agrippa were themselves Jews – a further reminder that the term ('the Jews') was probably used by Luke to denote the dominant Jewish or most representative Jewish opinion on a question.

26.4–5   The opening parallels that of the second account (22.3–4). At first it seems as though Paul is simply recalling his pre-conversion life-style (cf. Gal. 1.13–14; Phil. 3.5). But the difference is that the claim here envisages no break, no before and after (conversion): Paul is speaking of 'my way of life from my youth, from the beginning'; he expects the testimony of his contemporaries to his strict Pharisaism to stand him in good stead in the present; and he speaks to Agrippa of 'our religion', as of a religion still common to both. Implicit is the claim that his present way of life and gospel is directly continuous with what they had known of him earlier (cf. 21.24 – '. . . you live in observance of the law'; 23.6 – 'I am a Pharisee'). The assertion allows some adaptability since 26.4 may limit this form of life-style to his time 'among my people and in Jerusalem' (cf. I Cor. 9.20). We may note again that the description of the Pharisees as 'the strictest sect of our religion' uses one of the words used regularly by Josephus to describe the 'sect of the Pharisees' – 'strict, exact, scrupulous' (so also 22.3); Paul and Luke reflect a more widespread admiration for the Pharisees at the care they took over their religious observances.

26.6–8   Here the focus swings on to what has been one of the principal bones of contention from the first (4.2, 18; 5.28–32; 23.6–7; 24.15, 21; 25.19) – the claim of Peter and Paul and the others that God had raised Jesus from the dead. Paul's identification of himself as a Pharisee (26.5), a member of the principal Jewish sect which shared this belief, asserts implicitly an unbroken continuum from Pharisaic to Christian belief (so, more clearly, 23.6; cf. 15.5). But the explicit point of these verses is that the principal ground of complaint against Paul is actually the claim that the hope and promise given to their fathers and central to all Israel's daily worship and aspiration has been fulfilled. The 'our' in 'our twelve tribes' embraces both

Paul in the common hope and Agrippa in the claimed fulfilment. The question is posed to the assembly, but to the Jewish king in particular, 'Why is it judged unbelievable for you (plural) that (if in fact) God raises the dead?' (26.8). In answer, Agrippa might have replied: either that he (unlike Paul) was no Pharisee; or that his hope was to share in the final resurrection, not in the possibility of one-off resurrections prior to the new age. But in the present context the question makes its point: this (Christian) belief in the resurrection of Jesus is a Jewish belief and a Jewish hope realized.

26.9   Following the insertion of material particular to the setting (26.6–8), the familiar record is rehearsed (8.3; 22.4–5), but in significantly more detail (26.9–11). It is confirmed that 'the name of Jesus of Nazareth' was the banner under which the first believers came together and which provoked the hostility of their religious leaders (see Introduction to ch. 3).

26.10   The use of 'saints' here recalls 9.13 and the way in which this title seems to have been particularly associated with the first believers in Jerusalem (see on 9.13). New is the information that Paul's early persecution was authorized by the chief priests (plural); though given the priestly command of power in Jerusalem, such authorization would have been necessary anyway. That there was a judicial process which resulted in some being condemned to death probably strains the facts somewhat (see on 22.4), though Paul's own recollection of his career as persecutor uses very violent language (Gal. 1.13 – 'tried to destroy') which was reflected also in his reputation among the early churches (9.21; Gal. 1.22; cf. Gal. 4.29 and I Thess. 2.14–15).

26.11   Also new is the claim that Saul the persecutor 'punished them often in all the synagogues and tried to force them to blaspheme' (26.11). Quite what is in view here is unclear. 'Blasphemy' properly speaking was insult to the divine majesty. Luke can hardly mean that Saul tried to force Jewish believers to blaspheme God as such. But he could mean that Saul sought from them a confession which he would then have regarded as blaspheming God, that is, as making claims for Jesus which detracted from the honour due to God alone (cf. Luke 5.21; Mark 14.62–64). Or, less likely, that he tried to force them to deny Jesus as their Lord, and thus to blaspheme against his God-given status and glory, that is, blasphemy in Paul's (but not Saul's) ears. The reference to persecution 'even to foreign cities' is equally hyperbolic (no city other than Damascus is ever mentioned); but the phrase has an insider's perspective (literally, 'even to cities outside', that is, outside the land of Israel).

26.12–15 returns to the core testimony of all three accounts: the journey to Damascus, commissioned by the chief priests (9.1–2; 22.5; 26.12); at about midday a light shining from heaven (9.3; 22.6; 26.13) – here its brightness is emphasized, and that it shone on his companions as well (cf. 22.9); the falling to the ground (9.4; 22.7; 26.14) – but here again the whole company are involved and not just Saul himself (contrast 9.7); the voice addressing him (9.4; 22.7; 26.14) – but here the language (Hebrew or Aramaic) is specified. In this version, however, nothing is said of Saul's being blinded (contrast 9.8–9, 12, 17–18 and 22.11, 13) or of Ananias' role (contrast 9.10–19 and 22.12–16).

The snatch of dialogue is more or less word for word in all three accounts: 'Saul, Saul, why do you persecute me?' 'Who are you, sir?' 'I am Jesus, whom you persecute. Rise . . .' (9.4–6; 22.7–8, 10; 26.14–16). Here, however, a proverbial tag, well known in classical literature, has been added to the risen Jesus' first words: 'it is hard for you to kick against the goads'. The metaphor is obviously that of the ox being prodded to pull steadily or to make a straight furrow, though its reference to Paul's situation is unclear. The popular view persists that pricks of conscience were in mind, Saul struggling to free himself from the memory of his part in Stephen's death (7.58; 8.1), or from enslavement to covetous desire (cf. Rom. 7.7–12). The problem with both explanations is that none of Paul's own explicit recollections of his pre-Christian experience bear testimony to such pangs of conscience (cf. Gal. 1.13–14; Phil. 3.5–6); nor does the substantial persecution envisaged here (26.10–11) give any hint of such. The wonder of the Damascus road encounter for Paul was that Christ confronted him in his full fury as a persecutor (I Cor. 15.9–10), not as one eaten up with doubt or guilt over what he was doing.

26.16–18 Here the three accounts diverge again, though all three include at some point Paul's commissioning to the Gentiles (9.15–16; 22.15, 21). In this case, however, Paul's own final public self-testimony, the terms of the commissioning are important. It has several elements. (1) He was appointed, directly by the Christ from heaven, to be an 'assistant and witness' (26.16; cf. Luke 1.2); even here

Luke refrains from using the term 'apostle', but nonetheless the commission sets Paul fully at one with those originally commissioned by the risen Christ (1.8, 22; 10.41). Notable, however, is the content of the witness – 'both to what you have seen ('of me' may be an addition) and to what I will appear to you' (26.16). That 'the revelation of Jesus Christ' was the substance of Paul's gospel is certainly Paul's own testimony in Gal. 1.12 and 15–16; but the language seems to envisage further appearances (resurrection appearances? – cf. Luke 24.34; Acts 1.31; I Cor. 15.5–8). Or should we think here of visions like those in 18.9–10, 22.17–21 and 23.11 (cf. 9.15; II Cor. 12.1–10)? But were these latter meant to be the stuff of Paul's witness? In the continuing unclarity of the text, at least we can recognize Paul's (and Luke's) emphasis on the immediacy of divine direction and that witness-bearing needs to be able to reflect and express a continuing immediacy of communion between the witness-bearer and the one to whom witness is borne.

(2) Paul is promised that he will be kept safe or at least rescued from both his own people and the Gentiles (26.17). Even though the past few chapters have focussed on the opposition of 'the Jews', with the Romans presented more as the guarantee of Paul's safety, Luke does not forget the much more even-handed portrayal of Paul's earlier missionary work, where he was at peril as much from Gentiles as from fellow Jews (13.44–45, 50; 14.2, 5, 19; 16.19–24; 17.5–9, 13, 32; 18.6, 12–13; 19.9, 23–24). It would be of only some consolation to Paul that the promise echoed that given to Jeremiah (Jer. 1.8, 19).

(3) The principal part of the commission is that Paul is sent to the nations/Gentiles (26.17; cf. Jer. 1.5, 7). The commission itself (26.18 is spelled out in phrases which deliberately echo the commission of the Servant of Yahweh – a figure most likely understood to represent Israel itself: 'to open their eyes' (Isa. 42.7); 'to turn them from darkness to light' (Isa. 42.6–7, 16). Paul is evidently depicted here as fulfilling the role of the Servant, the role of Israel (see also 26.23). The commission is analogous to that accepted by Jesus himself, according to Luke 4.18–21; Paul is commissioned by the risen Jesus to continue his own mission. This is the crucial factor: for some reason not entirely clear, Paul understood that with the death and resurrection of Jesus the time and possibility had arrived for Israel's responsibility to be a light to the Gentiles to be fulfilled (Gal. 1.15–16; 3.13–14, 23–29; 4.1–7).

The remaining phrases (26.18) fill out the usual Jewish presumption that the Gentiles were without God, and so under the power of Satan and in dire need to turn to God (cf. particularly I Thess. 1.9; Eph. 2). 'Forgiveness of sins' was likewise assumed to be most or realistically possible only through faith in Christ (2.38; 5.31; 10.43; 13.38). The final phrase ('a share among those made holy by faith in me') recalls Paul's final testament (20.32) and carries the same overtones of a characteristic Pauline thought, that Gentile Christian identity is to be moulded into the distinctive Jewish heritage (see on 20.32). The themes of the whole verse are closely parallel to those in Col. 1.12–14.

26.19–20   Luke does not hesitate to call the resurrection appearance to Paul a 'vision' (the word used in Luke 1.22; 24.23; II Cor. 12.1). The implication is of immediate obedience, of Paul thrust at once into evangelistic preaching, presumably echoing Luke's own earlier narrative: Paul's initial mission (9.20, 28–29, and probably 9.31) and subsequent mission to Gentile territories (chs 13–20). It was evidently important for Luke (and Paul) that the even-handedness of Paul's outreach was maintained: for Luke he was never simply apostle to the Gentiles; Paul's own ordering remained important – Jews first and also Gentiles (Rom. 1.16). The emphasis on repentance and turning to God (of the Gentiles) is reiterated (26.18); the reference is particularly to the Gentiles (11.18, 21; 14.15; 15.19) but not exclusively so (3.19). The final phrase recalls a note of the Baptist's preaching (Luke 3.8) – a further reminder that Paul's message was as much for Jew as for Gentile (cf. Eph. 2.10).

26.21   is the only other reference to the immediate cause of the hearing (cf. 26.6–8), 'the Jews' once again signifying the representative weight of the Jewish populace opposed to Paul. Paul makes clear what the real reason for their hostility is: not any defilement of the Temple, nor even any question of his own apostasy (cf. 21.21, 28); but Paul's willingness to open up Israel's own distinctive heritage (26.18) to the other nations, thus calling in question Israel's own traditional identity as defined by its separateness from the other nations.

26.22–23   In contrast Paul repeats his strong conviction that his message is nothing other than what the prophets and Moses predicted: 'that the Messiah would suffer, and that as first of the resurrection of the dead, he was to proclaim light both to the people and to the nations'. This puts Paul's message not only on a direct line of continuity with the authoritative scriptures of Israel, but also with the earliest preaching of Peter and John in their similar emphasis on the necessity of the Christ's suffering and resurrection (see on 2.23 and 24). The identity of the Nazarene's core message in its continuity with Israel's hope is clear. What stands out more clearly now than it did earlier (even 2.39, 3.25, 15.16–17 and 20.32) is that the openness of the gospel to the Gentiles is equally part of that identity and of that continuity, as being part of Israel's own commission to serve as 'a light to the nations' (Isa. 49.6, already cited in 13.47). This final statement of Paul's testimony ('I stand here bearing witness to both small and great') has the same dramatic character as Luther's, 'Here I stand, I can do no other', and carries a similar weight of significance for Luke's portrayal of Paul. This is the bottom line for Paul.

26.24   Luke uses his regular device of indicating that the speech was interrupted before its end (cf. 2.37; 10.44; 22.22); but as usual, the speech was complete, Paul having said all that Luke could have wanted him to say. The device here has a double function: it helps highlight the last thing said as the point to be taken special note of (here, as in 22.21, Paul's divine commission to the Gentiles); and it helps maintain the dramatic climax attained in the speech, by focussing on the speech's impact on the other two principal characters in the scene. Festus' outburst is a double-edged compliment: 'much learning . . . mad'. Presumably Festus was reacting to the talk of resurrection (cf.17.32), though possibly also the thought of the same national religion for all the diverse nations would have made little sense to the representative of an empire whose policy was to respect the distinctive national features of their subject peoples.

26.25–27   The appeal to Agrippa to bear testimony on Paul's behalf is a dramatic masterstroke (Paul addresses the king boldly, man to man); but it also makes two substantial theological points. One is that there has been nothing underhand or secretive in the principal matters of which Paul spoke (26.26): the ministry, suffering and (proclaimed) resurrection of Jesus was a matter of public record (cf. 10.36); and the success in bringing Gentiles to faith in a Jewish Messiah (with positive personal and social consequences) no less so; as one well informed of Jewish affairs, Agrippa could hardly be unaware of or unimpressed by these events. The other is the well-worn Christian claim that all that had happened (Jesus' death and resurrection, and the outreach to the Gentiles) was simply the out-working of Israel's own prophecies (26.27), the claim just made climactically in 26.22–23; Agrippa as a good student of the scriptures could hardly fail to acknowledge that too.

26.28   The character of Agrippa's reply is not altogether clear. KJV's 'Almost thou persuadest me to be a Christian' has become more or less proverbial, with its tantalizing suggestion that Paul in his final throw in Judaea almost succeeded in converting the one remaining (and last) Jewish king. Some contemporary translations maintain something of this tradition: 'A little more, and your arguments would make a Christian of me' (JB/NJB; similarly REB). But most assume a note of irony or of questioning intended in the words: 'In a short time you think to make me a Christian!' (RSV, a too free rendering of the Greek); 'Do you think that in such a short time you can persuade me to be a Christian?' (NIV; similarly GNB and NRSV). Either way, the dramatic impact is powerful. None of these transla-tions, however, quite reflects the ambiguity of the final clause, which would be better rendered, 'to act (as) a Christian', possibly even 'to play the Christian', and which thus probably contains a stronger note of sarcasm. This is only the second time the term 'Christian' occurs, and significantly it appears in a formal Roman setting (see on 11.26).

26.29   Paul's reply has a noble dignity and brings the scene to a fitting end on a note of pathos: Paul truly believed that nothing would bring greater benefit to his audience than their acceptance of his message, to share his faith and vision – though not his chains.

26.30–32   Like the calm coda following the emotion draining climaxes of the second movement of Bruckner's Seventh Symphony or Tchaikovsky's 'Romeo and Juliet' overture, the final paragraph of this most dramatic of all Luke's scenes winds down quietly and gen-tly to a close. Surprisingly, nothing more is said in public by the principals; but dramatically that allows Paul to have the last word and the effect of his words to continue ringing in the ears of audience and reader. The concluding episode is in complete contrast – no formal gathering or consultation, but simply the sound of the depart-ing dignitaries talking among themselves. The point is that they are in total agreement: there are no grounds for Paul's imprisonment or death. And even if Agrippa has not been persuaded of what Paul affirmed, at least he is at the end quite clear that Paul is totally innocent. Nonetheless, Paul must to Rome: the privilege accorded the Roman citizen, even though the charges against him have been judged vacuous by the most competent authorities, still provides the occasion and means for the divine plan to be fulfilled. He must go to Caesar, and that meant, as any reader would know, to Rome! The most crucial step to 'the end of the earth' (1.8) is about to be taken.

The Voyage to Rome and Shipwreck
27.1–44

Following the slow paced chapters of much talk and little movement, ch. 27 comes as a welcome contrast. It is all action and little
talk. Dramatically it serves to slacken completely the suspense built
up over the past two chapters, and after a calm interlude (27.1–12)
it allows a quite different tension to build again, this time round
the prospect of natural danger and disaster. As noted earlier
(Introduction to ch. 26), the chapter's function is like that of the
Saturday following Good Friday and leading into the resolution of
Easter Sunday in the Gospel.

It is hard to doubt that Luke saw in this episode a paradigm of
Paul's mission: a laboured but definite progress; an unbelieving and
reactionary crew ('the Jews'?); a supportive Roman officer; above all
God's manifest reassurance and deliverance from the most perilous
of situations (see also on 27.21–26); and an outcome which can be
described as 'salvation' (27.20, 31, 34, 43–44; 28.1, 4). The parallel
particularly with the preceding events would provide redoubled
confirmation for the reader that as God delivered Paul from the
perils of the deep so his promise of deliverance from hostile Jews
and Gentiles (26.17) could be firmly relied on. Come what may, God
would fulfil his purpose by having Paul preach the good news in the
very heart of the Empire.

The shipwreck had been a favourite feature of ancient storytelling,
at least since Homer's *Odyssey*. And many assume that Luke has
simply followed ancient convention, drawing on such stories known
to him for the impressive range of nautical details which are a
feature of his account; there are, for example, echoes of Homer in
verses 29 and 41. On the other hand, stormy passages and ship-
wrecks were common in Mediterranean travel; in II Cor. 11.25–26,
written a few years prior to this episode, Paul recalls that he had
already been shipwrecked three times, had been adrift at sea for a
night and a day, and was no stranger to danger at sea. Luke himself,
presumably, had experienced his own share of such hazards,

whether with Paul or on other occasions. It would be a surprise, then, if his narrative was drawn solely from literary precedents; almost certainly he had his own memories, for example, of the details he records in verses 16–19.

If the details of the storm and of the desperate measures taken, vivid as they are, do not settle the question of the chapter's historical value, there are others which do suggest that through the story-teller's artistry there are clear historical reminiscences to be detected. We may mention, in sequence: the names of the centurion and his cohort and of Paul's companions (27.1–2); the details of the itinerary, including lesser known place names like Cnidus, Salmone and Cauda (27.7, 16); the name of the 'typhonic wind', 'Eurakylon (Northeaster)' (27.14); and the numbers involved (27.37). Notable also is the restraint of the storyteller. We read of no overtly super-natural intervention beyond the reassurance provided by an angel in a dream or vision (27.23–24): Luke, who elsewhere delights to draw parallels between Paul and Jesus (see Introduction §3), ignores the opportunity suggested by Luke 8.22–25. No miracle is attributed to Paul beyond the prediction of 27.26; otherwise his advice is simply good sense born of experience (27.10, 31). He is indomitable, but not divine (contrast 28.6).

Above all there is the appearance of the storyteller in first person terms ('we'), beginning at 27.1. Some suggest that this too is simply a feature taken over from the genre of sea journeys; but much the most obvious conclusion to draw from the 'we' form is that the writer intended his readers to understand that he himself had been present, an eyewitness of and participant in the events described. In fact, therefore, the simplest and most obvious conclusion to draw is that the chapter, as indeed the rest of the book, was written by one who had been a companion of Paul throughout this particular journey, and indeed, all the way to Rome (the final 'we' is at 28.16). Where so much remains unclear, the simplest and most obvious solution is probably the best.

The story is vivid indeed, and after a slow start (appropriate following the preceding drama) becomes absorbing in its own right. For the most part it tells itself, without requiring much comment. For the places mentioned it is simplest to consult map 4 on p.336.

27.1 Procurator Festus and the others need no longer be mentioned by name; they are the ones offstage who precipitate the next action. The storyteller reappears in person ('we/us'), for the first time since

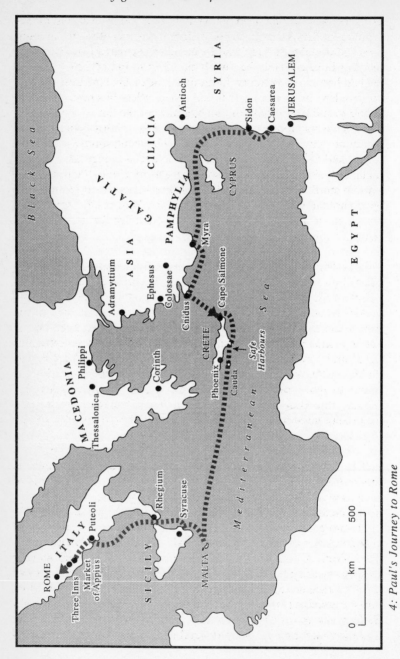

4: Paul's Journey to Rome

21.18. The implication need not be that Luke had been absent for the duration of Paul's time in custody, since in the meantime the account (Luke's normal technique) had focussed so exclusively on Paul himself; but Luke certainly had made no effort to indicate his presence (he had had an opportunity, for example, at 24.23). However, there is no problem in assuming that Luke had other business affairs to attend to and was absent for much or most of the time.

We have inscriptional evidence of auxiliary cohorts being granted the honorific title 'Augusta'. This detachment, under centurion Julius, had been given escort duty, whether as a regular or exceptional duty. Since the other prisoners are incidental to the story Luke says no more about them (until 27.42); how serious their crimes were we do not know, but as the sequel indicates, Paul as a Roman citizen would have higher status and be accorded free-er access to the centurion and the captain.

27.2–3   The ship was based in the Aegean and served the coastal cities; Julius presumably expected to pick up a more substantial vessel for the more demanding trip to Rome at one of the larger cities in Asia Minor. Luke mentions one other companion of Paul (apart from himself), Aristarchus from Thessalonica. He had been one of Paul's company when he came to Jerusalem (with the collection) (20.4), and may have continued with Paul to Rome (cf. Col. 4.10 and Philemon 24). We are to assume that the terms of Paul's custody continued to allow such favours (cf. 24.23), as also freedom to visit 'his friends' (the church) at Sidon (cf. 11.19; 15.3) and to enjoy some hospitality superior to the harshness of shipboard travel (27.3; cf. 28.14).

27.4–6   The prevailing wind of the region throughout summer is westerly or northwesterly, so a course to the east and north of Cyprus was able to use the island for shelter for much of the journey, before crossing to the south coast of Asia Minor where it could pick up a strong westerly current. At Myra Julius' hope was fulfilled: a larger vessel was there, bound for Italy. It had probably run northwards from Alexandria to Asia Minor where it could work its way westwards along the coast. The ship was presumably a grain carrier (27.37); Rome continued to depend on the grain of Egypt to feed its impoverished masses, and the maintenance and security of the grain traffic was a major objective of state policy. The orders of Julius the centurion might well have envisaged the likelihood of being able to combine his escort duty with that of supervising a grain shipment; hence, perhaps, his choice of a sea route in preference to the overland route.

27.7–8   The unfolding story makes it clear that the events took place late in the sailing season (27.9, 12). Both captain and centurion were evidently anxious to reach Rome before the season closed down: presumably the financial rewards for a late season cargo of grain made the risk worthwhile; and escort duty through the winter in foreign parts or the prospect of the lengthy overland route in early winter were evidently less appealing. In the event, however, the winds were against them (presumably the northwester), prevented them crossing the southern Aegean and forced them southwards, to the shelter of Crete's southern flank.

27.9–12   By tradition, and no doubt on the basis of earlier costly experience, no journeys were attempted in the open sea after 11 November (see also on 28.11). The two preceding months were regarded as dangerous. This fits with the timing indicated by Luke: 'the fast' is the Day of Atonement, Yom Kippur (the only national fast day in the Jewish calendar), which usually falls in late September or early October (in AD 59 it fell on 5 October). We should not overlook the clear implication that Paul and his companions continued to observe this distinctive Jewish holy day (cf. 20.6, 16). Since 'even the fast was already passed', they were well into the danger period.

The loss of 'much time' battling against the contrary winds would readily suggest to such a seasoned traveller as Paul that there was too little realistic hope of any further progress, let alone of reaching Italy without loss of life (his subsequent dream-vision, 27.22, changed his mind in part). It would be in character that he should choose to make his views known to those responsible for the voyage (even if he was unfamiliar with this particular route); the scene is not implausible. The centurion was evidently in charge: he had commandeered the vessel, or as a grain carrier it was on imperial service. But he evidently consulted not only the captain and owner (27.11) but also other experienced crewmen and travellers (27.12) before making up his mind or reaching a consensual decision. In the event, there was majority agreement that their wisest course was to winter in a Cretan port; the only disagreement with Paul was that the majority thought it worth taking the chance to reach a harbour which would be more secure from the winter storms. Phoenix faced 'southwest and northwest' (not 'northeast and southeast', as RSV).

27.13–15 The gentle southwester soon gives way to 'a violent (literally 'typhonic') wind, called the Northeaster'. Once round Cape Matala, about six miles to the west of Fair Havens, they would be unable to prevent themselves being driven away from the shore.

27.16–20 The measures taken would be the familiar emergency actions in such a plight: securing the dinghy, running stout ropes (literally 'helps') under the hull to help prevent the timbers starting apart or splitting, the use of a sea anchor (the Greek says simply 'letting down the gear') to prevent the drifting ship from turning broadside to the wind, and subsequently, and more unwillingly, lightening the ship by throwing overboard (some of) the cargo and then all but essential gear (cf. 27.29, 38). The danger was that they would be driven on to the Syrtes, the much feared sandbanks off the coast of Libya, where they would be pounded to destruction and almost certain death. Verse 20 catches well the mood of exhaustion and despair which all would experience after such constant buffeting.

27.21–26 The storm had been so unremitting that they had been unable even to eat. Paul is shown to give way to the so very human temptation to say, 'I told you so'. More positively, even in the extreme discomfort and distress of a ship pounded unceasingly, he had received one more vision (his last in Acts). This time it was not of Christ (18.9–10; 23.11), nor of a man (16.9), but of an angel (27.23) – the only time an angel appears to Paul in Acts (the last time an angel appeared was 12.7–11). That it was an angel could presumably be inferred from the message: he speaks as an emissary of God (contrast Paul's other visions). But why an angel here? Presumably because a Gentile crew would have no idea who 'the Lord' was; but then Paul could have provided an explanation sufficient for the occasion in a sentence or two. If this is Luke's contrivance it shows him to be an author sensitive to the severe constraints of the situation. Alternatively he recalls a Paul who displayed that sensitivity on the occasion itself. A pagan audience would find no difficulty in giving meaning to 'a messenger of the God whose I am and whom I worship'.

Nonetheless the God-centredness of the brief message is striking, as so often earlier in Acts (see 10.1–11.18; 14.15–17; 17.22–31): it is God to whom Paul belongs and who stands at the focus of Paul's worship (27.23); it is God who is affirmed to be in sovereign control of events and of those caught up in them (27.24; see on 4.12); and it is faith in this God which Paul affirms (27.25). To be noted is the fact that it is faith in a God who does not exempt from danger or cut it short miraculously, but who sustains endurance throughout the long drawn out crisis (cf. Luke 21.19); the verb used consistently in the climax of the account (27.43–44; 28.1, 4) means 'to bring safely through'.

Is the prospect of running on to some island (27.26) a prediction, a hope or a foreboding?

27.27–29   Thirteen or fourteen days would be about the time taken to drift from Crete to Malta. The Adria was the sea bounded by Italy, Malta, Crete and Greece. The soundings, using a lead weight, accord with an approach to Malta from the east.

27.30–32   Such action of the sailors is understandable in the circumstances, but their abandoning ship would have left it without skilled crew. That it was Paul who realized what was happening and alerted the centurion, who would likely be his closest companion apart from Luke and Aristarchus, makes for a better story but is not implausible. But did they (Paul and Luke) misunderstand what could have been a legitimate and praiseworthy attempt by the crew to anchor the bow? And did Paul mean the soldiers to cut the dinghy adrift, thus decreasing the chances of any kind of orderly disembarcation, should the weather improve?

27.33–34   That landfall had roused Paul's spirits is also in character. As one who had remained buoyant and resilient in the face of repeated setbacks in the past, and one who had demonstrated his natural leadership many times before, he takes the lead in giving encouragement. This was the nature and effect of his faith, as his letters repeatedly confirm (e.g. II Cor. 1.3–11; 4.7–18; 12.7–10; Phil. 1.15–26; 4.10–13). In this case in particular, he had been given an assurance as to the safety of his companions and he was not embarrassed to speak it forth as his own personal conviction. Therefore he urges them to take food 'for your preservation' (the same word means 'salvation'); the translations paraphrase – e.g. 'it will help you survive' (NRSV), 'your lives depend on it' (REB).

27.35–36 Some assume that the sequence, 'took bread, gave thanks to God, and broke it', must describe a eucharistic act. This is most unlikely. The actions are simply those of a normal Jewish meal, with the blessing and breaking of bread and its distribution (not mentioned here) as the first act of the meal by means of which all present can share in the blessing of the bread (cf. Luke 9.16; 24.30). In the circumstances what was needed was not a symbolic piece of bread, but sufficient bread to give them strength for the final stage of the long running crisis (27.34); and not a private celebration between Paul, Luke and Aristarchus, but a break-fast for everyone giving 'nourishment' to all (27.38). This conclusion is bound to reflect back on the earlier references to 'breaking bread' (2.46; 20.7, 11). In each case there is nothing in the text which points to the conclusion that Luke intended to describe any more than a shared meal (see further on 20.7a and 11–12).

The more significant feature for Luke is that Paul 'gave thanks to God before them all'. It is as a witness for God, the one God of Israel, that Paul stands out in his endurance, his perceptiveness and his leadership.

27.37 The exactness of the numbers is striking – 276. Was there a rollcall at this point, as would be appropriate with first light (27.33), given the likelihood of serious injuries or loss of crew overboard in the hazardous conditions of the last thirteen days? At any rate the number is best explained as a reminiscence; it seems to have no symbolical significance. An oceangoing ship would have been quite capable of carrying twice as many.

27.38 The long drawn out crisis was evidently about to be resolved; there was no point in trying to save any of the remaining cargo. The lighter the ship, the more likely that the waves would carry it through any shoals or over any rocks as they made the decisive attempt to bring her to safety or to beach her.

27.39–41 In the event the only hope was to try to beach the ship. Given the other identification mark (27.41), one of two beaches can be identified as St Paul's Bay. The desperate attempt met disaster at 'a place of two seas' (literally), that is, presumably, a sandbar or patch of shallows which divided deeper water on two sides or where two currents clashed; there they ran aground, and with the bow stuck fast the stern began to be battered and broken by the power of the surf.

27.42–44   The soldiers' plan to kill the prisoners (27.1) was the natural reaction of the escort; they would be held responsible should the prisoners have escaped in the confusion (cf. 12.19; 16.27). It is noteworthy that Luke does not attribute the centurion's counter-order to the urging of Paul; Luke makes no attempt to give Paul a leading role in the final denouement (contrast 27.9–10, 21–26, 30–32, 33–36). The centurion, presumably already impressed by Paul, might well consider that it would be in his own interest if he was able, after all and despite everything, to bring this probably innocent Roman citizen safely to Rome. But Luke no doubt would like us to deduce that the centurion was still more impressed by Paul's earlier reassurance (27.24); his detachment need have no fear of losing their charges – all would be saved. And so it proves: the swimmers make their own way and the rest using planks or 'some pieces (or persons?) from the ship' head for the shore. In a tone of appropriate thankfulness and triumph Luke concludes one of his most dramatic episodes – 'And thus came everyone safely to land'.

Paul Reaches the Goal and Final Centre of His Mission, Rome Itself
28.1–31

In the preceding chapters Luke gives the impression of over-indulgence in the space accorded to sequences which he could have treated much more sparely. But in this final chapter the proportions are carefully measured and the chief moments deftly sketched, leaving us in little doubt as to emphases which Luke wished to impress upon his readers for the last time. We have already noted the significance of the placing of ch. 28 as the conclusion to the Acts 'passion narrative' and to the whole volume (see Introduction to chs 21–28). Here we need simply highlight the impressions which Luke evidently wished his readers and auditors to take with them as they rose from this final reading.

In the first place he wished to leave no doubt as to Paul's innocence of the charges laid against him. Surprisingly for the uninformed reader, this declaration does not come in Rome itself, as the pronouncement of the Emperor. It is surprising, since it was to the Emperor, after all, that Paul had appealed for vindication (25.11), and since the execution of this appeal was the very means by which and reason for which Paul had come to Rome (25.21, 25; 26.32). But in Rome itself Luke says nothing more of all this beyond the reference back in 28.17–19. No hint is given in the closing scene of preparations being made for the decisive encounter or of initial consultations or hearings, let alone of the trial itself or of its outcome. The trial of Paul and the question of his even possibly being found guilty disappears entirely from Luke's view, even though Paul's custody continued for a further two years (28.30). Why should this be so? Partly, we may guess, because the outcome of the trial before Nero was unsuccessful in the event, and Paul suffered martyrdom (as tradition relates); evidently Luke, having already alluded to Paul's death (20.25), did not want to end his narrative on this note.

But partly also because in Luke's narrative the vindication has already been given, and not by the Emperor, but by divine warrant (28.1–7).

In the second place, Paul comes to Rome itself. This is the climax of Christian expansion. The programme of 1.8 has been fulfilled in its most decisive phase. To be sure, this is not 'the end of the earth' (though see on 1.8), but as the centre of the earth, Rome is the base from which the gospel can go forth to its ends. It is not that Luke wants us to believe that Paul was the first to bring the gospel to Rome; he is clear that there were already fellow-believers there before Paul (28.15). But after welcoming Paul and his party these fellow believers also disappear from the stage. The final scenes are dominated instead by Paul's two encounters with his fellow Jews (28.17–22, 23–28). In this way Luke makes it clear that the self-understanding of the believer in relation to 'the hope of Israel' remains at the heart of the gospel (28.20), and that, despite its being spoken against everywhere, the sect of Jesus the Nazarene is not antithetic to or opposed by the Jewish synagogues (28.21–22). This is the understanding of the gospel and of Christianity which Paul brings with him to Rome. This is the gospel and the Christianity which is to go to the end of the earth.

It is this emphasis which is elaborated in the final scene. At the heart of the gospel and of Christianity lies the dialogue of mutual self-understanding between Jews and believers in Jesus as the Christ. It is a testing dialogue, which easily leads to denunciation by one of the other. But it is an ongoing dialogue; the prophet Isaiah, despite being told that his people will not respond to his word from God, must still speak it (the implication of the quotation in 28.25–27). And so with Paul: in his case the offensive word is the good news about the kingdom of Israel's God and the Jewish Messiah given also to the Gentiles for their salvation (28.23, 28). But the implication is the same: that gospel must continue to be preached to all, Jew and Gentile alike (28.30–31); for that is the nature of the gospel and so also of its task.

On the question of the narrative's historical basis we can be confident enough about its basic structure. The aftermath of the shipwreck is the conclusion to the storm sequence of ch. 27, and the welcome and hospitality of the people is much as one would have expected (28.1–2). The episode with the viper has a circumstantial plausibility, and though Luke uses it to make his own point, his account is very sparse and he makes no attempt to elaborate it

(28.3–6). The sequel (28.7–10) recalls the name of the island's leading citizen (Publius) and the detail of the initial illness cured ('dysentry'), and otherwise could well reflect the enthusiasm which reports of Paul's double deliverance and initial healing occasioned; it is told as a rounded out tale complete in itself. The clearest historical unit is 28.11–16, with its well documented itinerary and timetable. Up to this point, we should also note, the narrative is that of a personal participant ('we').

Beyond that, however, it would appear that Luke has used tradition to complete the narrative in his own way. Certainly, an encounter with representatives of the Jewish community in Rome is historically plausible, as also the final picture of Paul's continuing residence in Rome (28.30–31). At the same time, the final scenes (28.17–28) clearly round off Luke's portrayal of the relationship between the movement Paul represents and its Jewish heritage (the other Roman believers are never mentioned again). And while the characterization of Paul's final speeches is Pauline enough, the Lukan emphases (e.g. 1.3, 6–8; 8.12; 13.46; 15.14–18; 18.6) are clear: the Pauline Paul is even more clearly the Lukan Paul.

The verdict is delivered on Paul
28.1–10

The episode on Malta is a cameo and summary of the long drawn out crisis confronting Paul. As with 'the Jews' earlier, events lead onlookers to the conclusion that he is a criminal; although he has escaped the perils of the sea, he has not escaped the due reward of his crimes; the goddess Justice has had the last word (28.3–4). But Paul's survival causes them to change their mind: not a murderer but a god; justice *has* had the last word (28.5–6).

In the overall construction of Acts this final judgment of the people ('He is a god') is remarkable. For a repeated feature of earlier scenes was Luke's determination to show how false ideas of God were rejected and to demonstrate the folly of confusing God with human beings or idols – Simon (8.10, 20–24), Peter (10.25–26), Herod (12.20–23), Paul and Silas (14.11–18), the Athenian shrines and idols (17.22–31). But here, quite exceptionally, Luke allows Paul to be reckoned a god and he makes no attempt to qualify or correct the opinion. We cannot conclude from this that Luke wanted Paul to be thought of in these terms, abandoning his earlier consistent strategy and emphasis. Rather he lets the judgment stand, precisely as the reversal of the earlier verdict of Paul's guilt (28.6): Paul's god-likeness here is rather the measure of his innocence and of his stature as the spokesman for the one true God.

Luke, then, evidently wanted this to be the final verdict on the accusations brought against Paul. This is indicated not only by the fact that Luke allows the verdict of the Maltese to stand unchecked: 'justice' has indeed spoken, and clearly in Paul's favour. It is indicated also by the fact, already noted, that the trial before Caesar stands suspended through the end of Luke's narrative: the final verdict has been given; nothing more need be said; and nothing that happens beyond the horizon of Luke's account can alter the verdict already given. But it is indicated also by the fact that the Jews in Rome have no accusations or complaints to bring against Paul (28.21): those ('the Jews') who have been the principal movers and instigators against Paul (28.19) now have nothing to say against the man himself. The verdict from on high has in effect quashed their accusations also; there is no charge or counter charge between Paul and his people to be resolved (28.19, 21). Paul can proceed as no longer an accused criminal and apostate. A fresh start can be made in preaching and teaching the gospel to his own people (28.22–31).

The sequel (28.7–10) functions as a corollary to the verdict just given: Paul is received as a celebrated figure; nothing is said of Paul as prisoner or in custody – these details are now irrelevant; the miracles confirm Paul's standing as a medium of healing power (divinely authorized and attested); the locals continue to be truer representatives of heaven's judgment on Paul as they heap his party ('us') with honours at the end of their stay. Nor, somewhat suprisingly, is anything said about Paul preaching to the people. Rather, the whole episode has a celebratory character – celebration in effect at the vindication of Paul.

28.1–2   The scene, though similar to other accounts of shipwreck, could be drawn from memory: the locals speaking in an unknown dialect (Luke calls them *barbaroi*, that is, not able to converse in the international language of the day, Greek); their uncommon kindness, nonetheless; the fire, the rain and the cold. As is usual in Luke's storytelling, however, the focus tightens on to the chief participants (Paul and the locals); the rest of the shipwrecked crew fade into the background.

28.3–4   The verisimilitude of the scene is sustained: Paul, not commanding but quick to help (cf. 20.34); the torpid viper caught up with the bundle of sticks and stirred by the heat of the fire; the superstitious but understandable reaction of the locals. But does Luke intend us to assume that despite being 'barbarians' their speech was understandable? 'Justice' is quite often personified as a goddess in Greek literature, in one case being named as Zeus' consort ('one who sits beside him'). For Luke, however, the point is that a higher justice than that of the Jerusalem council or the Judaean procurator or even that of the Emperor himself has been called into play. For all their lack of culture and primitive religious sense, the Maltese barbarians have recognized that Paul is a figure of significance before heaven who is about to experience the verdict of divine justice.

28.5   Unexpectedly, Paul is able to shake off the snake; what the barbarians assumed to be the instrument of divine punishment, itself perishes. This was one of the details which was used in the construction of the longer end added to Mark's Gospel (Mark 16.9–20) some time, probably, in the second century (Mark 16.18), and which more recently has been given special significance by snake handling sects.

28.6   The complete reversal of the spectators' verdict is as naive as their original judgment itself: Paul must be a god. But as the former judgment (28.4) represented a heightening of the unjust charges brought against Paul by his own people, so the latter verdict represents a truer account of Paul and his mission (cf. Luke 10.19). It is not that Luke intended their verdict to be taken literally: his earlier campaign against false ideas of God and of God's relation to humankind was too clear and sustained for such a conclusion to be possible (8.10, 20–24; 10.25–26; 12.20–23; 14.11–18; 17.22–31; 19.26); and those who speak the words are, after all, 'barbarians' (Luke would probably share something of the Greek contempt implied in the term). Nevertheless, the fact that Luke makes no attempt to refine or explain their verdict but lets it stand without qualification, indicates that he regarded their verdict as more commendable and final than any of the charges earlier brought against Paul. Those who saw the hand of divine Justice in the events (28.4) rightly conclude not only that Justice declares Paul innocent, but also that he is rather to be recognized as one divinely favoured and commissioned.

28.7   The hospitality accords with the traditions of hospitality of the time, though we should also note that it was limited to three days. Despite the further round of healings (28.8–9), Luke makes no attempt to suggest that Publius continued to entertain Paul for the remainder of their time on the island (three months – 28.11). Luke also continues to focus on Paul, or rather on 'us'; the reader is left to assume that the rest of the 276 survivors were given hospitality for an initial period too. Thereafter, presumably, they had to pay for their lodgings.

28.8   The description of the illness of Publius' father is remarkably detailed – not just a 'fever' (cf. Luke 4.38–39), but also 'dysentry' (a term which occurs nowhere else in biblical Greek). Such detail would normally indicate use of tradition, and here probably Luke's own personal recollection. The illness is not attributed to demonic interference, and Luke's description of the healing effected by Paul mirrors normal technique (prayed and laid on hands; cf. 6.6; 8.15, 17; 13.3), without reference to the name of Jesus (contrast 3.6, 16; 4.10, 30; 16.18). Unusually the healing is attributed to Paul himself (contrast 9.34), perhaps a reflection of his god-like status in the eyes of the onlookers.

28.9   In an echo of Jesus' similar success (Luke 4.40; 5.15; 6.18), the reports of Paul's double attestation from heaven generates an expectancy to which Paul was able to minister with effect. Paul himself had earlier recalled such occasions (Rom. 15.19; Gal. 3.5), so Luke's record of Paul's success as a healer is probably based on his own clear recollections of the time.

28.10   The episode is closed (but 28.11!) with all the indications of a triumph: Paul's party ('us') is 'honoured with many honours' (cf. Sir. 38.1), and all their needs met. Again nothing is said of the centurion or shipowner or any of the others. Nor, surprisingly, is anything said of the Maltese coming to faith. The period is represented solely as a celebration from beginning to end of Paul's vindication and authorization from on high.

'And so we came to Rome'
28.11–22

The most striking feature of the final phase of Paul's journey to Rome and of his first act in Rome itself is the interplay on the theme of brotherhood: on the one hand, the Christian 'brothers' who support and meet him on the way to Rome (28.14–15); and on the other, the Jewish 'brothers' who meet with him in Rome itself (28.17, 21). This indication of an overlapping spectrum of brotherhood is by no means new in Acts (see on 1.15), but it is particularly noticeable here. Luke may even see significance in the name under whose patronage Paul's ship sailed – 'the Twins' (twin sons of Zeus) (28.11) – perhaps suggesting that the Christian and Jewish brothers Paul was soon to encounter were likewise twin siblings of the one God, brothers of Paul and so of one another.

Be that as it may, it can hardly be accidental that Paul's encounters with the Christian brothers all take place outside Rome, even though the latter group were from Rome itself (28.15). In contrast, and surprisingly, these brothers do not reappear during Paul's time in Rome. The only brothers he encounters there are his Jewish brothers (28.17–22). It is not the portrayal of a supportive Christian community on which Luke chooses to focus his final description of Paul, valuable as that would have been (cf. e.g. 4.32–35; 9.31; 14.21–23). Rather his concern was evidently to sketch out the final encounters between Paul and the representatives of his own people settled in Rome.

Luke's purpose in relating this initial encounter (28.17–22) is evidently to clear the ground: to show that all the misapprehension and false accusations which had diverted and distracted the Jews encountered earlier from the gospel no longer pertain. 'The Jews' of Jerusalem might have laid complaint against Paul (28.17, 19), but Paul had already been afforded a divine vindication (28.1–6), and anyway the local representative Jews knew nothing of any such complaints (28.21). The way was therefore open for Paul to provide a final statement of the gospel as 'the hope of Israel' (28.20). The Jews of Rome, like their predecessors in Pisidian Antioch, Beroea and Ephesus (13.43; 17.11; 18.20), were eager to hear more (28.22). The stage is thus set for the final scene.

28.11 The account picks up again making a rather awkward overlap with 28.10; verses 11–16 evidently formed some kind of unit which Luke simply incorporated. The 'three months' take the story forward to February (probably of the year 60), the month on which more favourable winds began to blow and sea-travel became safe enough again. This ship was also from Alexandria (cf. 27.6), and probably also a grain carrier which had cut its timing at the end of the previous season just too fine. Its figurehead was the *Dioskuroi*, the heavenly twins, Castor and Pollux. These legendary twin sons of Zeus and Leda were regarded as the patron deities of navigation; the ship had taken their name as its own, for obvious reasons.

28.12–14   The detail of the route must surely be drawn from personal reminiscence, the timetable dependent on the variable winds. Puteoli, near modern Naples, was the main port in southern Italy, and passengers were usually disembarked there (five days vigorous walk from Rome) while the grain continued to Ostia, Rome's own port. The fact that Paul was still in custody and was one of a band of prisoners guarded by a detachment of soldiers remains out of view for Luke; the wishes of the Christian group (Paul, Luke and Aristarchus) are granted without demur. One could imagine the centurion giving Paul permission to enquire whether there were fellow believers in Puteoli (cf. 18.2; 19.1; 21.4), and even to accept their hospitality for a few days; but the implication that the centurion was willing to tolerate further delay in bringing his other prisoners to Rome seems more dubious. Conceivably, however, he left Paul with a token guard and proceeded directly to Rome with the rest of his party. At all events, it is significant that a church was already established in Puteoli (we know from Josephus, *Antiquities* 17.328, of a Jewish community there).

28.15   Christians from Rome itself give formal welcome to Paul and his party at Appii Forum (about forty-three miles south of Rome) and at the Three Taverns (about thirty-three miles south of Rome), both on the Appian Way – two different parties (cf. Rom. 14.1–15.6)? Who these 'brothers' were Luke does not say. As with the most significant breakthrough in 11.20, so with the foundation of the church in what Luke would regard as the capital of the world, Luke passes it over with the briefest of references (cf. Rom. 1.7–8). Whether these Christians are included in the 'we' of 28.16 is also left unclear. What is important for Luke is the arrival of Paul's party in Rome; even the Roman believers, having met them, are left on one side.

28.16   At the end of the journey Luke recalls (the last of the 'we' references) that Paul was after all a prisoner and briefly describes the conditions of his continuing custody. The terms of his custody remain as liberal as they had been from the beginning (24.23). The thought of Paul chained to his guard (28.20) has evoked many an imaginative scenario of Paul still preaching and seeking to convert his succession of captors; but they may well have some basis in historical fact (cf. Phil. 1.12–18).

28.17   There was a strong Jewish community in Rome, stretching back at least to the triumph of Pompey in 62 BC, when he returned to Rome with many Jewish captives to celebrate his annexation of Judaea to the empire; most of these would subsequently have been freed and gained citizenship. Putting together the various allusions to Jewish presence in Rome, the best estimate of its size in the middle of the first century is about 40,000–50,000, most of them slaves and freedmen. The Jewish population was concentrated mainly in Trastevere (across the Tiber). We know of some ten to thirteen synagogues, all of which may have been in existence at this time. However, we hear nothing of a Jewish council in Rome; so the 'first men of the Jews' would presumably be leading members of several at least of the synagogues. Nevertheless, we can assume a network of communication between the synagogue communities, so that those who responded to Paul's invitation can be regarded as representative of the Jews in Rome. The implication of verse 21, that there was regular contact between the Roman Jews and Judaea, is probably reliable also (cf. 2.10). The verb used, 'call together', need not indicate Paul's presumption of an authority he did not possess ('summon, convene'), since it can have the lighter sense of 'invite to a gathering' (cf. 10.24).

28.17–20   In the manner of the typical Lucan summary dialogue (cf. 25.14–21), Paul rehearses the basic facts of his case – from his own perspective. The salient points are: (1) his complete innocence of both the charges and the suspicions entertained against him – he has done nothing against either the people or the ancestral customs (28.17; cf. 21.21, 28; 24.12–13; 25.8); (2) Jewish hostility countered by Roman conviction of his innocence (28.18; a repeated motif in chs 21–26); and (3) Paul's denial of any antipathy towards his own nation (28.19; cf. 22.3; 23.6; 24.14; 26.4–5). (4) On the contrary, the issue for Paul remains completely 'in-house' – 'the hope of Israel'

(28.20; cf.23.6; 24.15; 26.6–7). In other words, from Paul's and Luke's perspective the coming together in Rome was not of representatives of different and hostile peoples or religions, but of fellow members ('brothers') of the same people and religion.

28.21–22   For their part the Roman Jews accept Paul's assurances. Surprisingly, in the light of the hostility of the Jews regularly recorded by Luke in his account of many of Paul's missions, none of the accusations regularly brought against Paul elsewhere (in Asia Minor, Macedonia and Greece) had reached their ears. Even the implacable animosity of the Jews of Jerusalem (sustained over two years) had not been reported to them. What are we to make of this? At the least we have to say that Luke did not wish to depict the opposition of 'the Jews' to Paul himself as so total and complete as his earlier narrative seemed to indicate. 'The Jews' of Jerusalem were not so representative of 'the Jews' elsewhere; so far as the whole body of the Jews in Rome were concerned, Paul's claim that the primary issue focussed on 'the hope of Israel' (28.20) was one they could examine without prejudice. On the other hand, they knew that 'this sect' which Paul represented was 'everywhere spoken against' (cf. 18.2!); but Luke was evidently concerned to show that the Roman Jews saw this to be distinct from any charges against Paul himself. They were anxious therefore to hear what Paul's views on the subject were. In other words, despite its bad reputation, they still saw the movement Paul represented as a Jewish sect (see Introduction to chs 1–5(6) [p.2]), and were open to Paul's account of it.

The final scene
28.23–31

Luke might have continued the previous scene without a break, but evidently he wanted to depict the encounter as a separate scene. The scene just completed had in fact simply cleared the ground of the now irrelevant accusations against Paul and had established the Roman Jews' openness to Paul's message. The final scene could then focus exclusively on this lasting image of Paul as Christian missionary and apologist.

And what is this image that Luke was so concerned to depict? Paul as preaching the gospel to Gentiles? Paul as building up the church?

Paul as bearing witness before Caesar? No. His concern evidently was to portray Paul making a final statement about the relation of his gospel to Israel and to the Gentiles. To the end of his defining description of earliest Christianity this remains his primary concern: that Christianity can only understand itself in relation to the people of the law and the prophets as well as by means of their message; and that the salvation which this Christianity proclaimed is also for the other nations as well.

Many assume that the scene depicts the final breakdown of relations between Paul and his own people; that Paul makes final pronouncement of God's rejection of Israel. 'God has written the Jews off' (J. T. Sanders 80–3, 297–9). But this is an unbalanced and ill-informed judgment. (1) We have already seen that Luke bends over backwards to affirm the openness of the Roman Jews to Paul (28.21–22). (2) This portrayal continues as he depicts the Jewish community divided over Paul's message – some being persuaded, while others disbelieved (28.24). (3) The citation of Isa. 6.9–10 (28.26–27) is no more a denunciation of the Jewish people than it was when first given as Isaiah's commission. (4) The turning to the Gentiles (28.28) simply repeats the earlier turns reported in 13.46 and 18.6. (5) The 'all who came to him' through the following two years presumably included Roman Jews (cf. 19.10); Luke certainly makes no attempt to exclude that deduction. (6) Not least, two elements remain at the defining centre of the message: the kingdom of God, with all its continuing overtones for Israel (cf. 1.6) – Paul the Jew continues to testify to the fulfilment of Jewish hope; and, above all, Jesus himself as attested by both the law and the prophets.

The mistake of those who see here the account of an irretrievable breakdown between Christianity and Judaism has been to assume that the third report of such a denunciation by Paul of his fellow Jews was intended to be final. On the contrary, Luke was well aware that real history continued beyond the limits of his narrative (cf. 1.11!). That was no doubt why he allowed the final scene to fade out with the image of Paul secure in Rome and preaching and teaching all who came to him openly and unhindered. That is to say, what Luke records is not so much a final scene as a definitively typical scene – the ongoing debate between believers in Messiah Jesus and traditional Jews as definitive for Christianity; the debate continues, some Jews being persuaded, others disbelieving. So it was and so it will continue to be, for this is the inevitable consequence of Christianity's own identity, given its foundational beliefs in the

353

kingdom of Israel's God and in Jesus as Messiah and Lord (see also on 10.27–29).

28.23   How big were Paul's lodgings (a room at an inn, or an apartment)? No matter: the point is that the Jews of Rome came to him 'in great numbers'. It was Paul's first task, as ever (13.5, 14; 14.1; etc.), to 'bear (solemn) witness' (a Lukan motif – 2.40; 8.25; 10.42; 18.5; 20.21–24; 23.11) to his fellow Jews, and at due length ('from dawn to dusk'), thus fulfilling the promise of 23.11.

The twin emphases of his testimony were the kingdom of God and Jesus. The fact that this twofold emphasis recurs in the very last verse (28.31) indicates that the choice of themes was neither accidental nor frivolous. As with the repeated emphasis in 1.3 and 6, Luke evidently wanted the continuity with Jesus' proclamation of the kingdom in the Gospel to be clear beyond doubt (see on 1.3). Equally fundamental to Paul's gospel was the claim that Jesus fulfilled the hopes of Israel as embodied in the law and the prophets (13.27; 24.14–15; 26.22–23; cf. particularly Luke 4.16–21; 24.25–27, 44–46; Acts 2.30–31; 3.18–26; 8.30–35; 10.43).

28.24   The response is as on the earlier occasions: some were being persuaded or convinced; others were disbelieving (13.43–45; 14.1–2; 17.4–5, 10–13; 18.4–6, 19–20; 19.8–9; 23.6–9). Luke uses the imperfect tense to indicate that this was not a once for all outcome (contrast the aorist tenses of 17.4 and 19.26); rather a process of ongoing debate and dialogue had been begun whose tendency and likely outcome followed the same twofold pattern but which presumably continued through the next two years (28.30–31). The implication is that that this twofold response continues to characterize the response of the Jews into the time beyond Luke's narrative.

28.25   To be noted is the fact that Paul's final word (28.25–28) does not follow a uniform rejection of his message by the Jews of Rome; in this final scene there is no more talk of 'the Jews' acting as a single body in animosity or hostility towards Paul (contrast 13.50; 14.4; 17.5; 18.12; 22.30; 23.12). Quite the contrary: Luke notes that the visitors leave, still disagreeing, even after Paul has made his denunciation. This confirms that Luke did not intend the quotation from Isa. 6.9–10 to be seen as Paul washing his hands of 'the Jews'; it simply indicates once more the mixed response that Paul's message would continue to receive from his own people.

28.25–27 The scripture cited, attributed to the Holy Spirit (as in 1.16 and 4.25), is from Isa. 6.9–10 more or less word for word. It was a passage much reflected on in early Christian writing, since it helped provide an answer to one of the most puzzling questions of all for the first Christians: why the Jews should have rejected their own Messiah in such large-scale numbers (Matt. 13.14–15/Mark 4.12/Luke 8.10; John 12.39–40; Rom. 11.7–8). The text serves this purpose here too (cf. the 'hardening' motif in 7.51, 19.9 and 28.27 with that in Rom. 11.25). But a significant factor in all cases, and here not least, is that the text was part of Isaiah's commission. Notable also here is the fact that the quotation begins with the words of Isaiah's commission to 'Go to this people' (28.26), which by implication functions also as Paul's commission. In its function within canonical Isaiah the text certainly was not intended to put Isaiah off from fulfilling his commission in prophesying to his people; another sixty chapters of just such prophecy follow on this commission! And in the context so skilfully set out by Luke, the probability is that he intended the quotation here too to be understood in this light: that is, that Paul, who had drawn so much of his own commission from Isaiah (see 13.47, 22.17–21 and 26.18, 23), would have understood Isaiah as indicating the course (and frustrations) of Paul's mission to his own and Isaiah's people, not as calling on him to end it in dismissive denunciation.

28.28 should not be understood as Paul's final turn away from and rejection of his people in favour of the Gentiles – any more than the earlier denunciations of 13.46 and 18.6 (cf. 22.21). The idea of 'the salvation of God' being known 'to the nations' is an allusion to Ps. 67.2 (cf. Ps. 98.3 and Isa. 40.5), passages which express the thought of God's faithfulness to Israel as part of his universal saving concern for all nations. The same point had been implicit in the multiple allusions to Isaiah in Luke 2.30–32 (Isa. 42.6; 46.13; 49.6; 52.10): the salvation of God for all peoples, Gentiles as well as Jews. In his description of John the Baptist (Luke 3.4–6) Luke had extended the quotation of Isa. 40.3–5 to climax in the phrase, 'all flesh shall see the salvation of God', to make the same point: Israel is most true to its heritage when it recognizes God's saving concern for the other nations as well. Just the same point was made by Luke in the opening scene of Jesus' ministry in Jesus' exposition of the prophecy from Isa. 61.1–2: the commission of Jesus was for Gentile as well as Jew (Luke 4.18–27).

The implication here, then, is that the turn to the Gentiles is simply part of God's larger scheme of salvation: that the turn to the Gentiles does not imply a rejection of Israel (see also on 13.46–47). In other words, the Lukan Paul is no different from the Paul of Rom. 9–11: the mixed and largely negative response of the Jews to the gospel of Messiah Jesus and the positive response of the Gentiles is simply a phase in the larger purposes of God to include all, Jew and Gentile, within his saving concern.

28.30–31   The fade-out scene is entirely positive. The implication is that Paul remained in custody (28.16, 20), but at his own expense (in a rented apartment?), sustained by the financial gifts of his supporters. Nothing is said of the progress of the case against Paul or of an appearance before Caesar (though note the implication of 27.24). And nothing continues to be said of the Roman believers, or even of Paul's own co-workers; the focus remains tight upon Paul himself. The significant points that Luke evidently wanted to remain with his readers were twofold.

(1) The chief features of Paul's message – 'proclaiming the kingdom of God and teaching what related to the Lord Jesus Christ' (the latter phrase used in 18.25) – continue to imply complete continuity with the preaching of Jesus and to centre the distinctiveness of the gospel and of the movement represented by Paul on Jesus. The concluding emphasis matches the initial emphasis (see on 1.3) and in effect answers the still hanging question of the first disciples (1.6). The kingdom will be seen to be most truly Israel's when it is proclaimed most freely to the other nations.

(2) Paul 'continued to welcome all who came to him', preaching this message 'with all boldness and without hindrance' (the latter a legal term). In context that can mean nothing other than a sustained proclamation to all, Jew as well as Gentile. Despite the depressing but realistic prognosis provided by Isaiah (28.26–27), the obligation to preach to all the good news of God's kingdom and of Jesus as Messiah and Lord remained unbroken, and the final picture is of Paul continuing to fulfil this commission into the undisclosed future.

And thus Luke gives his final answer to the question which has motivated the telling of his tale from the first (see Introduction to chs 1–5 [pp.1f.]). What is this movement, which we now call Christianity? It is the extension of Israel, of Isaiah's commission to Israel, of Israel's commission to be a light to the Gentiles. It is a movement which Paul embodies. It is a movement which can only understand itself in relation to Israel, to the hope of Israel, as fulfilling that hope and contributing to its further fulfilment. It is a movement which can be true to itself only in ongoing dialogue with Jews, both those who respect it and are open to its claims, but also those who dispute it and reject its claims. Only thus will it be true to its own character and commission as called by God to proclaim the salvation of God to all.